Lynn Smith Houghton
Pamela Hall O'Connor

The Kalamazoo Historic
Preservation Commission,
Kalamazoo, Michigan
2001

Maria A. Perez-Stable, Editor
Graphic Design: Brakeman
Contemporary Photography: John A. Lacko

COVER: Kalamazoo's Congregation B'nai Israel built its first temple in 1875, on the south side of South Street, near the intersection of Farmer's Alley. A graceful, wood-frame building unlike any other in Kalamazoo, it was "encased" in an addition shortly after 1910, following the Congregation's move to its new temple on South Park Street. In 1976, this temple and its wrap-around addition were razed, along with the Capitol Theatre next door, for a parking structure.

Portions of this book have appeared in the Kalamazoo Historic Preservation Commission's 1997 and 1998 calendars.

Copyright ©2001 by The Kalamazoo Historic Preservation Commission

All rights reserved.

Published by the City of Kalamazoo Historic Preservation Commission
City of Kalamazoo, 241 West South Street, Kalamazoo, Michigan, 49007.

Printed in the United States of America

ISBN: 0-9710682-0-8 (cloth)
0-9710682-1-6 (paper)

Table of Contents

Dedication . . . . *vii*

Funders . . . . *ix*

Acknowledgements . . . . *xi*

Preface . . . . *xiii*

Kalamazoo: Lost

    Introduction 1

    Commercial 9

    Health & Human Services 27

    Public Places 43

    Sacred Places 59

    Industry & Agriculture 73

    Homes 87

    Education 107

    Streetscapes 123

    Amusements & Entertainment 137

    Odds & Ends 157

Kalamazoo: Found 167

Architects, Builders, Contractors, Craftspeople & Artisans 257

Sources Consulted 265

Subject Index 275

*This book is dedicated to the memory of
Gilbert Edwin Smith (1929-1999)
whose belief in and support
of this project helped lead to its success.*

Funders

The Kalamazoo Historic Preservation Commission and the authors gratefully acknowledge the financial and other support of the following individuals, institutions and organizations whose contributions made this publication possible.

Anonymous donor
Sally Appleyard
Don & Lydia Blanchard
Jeffrey & Catherine Bonnes
Mary Cohen
Comerica Bank
The Dorothy U. Dalton Foundation
Fifth Third Bank
Mar-o-not Class, First Baptist Church
Beverly and John Folz
The Gary Sisters Fund
David Gernant
The Irving S. Gilmore Foundation
Jim Gilmore Enterprises
Rhonda Gilmore
Todd Groat
Nancy Hamilton
The Havirmill Foundation
Mark Hoffman
Huntington National Bank
The Kalamazoo City Commission

Kalamazoo Gazette
William Lawrence
Seniors Group, Lutheran Church
    of the Savior
Ken Potts & Ann Niedzielski
National City Bank
Chapter Q of the PEO Sisterhood
Maria Perez-Stable
Patricia Pierce
Don & Louise Rice
Susan Sonnevil
Jim and Mary Thorne
The A.M. Todd Foundation
James & Mary Little Tyler
The Burton H. & Elizabeth S. Upjohn
    Charitable Trust
The Harold and Grace Upjohn
    Foundation, Inc.
Robert Van Blarcom
Denis Warner
Diane Worden

Acknowledgements

The authors gratefully acknowledge the multitudes who have provided assistance with this project from its inception in 1994. We hope we have not missed anyone; however, if we have, please accept our sincere, unspoken gratitude. Special thanks go to the families of those who are no longer with us. We are fortunate to have had their assistance.

Mary Ann Ampersee
Sally Appleyard
Peter Brakeman and Chris Dilley, Brakeman
Zolton Cohen
Peter Copeland
City of Kalamazoo staff: Sylvia Pahl, Purchasing; Yvonne Wright, Community Development; John Urschel, Scott Borling and Tony Wright, Records Center; and former staff Daniel Bollman, Robbert McKay and Brice Sample
David Dunn
Eckert Wordell Architects
Elks Lodge #50, Kalamazoo
Del Farnsworth, Archivist, St. Luke's Episcopal Church
Sharon Ferraro
Mort Fisher
Ronda Gilmore
Nolia Goodwin, Allen Chapel, African Methodist Episcopal Church
Scott Grimwood, Fetzer Institute
Nicolette Hahn
Bill Hayes
Phyllis Herring
Ted Holden
John Houdek
Kalamazoo College's Upjohn Library staff: Elizabeth Smith, Robin Rank and Eleanor Pinkham
The Kalamazoo Community Foundation
Kalamazoo Gazette administration and staff: George Arwady, Dave Hager, Tim Broekema; retired editor Jim Mosby, and former employee Lisa Schade
Kalamazoo Public Library Local History Room staff: Catherine Larson, Susan Brower, Arlene Williams and David DeVries
Kalamazoo Public Schools, Facilities Management Division: Karen Jackson and George Herrity
Kalamazoo Valley Museum Collections Department staff: Paula Metzner, Tom Dietz and former employee Amie Mack
Lil Kyser, Archivist, First United Methodist Church
John Lacko
A. Rodney Lenderink
Corrin Markle
LouAnn Morgan, Morgan & Company
Jerry Oele, Joldersma & Klein Funeral Home, Inc.
Rodger Parzyck
Maria Perez-Stable
Anne Riopel
Rick Shields
Gilbert Edwin Smith
Sisters of St. Joseph, including Sister Marilyn Sullivan and the History Room staff
Nancy Sizer
Marjorie Spradling, Archivist, People's Church
Mary & Jim Thorne
Tim Turner
Mary & Jim Tyler
The Harold and Grace Upjohn Foundation
Western Michigan University's Archives and Regional History Collections staff: Sharon Carlson, Suzanne Husband and Shirley Campbell
Christine Weisblat
Diane Worden, WordenDex Plus
Douglas G. Worden
Raye Ziring

Finally, our gratitude goes to our families: Terry O'Connor, David Houghton, Jenn Houghton and Elizabeth Houghton — who lived every moment of this project with us.

Preface

WHY DID WE WRITE *Kalamazoo: Lost & Found?* How did we manage to immerse ourselves in a near decade of photo hunting, research, interviews and writing about Kalamazoo's historic architecture? Because the "truth" in architecture is about the way people relate to it; and to better relate to it, we need to know something about it. As we become informed, we are better prepared to determine future action. With this work, our goal is to provide some of that information.

> *"The past reminds us of timeless human truths and allows for the perpetuation of cultural traditions that can be nourishing; it contains examples of mistakes to avoid, preserves the memory of alternative ways of doing things, and is the basis for self-understanding…"*
>
> **Bettina Drew,** *Crossing The Expendable Landscape*

One of the responsibilities of the book's publisher, the Kalamazoo Historic Preservation Commission (KHPC), is to heighten public awareness of the value of preservation. *Kalamazoo: Lost & Found* is the KHPC's third publication in twenty-five years. It follows Peter Schmitt's 1976 *Kalamazoo: Nineteenth-century Homes in A Midwestern Village,* and Brendan Henehan's 1981 *Walking Through Time*. All three publications help us work toward fulfilling that responsibility.

Original plans for this book called for reprinting one of the earlier publications. But as we investigated that possibility, a new idea emerged. *Kalamazoo: Lost & Found* is based on a slide program that co-author and historian Lynn Smith Houghton created and presented beginning in the early 1980s. Titled "Lost Kalamazoo," Houghton's presentation reviewed some of Kalamazoo's lost historic architecture, both simple and elaborate. In it, she looked at buildings that were covered up or had vanished completely as the result of disaster or demolition, by design or neglect.

This work's concept is further fueled by the public's continuing interest in books published in the 1970s and 1980s about the "lost" architecture of great American cities like Chicago and New York. These books and others, published both before and after the nation's 1976 bicentennial celebration, continue to heighten the public's realization of these irreplaceable losses.

We have, however, purposefully strayed a bit from the format of the earlier "Lost…" books. While they focused only on buildings that were gone, we have not. We have broken this work into two major parts, the first of which discusses Kalamazoo's loss of buildings and places.

In this first section, readers will find a historic photograph of each featured site, showing it as it looked at an earlier time. Each historic photograph is accompanied by a contemporary view of the same site. This side-by-side comparison of past-to-present had an unnerving effect on us as we moved through the project. We believed we already possessed a well-developed sensitivity to Kalamazoo's significant losses, but this "before and after" proved to further heighten even our awareness of the beauty, elegant simplicity and functions of these sites that are now only memory. And even though these places no longer exist, we were exhilarated by what we discovered.

The *Found* or second part of the book focuses on preservation. There is no question that Kalamazoo has lost and continues to lose important and otherwise wonderful old buildings that could have been saved. At the same time, especially in recent years, we are finding more and more places restored, rehabilitated and reused—and these successes are celebrated here as well.

A warning: *Kalamazoo: Found* should *not* be misconstrued to mean that we are finished with preservation in our community. As we all continue to gain a better understanding of the many ways in which these places have the capacity to enrich our lives, we know that preserving our past is even more important today than ever before, especially in the United States. There is much more to do in Kalamazoo.

> *Old architecture prompts recollection of the personal histories which define us...*
> Arthur Cotton Moore, Architect & Planner

The historic photos and drawings used here come largely from three major public collections in Kalamazoo: The Kalamazoo Public Library Local History Room, The Kalamazoo Valley Museum, and the Western Michigan University Archives and Regional History Collections. We also included photos found in the *Kalamazoo Gazette's* archives, the City of Kalamazoo Records Center, and several private collections.

Many of the historic photographs were "posed," or taken in order to "show off" the building and community, and to demonstrate its prosperity. The photographers worked very hard to place both their subjects and the City in its best light, and through photographs, the buildings communicated stability, longevity and prosperity.

At the end, we asked ourselves: Do buildings still do that? Do they still communicate those ideals? And if they do, is that good? Our readers should decide.

> *Preservationists want to retain old structures not only for their obvious assets of beauty and scale but also because these buildings represent values ingrained in history, such as morality, integrity, and ethics.*
> Arthur Cotton Moore, Architect & Planner

Readers will not see many indoor photographs. Well-controlled artificial lighting and photographic technology were not well-advanced one hundred years ago, but when we found them, we included them.

You will notice quotations on most pages. These were sometimes taken from specific comments about a site, and occasionally from the same period as a site's construction. In other instances, we came across comments made by persons outside our community that seemed pertinent to the discussion. It is our hope that readers will find them insightful and entertaining.

Finally, we asked ourselves: What is "historic"? In response, we would like to be *very* clear. The sites identified here comprise only a small percentage of Kalamazoo's past and present historic places. In other words, a place or building need not be "designated" or named in a book to be historic.

As is clearly indicated within these pages, we have lost a great deal. In a study done several years ago, almost 50 percent of Kalamazoo's central business district was found to have been replaced with parking lots and single-story, post-World War II buildings. However, Kalamazoo remains rich with historic buildings and places, some unknown and many undesignated. Within the pages of this book, we have identified just a few.

Just like politics, many things historic are often *local,* and George Washington does not need to have slept somewhere to make it historic. And while having had a United States president in a Kalamazoo bed certainly bestows a level of importance on a place, there are literally hundreds of circumstances that could also impose an equally important "designation." The most important point is this: There are many parts to Kalamazoo's whole, and many good, *old* parts which should remain because they help us remember, have served us well, and have long lives left. A resource does not require historic "designation" to make it important. When we use a wider lens to observe and learn, we can easily agree about this, and make even better use of them in the future.

> *Memory is reality. It is better to recycle what exists, to avoid mortgaging a workable past to a non-existent future, and to think small. In the life of cities, only conservatism is sanity.*
> Robert Hughes, art critic

Lynn Houghton & Pamela O'Connor

You must remember this...

As Time Goes By, Herman Hupfeld, composer

c1894. A tremendous asset to its corner location at Rose Street and Kalamazoo Avenue and to the community. The building erected for Albert M. Todd's mint oil refining company headquarters and laboratories, survived until 1970.

Courtesy Kalamazoo Public Library Local History Collection

Kalamazoo: Lost

IT SEEMS ODD TO BEGIN this book with a collection of building obituaries. President of the National Trust for Historic Places, Richard Moe, probably said it best in 1996: "The soul of history is stories, and historic buildings have lots of stories to tell." Regardless of whether the buildings are still here or not, Moe's sentiment is true. We know because everywhere we went to conduct research on these places, we found stories. Tales about the architects and builders, the events, the designs, the materials, and on and on.

"The longer you can look back, the farther you can look forward."
— Winston Churchill

These "lost" buildings and sites fit one of three categories. Category One: they have disappeared from the landscape altogether. Category Two: they are substantially hidden under later alterations. Category Three: while the buildings themselves may remain, the primary activity for which they were built has disappeared, sometimes leaving behind a derelict building, and distant memories as a result.

These sites represent a tiny percentage of great Kalamazoo buildings and places. Indeed, so much is gone that we could have written an entire volume on each building type. However, decisions about what to include were largely dictated by the images we uncovered through research.

Over a three-year period, we scoured the three aforementioned local public collections and a number of private ones, looking for images as yet undiscovered, unidentified, or not found in earlier publications. Although not able to fully achieve this goal, we uncovered great treasures. Many are glimpses of Kalamazoo's past that few people, if any, have seen before. And the stories? Some are intriguing, some are surprising, others are just plain normal, but all of them represent pieces of Kalamazoo's history using buildings and places as points of reference.

The ten chapters in *Kalamazoo: Lost* are arranged generally by an "early-use" classification. For example, if the reader is particularly interested in religious buildings, he or she will find a some of the City's many old places of worship in that chapter; the same goes for commercial buildings, residences, public buildings and others.

Overall, *Kalamazoo: Lost* contains about one hundred places that well represent our community, and we point out the areas where Kalamazoo suffers from "photographic image shortfall." This malady is especially obvious in the residential chapter, where there is a distinct lack of photos of small- and medium-sized homes in public collections. Most home portraits in public collections were taken professionally and used to showcase the community.

1890. Kalamazoo resident and wool merchant James Cobb's large, beautifully detailed Queen Anne style home once stood in the 500 block of South Burdick Street.

Courtesy Kalamazoo Public Library Local History Collection

INTRODUCTION

We also discovered many other things about the community in the process of researching its architecture. For example, we noted that the recent past is clearly not the first time Kalamazoo has actively marketed itself, as evidenced by this proclamation provided by local real estate firm Cowgill & Miller, found in the 1892 book, *Kalamazoo Illustrated*:

MY NAME IS KALAMAZOO

I employ 3,000 Men in my Factories.
I have twenty miles of water pipe.
I have fifteen miles of sewers.
I have well-paved streets, handsome parks,
    twenty churches, and the best of education facilities.
I have two daily papers, five railroads
    and five banks.
I have the best of hotels and markets.
I have elegant stores and business places.
I have fine residences, and I am proud
    of them.
I have a cultured and enterprising population.
I am surrounded by celery gardens—
    the greatest in the world.
I am proud of myself and don't care
    who knows it.
I want more manufacturing enterprises.
    YOU can find out all about me by addressing my
    only exclusive real estate firm, Cowgill & Miller.

Most often, a newcomer first judges a community by its buildings. And if we live and work in the community, those buildings play significant roles in our lives, whether we notice this or not. Much of what we do daily takes place within and around architecture, and the means by which we physically interact with these buildings influences how we live. For example, an element as simple as where and at what time of day sunlight enters a house of worship can strongly influence how the building is sited, and how its interior space is perceived and used by those within.

Social scientists have long acknowledged that the physical design of an office environment strongly influences workers' behavior. Environments with full walls and doors discourage interactions between employees, while partitions that are short enough to look over, provide some quiet and privacy, while still allowing for important interaction.

Over their lives, most people will have the opportunity to experience many more building exteriors than interiors. Do the same principles apply? Do the exteriors of buildings influence how we feel or how we act when we are nearby? The answer is a resounding yes. Building size, massing, and especially, materials, clearly affect our behavior. For that reason, we think that the architecture of our more distant past is superior to much of what was produced in the past five or six decades. That is one reason why we produced this publication.

1919. Albert Barley moved his Roamer car production to Kalamazoo from Illinois in 1917, where he operated from this plant at Reed and Factory Streets until 1928.
Courtesy Kalamazoo Valley Museum

When architects and builders had an in-depth knowledge of how a building would serve both its users *and* its community, that knowledge was communicated through the building's design, materials and craftsmanship. As Kalamazoo developed, mostly in the 100 years on either side of 1900, that knowledge influenced the design of a great many buildings whose context was given serious consideration. How would they appear from the street, set in a particular place, within that block, the area, and the greater community?

People interact with buildings, the lack of them, and other elements of the street in predictable ways. In her seminal 1961 study *The Death and Life of Great American Cities,* Jane Jacobs addressed this issue and talked about one of the necessities: buildings should be close together, or dense in their arrangement. William Whyte, in *City, Rediscovering the Center,* studied how pedestrians interact when influenced by a number of variables, including building density, the length of blocks, empty lots and blank walls. When this arrangement is at its best — a high building density, lots of windows, especially at street level, short blocks, no blank walls or large unused open spaces — Whyte discovered that people are actually more friendly toward one another.

> *"The material fabric of old buildings — the heavy beams, rough brick walls, and solid woodwork — is one of their chief pleasures. That is why we feel cheated by hollow walls, flimsy doors, and shaky balustrades. Buildings should last — and feel as though they will."*
>
> **Witold Rybczynski,** *The Look of Architecture*

> *When we build let us think that we build forever. Let it not be for present delight, nor for present use alone; let it be such work as our descendants will thank us for, and let us think, as we lay stone on stone, that a time is to come when these stones will be held sacred because our hands have touched them, and that men will say as they look upon the labor and wrought substance of them, 'See! This is what our fathers did for us.'*
>
> John Ruskin, nineteenth century socialist and leader of the Arts & Crafts movement

But that discussion deals with groups and arrangement of buildings. What about the designs of individual buildings? They, too, elicit predictable, often subconscious responses. There are several specific responses to certain components. One component is size. Take, for example, large modern, or "mega" buildings, as Whyte called them. When placed in a city where the majority of surrounding, older buildings are of a smaller scale, the "megas" are found to "swallow" people who enter them. Once inside, people tend to stay inside for long periods of time, using the street less to access other buildings, and robbing it of its formerly rich and necessary pedestrian life. An active street life is an essential component of healthy communities, most especially in commercial districts.

A friendly component of most old buildings is fenestration. Referring to the arrangement of doors and windows within a building's facade, a well-fenestrated building invites people to look in while they use the adjacent street. Windows and doors are the eyes of buildings — and they allow human eyes to penetrate an otherwise solid exterior skin. Blank walls without windows are psychologically construed as a message that says: "Don't look!" or "Stay out!" — and people usually do, feeling a quiet hostility.

> *"Kalamazoo is now a progressive city of thousands of progressive people full of business and bustling and toiling tirelessly. Her citizens are pleased with her past, proud of her present and confident of her future."*
>
> Compendium of History and Biography of Kalamazoo County, Michigan

An old building's materials and ornament provided an opportunity for its designer or owner to make a statement, but again, they made their expression within the context of other nearby buildings. For example, a group of buildings of similar setback, size and massing can peacefully coexist and still express great individuality through materials and detail, including rooflines, window hoods, cornices, columns, use of glass, pediments, and so on. In groups, these buildings create a rhythmic streetscape that draws people to use it.

On the other hand, if setbacks, sizes and massing on a street vary widely, or buildings are missing entirely, it sends a very different, dissonant message to potential passersby. People read buildings and their contexts, and choose to interact or not.

James Howard Kunstler addressed this concept in his 1998 book, *Home From Nowhere*, particularly with respect to architectural element and materials:

> *...during America's richest period, 1950 to 1990, we put up almost nothing but the cheapest possible buildings, particularly civic buildings. Look at the richly embellished 1904 firehouse or post office and look at its dreary concrete box counterpart today.*

Kunstler also addressed another, weightier psychological aspect of old buildings:

> *...they [older buildings] paid respect to the future through the sheer expectation that they would endure through the lifetimes of the people that built them. They therefore evinced a sense of chronological connectivity — one of the fundamental patterns of the universe — an understanding that time is a defining dimension of existence... Chronological connectivity lends meaning and dignity to our lives. It charges the present with a more vividly conscious validation of our own aliveness. It puts us in touch with the ages and with the eternities, suggesting that we are part of a larger and more significant organism.*

This is the point that Kunstler and others have been making for decades: old buildings that once fully occupied traditional communities like Kalamazoo did far more for a community's people than look nice. Further, the ones that are still here will continue to positively influence people who experience them in the future.

Listening to a recent radio interview with a renowned musician who discussed her relationship with her instrument prompted us to reconsider these old-building relationships. However, those within the following chapters are mostly gone and those relationships no longer interactive. And although we would prefer them extant, through their loss we have gained a higher level of understanding about their influences.

We also feel as though we have developed similar relationships with the architects, builders and craftspeople whose names are so often repeated here. Who were they and what did they do? There are stories here as well.

> *Buildings are not biological species nor are they produced in toto by machine. They are created by human beings who respond to a complex variety of cultural as well as practical factors.*
>
> Richard W. Longstreth, *History On The Line*

Stories about buildings are stories about people, and in this case, narratives about Kalamazoo's growth and development from village to city. Although we have provided an index of architects, builders and craftspeople and the buildings they influenced, space does not permit us to tell each person's story. However, readers must know that these people played important roles, and so we share a few of them here.

They came to Kalamazoo from all over the world. Henry Vander Horst was one of the most prolific of the contractors whose work we studied. Beginning life in the Netherlands, Vander Horst's mother died when he was three years old, and he went to live with his grandmother. At about the age of 11, he again moved, this time to an orphanage. At 17, he found a job delivering bibles to Kalamazoo.

After he delivered those bibles, Vander Horst went door to door looking for carpentry work, vowing never to return to Holland. The persistence he demonstrated getting his first jobs paid off. By 1945, when Vander Horst died at the age of 71, he had constructed many of the finest residences, commercial and industrial buildings in Kalamazoo and the region. For many decades, he was responsible for all four buildings at Burdick Street and Michigan Avenue, Kalamazoo's best-known "Four Corners."

Contractor Albert J. White came to Kalamazoo from Indiana when he was 16, eventually finding work as a mason's apprentice. According to a *Kalamazoo Gazette* account based on earlier research, White's first boss initially discouraged him. However, White, a man of color, finally convinced the mason to hire him by offering to work for free in exchange for learning the trade. His persistence also paid off. In the 1880s, when White was in his late 20s, he started his own contracting firm, and shortly after 1900, had 50 men in his employ.

A short list of White's numerous local accomplishments include buildings at several former paper companies, including the National Register listed Illinois Envelope Building, the former Clarage Foundry and Parsons Business School, and a major addition to the former Borgess Hospital at Portage and Lovell Streets.

British-born builder Frederick Bush arrived here in 1840, and apprenticed as a carpenter from 1843 until 1848. Then sixteen, he went to New York City where he continued to work in the building trade. He returned to Kalamazoo in 1855, and a year later, enticed Thomas Paterson to join him.

c1909. Kalamazoo contractor Albert J. White's company was responsible for a long list of notable Kalamazoo buildings, including the extant National Register listed Illinois Envelope Building within the former Bryant Paper Mill site.

Courtesy Kalamazoo Public Library Local History Collection, from Michigan Manual of Freedmen's Progress.

INTRODUCTION

Paterson's Scottish parents had emigrated to New York City in 1816, and like Bush, he also apprenticed there as a carpenter. Starting small, Bush and Paterson's first significant jobs were the buildings at the National Driving Park, now part of the Washington Square-Edison neighborhood districts. From there, they quickly moved to homes and other commercial buildings in a partnership that lasted three-and-a-half decades.

Henry Coddington, builder, arrived in Grand Rapids in 1850 at about 20 years of age, and came to Kalamazoo in 1857. He worked for Bush and Paterson early in his career and later struck out on his own, eventually also working on both residential and commercial buildings.

Kalamazoo was also home to family partnerships. The Rickman family, father George and sons Alfred, Arthur, Peter and William, worked here together for over 30 years before and after 1900. The Kalamazoo-born DeRight Brothers, John and Stephen, worked together for decades as well, erecting many local schools, churches and public buildings.

Rockwell LeRoy, an architect who worked in Kalamazoo for many years, was raised mostly in Nebraska and while growing up, worked as a cowboy on his father's ranch. Architect Forrest Van Volkenburg was from Wayland, and came to Kalamazoo in 1903. He provided the community with many residential and public buildings influenced by the increasingly popular Prairie School style.

We cannot tell each person's story here. And although these pages are directed at Kalamazoo's buildings, we must not forget that it was people who created them — and that is where the stories really begin.

> *Buildings are sometimes referred to as timeless, as if this were the highest praise one could bestow. That is nonsense. The best buildings... are precisely of their time. That is part of the pleasure of looking at buildings from the past. They reflect old values and bygone virtues and vices.... That is why old buildings are precious, that is why we fight to preserve them. It is not only because we think them beautiful, or significant. It is because they remind us of who we once were. And of who we might be again...*
>
> Witold Rybczynski, *The Look of Architecture*

c1892. Builder Frederick Bush apprenticed here as a carpenter until 1848, went to New York City to continue his training, and returned to Kalamazoo in 1855 to practice his trade.

Courtesy Kalamazoo Public Library Local History Collection

Commercial

HISTORICALLY, the design of a building reflects both its purpose as well as some of the philosophy of its creators. The construction of commercial buildings in Kalamazoo followed this practice. In the periods during which Kalamazoo's public buildings were constructed, a sense of integrity was important. Those constructed for education needed to instill that same integrity, along with a functional design.

Commercial buildings enabled a growing economy and a continual line of entrepreneurs provided the opportunity. Soon after Titus Bronson founded this village, entrepreneurs arrived to provide the goods and services to an expanding population. Justus Burdick, one of the first (and destined to become one of the most famous), appeared in 1830 and soon after, invested the then significant sum of $800 for half of Bronson's Village.

In partnership with brother Cyren, Burdick erected the first commercial building in 1831, the Kalamazoo House hotel. And in a clever marketing scheme to attract customers, Burdick platted Portage Road so that it ended at the door to his hotel on East Main Street. From that place, Kalamazoo's first commercial district spread east to Burdick Street, and west to Edwards Street.

Stores, offices and more hotels went up, built to meet the needs of the community. Soon the downtown commercial district spread south down Portage Road, north and south on Burdick Street, and even further west down Main Street, flowing to Rose Street and beyond, with multiple-storied buildings. The customary arrangement was retail space at street level, with either offices or residential flats above.

As the community grew and moved outward from the center, each new neighborhood, those still close in but also the new "streetcar suburbs," developed its own miniature commercial district where meat markets, grocers, drug stores and restaurants could be found.

While these buildings dedicated to commerce fall within a variety of architectural styles, they were seldom considered "grand" structures, like many dedicated to the public. When it came to their design, function weighed more heavily in the process than symbolism. However, in Kalamazoo, as in most middle-sized Midwestern communities, the obvious exceptions to this practice were the "Halls of Finance." For example, the original design for the 1917 First National Bank building at South Burdick Street and Michigan Avenue, projected stability with the dignified Classical Revival elements in its "Arcaded Block" form.

This term "block" was found only in the commercial areas, and is a term used to describe the building's interior form, rather than a geographical measurement. When used in the context of this chapter, it refers to a large building, divided internally into particular units that serve separate businesses. Inside the Chase Block, for example, a visitor could find several stories occupied by lawyers, doctors, dentists, music teachers, real estate dealers, dressmakers, and other professionals.

"Here too [in commercial buildings], pleasing architectural effects may be obtained in an economical manner and will prove a decided asset in the investment."

Albert Kahn Inc.,
Architects and Engineers
Industrial and Commercial Buildings

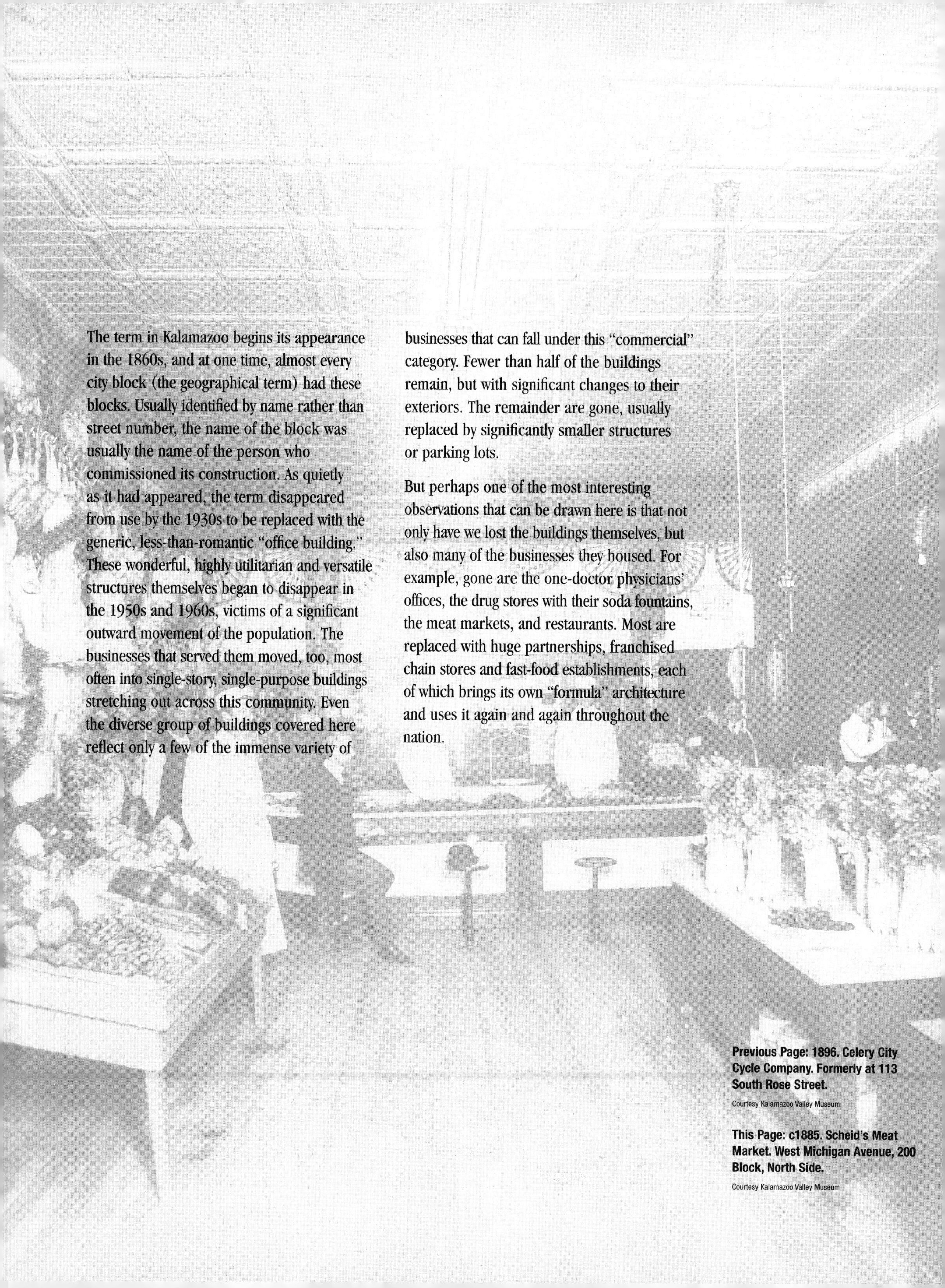

The term in Kalamazoo begins its appearance in the 1860s, and at one time, almost every city block (the geographical term) had these blocks. Usually identified by name rather than street number, the name of the block was usually the name of the person who commissioned its construction. As quietly as it had appeared, the term disappeared from use by the 1930s to be replaced with the generic, less-than-romantic "office building." These wonderful, highly utilitarian and versatile structures themselves began to disappear in the 1950s and 1960s, victims of a significant outward movement of the population. The businesses that served them moved, too, most often into single-story, single-purpose buildings stretching out across this community. Even the diverse group of buildings covered here reflect only a few of the immense variety of businesses that can fall under this "commercial" category. Fewer than half of the buildings remain, but with significant changes to their exteriors. The remainder are gone, usually replaced by significantly smaller structures or parking lots.

But perhaps one of the most interesting observations that can be drawn here is that not only have we lost the buildings themselves, but also many of the businesses they housed. For example, gone are the one-doctor physicians' offices, the drug stores with their soda fountains, the meat markets, and restaurants. Most are replaced with huge partnerships, franchised chain stores and fast-food establishments, each of which brings its own "formula" architecture and uses it again and again throughout the nation.

Previous Page: 1896. Celery City Cycle Company. Formerly at 113 South Rose Street.
Courtesy Kalamazoo Valley Museum

This Page: c1885. Scheid's Meat Market. West Michigan Avenue, 200 Block, North Side.
Courtesy Kalamazoo Valley Museum

Chase Block/Commerce Building
Northwest Corner, West Main [now Michigan Avenue] and North Rose Streets

Nehamiah Chase, owner of a successful Kalamazoo agricultural implements company, ventured into real estate in 1890, by completing a new building on the northwest corner of West Michigan Avenue and North Rose Street. This four-story Richardsonian Romanesque style building housed a variety of stores, restaurants, and offices. The massive, solid appearance of this style was very popular in Kalamazoo during the 1890s for both public, commercial and residential architecture.

By far, the most prevalent occupants on the second and third floors were lawyers, since the County Courthouse was just across the street. The entire fourth floor housed the Masonic Temple with a large dance hall and several meeting rooms. In 1913, the Masons moved to their new building on North Rose Street, just two blocks away, and the Knights of Columbus later filled their space in the Chase Block.

A disastrous fire struck the building on January 26, 1926, gutting the fourth floor and damaging those below. Firefighters failed to discover its cause. Rebuilt and renamed the Commerce Building the next year, the structure survived a second fire in 1932 that destroyed the basement and first floor. Although the owners razed the Commerce Building in 1974 citing plans for a new bank building, the land was used as a parking lot for almost twenty years until 1993, when the new building for Michigan National Bank-West opened.

↗1894. The heavy look of the Chase Block with its distinctive masonry window moldings contrasts with the delicate cresting at the top of the building and the finial at the corner.

↗1998. Opened in 1993 on the Chase Block site, Michigan National Bank-West has a distinctive corner tower.

↙1958. After a fire in 1926, the building's entire fourth floor was removed.

COMMERCIAL

Flynn's Soup'er Burger Restaurant
2838 Portage Street

Before the days of fast-food establishments, small locally-owned restaurants dotted Kalamazoo's neighborhood business districts. This establishment, Flynn's Soup'er Burger, located in the Milwood area, is a good example. Opened by Cale L. "Bud" Flynn in 1948, it offered the usual fare of hamburgers, sandwiches, soup and coffee. Mr. Flynn developed the catchy name. Erected in 1947, the building itself was a plain structure with cement block walls and a cement slab floor. Customers sat at tables and a U-shaped counter. Many neighbors and factory workers were part of the regular clientele. On Sundays, fried chicken was on the menu, originally cooked by his wife Margrete at home.

Mr. Flynn had a long-time interest in fast-pitch softball, both as a player and later as a sponsor, manager and administrator. Once, his local team even won the state championship in 1953.

He sold the restaurant in 1960 to Victor Gladysz who had managed a restaurant in Ohio and whose family owned a market next door. Mr. Gladysz changed the name to Victor's Restaurant and operated it for eleven years. For the next nine years it held various restaurants and a real estate office. In 1980, Bilbo's Pizza-in-a-Pan opened a restaurant which closed in 2000.

◤1952. The interior was renovated due to fire damage.

◤1998. One thing that has not changed with this building is its distinctive corner entrance.

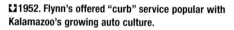
◤1952. Flynn's offered "curb" service popular with Kalamazoo's growing auto culture.

KALAMAZOO: LOST & FOUND

Gernant and Laning Meat Market
Potter Street, 500 Block, West Side

A generation ago daily trips to the neighborhood grocery store and meat market were a regular occurrence in Kalamazoo. Searching for an opportunity to go into business, friends Harry Gernant and Claus Laning discovered that Nicholas Bushouse, who owned a meat market on Potter Street in the Vine neighborhood, wanted to sell. Gernant and Laning opened in January 1909.

The structure, built in 1887, was a two-unit building with a meat market on the south end and a grocery store next door. In his unpublished autobiography, Harry Gernant said that neither he nor Claus knew anything about the meat business, but the Bushouses were willing to teach them. Mr. Laning, who wanted to be outdoors after working in a factory, drove the delivery wagon beginning at 7 a.m. Mr. Gernant noted that the horses, which came with the business, knew where to stop for each customer. Mr. Gernant ran the market, having been trained to cut meat by Peter Bushouse.

In 1913, they expanded, purchasing another meat market on South Burdick Street with Mr. Laning in charge. Six months later, he left the meat business to return to upholstering.

Mr. Gernant closed the Potter Street store to work exclusively at the one on South Burdick. He remained in the meat business until his retirement in 1955.

For over forty-five years, the south side of the building on Potter Street was the home for various owners of the grocery store next door. From 1958 until its demolition in 1985, it was vacant more often than occupied. Currently, an empty lot is on the site.

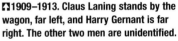

1909–1913. Claus Laning stands by the wagon, far left, and Harry Gernant is far right. The other two men are unidentified.

1998. The site for the Gernant and Laning Meat Market is now a vacant lot.

1909–1913. Harry Gernant stands behind the counter. He wrote later in his autobiography that a sharp knife was his "best friend" and a dull one his "worst enemy."

COMMERCIAL

First National Bank Building
108 East Main Street [now Michigan Avenue]

Designed by Chicago architects Weary & Alford, First National Bank's "Arcaded Block" design features a series of tall, arched openings extending across the north and west facades. The arches echo those first seen in Italian loggias during the Renaissance, and were a frequently-used bank design feature between 1900 and 1930.

The business heritage of First National began with Woodbury, Potter & Wood, a private bank founded in 1856. An 1863 reorganization of that bank produced Michigan National Bank. That same year First National was founded as a result of national bank legislation enacted by Congress. These two banks merged in 1912 and retained the First National name. Examiners who visited shortly after the merger reported that work space was tight — a predictable result of the company's growth. The expanded bank needed a bigger building.

In 1916, First National finally acquired remaining interest in their current home, the House Block, as well as a building next door to the east. Demolition ensued, and construction quickly followed on a grand, new building on the same site. Builder Henry Vander Horst oversaw the construction, and the public came to view his work on November 29, 1917. The *Kalamazoo Gazette* reported: "The design was made exclusively for this city's bank and the patterns from which it was made have been destroyed..." and "The interior walls are of Travennielle Clair marble...." and finally," These materials have been used in the construction of only five other buildings in the country."

First National's splendid new home remained unaltered for more than thirty years. Then, sometime between the late 1940s and the middle 1960s, another building to the east was demolished, and new construction there added a fourth, matched arch to the first three on the Michigan Avenue facade.

As the next 15 years passed, building design trends moved toward the less ornate, and First National followed suit. In 1974, architect Erwin Broeker oversaw the installation of white marble over the original terra cotta

◤ 1947. The main banking lobby of the First National Bank Building, before it was remodeled. This view looks toward East Michigan Avenue.

◤ 1948. This photograph shows the building as it was originally designed: three arches on the north facade, five on the west.

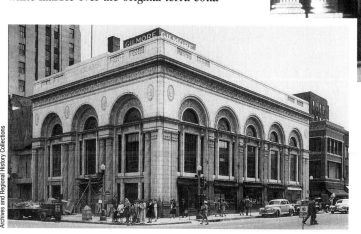

◤ c1965. Later construction gave First National Bank and Trust Building a fourth arch on its Michigan Avenue facade.

KALAMAZOO: LOST & FOUND

> "The terra cotta which forms the entire exterior of the First National Bank Building makes this the most perfectly designed terra cotta building in the whole United States."
>
> *Johnson-Howard Company, construction materials supplier*

▸ **1998.** This photo demonstrates the streamlining of the building's exterior with the application of white marble to its terra cotta facade in 1974. It retains its "arcaded" look, a distant reference to its past.

facade. Other streamlining measures included window replacement, and a remodel for both the lobby and basement at a recorded cost of $260,000. Six years later, a tornado blew through downtown, doing serious damage to the building. Repairs were estimated at $850,000.

Just four years later, in 1984, the bank raised the roof to accommodate a fourth floor. And finally, moving east once again, a new 18,000-square-foot addition went up, dressed in reflective glass and white marble. In 1997, then owner First of America Bank merged with National City Bank of Cleveland, Ohio.

COMMERCIAL

Little Michigan Restaurant
1018 West Michigan Avenue

Not the first "Little Michigan" building, this 1948 concrete block structure replaced a wood-frame one located about 50 feet northwest. With World War II over, and thousands of veterans returning home to pick up where they had left off — returning to school, marrying and starting families — success for a new, larger restaurant was assured. Local contractor Tom Schuring supervised the $7,500 construction project.

An example of Modernism, also referred to as the International Style, Little Michigan typically rejected all historical architectural references in its design and had no formal facade. The major function of its walls were to differentiate the interior space from the out-of-doors.

Its siting also represents a major departure from traditional development practice. Earlier development patterns created small blocks containing many buildings standing shoulder-to-shoulder, producing a dense, pedestrian-oriented streetscape. In 1948, planners and designers responded to a growing automobile culture by putting free-standing buildings in the middle of generous, off-street parking lots.

Longtime local Kalamazooan Harold Shoup flipped burgers for owners Lester and Doris Graybiel while he attended Western Michigan University, and recounts how the place received its name. Although the Graybiels had planned to locate the eatery in Ann Arbor near the University of Michigan's campus, their Kalamazoo market research changed their minds as to location. However, the earlier-chosen name remained the same.

Little Michigan closed in the middle 1950s. The building has since served as a branch bank, a clothing store, and most recently, a styling salon. The trees are gone and the horizontal effect of the building's deep eaves diminished when they were wrapped in a blue plastic awning.

"It was not only for college students, business people would go there too; and bring themselves up on Kalamazoo gossip."

Stefan Sarenius, *Kalamazoo resident*

c1948. This photo shows the restaurant shortly after its opening, looking west, toward Western Michigan University's west campus.

1953. When Little Michigan opened, coffee and rolls were the restaurant's only offerings. Over time, its menu expanded to include items like the T-Bone Special for $1.45 offered on the sign board above the counter.

1998. An awning wraps the formerly exposed, deep eaves, covering the building's single important architectural element.

KALAMAZOO: LOST & FOUND

American House/Park-American/Harris Hotel
East Main Street (now Michigan Avenue), 300 Block, North Side

First known as the American House, the fourth hotel of the village opened in 1844 on East Main Street. A new brick building was built on this site sometime between 1867 and 1869 after the first one burned down.

The hotel was in a good location across the street from the Grand Rapids and Indiana Railroad Station, which opened in 1870. By 1885, a fourth floor, a brick addition and dining room were added to the building. It became the first hotel in the City to be lit by electricity in 1891, and even had its own electric plant.

In 1905, local contractor Henry Vander Horst constructed a five-story addition to the west of the building. Kalamazoo businessman and developer Charles Hays purchased the hotel in 1910 and renamed it the Park-American. He tore down the 1860s-era building in 1914 and constructed a compatible addition.

Harry L. Harris & Associates purchased the hotel in 1947, renaming it the Harris Hotel. During the post-World War II era, the Harris was the hotel in the city housing many famous visitors and building a reputation for its excellent food. During these years, Kalamazoo was a "dry" town, serving alcohol by the glass only to members of a "club," many of which were located in hotels. The Harris had one of the most popular clubs, The Kalamazoo Riding Club, which met in its Cavalier Room.

The Hotel underwent one last transformation in 1961, but it closed its doors in 1968. The following year, the Hotel came down and the site remained vacant until 1974, when a Wendy's Restaurant opened. In 1985, the YWCA filled up the rest of the block.

c1920. The 1914 addition added an ornate small entrance and doubled the room capacity. A small park lay to the east of the hotel until a gas station replaced it in 1935.

c1963. Renamed the Harris Motor Inn in 1961, the hotel received a face lift both inside and out.

1998. Wendy's Restaurant and the YWCA currently use this site.

1908. The 1860s-era Italianate hotel is on the right; the 1905 addition to the left. A water tower on top of the older building helped operate the elevator which was the first one in the City.

COMMERCIAL

Downtown Gas Stations

Between 1905 and 1910, national automobile sales increased by 4,500 percent, and Kalamazoo's love affair with the car kept pace with the trend. At first, stations installed curb-mounted pumps, but their use added to growing traffic congestion. Cars formed long lines along the curb as they waited for a fill-up, blocking trolley tracks and intersections. In the 1920s, stations made the transition to off-street, free-standing "filling" stations, and America's first function-based architecture devoted purely to the service of the automobile proliferated. In larger towns like Kansas City, Missouri, estimators believe that as early as 1921, one station appeared in every two or three blocks.

In Kalamazoo as elsewhere, the appearance of the gasoline station brought with it a major change in land use. Demolition ensued in formerly built-up areas to accommodate "drive-in" stations. Sites that had earlier held homes and multi-storied commercial structures now began to see small, low-rise buildings, accompanied by several gas pumps, and plenty of space for driveways and parking.

Most station offices began as little more than rustic shelters, and proponents of the City Beautiful Movement soon had their say about them. One of the Movement's advocates, *The American City* magazine, stated it well in a 1921 issue: "The tumble-down shack had no place..." in the city, especially in residential areas; "...it would behoove cities to include in their ordinances regulations for the erection of such buildings, limiting them to certain types, insisting that the design be in keeping with other buildings of the neighborhood."

◘1958. 202 West Kalamazoo Avenue, northwest corner, Kalamazoo Avenue and Rose Street. A Standard Oil station first appeared here in 1921. This later building utilizes design principles from the Streamline Moderne movement— one design introduced by the major oil companies in the 1930s and 1940s.

◘1998. The Standard station was demolished about 1965, making way for Thurman's Restaurant and parking lot. A McDonald's fast-food franchise later replaced Thurman's.

◘1954. 1200 block of North Burdick, southwest corner, Burdick and Paterson Streets. Edward's Gulf Station, as it was known when this photograph was taken, was originally owned and operated by local filling-station and gasoline pioneer L.V. White, creator of "Dixie" gasoline, a nationally-known brand. The station served jointly as an auto sales lot for many years, and was demolished about 1965.

◘1998. A parking lot replaced the Gulf station on this corner.

◁ 1958. 402 South Rose Street, southwest corner, Lovell and Rose Streets. This Sinclair station was a downtown fixture for many years. Constructed c1925, and demolished in the late 1950s, it had a number of owners during its 30-year life.

> "A certain number of cars passing by would always be in need of gas."
>
> **Chester Liebs,** *author*
> Main Street to Miracle Mile:
> American Roadside Architecture

Oil companies soon responded, producing stations in an assortment of styles—from those that looked like small civic monuments to prefabricated models that could be selected from a catalog, shipped en masse, and assembled in two or three days. Especially popular catalog models resembled petite houses, and ranged in style from English cottages to bungalows, which fit particularly well within residential areas.

▷ 1998. The demolition of the Sinclair station made the space available for a District Court Public Safety Building in the International Style.

Beginning in the middle 1930s, larger companies like Texaco began developing new prototypes, utilizing design principles from the International Style and Streamline Moderne movements. The new designs put office, service bays, storage and restrooms under one roof. Each company geared its design toward promoting the concepts of neatness and efficiency, and establishing an instantly-recognizable corporate image. The stations on Kalamazoo Avenue (Standard Oil) and Portage Street (Texaco) are examples of these models, which appeared nationwide.

◁ 1939. 201 Portage Street, southeast corner of Portage and East South Streets. This corner first housed a Standard Oil station in 1921. This photo shows its incarnation as a newly-redesigned Texaco station in the International Style, one that gained national prominence in the middle 1930s.

All of these examples were constructed between 1920 and 1930, and although one lasted until the late 1970s, the remainder all disappeared in the early 1960s—a time that capped the greatest city-to-suburb, urban-outward migration in American history. The gas stations soon followed.

▷ 1998. The Texaco station was razed in the late 1970s and replaced with a parking lot.

COMMERCIAL

Greyhound Bus Station
West Main Street [now Michigan Avenue], 300 Block, North Side

Through the years, getting to and from Kalamazoo never seemed to be a problem using the stagecoach, train or interurban, and beginning in 1921, the "motorbus." By 1926, there were 67 daily buses connecting Kalamazoo to cities and villages across the State. During these early years, the waiting rooms were in a building on North Rose Street, but in 1941, Eastern Michigan Motorbuses constructed a new bus terminal on West Michigan Avenue housing seven different lines, including Greyhound.

The Cleveland, Ohio, firm of Bonfield and Cumming designed not only this Art Deco building, but also other terminals across the Midwest, including one in Ann Arbor that still exists. Pearson Construction Company built it for $90,000.

Sandstone, polished marble and stainless steel trim decorated the building's facade. Its vertical sign was typical of many bus terminals. The interior had a walnut ticket counter, a light blue ceiling and silver chrome chairs, all prevalent colors in buildings of this type. Because of World War II, materials were not available to finish the restaurant until later.

The building remained the bus station until 1977, when all operations moved to the Intermodal Transportation Center on North Burdick Street. First Federal Savings and Loan Association remodeled it two years later and it now serves as branch for Standard Federal Bank.

⬉ 1998. In 1997, renovation of the building's exterior took place.

⬉ 1943–1948. Buses entered from behind Water Street and departed onto West Michigan Avenue.

Browne Block/Peck Building
Southeast Corner, South Burdick (Kalamazoo Mall) and East South Streets

Ella Drake Browne was the granddaughter of Kalamazoo pioneer Benjamin Drake, and step-granddaughter of Henry Brees, a wealthy local investor. Upon Brees' death, Browne inherited $80,000 from him. From the pioneering side of the family, Browne clearly inherited the courage to do something bold. She erected a first-class commercial building in the central business district. Likely a difficult enough task for a woman at the turn of the century, this project proved even more arduous.

Henry Vander Horst was 31 years old when he contracted to erect the brick and steel building, and followed a popular design: the "Three-Part Vertical Block." This form, used in cities between 1850 and 1920, is characterized by column-like sections: base, shaft and capital. On the Browne Block, each section was topped with a dentilled beltcourse.

About the same time Vander Horst added finishing touches to the building, Browne engaged in a battle to keep the inheritance that made its construction possible. Following a well-publicized trial, Browne, the Kalamazoo Savings Bank and the Brees' estate executors were exonerated of charges claiming misrepresentation of the estate's value, and that Browne had received her inheritance illegally. The Michigan Supreme Court upheld the "not guilty" verdict, but the stress may have been too much for Browne. In 1908, she sold the building to capitalist Charles Peck for $75,000, who renamed it after himself.

The Peck Building had other prominent owners,

c1934. The *Kalamazoo Evening Telegraph* called it: "Kalamazoo's pioneer office building, embodying all modern improvements…." Walgreen Drugs occupied the street level bays for almost 30 years, beginning in the 1930s.

including developer Charles Hays, and businessman and former Kalamazoo mayor Jim Gilmore. Over the years, a mix of businesses, including retail, service agencies, dressmakers, dentists and others helped the building maintain its healthy occupancy rate. But Fidelity Federal Bank's 1968 purchase of The Peck signaled impending doom. Fidelity, operating from the Elite Theatre site next door since the 1950s, needed to expand. They razed The Peck in 1975, replacing it with a building of contemporary design.

1998. Most recently home to Standard Federal Bank, this 1970s building was actually constructed on the earlier Browne Block/Peck Building foundation.

1907. The Browne Block, shortly after construction. The upper-floor windows are filled with names of physicians, dentists and lawyers.

> *"Its location just opposite the post office and within a short distance of the courthouse and business center, together with its convenient arrangement and good elevator service, make it one of the most desirable properties in the city."*
>
> Kalamazoo Evening Telegraph
> *May 21, 1908*

COMMERCIAL

Railroad Depots

- Michigan Central Depot No.2, West Willard Street, 100 Block, North Side
- Lake Shore and Michigan Southern, Northeast Corner, East Main Street [now Michigan Avenue] and Porter Street
- Chicago, Kalamazoo & Saginaw, East Main Street [now Michigan Avenue], 500 Block, South Side

The second half of the nineteenth century has been characterized as the Great Railroad Era. Railroad builders laid thousands of miles of track, and put up over 80,000 stations which quickly became major community social and commercial centers.

On a Sunday in 1846, Kalamazoo joined the movement. The locomotive, St. Joseph, arrived in town, pulling its single passenger coach. The 1860s brought the boom into full swing and by 1892, forty, first-class passenger trains operated by five different railroad companies visited daily.

Most early depots were simply built and designed with several essential components: an agent's office, one or two waiting rooms, and one or two rooms for baggage and small freight. Simply designed as well, they were often wood-framed, and served both passenger and freight functions. As business grew, separate warehouse-style buildings for freight were constructed.

The second Michigan Central (MC) depot was erected in 1853, after fire consumed its predecessor. Of the three passenger depots to serve the line over the years, this second building, finished in the Gothic Revival style, was the only one to sit north of the track,

on Willard Street, between North Burdick and North Rose Streets. Its site is now occupied by the City's municipal bus garage.

In 1869, Lake Shore and Michigan Southern (LS&MS) owners finally secured access to Kalamazoo and brought the second railroad to town. This feat was accomplished when they

1998. This photo looks northeast at the empty site of the former Lake Shore and Michigan Southern depot.

c1895. The Lake Shore and Michigan Southern line was Kalamazoo's second railway.

1998. Municipal bus garage, site of the second Michigan Central Depot, north of the railroad tracks, across from the current depot, also known as the Intermodal Transportation Center.

Several miles of narrow-gauge road bed had been graded when the 1873 financial panic hit. The company failed, but the idea did not. In 1883, the line was reorganized as the Chicago, Kalamazoo & Saginaw. The second CK&S passenger depot, featured here, was constructed in 1899, on the south side of the 500 block of East Michigan Avenue. It was also a simple, wood-framed, two-story building with a gabled roof.

Business was good for the CK&S. In 1909, they carried almost 110,000 passengers. Many were local vacationers and "drummers," as traveling salesmen where then called. The popularity of the automobile forced ridership down in the 1920s, and the CK&S passenger depot was closed in the 1930s, although the building continued to be used by CK&S and later Michigan Central employees. The E.M. Sergeant Company owned it for many years, and after surviving to almost 100, the building was razed in 1993.

> "A visit to the ticket offices discloses a very busy state of affairs...."
>
> Kalamazoo Illustrated, *1892*

◤ The second Michigan Central depot had a graceful, "pagoda" style roof. This photo was taken between 1853 and 1887.

took control of lines from White Pigeon and then leased additional track to Grand Rapids. The LS&MS passenger depot sat at the corner of Porter Street and East Michigan Avenue. Like many across the country, it was a simple two-story building, created for function and little else. About 1900, after new track was laid to allow its trains to use Michigan Central's yard, the LS&MS passenger depot was demolished. The site sits empty today. The Chicago, Kalamazoo & Saginaw (CK&S) became Kalamazoo's only locally owned company. In 1871, two Kalamazoo merchants, Thomas Cobb and George Kidder, joined Andrew Browne of Hastings to form the Kalamazoo, Lowell and Northern Company.

◤ 1998. A pole building now occupies part of the former Chicago, Kalamazoo & Saginaw passenger depot site on the left side of this photograph.

◤ c1909. The Chicago, Kalamazoo & Saginaw railroad depot building on East Michigan Avenue.

COMMERCIAL

J.R. Jones Sons and Company
Southeast Corner, West Main [now Michigan Avenue] and South Rose Streets

J.R. Jones Sons and Company quickly became one of Kalamazoo's most popular local dry goods/department stores after it opened in 1872, at its original location on East Main Street near Exchange Place. In 1901, they purchased the business of the late Joseph Speyer who had a store on the southeast corner of West Main and South Rose Streets. Mannes Israel, Kalamazoo's first Jewish settler, constructed this Italianate building in 1864 for his dry goods business. Both Speyer and Simon Rosenbaum had worked for Mr. Israel, later taking over the firm.

J.R. Jones Sons and Company moved into the building in 1902, and for the next forty years it was a necessary stop for anyone in Kalamazoo who needed clothes. Many shoppers still recall the small baskets which traveled up a wire track with sales slips and cash to a caged office above and returned with change. Dollar days were an annual event. It was easy to identify the clerks since they were the ones not wearing hats.

Godfrey, Hammel and Associates purchased the company in 1938. A separate men's store opened nearby in 1939, on South Rose Street and Exchange Place.

An explosive fire destroyed the building in February 1945, but wartime restrictions made rebuilding impossible. The store reopened almost immediately in temporary quarters at the men's store and later moved in 1949 to 111 West Michigan Avenue, just up the block. At this point they now exclusively sold clothes and other accessories for women. In 1964, J.R. Jones Sons and Company suffered another disastrous fire when this building, and four others next to it, burned. The store never reopened.

The corner site for the company on South Rose Street and West Michigan Avenue has remained vacant since 1945 and is now a parking lot.

c1925. Before long, J.R. Jones Sons and Company moved into the building to the east. Displays in front windows were a critical part of advertisement.

1998. The former site for the J.R. Jones Sons and Company has been a parking lot since the building burned down in 1945.

1909. This 1864 Italianate building, with its ornate, bracketed cornice, had long narrow windows with moldings and several unusual circular oculus windows on its west side.

KALAMAZOO: LOST & FOUND

Ray and Ella Van Avery Drug Store Building
Northwest Corner, West North Street and North Westnedge Avenue

Over the years, Kalamazoo had three different Van Avery Drug store locations. Charles and Elsie Van Avery opened the first one around the turn of the century at 735 Portage Street. That business moved to its second site on North Burdick Street in the early 1920s. Charles' brother Ray and wife Ella Van Avery opened the "other" Van Avery Drugs in the third location in 1907. On the northwest corner, it faced the intersection at West North Street and North West Street, later renamed North Westnedge Avenue.

The building that housed Van Avery's — a two-story, Two-Part Commercial Block — is a form used since the Middle Ages when urban buildings contained living quarters above street-level shops. Also called "shop-houses," they were constructed beginning in the late 18th century in emerging commercial centers in towns and cities all over the United States until the 1940s. The designers of the Van Avery's simple brick building added grace to this neighborhood commercial district by

c1920. A two-story, Two-Part Commercial Block, the Van Avery Drug Store Building had shops at street level and offices above.

gently wrapping the building around the corner, and adding a Roman-style arched entryway. Its large awnings both protected goods in the window from the southeast sun and pronounced the division between lower and upper stories.

The store occupied the building's center and north street-level spaces, while the west end spent the most of its life housing a grocery. Physician Paul Woolsey had his office above the drug store for many years.

Gerald Van Avery bought the drug store from his uncle in 1924. After his own retirement in the late 1940s, new owners continued the store's operation until the middle 1950s. After a short vacancy, the space housed a laundromat for 15 years, and later, a restaurant. The building came down in 1980, and its lot remains vacant today.

1998. The former Van Avery site remains undeveloped today.

Health & Human Services

FEW PROFESSIONAL FIELDS have seen as much change as those that provide welfare and healthcare services in Kalamazoo. Early residents and physicians, faced with epidemics of cholera and diphtheria, fought back with primitive medicines and home-concocted remedies, and sent the serious cases to a pest house outside the Village limits. Until the 1890s, most patients were treated from birth to death at home, not in a hospital.

Interestingly, Kalamazoo's health and welfare history did not begin with its first hospital for physical illnesses; it really began with its asylum for the treatment of mental illnesses and disabilities.

Lacking modern medical and psychiatric treatments, some mental illnesses could not be accommodated at home, and those afflicted were sent to the poorhouse, wandered the streets or were locked up in attics and jails. Less than 20 years after the Village was established, the state legislature chose Kalamazoo as the site for its first asylum.

Village leaders, with a small dose of charity and a large dose of business acumen, lobbied for Kalamazoo when various sites were considered. Their inducements and legislative connections paid off. At the height of its operation in the early-to-middle 1900s, the Michigan Asylum for the Insane, later called the Kalamazoo State Hospital, had patient populations of as many as 3,600 in one year. As a result, the hospital was a major employer. Even as late as 1966, it still employed 900 psychiatric attendants, and that figure does not include physicians, nurses, maintenance crew members or other staff. Further, the hospital exercised great economic influence through its purchases of local goods.

The institution set examples architecturally and medically as well. The Thomas Kirkebride-Samuel Sloan collaboration that guided development of the original site and building design, as well as the other innovative therapy theories and practices introduced there, made it a national leader. However, for many good reasons, those theories and practices are no longer subscribed to, and sadly, many of the physical reminders of that time—the buildings—are mostly gone.

Over the years, women played a vital role in the healthcare field. Dr. Maltilda Towsley became Kalamazoo's first woman physician in 1869, closely followed by Dr. Della Pierce, two of just several female doctors who had private practices here. Helen Bissell, M.D., was appointed to the medical staff at the State Hospital in 1879, and was the earliest of a group of women pioneers at that institution. Linda Richards, chief of nursing between 1906 and 1909, was the first professionally-trained graduate nurse in the nation; and Marion R. Spear is largely credited with developing the first occupational therapy program in the state. Borgess Hospital's Sisters of St. Joseph provided nursing, surgical and administrative services to that facility for nearly a century. And finally, the work of the Women's Auxiliary at Bronson Hospital was crucial to that hospital's early success.

"Hospital equipment and accommodations offered in Kalamazoo are unsurpassed by cities of its size in the United States."

Kalamazoo Gazette
October 18, 1925

Before the early days of municipal departments of health, private organizations worked to improve the welfare of the citizens. Kalamazoo's Women's Civic Improvement League, established in 1904, became one of the largest. Spearheaded by local reformer and minister, Caroline Bartlett Crane, thirteen groups joined to form the League. Its long list of accomplishments includes: promoting street sanitation, procuring financial aid for medical emergencies, creating day nurseries for children of working mothers, construction of Pretty Lake Vacation Camp, implementing savings programs for low-income residents, and helping build public playgrounds and medical clinics. The Child Welfare League, another organization, promoted pre- and post-natal programs that led to the creation of the first Infant Welfare Station on Gull Street.

Gone are the days when physical illnesses such as diphtheria, smallpox and tuberculosis required people everywhere to either recuperate or pass on in "sanitariums." Built in remote areas from the center of town, these institutions provided a home away from home for those with highly contagious and chronic physical diseases, and were often run by municipal or county governments.

As the 19th century ended, healthcare became even more professional and business-like. Local physicians banded together to form the Kalamazoo Academy of Medicine in 1883 to improve their own education and professionalism. In 1889, the State of Michigan created a system to examine, regulate and license physicians and surgeons. This period also saw major improvements in surgical techniques, and hence, improvements in the public's perceptions of surgery.

All of these developments helped lead to the creation and growth of hospitals, and Kalamazoo moved right along with the trend. By 1886, Father Frank O'Brien took the first steps towards the establishment of a hospital here. And during the next two years, the City also worked toward that same end: the voters approved a measure, but the necessary funds could not be raised. Father O'Brien won the race when his Borgess Hospital opened in December 1889, more than a decade before Kalamazoo Hospital, now known as Bronson, was finally opened. Both institutions grew slowly at first, but now play a major part in the medical and economic life of this community, similar to that played earlier by the Asylum.

Several of Kalamazoo's healthcare institutions no longer exist, and in many cases, their buildings are gone as well. Some, like the Queen City Hospital, were here for a very short time. Established by Dr. O.H. Clark at his house on the southwest corner of Rose and Park Streets across from Bronson Park, it existed only for two years between 1898 and 1900. But in that time, it reported that medical personnel performed over one hundred operations.

The buildings featured in this chapter reflect the popular architectural styles of their periods, but because their purposes were utilitarian and their construction budgets Spartan, they rarely had the more elaborate ornamentation often found on public, commercial or residential structures. Instead, they were mostly simple buildings, very well-designed, and constructed to help fulfill important purposes.

Previous Page: c1890. Trask Cottage. Brook Farm, Kalamazoo State Hospital.

Courtesy Western Michigan University Archives and Regional History Collections

This Page: c1900. Borgess Hospital. West side of Portage Road between Spring and East Lovell Streets.

Courtesy Kalamazoo Public Library Local History Collection

Borgess Hospital
Portage Street, 300 Block, West Side

About 1853, James and Eliza Walter moved into their new home three blocks south of Main Street (now Michigan Avenue) on Portage Street. The Italianate style was popular in the Midwest and their home expressed its best features. Underneath the deep eaves, large, paired brackets were set onto a wide cornice. Above, the cupola's triple windows offered grand views.

Around 1885, Reverend Moses Hill bought the Walter home. In 1889, Hill sold the property for $10,500 to Father Frank O'Brien, who, with a gift of $5,000 from Detroit Bishop Casper Borgess, soon began Kalamazoo's first hospital in the Walter home. O'Brien wasted no time, contracting immediately with architect Martin Roberts and builder William Ritchie for a rear addition—one that would help accommodate both the soon-to-arrive Sisters of St. Joseph and their patients.

Shortly after the turn of the century, another, much larger front addition was built by contractor Albert White. A $50,000, four-story building of brick and stone, the addition closely fronted Portage Street. Less than a decade later, additional floor space was added to the south.

A little more than fifteen years later, space was tight again. A second Borgess Hospital was built on Gull Road in 1917, and the two operated simultaneously until 1929 when the Portage Street site was vacated. In 1933, the Upjohn Company purchased the property and cleared the land for future development. The building Upjohn later constructed on the site still stands today, now owned by Pharmacia.

c1884. Trees on the north and south sides framed the Walter home's setting in this photo. Later, as part of Borgess Hospital, additions were made first to the rear and then to the front.

c1905. This substantial frontal addition added 53 rooms to the facility. The original house still stood behind this new edifice.

1998. This Pharmacia building now occupies the former Walter/Borgess property.

"Soon, sisters of mercy, easing pain, watching health return to tired eyes, giving comfort as lives ebbed, passed quietly and efficiently through its halls. Now, its service to the city ended, it must give way to the demands of time and industry."

Kalamazoo Gazette, *1933*

Fairmount
North Prairie Street, 1100 Block, East Side

A cluster of buildings once stood on this hill in the northwest corner of the City, on land bounded by Alamo Avenue, and Denner, Blakeslee and Prairie Streets. Together, they served the community for almost three-quarters of a century, providing respite for patients with diseases like smallpox, diphtheria, and tuberculosis. Medical researchers had yet to discover their causes or cures so patients were quarantined.

Restoring residents to good health was earnest business, and Forrest D. Van Volkenburg's original designs echoed that seriousness. The hospital's unadorned facades were similar to others of the period, and Van Volkenburg relied on the natural beauty and skilled application of the stone and brick to create a sense of stability. The two smaller buildings, or "cottages," were scaled-down versions of the larger. All were completed in 1914.

The County assumed responsibility for the hospital from the City in 1918 and named the complex "Fairmount." Over the next several years, they contracted with Ernest Batterson to design a second-story addition to the contagious disease cottage and a new Nurse's Home. In the early 1930s, Billingham and Cobb designed and O.F. Miller constructed even more space — an addition to the large administration building which already housed the tuberculosis ward.

Fairmount's tuberculosis unit was discontinued in 1953. Over the next fifteen years the complex served the impoverished as well as older and disabled patients. The buildings' demise began in 1969 when the County announced that the facility would be shut down. The contagious, smallpox and nurses' buildings were razed in the early 1970s.

The City bought the land back from the County in 1980, and later demolished the remaining buildings. In 1990, a retirement-home development for the site was denied, in part due to response from neighborhood residents. Later that same year, the property was designated City park land.

"Located on a spot high and dry, the air is at all times invigorating. Unshaded, the purifying rays of the sun touch every corner and crevice of the place."
Kalamazoo Gazette, c1916

1998. The Fairmount property is once again City-owned and now serves as park land. Remnants of the original hospital's foundation can still be seen on the grounds.

1914. Fairmount's largest building stands facing west toward Prairie Street. The small building at the far right is the contagious disease cottage. The smallpox cottage peeks out from behind. The Nurse's Home was later constructed between the two small buildings.

KALAMAZOO: LOST & FOUND

Infant Welfare Station No. 1
Southwest Corner, Gull and North Streets

This little place had a big name: "Infant Welfare Station No. 1." Completed in 1916, it was located on what is now City park land in the 600 block of Gull Street. It serviced the community for almost 70 years in several capacities, beginning as the culmination of a dream of the Child Welfare League, formed in 1913 as a study group to investigate the health and well-being of Kalamazoo's children.

The small scale of this simple bungalow was equal to the relative size of its patrons — babies. Physicians and public health nurses examined those aged two and under here several days a week. Weights, heights, habits and other information was recorded, mothers were advised in care and feeding, and then encouraged to return for regular check-ups. In the 1940s, "expectant fathers" were invited to special sessions instructing them in the fine arts of lullaby-singing and cod-liver-oil dosing, as well as the more routine feeding and diaper-changing.

This clinic was the first of several that were eventually opened by the League. Originally covered in stucco, wood shingles were later applied, and a 1941 rear addition doubled its original size.

In 1952, the League transferred ownership of the building to the City. Around 1965, several years after the building's use as a clinic ended, the congregation of the Pleasant View Primitive Baptist Church moved in. About 1970, the little place was recycled again for use as the City's Community Relations Department. They moved out five years later, and the building stood vacant until its demolition in 1979.

1998. The site is now a City park.

c1935. This photo shows the Infant Welfare Station after its original stucco exterior was covered with wood siding, but before the rear addition was constructed in 1941.

"If it happens to be a Tuesday or Friday morning this porch will be crowded with go-carts and baby carriages, and inside there will be a chorus of many childish voices...."

Gazette-Telegraph, *1916*

HEALTH & HUMAN SERVICES

Kalamazoo Radiology
458 West South Street

This building was the third home of a long-standing practice founded by Kalamazoo radiology pioneer Dr. Augustus Crane. Beginning around the turn of the century, Crane worked alone from an office in the former Chase Block, but as his practice grew, he moved to a new office-home at Lovell and Rose Streets. There, doctors Jackson, Hildreth and Volderauer joined him over the next 35 years.

Shortly after Crane's death in 1937, the partners commissioned local architect M.C.J. Billingham to design a new building for a site on South Street, across from the grand Marlborough Apartment building. Billingham's design work turned out a functional, compact edifice with a demure street presence. One story with an attic, the 1939 structure had details culled from several different architectural styles: twelve-over-twelve double-hung windows, a front door with an elliptical fanlight and sidelights, and a hipped roof with double chimneys.

The radiology practice grew substantially over the next 30 years and in 1971, Haughey, Black & Associates designed an addition. Contractors Neil Blok and Roy Sheridan raised the roof

c1940. This photo was likely taken soon after construction of the South Street home of Kalamazoo Radiology.

and expanded the attic space to add a full second story, which they topped off with a mansard roof. With its original front windows now blocked in, the building took on a completely different street presence.

Kalamazoo Radiology moved to a new office on South Park Street in the middle 1970s, and the South Street building has since been home to a number of businesses and organizations. A recent occupant was the Kalamazoo Institute of Arts, which resided there temporarily while its own building was expanded and remodeled in 1998. A law practice now calls the building home.

1998. The building's 1970–71 renovation dramatically changed its character.

Bronson Methodist Hospital
East Side of John Street between Lovell and Cedar Streets

Kalamazoo's second hospital traces its origins to 1896 when six local physicians decided to establish a non-religious institution. Henry Brees aided their cause by donating land on John Street near the intersection of Cedar Street. That same year the doctors purchased a house next door and opened it as the Kalamazoo Hospital four years later. The Women's Auxiliary, created in March 1901, spent the next four years holding fund-raisers including card parties, dances, concerts, theatricals, bazaars and baseball games. Other institutions and businesses helped raise money. By 1903, plans were underway for a new $24,000 hospital building. It opened on November 4, 1905 with forty-six beds. The Women's Auxiliary saved money by getting individuals to pay for furnishing the rooms.

During its early years, the Hospital was never on firm financial ground. At its opening, it was already $16,000 in debt. At a time when hospitals had no endowments and patients had no medical insurance, the debt increased. It reorganized in 1907 under the State Charities Act and was renamed Bronson Hospital. Both the Hospital and community spent years raising money to erase the debt.

In 1920, the Methodist Episcopal Church took over the institution, renaming it Bronson Methodist Hospital. An addition to the north, built by the David Little Construction Company, added sixty beds in 1928. These two buildings served as the hospital until the construction of a five-story building to the east in 1940. In 1958, the hospital removed the gabled roof from the 1905 and 1928 structures. In 2000, the entire Hospital moved one block south to a new facility. The Hospital demolished these two oldest buildings in May 2001, to make room for underground parking access, part of a redevelopment project for the remainder of this complex.

> *"The building is most thoroughly equipped with every convenience necessary for the ease and comfort of the patients and nurses. It is not equaled in most respects by any hospital in Michigan."*
>
> Kalamazoo Semi-Weekly Telegraph
> *December 5, 1905*

▸ **2001.** Bronson demolished the first dedicated hospital building in Kalamazoo in May 2001. Community members, preservationists and the hospital worked to save the grand entrance portico.

▸ **c1908.** An example of Tudor Revival influence with a parapeted, gabled roof, dormers and a bay window in the front. An unusual feature is the classical entrance.

▸ **1928.** The addition to the north continued the gabled roof line.

HEALTH & HUMAN SERVICES

Kalamazoo State Hospital
Oakland Drive, 1000 Block and South, West Side

The existence of this institution has long impacted many areas of Kalamazoo's culture. Early community leaders knew this would be true — so luck played no role in locating it here. As social reformer Dorothea Dix and others campaigned for better treatment of the insane and indigent in the middle 19th century, Michigan Governor and Kalamazooan Epaphroditus Ransom responded to their appeal, and in 1848, he helped convince the legislature to establish an institution for the "insane." Allowing their incarceration in jails or poorhouses was no longer acceptable.

Another Kalamazoo man, Ransom's law partner and later Senator, Charles Stuart, was appointed to the Board of Trustees for the Michigan Asylum for the Insane, the authority charged with choosing a site. Incentives dangled by the community further helped secure a decision: $1,500 and ten acres of land near the center of town. The State later sold the land and purchased the Oakland Drive site. Insufficient funding delayed the project for years. Finally, in 1853, Philadelphia architect Samuel Sloan received a commission for the first building, later known as the Female Department.

Sloan received the commission based upon the recommendation of the State's hospital consultant, Dr. Thomas Kirkbride. A well-known progressive East-coast physician, Kirkbride advocated turning asylums into real hospitals. In a departure from traditional asylum practice, hospitals run under Kirkbride's plan admitted, classified and actively treated patients according to the nature of their disorder rather than merely providing custodial care.

Building design played a large role in meeting these patient objectives. Kirkbride's "Linear Plan" provided for everything: building placement, style, materials and finishes inside and out, heating and ventilation, and landscaping.

c1875. The approach and entrance to the original State Hospital building, later known as the Female Department. It captures the effects of consultant Dr. Thomas Kirkbride's attention to every detail of the building and grounds, including its extensive landscaping. The building was designed by Kirkbride collaborator, Philadelphia architect Samuel Sloan. (a)

The Linear Plan called for multiple wings projecting in two opposite directions from a central building, with transverse sections separating each wing from the next. This isolated patients with different disorders and economically provided space for separate entrances, stairways, bathrooms and mechanicals. During their thirty-year design collaboration, Sloan and Kirkbride created Linear Plan hospitals all over the United States.

The State appointed Dr. John Gray to the superintendent's position in 1854. Two years later, Dr. Edwin Van Deusen succeeded Gray. Along with master builder James Heneika, Van Deusen oversaw the construction of the central, Linear Plan building (reconstructed after an 1858 fire) and its south wings, accommodating male and female patients. Work began in 1859, eleven years after the Asylum act passed. A decade later, mason Tobias Johnson completed the building's north wings for 300 women patients, using two and one-half million bricks. The male patients remained in the south wings.

c1900. The first building on the hospital grounds, the 1859 Italianate style center section, with south wing and transverse sections of the original building, later known as the Female Department. The matching north wings were completed a decade later. (a)

Van Deusen acted as chief care-giver, campaigned for additional appropriations for better, larger facilities, and educated the public about mental disability. His hospital construction oversight included the relocation of the greenhouse, construction of the extant Gate Cottage and the new, separate 1874 Linear

⬆c1916. This photo presents the Female Department after its roof was raised, about 1910. The central cupola disappeared and the corner towers were enclosed. The upper triple-arched windows in the original gave way to ones of rectangular shape. It was 107 years old when demolished in 1966. (a)

Plan Male Department south of the original structure, then renamed the Female Department.

Dr. George Palmer succeeded Van Deusen, and oversaw the addition of a hospital to the Female Department in 1883; one for the men at the Male Department in 1886; and a new chapel about 1890. Palmer also acquired the 19-acre Trowbridge parcel for the Asylum, and in 1885, instituted the "Colony System"—removal of certain classes of patients to farm colonies in remote locations.

⬆c1875. This photo shows a long interior hall of the original building, or Female Department, as specified in Dr. Kirkbride's "Linear Plan."

> *"Although it is not desirable to have an elaborate or costly style of architecture, it is, nonetheless, really important that the building should be in good taste, and that it should impress favorably not only the patients, but their friends and others who may visit."*
>
> **Dr. Thomas Story Kirkbride,**
> *State Hospital consultant, from:*
> The Art of Asylum Keeping…

c1900. Burns Hospital had brick work courtesy of local mason Benjamin Roe. Upon completion, it accommodated 100 patients in rooms of 1,000 square feet each. It was razed in 1988. (b)

c1908. Detroit architect Joseph Mills designed the Edwards building with design details similar to those used on Fletcher Hospital, characterized in a 1987 report as "Institutional Queen Anne." Edwards was torn down in 1988. (c)

Dr. William Edwards took over in 1891 and began a 15-year expansion to accommodate a growing hospital population. Edwards supported the Colony System, but also felt that another treatment should be commenced for patients who did not require ward supervision, but for whom the rigors of a farm setting were inappropriate. After opening a training school for nurses in 1892, and overseeing the construction of the 1896 Water Tower which still stands, Palmer contracted with Chicago architectural firm Holabird and Roche for the design of the first "cottage" or "detached" building on the main hospital grounds.

The Kalamazoo firm of Kehoe and Nicols won the plastering contract, and in 1897, "Hall M," or Fletcher Hospital received its first occupants. The brick and stone Queen Anne style building accommodated 110 men, and the completed Fletcher cast a dignified shadow with a nine-foot foundation of cut stone, brick facades with limestone beltcourses, and multi-paned casement windows. A raised porch with arches over its bays mirrored those over the windows.

In 1898, the detached Potter Hospital for women opened, followed in 1900 by the Burns Hospital for men. Also Queen Anne in design, Burns had a jerkin head roof and fewer facade details than the Fletcher building. Local mason Benjamin Roe, who had just completed work on Potter, laid the brick for Burns, which accommodated 100 men in sleeping rooms of 1,000 square feet each. Its two-story porch was later raised to three.

1902 brought the opening of the Monroe Cottage for women. Edwards Hospital, named for the former superintendent, opened for men in 1905. Like Potter, Edwards' purpose was for receiving and diagnosing patients who were then either retained for further treatment, or sent to a ward, hospital cottage, or colony farm. With the hospital population still rising, Detroit architect Joseph Mills planned Edwards for 74 patients, again employing the Queen Anne style. He gave it features like those Holabird and Roche had created for Fletcher, including the arched porches and parapetted roof gables.

Dr. Alfred Noble succeeded Palmer. Noble, remembered for his abolition of all mechanical means of constraint, oversaw the completion of the 1908 Van Deusen Hospital. Despite its three and one-half stories, Van Deusen had a low, solid appearance. Its elevated and rusticated main floor, its double-hung windows encircling each floor, and deep, ornamented

c1880. The Male Department, finished in 1874, sat just south of the original hospital building and also followed Kirkbride's "Linear Plan." It was 101 years old the year it was demolished. (d)

c1900. The Chicago architectural firm of Holabird and Roche designed Fletcher Hospital, the first structure finished under the "cottage" or "detached" building treatment theory. It was demolished in 1988, along with the Edwards and Burns buildings. (e)

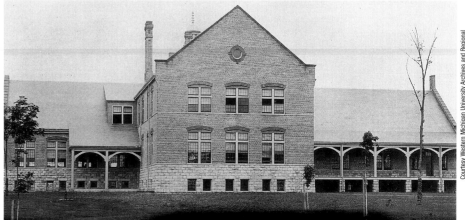

KALAMAZOO: LOST & FOUND

cornice topped with a balustrade, all worked together to give the building a strong horizontal presence.

In 1908, Potter was remodeled to serve as a nurses' home, and about 1910, the roofs were raised on parts of the Male and Female buildings for additional space. The State purchased the Montague estate about that same time, forming the hospital's north boundary along Oliver Street, and changed the institution's name to "The Kalamazoo State Hospital." One history declares: "In 1914, the institution had 73 buildings and a tract of land of 1,053 acres, which was valued at $4,585,189.15."

Over the next half-century, about 25 additional buildings were built at the hospital and farms, including the few which survive today on the main grounds. Social and medical developments after the 1950s teamed to bring about the demise of the institution's physical presence. Medical research provided new drug therapies, resulting in significant patient improvements, and decreasing the need for institutional care. This development coincided with a nationwide trend to get patients out of the hospitals and provide them with opportunities to live within the community.

The 1859 Female Department was razed in 1966, the same year Congress passed The National Historic Preservation Act. Had the Act been passed a decade earlier, both the State and the community may have better understood the importance of this historic first Asylum structure — whose innovative programs helped lead the nation in creating our first organized care and treatment system for people with mental disabilities. Rehabilitation and reuse of well-constructed historic buildings was not a popular consideration in the 1950s and 1960s however — a period when more historic buildings were razed than ever before.

The 1874 Male Department came down in 1975, along with the Monroe, Potter and other buildings. Although increasing public recognition of historic places saved the water tower in the 1970s, sentiment was not yet strong enough to save the Fletcher, Burns and Edwards buildings in the late 1980s. Western Michigan University assumed title to the property in 1998, and the extant buildings serve both the Hospital and the University.

c1908. The Van Deusen Hospital represents another phase of the institution's expansion. The Potter building is left. Van Deusen was demolished. (f)

This schematic map, based on a 1961 drawing courtesy of the Kalamazoo Public Library Local History Collection, shows the Hospital grounds as they were both before and after the demolitions that began in the middle 1960s. The 13 buildings that are still standing today are in black, while the 14 that have been razed since that time are in gray.
(a) Female Department
(b) Burns Hospital
(c) Edwards Hospital
(d) Male Department
(e) Fletcher Hospital
(f) Van Deusen Hospital

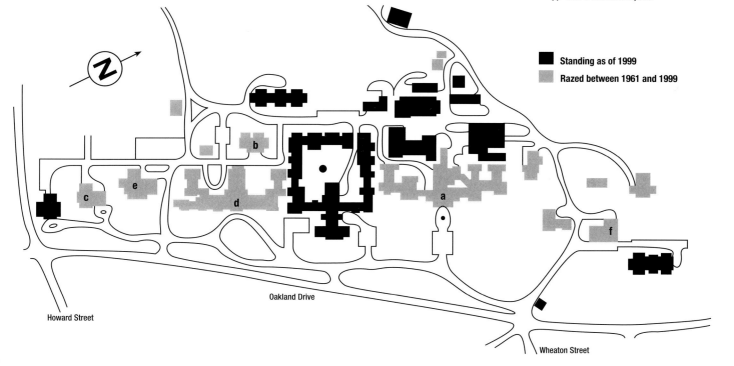

HEALTH & HUMAN SERVICES

Children's Home
Southeast Corner, South Westnedge Avenue and Ranney Street

Concern for the welfare of local girls in the middle 19th century led businessman and his wife, William G. and Jane Tuttle Dewing, to establish the Industrial School for Girls that taught such skills as sewing and knitting. The Dewings later established the Children's Home in 1883, providing girls, ages five to fourteen, with a place to live. All were either orphans or from broken families. Support came from donations and a small endowment.

The Children's Home constructed this building in 1885 on the corner of South West, now South Westnedge, and Ranney Streets. The total cost was $11,000 with many of the furnishings contributed by various individuals. Over four hundred people attended the opening on September 29, 1885, where local residents provided the entertainment. Admission to the event was ten cents.

This Second Empire style building has a distinctive mansard roof which encloses the entire third floor, multiple dormers and long, narrow windows with arched moldings.

The home housed an average of twenty-eight girls who attended local public schools and received instruction in cooking and sewing. Beginning in the 1930s, the Children's Home mission changed and it became a residential facility for the "rehabilitation" of adolescent girls. In 1960, the administration renamed the building Dewing Hall as a tribute to the founders.

In 1964, Dewing Hall joined the Lake Farm for Boys to create Lakeside, located on White's Lake off of Oakland Drive. Interestingly, the Lake Farm for Boys was created in 1907 by the Dewings' son, William S. Dewing.

Dewing Hall became a boarding house for veterans from Fort Custer, but it was razed in 1971. The lot remained vacant until Ye Olde Central Laundry was built in 1985.

c1910. Several of the young residents are standing on the porch wearing what appears to be their best white dresses.

1998. Ye Olde Central Laundry is now on the site of the Children's Home.

c1910. Along with a library, sitting, dining and play rooms, the Children's Home had fifteen "chambers" or bedrooms.

> *"The Home, located on South West Street, just south of Vine Street, is handsome looking and is a very commodious building, admirably adapted for the purposes for which it has been brought into being."*
>
> Kalamazoo Daily Telegraph
> September 30, 1885

Wilbur Home and School for the Feeble-Minded
Michigan Avenue, North Side, between North Dormitory Road and North Hays Drive

In May 1884, a new private institution opened for children classified as mentally deficient. This stately structure, located on old Paw Paw Road, now Michigan Avenue, served as the site for the Wilbur Home and School for the Feeble-Minded. Its founder, Dr. Charles Wilbur, wanted to create a home environment for children whose parents did not want to send them to a state hospital and could afford sending them to a private facility. Local businessman Benjamin Austin built the house in 1868 on a forty-two-acre parcel. It is a classic Italian Villa with a central tower, long windows with arched moldings, a cornice with paired brackets, and a front bay window. Girls lived at the main house and boys lived in two cottages on the property.

Wilbur divided the children into three different classes based on their abilities. With the understanding that if they could not be cured, they were taught to read, write and perform light tasks. A *Kalamazoo Gazette* article from 1926 reported that some of the original patients were still living there after almost forty years.

After Wilbur's death in 1909, his son Joseph took over until his own death in 1924. The home remained under the operation of Joseph's wife Helen and his brother,

c1885. Looking northwest. The porch in the foreground belongs to one of the cottages used by Dr. Wilbur, now home of the Lutheran Student Center on Western Michigan University's campus.

Dr. Edward Wilbur, until 1950 when it closed. Local realtor Charles B. Hays purchased the house and rented it two years later to Sigma Alpha Delta, a Western Michigan College fraternity. They lived there until 1955 when WMU tore down the house. Between 1956 and 1961, the University built the Bernhard Center and four dormitories on the site.

> *"Dr. Wilbur at his school for the feeble minded children received his first pupil yesterday. He came from Illinois."*
>
> Kalamazoo Gazette
> May 16, 1884

1892. Looking northeast. Benjamin Austin reportedly traveled to England to get ideas for this house completed in 1868.

1998. Western Michigan University's Bernhard Center along with Ellsworth, Hoekje, Bigelow and Henry Halls are on the general site of the Wilbur Home.

1953. Three members of Sigma Alpha Delta on the front porch.

Colony Farm
Kalamazoo State Hospital; Parkview Drive and Drake Road

In 1885, the Kalamazoo State Hospital became the first institution in the nation to begin a new innovative alternative to the care of chronic patients. Called the "Colony System," it advocated the creation of a large farm. This plan was considered both economical and beneficial because it produced food for the entire hospital community and provided work for patients who were capable of it. Administrators also claimed that it would cost a third less to care for a patient in a colony as opposed to being housed in a hospital.

Brook Farm, located three miles north of the Asylum on Douglas Avenue, was the first farm purchased that year. Encompassing 250 acres, it was primarily a dairy farm and accommodated forty men on average in the house built for them called "Trask Cottage."

The Hospital hoped to buy more land to multiply Brook Farm threefold. However, the land was not for sale so in 1887, it purchased the Hind's farm two and one-half miles southwest of the Asylum. The 357 acres included oak groves, farmland, pasture, and Loren's Lake, renamed Asylum Lake. The farm became known as Fair Oaks, and later, Colony Farm.

1890. Palmer Cottage, built in 1889, could house up to seventy-five women on its three floors. Similar to Van Deusen with its wrap-around porch, side tower and gabled roof, Palmer had dormers and a decorative cornice.

By 1892, there were four substantial Queen Anne brick buildings, called "cottages," for about 350 men and women patients. Considered "quiet," they were given work deemed to be healthy and stimulating. Women did general housework, including cooking, washing, sewing, gardening and picking fruit. The men did the major farm, garden and dairy work. Attendants and a physician also resided

"In planning these cottages, efforts were made to relieve them as far as practicable of institutional appearance... so that in viewing them... one might easily get the impression that the persons seen sitting upon the capacious porches... were summer resorters rather than patients suffering from mental disease."

Report of the Board of Trustees of the Michigan Asylum for the Insane, 1889–90

1890. Completed in 1888, Van Deusen Cottage housed an average of forty women patients. Queen Anne in design, it had a gabled roof, side tower and cresting at the top of its long porch.

1999. Western Michigan University has owned this land since 1976.

on the Farm. Construction of several barns and a slaughterhouse followed, along with a cannery on the main hospital grounds to process the fruits and vegetables. In its 1885–86 *Annual Report,* the Hospital emphasized that it would not take advantage of the patients' labor by selling its products. Everything they produced, they used on site.

By the 1920s, things began to change. Beginning in 1929, repeated attempts to sell Brook Farm failed. By the 1950s, all farm activities were consolidated at Colony Farm. By 1958, the Hospital sold both dairy herds as it was more economical to buy milk than produce it. That year, it learned that the new U.S. 131 interstate highway would cut 250 feet through the orchards at Colony Farm, taking 15 acres of fruit trees.

Brook Farm finally sold in 1960, and Colony Farm operated until 1969. At that time, the Hospital took over the Southwestern Michigan Tuberculosis Sanitarium on the City's north side and began to house patients there from the Oakland Drive facility. Patients from the Farm then moved to Oakland Drive. The State razed the Colony Farm buildings in 1971 and declared it surplus land until 1976 when it transferred title to Western Michigan

1895. Mitchell Cottage was the third cottage for women, that all faced Asylum Lake. Completed in 1892, it was home to about seventy-five patients.

University. The area became the center of controversy between 1990 and 1993 when the University announced plans to build a research business park. In early 1999, an announcement was made that the Asylum Lake property would be preserved for passive recreation. The research business park is located to the south.

1895. Pratt Cottage, built in 1892, housed male patients, thus its location which was one-half mile from the women's cottages on the west side of Drake Road.

"It [the cottage] is inviting and homelike and is destined to aid the economical prosecution of the great humane purpose of the institution for which it is attached."

Kalamazoo Gazette
November 11, 1889

Public Places

AS SETTLERS ESTABLISHED their villages, no matter where, they quickly created public institutions that would provide governance for their communities, giving them stability and permanence. In doing so, they declared their intent to stay. As the institutions were established, plans for proper buildings to house them quickly followed.

The Village of Bronson, now Kalamazoo, followed this pattern closely. Within a year of its founding by Titus Bronson in 1829, the new residents did their best to have the Village declared the county seat. The Village of Comstock vied for this honor, but Bronson's petition was aided by his accompanying offer of four squares of land to the County for a courthouse, jail, academy and four churches. The seat was named in 1831, and it gave the Village of Bronson both prestige and increased business.

The first official public building here, constructed in 1835, was a jail. Early records do not indicate how many prisoners were housed there, but an 1867 history stated the jail was constructed primarily as: "…a precaution—as a flaming sword held before the eyes of the evil-minded to terrify them from deeds of evil."

Not long after the jail was finished, plans were drawn up for a courthouse. The *Kalamazoo Gazette* declared of the Courthouse plans in 1837: "…when finished would prove to be an ornament to the Village."

Many of the institutions in this chapter were created long before their buildings were completed. In many cases, their earlier homes left much to be desired. The Public Library occupied the second story of a store before its own first building was finished in 1893. The Fire Department was located on the first floor of Corporation Hall and shared space with City offices and the Police Department for many years. The Fire and Police Departments both received buildings of their own early in the twentieth century. About that same time, the National Guard moved from the second floor of a building on North Burdick Street to their new Armory on Water Street.

Our predecessors followed popular trends when choosing designs for their community-owned buildings. "Richardsonian Romanesque" was very popular during the late nineteenth and early twentieth centuries, and its elements are visible in a number of the buildings featured in this chapter.

Locals contractors and architects, like Bush and Paterson, the DeRight Brothers, and Charles Fairchild, built strong reputations for themselves over many years of practice here. Those from outside the Village, like Edward Fallis, designer of the second County Courthouse, were chosen for their regional and statewide reputations.

It is not coincidental that almost all of these structures were eventually demolished because they were considered overcrowded. This was happening everywhere. Less than ten years after the Post Office on South Burdick Street and the first Library building were occupied, complaints declaring that space was again at a premium abounded. Was this poor planning? Or was it simply failure to meet the dual building objectives of well-designed and practical?

When completed, these places served as sources of pride for the community. Over the years, the *Kalamazoo Gazette*, the *Kalamazoo Telegraph* and organizations like the Chamber of Commerce published commemorative editions and booklets promoting our town, and each prominently featured our public buildings. The September 8, 1894, *Kalamazoo Daily Telegraph* issue claimed, "It can be safely said that Kalamazoo is not surpassed by any city of equal size in the number and architectural beauty of public buildings."

These public structures, most which were owned by the people, served as symbols of pride, and helped establish a sense of place for our growing community.

> "...*the citizen is the reason for the state... public architecture should be generous, bold and finely built.*"
>
> **Robert Hughes,** *art critic*

Previous Page: c1935. Central Fire Station. Northeast corner, South Burdick and East Lovell Streets.
Courtesy City of Kalamazoo Records Center

This Page: c1945. Main entrance of Kalamazoo Public Library welcoming World War II veterans home. Southeast corner, South Rose and West South Streets.
Courtesy Kalamazoo Public Library Local History Collection

Kalamazoo Public Library
Southeast Corner, South Rose and South Streets

Excitement was in the air in July of 1890 when the School Board announced that an unknown Kalamazoo resident would donate $50,000 to build and furnish a new Kalamazoo Public Library. The benefactors later were revealed to be Dr. Edwin Van Deusen, a former superintendent at the State Hospital, and his wife, Cynthia.

The Library began as a school library in 1860 and opened to the public in 1872. It needed this gift desperately due to its cramped quarters in a store on Main Street. The School Board purchased the land on the southeast corner of Rose and South Streets for $16,000. Patton and Fisher from Chicago designed the Richardsonian Romanesque three-story building of pressed stone. The massive arched entrance, windows with stone transoms, gables, and towers with conical roofs are common to this style. Kalamazoo resident Ulysses D. Wheaton constructed the building. The Van Deusens wanted no formal ceremony when it opened in May 1893.

Fifteen years later, staff reported the building was overcrowded. This began a fifty-year search for sufficient space. In 1926 and 1929, the Peck and Kauffer houses just south on

▸ c1900. Dr. Van Deusen chose the building site on the corner of Rose and South Streets.

Rose Street were purchased for various Library departments. Studies conducted throughout the 1920s and 1930s commented on the Library's crowding and deterioration.

Finally in 1955, voters approved a bond issue for a new combined Library-Museum. The old Library was demolished in March 1958, and the new one opened in May 1959, with the auditorium named for the Van Deusens.

The building underwent a major, two-year renovation between 1996 and 1998. The Van Deusen name stayed with the auditorium, and three of the first Library's original mosaic glass windows are installed on the second and third floors.

> *"A building that is in itself an education in beauty and an inspiration to strive for the best in the decoration of our homes and public buildings, it aims to serve the public in all educational ways."*
>
> Kalamazoo Telegraph-Press
> *April 30, 1912*

▸ c1959. Local firm Kingscott and Associates designed this Library-Museum building.

◂ c1893. The interior was decorated with tile floors, wood paneling, ornate wall coverings and mosaic glass. Initially, only the librarians had access to the books.

▸ 1998. It took two years to complete the $13 million redesign of the building by Dave Milling and Associates.

PUBLIC PLACES

Post Office
Southwest Corner, South Burdick [Kalamazoo Mall] and South Streets

There was little fanfare on February 14, 1892, when the new Post Office on the southwest corner of Burdick and South Streets opened. However, the difference between this building and its previous headquarters in a bookstore on South Burdick was significant.

The Federal government appropriated $125,000 for this structure. Bush and Paterson received the construction contract, but the architect is unknown. Local mason Benjamin Roe laid the brick and stone, and Henry W. Coddington supervised construction.

This structure is Richardsonian Romanesque, with massive entrances, windows decorated with masonry arches and a distinctive, rounded tower. They used Vermont marble in the lobby, and the winding, Italian granite stairway was called a "marvel of beauty." The main floor had several windows for service and over 900 mail boxes. The second floor held offices for the postmaster, U.S. Pension Board and the U.S. District Court.

Due to a rapidly growing postal service, an addition completed in 1904 doubled the size of the building. Further growth led to improvements in 1924, adding an elevator, mail chute, loading dock, and larger work rooms.

Discussions began in 1930 for a new Post Office. A site on Michigan Avenue and Park Street was chosen three years later. Funds finally became available in 1938. The old Post Office was vacated in April, 1939, and demolished a year later. The site remained vacant until 1956 when J.C. Penney built a new store. Penney's moved out in 1980, and the building was empty until 1984. The Hinman Corporation now owns the building.

1891. Taken before the building opened with many of the construction workers in front. The 1904 addition was built to the rear, at right.

"Tomorrow Kalamazoo's new government building which is one of the most elegant and substantial structures in the city will be thrown open to the public."

Kalamazoo Daily Telegraph
February 13, 1892

c.1900. Mail room. In 1893 the City began free delivery service.

1998. This building, now known as Century Plaza where the Post Office once sat, contains offices, shops, a restaurant and a school.

KALAMAZOO: LOST & FOUND

Kalamazoo County Jail
Courthouse Square: Southwest Corner, West Main [now Michigan Avenue] and South Rose Streets

In 1868, voters approved $40,000 for the County's third jail, to be located next to the courthouse. Completed by Bush and Paterson the next year, this brick Italianate had long narrow windows topped with decorative moldings and paired cornice brackets. The central roof pediment matches the ones added to the first county courthouse by Bush and Paterson in 1866. This building features a distinctive round window as well. There were twenty-seven cells and living quarters for the sheriff or jailer. The *Kalamazoo Gazette* declared it to be, "…the best and handsomest building in the state devoted to a like purpose."

Over the years, both the County population and jail population grew. Overcrowding at the jail became a real problem, as did its deteriorating condition. Officials claimed it was easy to break out of jail with just a spoon or fork to dig the brick mortar away.

The County Board of Supervisors received both a grant and loan in 1934 from the Public Works Administration for a new combined courthouse and jail. Voters even approved a bond issue at the height of the Great Depression to pay for the loan. Prisoners and staff were moved to the new jail in April of 1937. The old building was torn down that month.

↗ 1998. A flower garden and greenspace mark where the jail was located.

↙ 1885. The entrance faced Rose Street.

> "…it is really one of the finest buildings and conveys to the beholder scarcely a suggestion of its real purpose."
>
> Kalamazoo Gazette
> *April 1869*

PUBLIC PLACES

Kalamazoo Public Museum
South Rose Street, 300 Block, East Side

When Horace and Helen Peck built their house on South Rose Street next to the Kalamazoo Public Library in 1893 for their family, which included daughters Katherine and Frances, little did they know it would become a site for adventure and mystery for many of Kalamazoo's children.

The Kalamazoo Public School Board purchased the house in 1926 for the Library's art department and museum collection. Within a short time it exclusively became the location for the newly named Kalamazoo Public Museum. Mr. Peck's father, Horace M. Peck,

1928. Programs for all ages, especially children, has been a hallmark of the Museum.

gave the first gift in 1881 to the Library of shells and corals that formed the nucleus of the Museum's collection.

Local collectors like A.M. Todd, Donald Boudeman and D.D. Porter loaned and later donated their collections to the Museum. The *Kalamazoo Gazette* ran weekly articles about upcoming exhibits of costumes, fire equipment, arrowheads, paintings, porcelain, and artifacts from different cultures. Scores of residents remember the Pioneer Room in the attic and the mummy in the Egyptian room on the second floor.

As the Museum grew, it, like the Library, experienced cramped conditions. Voters approved a bond issue in October of 1955 for a new Library-Museum building. The Peck house was razed early in 1958 and the new building was completed May 1959. The second floor housed the Museum, with the Library downstairs. In 1996, the Kalamazoo Valley Museum opened its new building on North Rose Street. On display there is the stained glass window from the front stairway of the Peck house.

1955. Built in the Queen Anne style, this red brick house had a distinctive tower decorated with a finial.

1998. This portion of the redesigned Kalamazoo Public Library now occupies the site of the first museum.

"If you have never taken the time when in Kalamazoo to visit our museum, we have a surprise and an unusual treat in store for you. We say a surprise because you would not ordinarily expect to find a museum of this caliber in any except the largest cities."

Gateway
Kalamazoo Chamber of Commerce
January 1929

Central Fire Station
Northeast Corner, South Burdick [Kalamazoo Mall] and West Lovell Streets

The 1907 Village *Annual Report* announced: "The sites for the new fire stations have been selected and paid for. We are having plans prepared...."

Those plans provided for one of the most attractive civic buildings ever constructed in Kalamazoo. Completed in 1908 at a cost of $36,500, the Central Fire Station was one of architect Forrest D. Van Volkenburg's finest achievements. The building perfectly reflects this evolutionary stage of American fire protection practice, taking its buildings from simple sheds that housed equipment for voluntary, fraternal organizations, to those reflective of a new, post-Civil War sense of municipal responsibility.

The building's well-grounded appearance suited its unusual combination of civic functions. The main floor was public and institutional, and provided office space and areas for horses (later engines), trucks and equipment. The second floor was largely private and domestic, and in addition to offices, included sleeping and lounge spaces, bathrooms and lockers for the firefighters. The building faced South Burdick Street and the hose-drying tower was located at the rear.

Its design, based on Renaissance Revival principles, provided for the building's massive appearance and strong horizontal lines. On the front facade, the architect separated the second-floor windows by Ionic columns and topped them with arched-brick detail and circular windows that provided additional interior light. The large, street-level arches borrow from Romanesque design, resolving the challenge of enveloping the huge firehouse doors while keeping the station attractive to passersby.

In 1959, Van Volkenburg, then 84 years old, sadly witnessed the station's August demolition, allowing for the construction of Jacobson's Department Store. At his request, the crew saved a portion of one of the columns from the front facade for his tombstone.

> *"He has been one of the most faithful in the large crowd of spectators watching as a huge steel ball smashes one of his finest achievements to rubble."*
>
> Kalamazoo Gazette, *1959, referring to F.D. Van Volkenburg, the Fire Station's architect*

↗ 2001. In the early 1960s, Jacobson's Department Store completed their new building on the site, which was later expanded and remodeled. The space is now used as a cultural arts center.

↙ c1920. Horse-drawn and motorized vehicles were both in use at the time this photo was taken.

Kalamazoo County Courthouses
Courthouse Square: Southwest Corner, West Main [now Michigan Avenue] and South Rose Streets

Plans for Kalamazoo County's first Courthouse began in 1836 after years of holding court in various locations including the schoolhouse. The Supervisors voted to raise $6,000, which they borrowed from the State of Michigan's University and School Fund.

Accounts differ on the building's architect. Several give credit to Ammi B. Young from Vermont. Others claim it was E.R. Ball, a builder who was working on Justus Burdick's Main Street mansion. Whoever the architect, he designed a very plain, clapboard Greek Revival building. Typical of that style, its double-hung windows were divided into multiple panes with moldings at the top and shutters at the side. Each corner of the building was decorated with a pilaster. Originally, its rear tower rose 20 feet above the roof, causing some residents to comment the building was built "hind side before." The first floor contained the county clerk, registrar, treasurer, prosecutor and sheriff's offices. The second floor courtroom seated 300.

The Courthouse became a county community center. Along with providing space for its daily functions, it also was the site for elections, patriotic celebrations, Village picnics and speeches by visiting dignitaries.

c1870. The entrance for this first courthouse was off Main Street. Taken after the major 1866 renovations.

The County spent $7,000 in 1866 to enlarge the Courthouse. Contractors Bush and Paterson removed the tower, moved the building back a few feet, and rebuilt the courtroom. They also extended the two entrances into the building and added central roof pediments.

c1890. The second courthouse sat in the middle of the grounds of courthouse square. The statue *Justice* can be seen at the top of the building.

c1870. This first courtroom was known for its judicial bench which spanned almost the entire room. Also shown is the prominent cast iron stove.

KALAMAZOO: LOST & FOUND

The new Courthouse was completed in 1885, designed by Edward Fallis from Ohio, who was well-known for his courthouse designs. His Kalamazoo example was Renaissance Revival with long, narrow windows, pedimented entry, brick pilasters and large cornice. Like most courthouses of its day, this brick and stone building had a central tower complimented by four others, all topped by mansard roofs. The statue *Justice* stood prominently atop the central tower. Her origins unknown, she appeared on many courthouses from this period.

This building served the County well, but by 1931 there were calls for a newer combined courthouse and jail. In 1934, the County received both a Public Works Administration grant and passed a bond issue for $563,000 for the present building. The old Courthouse was torn down in 1935 and the present one, the third building, opened in October 1937.

Today, the statue *Justice* is displayed prominently at the Kalamazoo Valley Museum.

> *"Nothing was wasted on sentiment, fancy or adornment. That was supplied, at times, by the eloquent young attorneys of the period, some of whom were destined to attain the highest distinction as statesmen, judges and lawyers in after years."*
>
> **A.D.P. Van Buren,** *Michigan Pioneer & Historical Society, regarding the first courthouse*

The brackets on the cornice may have been added at this time. Some people remarked "friends of the old temple of justice would not have recognized it."

Like many other Michigan counties, Kalamazoo replaced its pioneer Courthouse with a larger, more grandiose structure in the 1880s. Voters approved $60,000 for the project. The first building was not abandoned, but moved to the northwest part of the square in 1884 and used while the new building was being constructed. It was sold for $100 and moved again one year later to the south side of West Water Street between Rose and Church Streets, where it served as a laundry and later a livery stable. It was torn down in 1921.

1998. Local architect M.C.J. Billingham designed this current Art Deco building.

c1890. Little has been written about the second building's courtroom. The tall ceilings were a typical feature in many structures of the period.

PUBLIC PLACES

Michigan State Armory Building
East Water Street, 100 Block, South Side

A medieval fortress in the middle of the City? Exactly. Local architect Charles Fairchild designed an Armory that followed a trend established a quarter of a century earlier. In keeping with the concept of "Functionalism"—that a building should express its purpose through its design—Fairchild provided an imposing structure, topped with towers and crenelations to inspire awe and respect.

Kalamazoo donated the land to the State, and after the DeRight Brothers completed construction of the $50,000, "absolutely fireproof" building in 1913, our "Citizen-Soldiers," known as the National Guard, moved from their earlier site in the 300 block of North Burdick Street.

At the building's opening, hundreds of residents and guests gathered to celebrate with a parade. Governor Woodbridge Ferris presided over dedication ceremonies, including a formal ball. The auditorium, decorated with flags and bunting, created a backdrop for Fischer's Orchestra.

The new Armory was home to Company C, originally organized in 1856 as the Kalamazoo Light Guard. Its history includes battles at Bull Run during the Civil War, and pursuit of Pancho Villa with General Pershing in Mexico. Under the direction of hometown hero Colonel Joseph Westnedge, the Company formed part of the famed 32nd Division in World War I. Members served in that division in World War II as well. In 1967, Company C found itself on the other side of the State, patrolling Detroit's riot-torn streets.

The Guard began looking for a new home in the middle 1950s. Twenty years later, it found land outside the City, just as the City determined it needed additional parking downtown. During its life, the building not only provided space for the Guard, but served as a community convention, meeting, and dance hall. It was 65 years old when it was razed in 1978.

> *"It was supposed to look like what it was, namely a building that housed a military organization... and in the event of siege, a fortress."*
>
> **Robert M. Fogelson,** *author,*
> America's Armories...

◪ **1998. The Armory and Police Station sites are now used for parking. A remnant of the Armory building survived, mounted in the NW corner of this lot—until a snow removal crew accidentally knocked it down and hauled it away during the winter of 1997–1998.**

◪ **c1913. Located just west of the new Police Station, the design of Kalamazoo's new Armory on Water Street followed a national trend.**

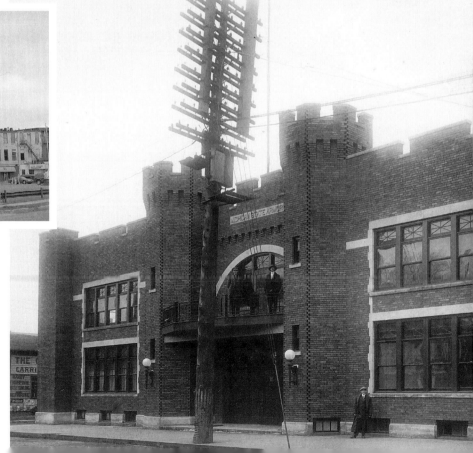

Police Station
East Water Street, 100 Block, South Side

The Water Street site of the former municipal hay market saw considerable activity during 1912 and 1913. At the same time the new Armory was being constructed, the community gained this prominent building—a new Police Station. Less than half the size of the new armory next door, the Police Station still managed to add a sober, imposing facade to the streetscape.

Several years earlier, the 1908 Village *Annual Report* included this claim: "We believe at this time it is well to call the attention of your honorable body to the condition of the place known as police headquarters" [then in Corporation Hall on South Burdick Street] "which is entirely inadequate for the proper discharge of duties of this department." Administrators took this advisement to heart. They floated a $35,000 bond issue in June 1912, and later that same year, approved architect Rockwell A. LeRoy's plans and gave Thomas Foy the

1914. Cell block corridor, just after construction.

construction contract for the new headquarters. With the three and one-half story building substantially complete, the department moved in August 1913. Former policeman Donald Rowe remembered the building as it was when he worked there in 1934. The lowest level housed the garage, and two cell blocks with four cells each. The main floor provided space for the information and complaint desk, and offices for the Chief, the detectives, and the policewoman. The second story contained chambers for the municipal judge and the traffic bureau. The third floor held locker rooms.

In the late 1950s, after a new station was constructed on the southwest corner of Lovell and Rose Streets, the City floated a $625,000 bond issue to provide more downtown parking space. The Water Street Station was razed for that purpose in 1960.

"I was probably six or seven then. In the summertime the jail windows would be open down below, and you could talk to the prisoners through the bars. I would stay on the far side of the alley, though."

Roger Hall, *whose father had a shop on Water Street, across from the Police Station*

c1914. This photo was likely taken just after construction of the new station. Note the bars on the lower level jail windows.

Public Comfort Station
Academy Street, between Bronson Park and the County Building

Discussion to provide a "Public Comfort Station" somewhere downtown first occurred about 1912. In 1914, it came up again and was referred by the City to the Committee on Public Grounds and Buildings. That committee discussed it again, but the project seems to have languished.

In December 1919, the issue arose yet again, and this time the record refers to a location for the Station: "...on the corner of Rose and Main Streets." The July 12, 1920, entry further defines it as "...on the north driveway leading to the Jail on S. Rose Street, east of the Court House." The Comfort Station would become a City building on County land.

After eight years of discussion, in the summer of 1920, with the preparation of architectural plans by Ernest Batterson, the project moved ahead. But several weeks later, the League of Women Voters made an ill-fated plea for a better building, further stalling the project. The Commission finally sent out requests for construction bids and awarded the job to the DeRight Brothers in November.

The building's design seems derived from two popular styles of the time. Craftsman principles

◤1921. Public Comfort Station, shortly after construction.

account for the building's shape, its hipped roof, eave brackets and entrance pergola. The presence of the fanlight and sidelights around the entrance, and the symmetrical proportions of the front facade come from Colonial Revival design.

Opened in 1921 at a cost of $13,000, Royal E. Blodgett and his wife, whose name was not included in City records, signed on as the station's first attendants.

But where was it located? It was erected on the southwest corner of the County Courthouse property, instead of the northeast as originally planned. It served the public until sometime between 1932 and 1937, and was likely demolished when the "new" Courthouse project began in the summer of 1935.

"The location must be thrashed out…"

City Commission meeting minutes December 29, 1919, in reference to the various options for siting the Public Comfort Station

◤1998. The Comfort Station sat to the left of the large tree in this photo.

KALAMAZOO: LOST & FOUND

Corporation Hall
South Burdick Street [Kalamazoo Mall], 100 Block, West Side

Kalamazoo's first Village hall was constructed in 1867 by the local firm of Bush and Paterson. Corporation Hall, or "Quick to the Rescue Hall" as it was nicknamed, cost $15,500 to build, and its design reflected its status as a prominent public place. Rich in detail with just a few felicitous elements, the large central roof pediment is uncommon for this style, but the pedimented, four-over-four window sashes clearly declare the building's Italianate heritage.

Its fire hose drying tower was constructed at the rear of the lot first, in 1860, because at that time, Fireman's Hall was located just to the north. When Corporation Hall was constructed seven years later, government offices and fire protection were combined under a single roof. The Fire Department occupied the main floor, and Village offices were above. The City renovated the main floor for additional offices after the Fire Department moved to new quarters in 1908.

The Hall had its interior remodeled several times during its civic life, including major work as documented in the 1879 Village *Annual Report:* "Corporation Hall has been thoroughly overhauled and improved, and put to valuable good uses." Several of these included space for the first Public Library, the Ladies' Library Association and the Board of Education.

City offices moved to the Milham and Orcutt homes on West Lovell and West South Streets during April 1925, and Corporation Hall was leased to the J.C. Penney Company. In 1936, the front facade, with all of its fine detail, was removed entirely and replaced with a contemporary design, and the rear of the building expanded — at a cost of $60,000. An even later remodeling gave the facade its present appearance.

c1897. Pediments over the second-story windows reflect those at street level, but are more delicate.

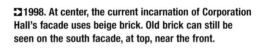

1998. At center, the current incarnation of Corporation Hall's facade uses beige brick. Old brick can still be seen on the south facade, at top, near the front.

1950s. This photo of the J.C. Penney store shows Corporation Hall's second facade.

c1913. Corporation Hall's elegant tower contributed to the building's dignified street presence.

Water Works
Northeast Corner, South Burdick Street and Crosstown Parkway

Water, or to be more specific, its delivery to homes and businesses, was the topic of serious conversation in Kalamazoo in the late 1860s. Fire protection was the major concern, and the existing system of reservoirs and cisterns was considered inadequate for present and future needs. The Village Council chose a waterworks site on South Burdick Street, overriding one earlier considered on Eleanor Street.

Mr. Birdsill "Burt" Holly of Lockport, New York, had recently developed "The Holly System of Fire Protection and Water Supply." Mr. Holly's patented "Improved Turbine Water Wheels" powered his patented "Rotary Power Fire Pumps" which the company claimed could throw 1,200 gallons of water per minute.

The Holly system became Kalamazoo's new system, and the first water works was soon constructed on the South Burdick Street site. Less than 15 years later, that original system and building showed signs of serious overuse. The 1883 Village *Annual Report* advised: "The old building is also needing repair, owing largely to the foundation being of such a nature as to cause settling...."

c1900. The 1884 Waterworks building is shown here on the left. Its smaller companion to the right was constructed in the early 1890s.

In 1884, Kalamazoo architect Martin W. Roberts designed the building. Local contractor William Ritchie handled the construction. The stone and brick structure cost about $10,000 to build and owes its architectural allegiance to many elements commonly used during the Victorian period: decorative, arched and paired windows, as well as the cupolas and cresting atop the roof. About a decade later, the City added a smaller, look-alike companion building.

Administrators sold the property in 1960, when a new pumping station was completed two blocks south. The new owners razed the buildings in 1961 for a gas station, which was never constructed. Since 1968, a branch bank occupies the site.

> "*Happily, these two most important objects of fire protection and water supply, are fully accomplished by the new system of waterworks, invented by Birdsill Holly....*"
>
> B. Holly's System of Fire Protection and Water Supply for Cities and Villages

1884. Although utilitarian in purpose, the Waterworks building was both graceful and demure.

1998. The former Holly Waterworks sat close to the street, approximately where the right half of this branch bank building now stands.

Sacred Places

THE FIRST organized church in Kalamazoo appeared in 1833, just two years after the Village was settled. When it came to houses of worship, Kalamazoo was right in step with the rest of the country. Beginning with "Church Square," bounded on the east by Church Street, the south by Academy Street, on the west by Park Street, and the north by West Main Street (now Michigan Avenue), Kalamazooans followed traditional settlement patterns.

As the population radiated from the center of the Village, the churches, meeting houses, synagogues and temples followed. After the initial Village center construction, "second waves" of construction took place. Between 1887 and 1925, four churches and a temple were constructed in just a three-block stretch on South Park Street, between Lovell and Dutton Streets. These included Second Reformed Church, 1887; People's Church, 1894; Third Christian Reformed Church, 1907; Temple B'nai Israel, 1911; and Grace Christian Church, 1925 — the only church which remains today.

For the most part, the architecture of these and other congregations followed national trends. Although no local examples of the earlier Greek Revival style were found, the period roughly between 1840 and 1870 brought Gothic and Romanesque design examples in their many variations and hybrids, including most of those included in this chapter.

While others were more "pure" in design, the Methodist Episcopal Church, formerly at the corner of West Lovell and South Rose Streets, was an example of a Gothic-Romanesque hybrid. Apparently, the original project architect designed a Romanesque structure which would have called for a symmetrical, in this case rectangular, footprint, with a regular pattern of round-arched windows and doors. He may have also planned a tower front and center. However, several alterations of the building's original plans took place, and church records indicate that the last consulting architect made a number of changes, giving the building a more Gothic look. These changes included a new window design, substituting brick for stone, and locating its tower on the corner of the building rather than in the center.

Just as important as the physical realm of these buildings, however, are the people who built them. Again and again, we discovered stories of dedicated congregations — people who moved ahead in these acts of creation with great faith. No matter the size of their assembly, the personal sacrifices they made to secure these buildings vastly exceeded the buildings themselves. Regardless of the financial requirements for a project, none failed for lack of funds. And although outside events and influences sometimes slowed their progress, no examples could be found where members failed to obtain their goals to either buy or construct a new congregational home.

Examples of this determination abound. When informed by the City Council that their building was unsound and could not be moved from its site at the intersection of Pitcher and Water Streets, the members of Allen Chapel did not fall to defeat. Instead, they held services at the corner of Porter and Lockwood Streets while they awaited completion of their new building. And according to the members of its current-day

"If churches were the expression of the piety of a people then the Americans would be the most pious in the world."

Unknown

congregation, the church's own rector, Reverend Joseph Pettiford, had a hand in the construction of the new building.

"The Immortal Thirteen" at the Methodist Episcopal Church, including Edwin Phelps, James Turner, Henry Wood and others, joined their pastor on April 20, 1868, committing their personal financial resources to completing their building if the money could not be raised through regular fundraising campaigns. In another example, Father Anthony Label personally purchased many of the materials for the construction of St. Augustine's 1869 church building on Kalamazoo Avenue, while his parish members supplied much of the labor for the carpentry and masonry work.

Once completed, these buildings did not remain static. There were additions made to almost all of them over their lives, including aggressive campaigns undertaken by a number of them in the 1950s and 1960s to construct educational wings or annexes. Some of these included Second Reformed and Park Street Church of Christ in 1952, Third Christian Reformed in 1956, and People's Church in 1962.

After area congregations finished their own buildings, they also assisted the community by providing temporary homes for others in transition. People's Church in particular has a history of offering quarters for other groups at their South Park Street and current Oshtemo locations, including service twice as home to B'nai Israel's congregation, once beginning in 1946 and again in the middle 1970s.

Beginning in the late 1800s, settlement patterns took another course that continued into the 1940s, 1950s and 1960s, fueled by the end of World War II and federally-sponsored mortgage loans which encouraged suburban growth. Earlier, residents moved to the second ring "suburbs" such as the Vine and West Main Hill neighborhoods, and later, outward toward third or fourth ring suburbs such as Milwood and Oakwood. In almost all cases, when the population shifted, their houses of worship followed.

This movement took two forms. In many instances, the centrally located church closed, constructed a new home, and physically moved its congregation to a suburban location. A second phenomenon, commonly referred to as "mothering" also occurred. In these situations, a centrally located "mother" congregation birthed one or more "daughters," each of which then operated more or less independently. Multiple examples of this process existed in the Methodist, Catholic, and Reformed Christian churches, as well as others. And in some cases, the mother actually later joined the daughter, closing the centrally located house of worship. One example of this took place when the Park Street Church of Christ mothered a "daughter" mission church. The daughter church constructed its own building on Winchell Avenue in 1962. Then, in the early 1970s, the mother congregation joined the Winchell members and sold its downtown building and property.

This phenomenon of "mother joining daughter in the suburbs" actually coincided with the last major trend in the location of houses of worship — to the outer suburbs and rural areas. While those remaining downtown demolished nearby structures to provide parking lots, congregational homes that moved further and further outward began to look very different. The increase in automobile use and subsequent decrease in pedestrian and mass transit placed houses of worship either within or next to large parking areas to accommodate their driving congregations.

Even though the designs and locations of Kalamazoo's houses of worship have changed somewhat, the dedication and support of their memberships has not. These congregations continue today as examples of what is good in the community.

Previous Page: c1910. Simpson Methodist Episcopal Church. Northeast corner of West North Street and Cobb Avenue.
Courtesy Kalamazoo Public Library Local History Collection

This Page: c1915. First Congregational Church. Northeast corner of Academy and South Park Streets.
Courtesy Kalamazoo Public Library Local History Collection

Third Christian Reformed Church
Northwest Corner, South Park and West Walnut Streets

Third Christian Reformed Church began because the Christian Reformed Church in Kalamazoo felt there was a need to create a congregation that would conduct services in English rather than Dutch in the hope of retaining young people. Incidentally, Second Reformed Church which began for the same reason, offered to sell their building to Third Christian Reformed Church in 1907 when it organized. The new congregation declined, but decided to build a new structure just to the south of Second Reformed Church on the northwest corner of South Park and Walnut Streets. Designed by Detroit architects, Spiers and Rhone and built by Scheid and Herder of Kalamazoo, it could seat five hundred worshippers. The English Tudor style had a steeply pitched cross-gabled roof, arched windows and stucco walls with a half-timbered pattern. The dedication took place on January 1, 1908. The church had gas lighting, a hand-pumped organ and several hitching posts.

Basic interior changes including new organs, a new balcony, and replastering occurred in the next fifty years. In 1956, the church added an educational wing. Its situation was along South Park Street just north of the church.

In the middle 1960s, planning took place for a new building. As with most downtown churches, finding sufficient parking for parishioners proved to be a major challenge for Third Christian Reformed Church. Less than ten years later, the church decided to locate in the Winchell neighborhood on the corner of Winchell Avenue and Broadway Street. Kalamazoo Radiology acquired the old church property in 1974. They demolished the church in the spring of 1975, but retained the education wing which was incorporated into their new facility completed a year later.

c1910. The church had a corner tower and a small portico. It also had a symmetrical fenestration.

1999. Kalamazoo Radiology has been on this site since 1976. The church's 1956 education wing is to the north of the building.

1950. The interior contained a central arch with a decorative molding. A new Moeller organ had been installed the previous year.

"The interior of the church is imposing and at the same time comfortable and the congregation is to be congratulated on the acquisition of such a fine new church."

Kalamazoo Gazette
January 1, 1908

People's Church
Southeast Corner, Lovell and Park Streets

Caroline Bartlett Crane came to Kalamazoo as its seventh Unitarian minister and brought "Social Christianity" with her. Member Silas Hubbard liked the idea, and started a church building fund with $20,000. Crane and committee members laid the groundwork and used her philosophy to shape the building's design — it would be "institutional" and open daily for community activities.

Architect C.A. Gombert (brother-in-law of building committee member Otto Ihling), designed what might be called an "Institutional Queen Anne," similar to buildings erected at the Kalamazoo State Hospital just after the turn of the century. With few embellishments, it is unlikely that passersby would immediately identify it as a church. On the inside, Crane said the committee "…planned for the uses of the same rooms for several purposes in rapid succession in the same day."

After masons Rickman and Atkins laid the last brick and the building was finished, Crane threw a banquet for all the builders, including general contractors Frobenius and Huwiler. The next day, December 19, 1894, the congregation dedicated the building.

▲ 1910. The sturdy, unadorned People's Church reflected its purpose and mission of "Social Christianity."

Members put community programs into place immediately. Their kindergarten was the first in the City. They began manual training and household science classes. The Frederick Douglass Literary Club met there. The "Evening Rest" program for independent working women ran six days weekly for a decade. And throughout its life, the church provided a home as needed for other area religious congregations.

An educational annex was completed in 1963. But a few years later, suburban demographics forced a difficult decision, with most of the congregation commuting by car and limited parking space. With regret, the congregation sold the property and moved to Oshtemo Township. The annex remains, converted to business use, but the former church building was razed for a parking lot in 1968.

▲ 1968. Taken just before the old church building was razed, this photo also shows the annex (on the far right) designed by James Parent of Stone, Smith & Parent.

▲ 1999. Although the annex at far right remains, the church site serves as a parking lot.

"Come ye all, Jew or Gentile, you need not renounce the ancient faith of your fathers, if thou canst love thy neighbor, be charitable, do justice, thou shalt be one of ours."

Meyer Desenberg, *from his hand-written memorial piece for the cornerstone at People's Church*

KALAMAZOO: LOST & FOUND

Second Holland Christian Reformed Church
South Burdick Street, 900 Block, East Side

Not all churches in Kalamazoo were large, impressive structures. This simple wooden church located south of downtown near the City water works served as least three different congregations over the years. Reverend Henry H.D. Langereis arrived in Kalamazoo in 1894 and organized the Second Holland Christian Reformed Church. They held services in his home on South Burdick Street until 1901, when a small clapboard church was built adjacent to his house.

The Colonial Revival church contained elements distinctive of that architectural style including a symmetrical design, rounded arched windows, a central portico with a fanlight window, a steeply-pitched roof with a cornice return, and a central tower that may have contained a steeple. The only photograph located shows a type of railing at the top of the roof.

After Reverend Langereis' death in 1903, the church continued under a different name, the Free Holland Christian Reformed Church. Unfortunately not much information is available about this congregation. The Netherlands Reformed Church purchased the building in 1952. They remained here until 1967 when they sold it to the Central Church of the Nazarene.

In 1976, after seventy-five years of serving as a church, the building was sold and today it houses the Alano Club which provides support for people who are recovering from alcoholism.

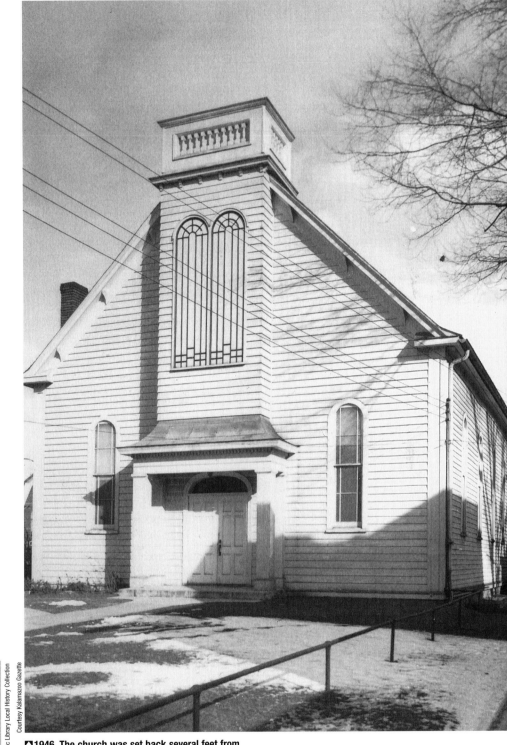

1946. The church was set back several feet from the street.

1999. The basic shape of the original church can still be seen.

Methodist Episcopal Church
Southeast Corner, Lovell and South Rose Streets

The beginnings of this congregation took root in 1830 and proved tenacious. In 1866, they sold their first building at Academy and Church Streets to finance the construction of this new church.

Considering five locations, the Methodists paid $6,000 for the new site. Eager to begin, the Trustees quickly approved plans by architect David Hopkins, but that decision was quickly followed by another decision to halt construction. Shortages of workers and cash for materials aborted the plan. Returning to Hopkins, the Trustees approved a scaled-back plan, but church records indicate that even this plan was curtailed dramatically. They completed this "chapel" with lectern and audience room only in 1867.

In March 1868, the building committee moved to have Hopkins' second plans reviewed. They engaged a Mr. Coddington (believed to be local builder/architect Henry W. Coddington), as construction superintendent, and gave him authority to consult with another architect. Coddington consulted with Chicago architect O.S. Kinney, who made radical changes to Hopkins' plans, and construction began anew. Kinney changed the window and cornice designs, and substituted brick for much of the earlier specified stone. The Methodists dedicated their church in 1869.

Between 1873 and 1905, a tower, spire and new front entry were added. Unfortunately, the spire was lost in a fire in 1922. Shortly afterward, planning began for another new church at Academy and Park Streets, a process significantly hastened by a second fire on March 13, 1926, which leveled the old church.

A gas station appeared on the lot in the early 1930s, disappearing about 1968. In 1972, construction of the Michigan Bell Telephone Company Business Office filled the corner and much of the block — a building which remains there today.

c1888. The rectangular form and regular fenestration with round-arched windows demonstrate a Romanesque Revival influence on the church's design, although the tower and spire are usually associated with Gothic Revival, another popular style of the time.

"The work was begun, the foundations of the church were built, and the chapel completed. The work on the main building was stopped because of lack of funds."

E.J. Phelps,
Seventy-Five Years of Methodism — 1833–1908

c1888. The interior of the Methodist Episcopal Church at the corner of Lovell and Rose Streets. Note the balcony around the exterior of the "audience" room or nave.

1999. This 1970s building now houses Ameritech, formerly Michigan Bell Telephone Company. Its right half occupies the former church site.

KALAMAZOO: LOST & FOUND

Second Reformed Church
South Park Street, 500 Block, East Side

In 1885, Dutch was the only language spoken during services at First Reformed Church. Their pastor, Reverend H.N. Dosker, proposed to create another congregation that would use English to keep young people in the church. Second Reformed Church organized and purchased property on the east side of South Park Street between West Cedar and West Walnut Streets in 1886. They raised funds for a building from members and friends, including Reverend Dosker who loaned $1,000. Designed by local architect Martin Roberts and constructed by Kalamazoo builder William Welsh, dedication of this Gothic Revival church took place on August 9, 1887.

Approximately twenty years later, the first major change to the building occurred when a central entrance replaced the original corner ones. The need for more space led to the construction of a kitchen and meeting room in 1920 at the rear of the church. Added to the site five years later was a parsonage. By 1952, funds permitted the building of a new education wing.

The need for more space led to plans in 1961 to build a new church. Debate occurred over whether to stay on the same site, or move to a different location. Over the years, finding sufficient parking was a major challenge. The congregation decided in 1970 to build a new church on Stadium Drive. They sold the church on South Park Street in 1971 to the Fraternal Order of Police.

A fire destroyed the church in February 1976. The F.O.P. built a new building one year later on the same site, retaining the 1920 kitchen and 1952 school wing. They sold the building in 1988 to the Kalamazoo Probation Enhancement Program, which is still there today.

◤1909. A side tower, pointed arched windows, a steeply pitched roof and corners decorated with battlements embellish this Gothic Revival building. This photo shows the church after a central entrance replaced those on the corners.

◤1999. The kitchen and school wing of Second Reformed Church remain as part of this building which now houses the Kalamazoo Probation Enhancement Program.

"It is to be made a fine structure with all the appointments which distinguish the modern house of worship from those of a half century past."

75th Anniversary of the
Second Reformed Church

◤1943. The new acoustical ceiling and rebuilt organ are visible in this photograph.

First Temple and Second Temple B'nai Israel, later the Congregation of Moses
East South Street, 100 Block, South Side and South Park Street, 600 Block, East Side

In 1843, Mannus Israel, believed to be Kalamazoo's first Jewish resident, arrived just a decade after the Village's founding. In 1866, he and others, including members of the Desenberg, Lilienfeld and Rosenbaum families who believed in Reform Judaism, joined together officially. Another decade passed, and in 1875 they constructed their first Temple. Located at 5 South Street (now known as East South Street), the temple cost $15,000 to construct. And although less than 50 feet wide and 100 feet long, Temple B'nai Israel graced South Street with its vertical, skyward reach which seemed to echo the words inscribed on its shrine inside: "This is none other but the house of God, and this is the gate of heaven!"

An unidentified newspaper piece describes the first temple's interior: "The walls and ceiling are beautifully frescoed in a style of great richness of ornamentation" and "...at the south end of the audience room is a beautiful altar and shrine, made of inlaid woods." Twenty-five years later, the Temple gained a neighbor. A group of residents who believed in Orthodox Judaism dedicated their own first synagogue several blocks east on South Street. This group became known as the Congregation of Moses. Later, the two congregations would literally cross paths.

About the same time the Synagogue was finished in 1907, a theater opened next door to the Temple. Was it the theater's construction that stirred the Temple's members into thinking it was time to move? Their records do not indicate this, but do say that there was "...considerable discussion on whether the congregation should sell its current building and build a new, modern one." They purchased land on South

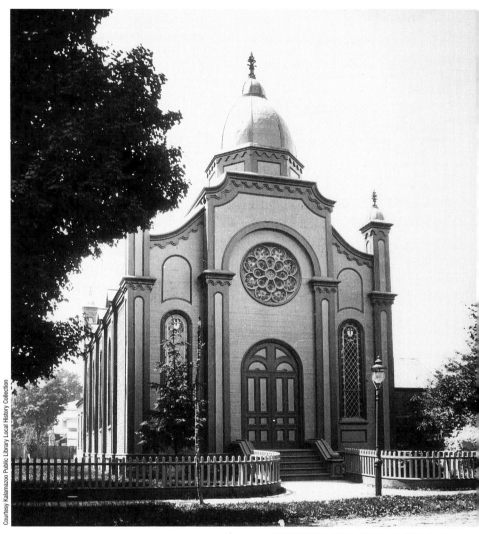

c1880. The simple elegance of the first Temple B'nai Israel on E. South Street gave this petite building a strong, yet inviting presence.

c1954. Temple B'nai Israel first building's "structural cocoon" covered everything except the dome, its shoulders, and the roof. Its earlier spire has disappeared.

1999. Temple B'nai Israel's first home on South Street was demolished in the middle 1960s to accommodate an automobile parking ramp.

KALAMAZOO: LOST & FOUND

Park Street in 1910, and asked architect Robert Gallup to design a new building for that site.

Described as Greco-Roman, the term "temple front" also summarizes this building's principal facade, with its colonnade and triangular pediment above the entrance. And although it was a small building, this combination of elements provided it with a monumental street presence. Local contractor Albert J. White helped turn Gallup's plans into reality.

Back on South Street, the old Temple building underwent a major transformation. Now owned by John J. Knight, it soon became known as the Knights Hotel, and later the Capitol Hotel. Contractor Frank Flaitz undertook alterations, beginning with a two-story front porch. Eventually, the temple was wrapped entirely by another new building, leaving only the original dome exposed to view.

B'nai Israel met in their second Temple on South Park Street until 1946, when declining attendance led them to sell the building to their former neighbors on South Street, the Congregation of Moses, who needed larger facilities. B'nai Israel moved to People's Church for their services, and the Congregation of Moses moved into the South Park Street building, remaining there until the early 1960s.

The Congregation of Moses changed its affiliation from Orthodox to Conservative Judaism almost a decade later, and in 1959, it faced another important decision—to either expand the South Park Street building or construct a new structure elsewhere. They relocated to Stadium Drive where they remain today.

Suburban migration was well underway when the South Park Street building came down in the middle 1960s. Ironically, its predecessor outlasted it, wrapped in its structural cocoon until 1976 when it and the Capitol Theatre next door were demolished for a parking ramp.

The Temple B'nai Israel congregation, after several additional moves, now resides on Grand Prairie Avenue in Kalamazoo Township.

"My House Shall Be A House Of Prayer For All People"

Inscription over the portico of Temple B'nai Israel, later the Congregation of Moses, on South Park Street

◨1999. The site of the second Temple is now occupied by this office building.

◨c1913. Temple B'nai Israel's second home on South Park Street, later occupied by the Congregation of Moses, was designed in the classical manner.

SACRED PLACES

Park Street Church of Christ
Southwest Corner, North Park and West Water Streets

Little did residents Charles Rounds and A.L. Dean know that a casual conversation between them in 1891 would lead to the creation of a Church of Christ denomination in Kalamazoo. After meeting in various locations for ten years, the congregation purchased land on the southwest corner of North Park and West Water Streets and built a small chapel.

Four years later in 1905, they completed a Victorian Gothic church designed by architect E.C. Van Leyen and built by William Case. Located to the north of the chapel, it sat 420 people. It initially had no baptismal font, however, and Reverend H.H. Halley took care of this by maintaining a tank of water in his backyard.

In 1937, plans for the new Federal building on West Michigan Avenue necessitated the demolition of the small chapel. The year 1952 saw the completion of a small two-story education wing to the west. Six years earlier, the congregation, now known as the Park Street Christian Church, created a mission church which eventually built a building on Winchell Avenue.

Both congregations grew. The newly renamed Central Christian Church downtown felt a need for a larger building and for more parking space. They sold their building in 1969 to Humphrey Products, owners of the Valley Inn Motel across the street. They held joint services with the congregation on Winchell Avenue, eventually merging one year later to form what is now known as the Christian Church—Disciples of Christ.

Torn down in 1971, the site for the Park Street Church of Christ is now a parking lot. The 1952 education wing became a law office and it remained standing until it came down in the 1980 tornado. Six months later a new law office was built on the original foundation.

c1905. Made of glazed brick and graystone, the main church had broad gables and a corner tower topped with a parapet and triangular roof. It also had a symmetrical fenestration with broad-arched windows. Just to the left of the church on the south side is the small chapel built in 1901.

1999. A parking lot for a law office is now on the church site. The present law office sits on the original foundation of the education wing.

1946. Taken after the completion of the Federal building and before the education wing was built. Note the church's arrangement on the corner.

KALAMAZOO: LOST & FOUND

Allen Chapel African Methodist Episcopal Church
Northwest Corner, Edwards and Frank Streets

Reverend Robinson Jefferies of South Bend, Indiana, came to Kalamazoo with a purpose: to organize the African Methodist Episcopal (A.M.E.) Church. Assembled in 1855, the congregation flourished until it outgrew its members' homes. In 1867, they moved into their first church building on the northeast corner of Pitcher and Water Streets.

The frame structure served them until 1912, when the congregation sold the land intending to move it to their new lot on the northwest corner of Edwards and Frank Streets. However, the City Council's Building Committee recommended against that plan when they judged the structure unsound. Left without a building, old or new, the congregation found themselves homeless. As they planned for their new building they again approached the City Council, seeking permission to hold services out of doors, which was granted for the corner of Porter and Lockwood Streets.

Soon, construction was underway for their "Allen Chapel" building, with Reverend Joseph Pettiford and members of the congregation acting as its builders, laying bricks and performing other tasks themselves. On January 9, 1914, Reverend Pettiford made a special appeal to the community in the *Kalamazoo Semi-Weekly Telegraph*, requesting assistance in completing the $4,000 structure.

When finished, three corner towers accented the rectangular building. The tower on the street corner housed the church's bell. Simple, matching entrances fronted Frank Street, each topped with a pointed, Gothic-style stained glass window similar to those on the east and west sides of the building.

In 1980, the A.M.E. congregation left "Old Allen," as they called it, and relocated into the former Simpson Methodist Church. The Church of God in Christ Pentecostal purchased Old Allen, and remained there until February 1990, when a major fire severely damaged the building. In 1991 the remains were demolished, and the lot remains vacant today.

> *"The building when completed will cost about $4,000. We must raise about $1,200 to complete our work."*
>
> **Reverend Lewis Pettiford,**
> *in a letter to the* Kalamazoo Semi-Weekly Telegraph, *January 9, 1914*

c1985. "Old Allen," as church members call it, was a sturdy, dignified structure which its members helped build.

1999. The site of "Old Allen" has remained empty since its remains from a 1990 fire were cleared from the lot.

St. Augustine Roman Catholic Church
West Kalamazoo Avenue, 400 Block, North Side

For over eighty years, the center for Catholic life in Kalamazoo could be found on the block bounded by North Park Street, West Kalamazoo Avenue, Cooley Street and the railroad tracks. The area contained an elementary school, a high school, a rectory, and most prominently, St. Augustine Church.

Completed in 1869, the church replaced a smaller nearby structure originally built in 1852. In 1864, Father Anthony Label wanted to build an academy and vocational school, but parishioners pressed for a new church. A year later, Detroit Bishop Paul LeFevre came to bless the cornerstone and donated $100, encouraging others to be just as generous. He hoped one day this church would be a cathedral and later personally paid to construct a much larger structure.

Local architect David S. Hopkins designed the red and cream colored brick Romanesque Revival structure. Father Label purchased many of the building materials himself which according to records actually increased their costs rather than decreased them. Supplies came from many places including Plainwell, Chicago, Buffalo and Europe. Many of the male

c1910. New great and side altars were dedicated in 1907. The main altar contained statues of St. Ambrose baptizing St. Augustine with his mother, St. Monica, nearby.

c1940. A new front entrance to the church was built in 1907 carrying over the triple rounded arches prominent in the original entryway. LeFevre Institute, the elementary school, opened next to the church in 1891.

c1875. A central rose window could be found between the church's twin spires that contained several oculus windows. The church also had a triple-arched entryway. The original school, built in 1873, is to the northwest of the church.

KALAMAZOO: LOST & FOUND

parishioners, who were bricklayers and carpenters, supplied the labor. Women raised the money needed to complete the project through bazaars. The dedication took place on July 4, 1869, with several prayer services, a festival and over 300 people confirmed. The entire cost of the structure, including furniture and fixtures, was $59,883.

Over the years, more buildings including several schools, a convent and a rectory were added around the church to house staff and students. Renovation of the church occurred in 1896 and 1907. This last work included new grand and side altars and an extended main entrance. One disadvantage of the church, however, was its location right next to the railroad tracks. For years, sermons, masses and general prayers would be interrupted by the noise of both trains that passed and stopped nearby at the station.

In the 1920s, the church decided to shift its facilities from Kalamazoo Avenue to a new location on West Michigan Avenue. A new high school was completed in 1926, followed by a new elementary school thirteen years later. Plans for a new church were delayed until after World War II. Dedication of the new St. Augustine's Church occurred in December of 1951. The last mass was held at the old church that morning. Four months later the outdated church was torn down with its interior stripped of pews, altars, statues and fittings which were sent to other churches. The site remained vacant until 1954 when the Detroit Automobile Inter-Insurance Exchange completed a regional office. This building also has served as the site for the Kalamazoo County Health Department and presently, Kalamazoo Community Mental Health Services.

St. Augustine's Church on West Michigan Avenue eventually did become a cathedral in 1971, 105 years after Bishop LeFevre's wish.

> *"As I looked over the buildings of the church property, the church itself seemed to be a cathedral in miniature... I had never seen anything like that before nor do I think that anyone else since has even seen anything exactly like it."*
>
> **Msgr. John Hackett,**
> *St. Augustine Church Dedication Booklet, December 4, 1951*

◤1999. Kalamazoo Community Mental Health is now housed in this building, built on the site of St. Augustine's Church in 1954.

◤1946. The rounded Romanesque arches are prominent everywhere on the church. A parking lot replaced the LeFevre Institute which was torn down in 1942. The church remained the only building on the block until its demolition in 1952.

SACRED PLACES

Industry & Agriculture

A COMMUNITY'S IDENTITY can be derived from many different sources — its location, its place in history, and in Kalamazoo's case, its industries. Kalamazoo was well-known for a variety of products, and in some instances was a leading producer for many of these goods. For years Kalamazoo had a diversified industrial base supplying paper and paper-related products, celery, cigars, pharmaceuticals, agricultural implements, buggies, corsets, cigars, stoves, fishing tackle, musical instruments, springs, uniforms and regalia all over the United States and the world.

The location of these factories was very important to their success. Most crucially, a source of power needed to be available to run machinery. Many of the first factories of the middle 19th century were located near the Kalamazoo River or any of the various creeks that surround it. The most famous example is the Lawrence and Chapin Ironworks whose building remains on the northwest corner of North Rose and West Water Streets. It used Arcadia Creek as a power source. The introduction of gas and electricity to the area freed factories from relying on water for power, but many continued to use both the river and creeks for sewage. This resulted in environmental challenges that continue today.

While location for power became less of an issue, it remained important for transportation. Almost every factory building in Kalamazoo was sited either next to railroad tracks or within several blocks. In some cases, the railroad siding was constructed at the same time as the building. Until the 1960s, rail was the primary means of getting raw materials to factories and finished products to market. To this day, while railroads may not be the major means of moving goods, they still play an important role.

Architecturally, Kalamazoo factories during the middle 19th and early 20th centuries, like those across the nation, were very plain with little ornamentation. The critical part of the building was not the exterior, but the interior where the manufacturing took place. Very important was the efficient use of space where raw materials would enter and finished products would exit. Some buildings had exterior architectural flourishes, including decorated cornices, arched entrances and even small towers, but they were very subtle. The majority of the funds spent for the construction was directed towards the space and machinery inside.

There was never any doubt that each of these factories would have additions due to the growth of these industries. Some of these newer structures blended well with the original ones; however, others were added later with no thought as to how they would look. Adding space was more important than making an "architectural statement."

For many of Kalamazoo's factories, there is little knowledge of the architects who designed them or the contractors who built them. These people chose to remain, for the most part, anonymous, for these buildings did not have the prestige of a county courthouse, fire station or bank. Over the years there did develop,

"Diversification, that one word slogan ... has been for Kalamazoo the industrial open sesame to a business well-being that few citizens in Michigan have been able to rival."

Kalamazoo Gazette
January 24, 1937

not only in Kalamazoo but across the country, a separate group of architects, builders and engineers who specialized in industrial buildings.

Factories, like many other building types, cannot be dated by their architectural style. More commonly, one dates them through the construction methods used to build them. During the middle 19th century, basic factory construction consisted of brick walls and open wood joists. Typically, these buildings had a series of double-hung windows which allowed some ventilation, but a limited amount of light compared to the large space within. Change came in the early part of the 20th century, just before World War I, with the introduction of reinforced concrete strengthened by iron or steel. This stronger framework supported "day-light" windows which were taller and wider than double-hung, and allowed a greater amount of light between jambs. After World War II, new types of artificial light, such as fluorescent, allowed factories to be built with few windows. Aluminum and other types of artificial siding replaced bricks for the exterior. These structural changes meant less expense for the company, but also made a less attractive building.

Today, many of the factories are located outside Kalamazoo in the suburbs and outlying areas. Many communities attract companies with industrial parks which provide all the services needed. Urban core communities like Kalamazoo are working to bring industries back into the central city with brownfield redevelopment programs.

This chapter includes not only lost industrial buildings, but also lost industries. No longer is Kalamazoo the leading producer of corsets or loose-leaf binders, but fortunately, almost all of Kalamazoo's factories were photographed both outside and inside for catalogs, advertisements, newspapers and articles. Still to this day, Kalamazoo's local library, museum and archives continue to receive questions about these companies from around the world. The community may not make these products any longer, but it is still known for them.

Previous Page: c1885. Burrell and Son Carriage and Wagon Shop. Northwest corner of West Michigan Avenue and North Park Street. Present location of Federal Building.
Courtesy Kalamazoo Public Library Local History Collection

This Page: c1900. Kalamazoo Paper Company. Portage Road near Cork Street.
Courtesy Western Michigan University Archives and Regional History Collections

Henderson-Ames Company
Southeast Corner, North Park and West Water Streets

In March of 1901, the Henderson-Ames Company announced plans to build a new factory downtown that would allow them to consolidate their operations which were spread across four different locations in the City. The company produced uniforms, regalia and other supplies for the military, civic organizations, and lodge and fraternal orders.

The four-story structure, completed in November 1901, contained three acres of floor space. Steam-powered and lit by electricity, it also had two large interior courtyards for ventilation. Employees at the factory made more than one-half of all lodge uniforms used in the United States.

In 1909, the company built a woodworking and furniture plant on Paterson Street. They completed a new office building in 1924 on the northeast corner of West Michigan Avenue and North Park Street. A second-floor passageway connected it to the main factory.

In 1933, the Henderson-Ames Company merged with the Lilley Company to form the Lilley-Ames Company, and all operations moved to Columbus, Ohio. For the next few years the factory building stored furniture for Vermeulen's and housed a printing company.

Demolition of the Henderson-Ames factory took place in 1940. The area became a parking lot. The Henderson-Ames office later housed a grocery store, law practice and a bank.

In 1997, the Kalamazoo County Chamber of Commerce purchased both the former Henderson-Ames office building on West Michigan Avenue and the parking lot to the north for their headquarters. They moved into the building in 1998.

c1905. Boning and Eyelet Department. At one time the Henderson-Ames Company employed close to six hundred people, over sixty percent of them women and girls.

1999. The site of the Henderson-Ames Company factory is now a parking lot for the Kalamazoo County Chamber of Commerce.

c1910. Looking southeast from North Park Street. Four corner towers decorate the building along with a corbel course at the cornice. Two arched entrances are on West Water Street. The office building, completed in 1924, was to the south of the factory.

"The eye of the passer-by is pleased with the solid and substantial structure erected...."

Kalamazoo Gazette
October 20, 1901

INDUSTRY & AGRICULTURE

Kalamazoo Loose Leaf Ledger Company
West Kalamazoo Avenue, 400 Block, North Side

In 1903, Kalamazoo's Ihling Brothers and Everard Company purchased the patent rights for a loose-leaf binder. The popularity of this product led to the eventual formation of a separate company, the Kalamazoo Loose Leaf Ledger (later renamed Binder) Company.

Need for a factory led to the completion in 1906 of a four-story brick structure built by the local firm George Rickman and Sons. Over the next 17 years, the building more than tripled in size to meet the growing demands of the company. Additions were completed to the west in 1913 and 1917, and to the east in 1921. The building eventually spanned the entire block.

The company merged with the Remington-Rand Company in 1927, which led to the building being renamed the Remington Building. Despite the merger, two years later operations moved to Benton Harbor, Michigan. However, several employees remained in Kalamazoo creating a similar company called Mastercraft that remained on West Kalamazoo Avenue until 1935. During these years, the building also filled its space with all types of light manufacturing industries and service related companies.

In 1950, the Saniwax Company, which produced waxed food wrappers, purchased the newly renamed Saniwax Building to house some of its operations. Since 1918, they had been located in an adjacent building on North Park Street.

In addition to Saniwax and other companies, artists and craftspeople began to rent space in the building during the 1970s. Even though the Saniwax Company left in 1971, the building is still filled with the same types of tenants. Purchased by the 436 Park Corporation in 1982, the structure is now called the Park Trades Center.

↖ c1925. The original building, at center, can be distinguished by its six rows of long, narrow rounded windows. The entire building is topped by a corbel course at the cornice. The large windows throughout the rest of the structure is a characteristic of "day-light" construction.

↖ 1999. The building continues to be filled with a variety of artists, craftspeople and small businesses.

"The finished building housing offices and factory, is one of the most convenient and best arranged of concerns in America devoted to the manufacture of loose leaf devices and systems...."

Kalamazoo Gazette
June 26, 1921

↖ c1925. The company made not only binders, but also ledgers, catalog covers, ruled sheets, indexes and even hand accounting equipment. It became the largest loose leaf manufacturing plant in the world.

Kalamazoo Sled Company
East Crosstown Parkway, 800 Block, South Side

There were times when older businesses in Kalamazoo made way for newer ones. In 1894, a group of local investors bought the Page Manufacturing Company on Third Street, now known as East Crosstown Parkway, that made hardwood products like broom handles. They merged it with the Columbia Sled Company to form the Kalamazoo Sled Company.

In 1895, the company finished a new three-story factory, designed by local architect Charles Fairchild, to join the buildings that remained. Sleds would be painted, decorated and varnished in this new structure. It was a basic building with four-over-four rounded double-hung windows and a pitched roof. Added later was a pedimented side entrance.

The company soon produced eighty different sled styles ranging in price from $0.20 to $3.50. They also branched into manufacturing lawn furniture and folding chairs, the latter widely used by circuses. By 1906, the Kalamazoo Sled Company employed one hundred people and made more children's sleds than any other company in the world.

Throughout the next fifty years, older buildings were torn down and new ones erected in their place. The company soon added educational toys to their inventory. The Gladding Corporation bought the company in 1968 and moved all operations out of Kalamazoo in 1972. The buildings were for sale, but a fire in April 1974, destroyed several, including the 1895 structure. Most were torn down over the next few years. At least two buildings remain, covered with aluminum and other materials. They are a reminder of a business long since departed that helped put Kalamazoo on the map, especially during the holidays when children found these sleds under their Christmas trees.

> "The building is three stories high and about as near fire proof as a building can be made."
>
> Kalamazoo Gazette
> *January 4, 1895*

c1960. The entire complex sat right next to the railroad tracks making it easy to get sleds to market.

c1960. The simple interior of the 1895 building included wood and metal beamed construction. Lawn furniture and folding chairs were by then a considerable part of their business as evident by this photograph.

1999. Some of the foundations remain from the Kalamazoo Sled Company and two others buildings.

Consumers Power Company Power Plant
East Michigan Avenue, 700 Block, North Side

Kalamazooans first enjoyed electric power in the middle 1880s, when Frederick Bush organized the Kalamazoo Electric Company with $50,000. The first commercial customer received electric lighting power in 1886, and by 1898, the Foote Brothers, W.A. and James B., had moved into town to add to their own inter-connected system. Their plan soon came to fruition. Just like finished goods off the assembly line, they consolidated the generation of electricity in several locations and then shipped it out to multiple regional customers.

W.A. Foote, as principal of the newly reorganized Kalamazoo Valley Electric Company, joined Bush's original plant with others in Jackson and Battle Creek, Michigan, in 1898. The following year, he and brother James became electrical pioneers as they successfully transmitted power over a new twenty-mile line stretching from the Trowbridge Dam in Allegan County to Kalamazoo. Over the next decade, a series of mergers gave birth to Commonwealth Power in 1903, who announced construction of this building in 1910.

Easements were obtained, transmission poles set, and a railroad siding was built to accompany the construction of the new building. Its

↑c1928. From the southwest, the multi-storied east addition to the plant rises adjacent to the stack on the right.

materials were those that best suited its purpose and the era — steel and concrete. Dressed in brick, the one and one-half story structure had a dignified look. Ground to frieze windows, separated by capped pilasters, allowed plentiful light inside. Along the Michigan Avenue facade, frieze windows gathered additional southern light while further heightening its stately yet sturdy appearance.

In 1915, Commonwealth became Consumers Power, and in 1927, Consumers added a building on the east side to house a new generator. This addition doubled the square footage, providing space for a new generator and increasing the plant's capacity to 72,000 horsepower.

Construction of a new plant at Morrow Dam in 1936 signaled the beginning of the end for the Michigan Avenue buildings. Demolished in 1976, the site remains empty.

↑1999. The site, cleared in 1976, remains vacant today.

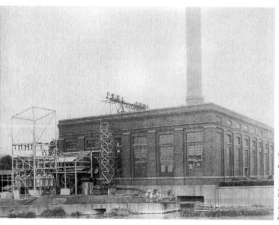

↑c1912. This photo illustrates a basic principle of post-1900 industrial design: great expanses of wall that could now be dedicated to windows because the concrete and brick walls were reinforced with iron or steel.

"...linking these together and then in turn chaining them with the other plants and dams and they have a regular octopus of efficiency."

Kalamazoo Gazette, February 1, 1910, speaking of Commonwealth's announcement that a new plant would be built on the river

City Union Brewery/Kalamazoo Creamery Building
Lake Street, 700 Block, South Side

The exact date of the first brewery on this site is unknown, but Kalamazoo's 1873 *Atlas* shows a "brewery" on Lake Street. Consistent in design with others being built at that time, the original structure had two stories and a tower for lifting water and malt into large cookers. By 1883, brewer George Neumaier was proprietor of the Coldstream Brewery; Neumaier lived directly next door.

By 1886, Neumaier bought out his major competitor, the Kalamazoo Brewing Company, thus expanding his market. In the following decade, he changed the company's name to City Union Brewery and then sold the business to his son Fred. During the 1890s, important technological advances appeared, including electricity to run refrigeration units. During that same time, the building grew larger and gained a distinctive personality.

The addition filled in the north side of the original building and the street. Faced in brick, it was three stories, with a center portion that climbed another two. Brick beltcourses encircled it between floors and the windows on each level were each treated differently. The tallest parts were corbelled underneath the cornices, where the brick was stepped out with each course.

Another addition just after the turn of the century more than quadrupled the total floor space of the original building. Shortly afterward however, Kalamazoo joined the prohibition movement in 1915, putting Fred Neumaier out of business. Less than five years later, Kalamazoo Creamery, formerly located on South Street, moved into the complex.

As years passed, the pre-1900 addition to the building became obscured by later additions as the Creamery grew both east and west toward Portage Street. The earlier decorative facade is difficult to find, but its outlines remain within the brick. The Creamery closed in 1997.

◹1909. This shows the Brewery after its major addition and character change. The original building and tower are marked "Kalamazoo Brewing Co." at the right rear.

"This brewery is noted for producing beer that is seldom equalled and never excelled…."

Kalamazoo Daily Telegraph
January 16, 1901

◹1999. The outlines of the decorative facade and windows of the building can barely be seen today.

◺c1925. This photo, after the Creamery moved in, also shows another two-story addition to the complex on the right.

◹c1945. The Kalamazoo Creamery bottling operation.

INDUSTRY & AGRICULTURE

Bryant Paper Company, Power Plant and Office Building
Alcott and Bryant Streets, West of Portage Street

Although not the first paper mill in Kalamazoo, with its 1895 opening, the Bryant Company grew to a formidable size. As it competed successfully with Kalamazoo Paper, King Paper and others, their combined activities gave Kalamazoo its new name "The Paper City." Noah Bryant, an Englishman with years of experience, headed the organization, John King served as superintendent, and Frank Milham as treasurer.

The men located the company a little more than a mile south of downtown, on a large parcel of land on the east side of Portage Creek. The complex doubled in size by 1902, and by 1908, it grew by another 50 percent. That growth continued, and in the early 1920s, two buildings went up at Bryant, one of which barely survives.

The tall Power Plant was designed in the early 1920s by engineer V.D. Simons of Chicago, who gave it a dynamic look with a stepped cornice, that he repeated on its dual cupolas. Like its counterparts of the period, the building offers large expanses of glass—concrete and steel structures carry heavier structural loads with far less material.

In 1920, then president Frank Milham announced that contractor O.F. Miller's engineering department was working on a new office building design. A *Kalamazoo Gazette* article reported: "…the edifice will embody many interesting innovations." A favorite feature, guided by Milham's ideas, was the "welfare" hall on the top, or third floor, to be used for meetings, exhibits, and employee events like dances and motion picture shows.

Milham did not live to see his offices completed, but new president Felix Pagenstecher and his staff moved there in 1921. From the outside, the classically-styled building would have been at home in the downtown commercial district or on campus at the Teacher's College. This time, round arched windows topped vertical stretches of glass, each with its own keystone. This, and the two-story pedimented entry, combined to give a monumental appearance to a small building, whose footprint was just 60 by 90 feet.

Bryant Paper continued to grow. Between 1908 and 1930, the complex again doubled in size. By the middle 1950s, the Chamber of Commerce reported that of the 24,200 people

◪ 1942. This photo, from the *Bryanteer* shows the Power Plant Building in its glory, releasing a large cloud of steam as it goes about its work.

◪ 1999. The Power Plant today is a sad reminder of the paper industry decline in Kalamazoo.

locally employed in manufacturing, almost 10,000 of them manufactured paper and related products. However, by the end of the 1960s, Bryant and other Kalamazoo paper companies declined. New manufacturing processes and consolidation took its toll, and serious concerns were raised about pollution resulting from paper-making. The company and its property changed hands several times.

The Power Plant building still stands despite its lack of maintenance, although tenuously, awaiting its fate. In 1969, the City of Kalamazoo issued a list of office building code violations to then owner Allied Paper. They responded several years later by erecting a small, single-story building closely fronting Portage Street, and demolishing Frank Milham's dream the following year.

The 1905 Illinois Envelope Building, located just west of the Power Plant, is still standing and occupied today within the Bryant Paper complex. It, unlike most other extant buildings there, is well-maintained, and was listed on the National Register of Historic Places in the early 1980s.

↗1999. A parking lot occupies the former Bryant Paper Office Building site.

↙c1921. A 1920 *Kalamazoo Gazette* article said of the new office building: "Black walnut will be used for the interior finish, with high panel wainscoting for the side walls. The floors will be of cork, insuring maximum quietness."

"The location is on the banks of Portage Creek, only a short distance from the old state fair grounds, and in a pleasant section of the city, or rather it should be said upon the borders of its suburbs."

The Paper World, *describing the new Bryant Paper Mill*

D'Arcy Spring Company
Northwest Corner, Paterson and Pitcher Streets

Frank D'Arcy arrived in Kalamazoo in 1884 as a jeweler. Over time, his interests involved him in multiple businesses. He opened his own jewelry, had a ceramic painting studio, and beginning in 1912, a theater. But his largest and most lucrative endeavor was his spring company.

About 1905, he moved the spring company from North Rose Street to the northwest corner of Paterson and Pitcher Streets, into the former home of St. John Plow. D'Arcy made his first architectural change when he joined two separate buildings around 1906. Contracts with Hudson Motor Car in 1916 and with Roamer and Velie in 1917 undoubtedly increased his wealth. By 1924, D'Arcy did one half million dollars of business annually.

By the middle 1920s, D'Arcy held 60 patents, including springs for everything from upholstery to typewriters. Now a true success, D'Arcy decided to again indulge his obvious artistic side, earlier evident in his jewelry and ceramics endeavors. Most likely in the early 1920s, he orchestrated a major addition to his factory, adding on, squaring it to the street and rounding it out at the rear, next to the railroad siding.

In remodeling his factory, D'Arcy did something unusual. He made it attractive. Facing Paterson Street, colossal columns framed the two new entrances, which were topped with monumental decorative fanlights. Giant brick pilasters punctuated the broad expanses of glass and rose to meet a frieze of triglyphs trimmed with dentils, and capped by a handsome, stone-trimmed brick parapet. In a finishing touch, the building was fronted by spectacular grounds with formal plant beds, walkways, pergolas and many shady trees.

D'Arcy died in 1931, and shortly afterward, the company moved to another location. Sutherland Paper Company bought the building in 1936. Later owned by Brown Paper and James River Corporation, it was demolished for a parking lot in 1996.

"North Side Plant Is Made A Beauty Spot by Its President."

Kalamazoo Gazette
October 18, 1925

1999. The former D'Arcy site now serves as a parking lot. A few trees remain fronting Paterson Street.

c1925. This newspaper photo shows the full Paterson Street facade of the newly completed D'Arcy Spring Company addition, along with its formal garden.

c1925. This photo shows the well-lit interior of the new D'Arcy Spring Company addition, with its large expanses of glass.

Little Brothers
East Kalamazoo Avenue and Water Street, 400 Blocks

The Little family has a long agriculture industry history in Kalamazoo, beginning in Yorkville, Michigan. The Kalamazoo chapter began when George Little entered into the feed grain business in 1904 with A.K. Zinn. Little bought Zinn out in 1908, and two years later, paid Sam Curry $500 to move the 1864 elevator from its original Michigan Avenue site to Kalamazoo Avenue.

After the move, a poultry building was added, and in 1911, a warehouse. Brother Charles joined the business in 1912 to form "Little Brothers." Growth continued, and in the 1920s, George's sons, Alvin and George R., joined the business. Over the next decades, in addition to buying and re-selling grain, Little Brothers prepared custom-mixed livestock and poultry feeds and bred poultry.

The company acquired the Kent grain elevator directly south on Water Street in 1926. Two more new buildings were constructed on Kalamazoo Avenue in the 1940s—a poultry breeding house and a hatchery. Together, these buildings housed 8,000–9,000 roosters and hens, who produced 250,000 chicks each year.

In the early 1960s, Little Brothers employed about 50 people, but suburban development continued to encroach on farming, and by 1965, that number had dropped to twenty. That same year, Little Brothers announced the sale of their business to the Farm Bureau, while they retained the land and buildings. The original elevator reached the end of its more than 100-year life in 1967 when it was razed, along with a number of other buildings in the complex. The City of Kalamazoo received the title to the Water Street elevator and demolished it in 1974.

Parts of the Kalamazoo Avenue complex remain, and are occupied by the Emporium, a high quality antiques dealership. The Water Street elevator site was recently re-occupied by a building moved there from another location.

c1965. This photo shows the front of the Kalamazoo Avenue complex. Over the years, additional buildings behind these stretched to the rear of the block. The original elevator building is the second-highest gable-end building on the right.

1947. Looking north from the Kent elevator site on Water Street, the Kalamazoo Avenue Little Brothers complex is visible at the right rear.

1999. What remains of Little Brothers on Kalamazoo Avenue includes the former straw storage building on the left, and the flour and feed warehouse on the right. Today, both are occupied by The Emporium Antiques.

"Many acres that produced grain in the past have been taken by housing development, manufacturing development, free-ways and what else."

1965 letter to Alvin Little from a friend, upon Mr. Little's announcement that Little Brothers would discontinue their business in Kalamazoo

INDUSTRY & AGRICULTURE

Kalamazoo Corset Company
Northeast Corner, Eleanor and North Church Streets

Ninety years ago, turkey feathers, of all things, were the major component of corsets made in Kalamazoo by one of the largest employers in the area. The Featherbone Corset Company moved to Kalamazoo in 1891 from Three Oaks, Michigan, where the technique to use turkey feather quills to make durable materials for such items as buggy whips and corset stays began.

After renting space downtown, the company moved to a new four-story brick factory on North Church Street just north of Eleanor Street in 1894, built by Rickman and Atkins. It changed its name to the Kalamazoo Corset Company three years later. The company continued to grow at a tremendous rate, necessitating the construction in 1899 of a new building around the corner facing Eleanor Street. A third building on the vacant corner site joined these two structures in 1905, completing the complex.

All three brick buildings had street-level foundations and double-hung windows with stone lintels. The arched entrances and diagonal corner section with paired double-hung windows and a dentiled cornice were the buildings' only ornamentation.

By 1906, the Kalamazoo Corset Company produced over 1.5 million corsets yearly in one hundred different styles. Six years later, over 800 people were employed, many of whom were women. A strike that year which lasted almost four months financially damaged the company. It went into bankruptcy, but reorganized in 1915.

Changes in fashion after World War I led to different types of undergarments many which bore the "grace" name. To reflect this new image, the name of the company changed to the Grace Corset Company in 1921. Over

c1922. The three buildings, left, center and right, are visible in this photograph. Each arched entryway is decorated by a keystone.

c1910. Over 90 percent of the workers were women who were skilled at sewing, but paid less than men. Working conditions in the factory were crowded and noisy.

c1910. Men were employed in such positions as pressers, assemblers, sales and administration.

> *"This rapid growth of the business is due to both the efficient management of the company and the superior workmanship, style and material employed in the manufacture of its product."*
>
> **David Fisher and Frank Little,**
> Compendium of History and Biography of Kalamazoo County, Michigan, *1906*

the next decade, sales of foundation garments plummeted and by 1932, the company employed only 175 people. Six years earlier they had begun to lease out empty space in the factory to other companies.

In 1956, the Flexnit Company of Elizabeth, New Jersey, purchased the Grace Corset Company and ended operations in Kalamazoo the following year. Over the next twenty years, many small manufacturing companies leased space in the buildings. Portions of the structure even housed the Kalamazoo Public Library and Museum between 1958 and 1959 during the construction of the new library building on South Rose Street.

Demolition of the Kalamazoo Corset Company buildings took place in 1972 and 1974. The site remained vacant until the completion of a parking ramp for Kalamazoo County employees in 1979.

1999. For the last twenty years a parking ramp for Kalamazoo County employees has been on this site.

INDUSTRY & AGRICULTURE

Homes

THE FIRST STRUCTURES in any community are those which provide personal shelter. And so it is true of the Village of Bronson; the first "buildings," as distinguished from more temporary shelters used by Native Americans, were for the settlers of European descent.

Titus Bronson constructed his first home shortly after he arrived here in 1829. This first shelter was, in fact, temporary, and devoid of any developed architectural "style." Made of tamarack poles and marsh grass, it likely resembled those Native American shelters more than the homes constructed just a few years later, but it helped him stake his claim.

In 1831, Bronson and his wife, Sally, built a larger, log house near what is now the corner of Water and North Church Streets. Several other residents built log houses in the new Village of Bronson. However, within a year, Bronson opened the first sawmill, providing wood for more permanent frame homes.

Over the years, Bronson, like most Midwestern villages, reproduced the popular styles of each period. Greek Revival was the first style adopted here, and evidence of this form can still be seen in some of its remaining homes. The oldest surviving example is the 1838 Justus Burdick House, moved 43 years after its construction from downtown to its present location, at the southeast corner of Vine Street and South Westnedge Avenue. Another remaining example of the Greek Revival style lives on at the Austin-Sill House on Lovell Street, one lot west of its own original site at the northwest corner of Lovell and Rose Streets.

As the nation moved forward in time, house style preferences changed in Kalamazoo, just as they did elsewhere. Italianate, Octagon, Queen Anne, Colonial Revival, Craftsman and other forms each enjoyed popularity here, designed and built by both local and regional architects and contractors.

Many old houses survive today in Kalamazoo. Unfortunately, many are lost. To piece together a complete representative sampling is vexing because almost all of the photographs existing in the public collections illustrate a limited range: they are primarily the homes of the town's wealthy and influential. Photos of these houses were widely distributed, used in advertisements, commemorative newspapers and picture books — all demonstrating how prosperous Kalamazoo had become. To uncover photographs of smaller, less pretentious houses, those built for residents of more modest means, is a rare event. So, as one reads this chapter, it is important to keep in perspective that not everyone here lived

> *"The strength of a nation is derived from the integrity of its homes."*
> **Confucius**

in mansions of twenty-plus rooms, fronted with broad lawns, and porte-cocheres in the rear.

Even rarer than photos of modest houses are pictures of home interiors. This is understandable when one remembers that home interiors are private places, as well as the restrictions placed on early photography by limited interior lighting.

The one major exception to this rule, just before and after the turn of the past century, are photographs taken and commissioned by Unitarian minister and social reformer, Caroline Bartlett Crane. There are boxes of photographs in her collection at the Western Michigan University Archives and Regional History Collections, many of which were taken inside not just one, but many of her homes in Kalamazoo. The existence of this collection, which also includes diaries and business and personal papers, not only illustrates her social awareness, but her meticulous nature. Her life was important to her and to many others, both then and now.

Crane's homes, as many that are represented here, were found in what is now considered the central business district, and in coming to their ends, experienced a variety of fates. Some remained residences up until the time of their demolition. Others were adapted for use as stores, schools, funeral homes and offices. Two of the homes featured remain, but are hidden underneath the shrouds of one or more later, surrounding buildings.

As the community and the streets grew and changed, so did the houses. South Burdick Street, West Michigan Avenue and South Street ceased to be grand residential avenues, and gave way to office and public buildings, parking lots and wider streets. Several homes were demolished not because they had deteriorated, but simply because their owners did not know what else to do with them. It was simply a matter of bad timing. Fortunately, there are now alternatives to demolition; some of Kalamazoo's historic houses have been adaptively reused, and others moved to new locations.

Although much has changed, what has remained is the shared pride in Kalamazoo's extant historic residences. These houses provide not only shelter, but still do, as they did then, provide an opportunity to express individual choice, style and taste. This has not, and never will, change.

Previous Page: c1890. The Peck House was in the 300 block of South Rose Street, east side.
Courtesy Mary Burdick Thorne Collection

This Page: c1900. The Simpson House was in the 100 block of West Cedar Street, south side.
Courtesy Kalamazoo Public Library Local History Collection

Bassett House
Northwest Corner, South Burdick (Kalamazoo Mall) and West South Streets

The Bassett House is one of Kalamazoo's hidden architectural secrets. Many people pass by this corner daily, completely unaware of this building's existence.

The home dates from 1860, constructed by local builders Sprouge and McGoff for dry goods owner and real estate developer John C. Bassett. The elegant Italianate with its traditional cubic shape, long, narrow windows, bracketed cornice and cupola was set far from the street. The first floor was high off ground level.

Bassett died in 1870 leaving his five-year-old son, George, in the care of his sister Louisa. Both continued to live here until George turned twenty-one, received his inheritance and married. He eventually sold all his real estate except this property. Used as a boardinghouse and later a private social club, the house in 1899 began to be rented by George's widow Eda to physicians, dressmakers, dentists and music teachers. She increased the rental space in 1901 by adding three, two-story buildings in front of the house on the wide lawn. She built another addition to the west of the house on West South Street, completely surrounding it with the exception of the south side.

Local lawyer Dallas Boudeman built around the property himself, first to the north in 1904 and then to the west in 1906. He purchased the entire Bassett property from Eda in 1907. Years later, a small fire destroyed the house's cupola.

Over the years, space in this building has housed stores, restaurants and offices. Oftentimes customers step up or down to a different level, not realizing they are stepping into a building that has been a part of Kalamazoo's architectural landscape since before the time of the Civil War.

1890. The *Kalamazoo Gazette* in its description noted the house's ornamental cornice with its paired brackets. Decorated cast iron railings are on the first floor windows, all of which are topped by stone moldings.

1999. The bay window still can be seen on the south side of the house.

> "...*for elegance, convenience and the pleasantness of its rooms, we know of none that equals the place.*"
>
> Kalamazoo Gazette
> *January 27, 1860*

Merrill House
Southeast Corner, West Lovell and South West Streets [now South Westnedge Avenue]

David Merrill came to Kalamazoo in 1858 at the age of twenty-five, purchasing his first flour mill. Eventually, he would own four, and also invest in real estate.

By 1883, he and his family lived in a house on the southeast corner of West Lovell Street and South West, now Westnedge Avenue. By 1890, that structure came down, replaced by this larger Queen Anne house. Facing West Lovell Street, it had a prominent corner tower with fish-scale shingles, gabled roof and a front porch with paired and triple columns. The east side had a porte-cochere and extensive garden.

Merrill died nine years later. His wife Ida remarried Homer Manvel, president of the

1959. Taken a year before its demolition.

Kalamazoo Tank and Silo Company, in 1907. Merrill's will stipulated that his house would be turned into a home for widows once his wife passed away. The Merrill Home opened in 1921 for women over seventy years old of "provable respectability." They needed an entrance fee of $1,000 and were promised a home, free from work, for the rest of their lives. On average, fifteen women at a time lived in the house.

The Merrill Home merged with the newly created Senior Citizens Fund in 1952. Three years later, sufficient funds were raised to construct the east wing of the Merrill Residence, just east of the house. The original Merrill home continued to be used for additional housing.

In 1960, the Merrill home came down to make way for the west wing of the Residence completed that next year. David Merrill's house may be gone, but his name and desire for improved senior citizen housing continue.

c1925. Each woman had her own room that she could decorate with personal possessions.

1999. The Merrill Residence today.

"The home [at] 449 W. Lovell Street is one of the most desirable, modern residences in the city, very pleasantly located."

Kalamazoo Gazette
January 7, 1899

Severens House
Thompson Street, East Side

Situated on the top of a hill west of downtown called "Mt. Carmel," the Severens House was one of the most unusual residences that graced Kalamazoo. Currently, only one photograph exists in public collections, showing an elaborate Second Empire structure with a central tower covered with a mansard roof. The gables are decorated with bargeboard and topped with scrollwork and finials.

Local architect L.D. Grosvenor designed it in 1871 for the family of Henry and Sarah Severens. Severens was a lawyer and later appointed a Federal district judge. He located his new house just to the north of Kalamazoo College. In July 1871, the *Kalamazoo Gazette* provided an extensive description of the house. The first floor included a reception room, dining room, library, parlor, kitchen and veranda that provided picturesque views of the Village. The second floor had four rooms, all connected to each other.

At the same time, Grosvenor was in the process of designing a much larger Second Empire building downtown for the Lawrence and Chapin Iron Works that still stands.

By 1923, both of the Severenses had died and the house became vacant until purchased by the Fred and Anna Scheid family. A lifelong resident of Kalamazoo, Scheid, then president of Star Brass Works, had gone to Alaska searching for gold in 1898 and stayed for fourteen years.

After Scheid's death in 1959, his second wife and widow Winifred lived in the house until 1961. Purchased by Kalamazoo College, it was demolished the next year to provide parking for their new fine arts building.

c1897. The home had a variety of different windows including several circular oculus windows.

1999. The parking lot for Kalamazoo College's Light Fine Arts Building was the site of the Severens House.

Burnham House
Southwest Corner, West South and South West Streets (now South Westnedge Avenue)

Three growing daughters was one of the reasons local grain merchant Jay Sebring decided to build a new house on the southwest corner of West South and South West Streets, now Westnedge Avenue, in 1882. During its construction, Battle Creek businessman Harrison Horton somehow convinced Sebring to sell it to him for his daughter and son-in-law, Mary and Giles Burnham. Sebring took the money and built a new house one block east.

Even though the owners changed, plans for the house did not. Greenstone, a volcanic rock, comprised the exterior of the Queen Anne structure. It arrived in slabs on railroad cars from the Northeast, and was hand-carved upon its arrival. A total of twenty-four rooms were decorated with a variety of woodwork such as butternut, mahogany and oak in addition to sixteen crystal chandeliers and several stained glass windows. The Burnhams were avid gardeners and maintained a conservatory next to the house.

In 1925, the Burnham family sold the house to Helen Boylan who with her sister Anna Boylan Travis, owned the Gown Shop, a well-known woman's clothing store that had both ready-to-wear and designer fashions. At its peak, the store drew customers from Detroit and Chicago and employed over fifteen people. Many local women still can remember modeling their prom or wedding dresses from the grand staircase.

Thirty years later, in 1959, Boylan sold the property and the house became Sharpe's Colonial Furniture. The W.E. Upjohn Institute for Employment Research purchased five pieces of land in March 1964, including this house, for future expansion. The Institute demolished the house in the spring of that year and its new offices were completed in January 1965.

c1961–1964. Taken shortly before its demolition. The Boudeman House at 515 W. South Street can be seen to the west of the Burnham House.

1999. The north side of the W. E. Upjohn Institute for Employment Research now sits on the site of the Burnham House.

1892. The house had a gabled roof with ornamental cresting at the top. Set back from the street it had a wide front and side lawn.

KALAMAZOO: LOST & FOUND

Perrin-Milham House
Southeast Corner, West South Street and St. John's Place

Currently Bronson Park is surrounded on all four sides by religious, civic, commercial and government buildings. Over eighty years ago, however, houses dotted the majority of the perimeter, including this one built between 1888 and 1889 by businessman Joel J. Perrin. It replaced a smaller Italianate house that Perrin had lived in for over fifteen years.

This larger wooden Queen Anne house had a prominent tower with arched windows at each side, and a front-gabled roof decorated with fish-scale shingles. Turned supports and delicate spindlework decorated the front porch.

Perrin died in 1900. Four years later, Frank and Elizabeth Milham purchased the house. A life-long resident of the area, Milham, president of the Bryant Paper Mill, served as mayor and gave the family farm to the City for a park which still bears his name. Also living with the Milhams was Elizabeth's father, Noah Bryant, an owner and investor in several paper companies.

After Milham's death in 1921, Elizabeth continued to live in the house until 1924 when she sold it to the City. Plans were underway for a new City Hall, with this site chosen. The Perrin-Milham house became a temporary home for such offices as the city manager, treasurer, clerk, and auditor. In addition, another home behind this house also was utilized for city offices. Within five years, both houses were torn down to make way for the new Art Deco styled City Hall completed in 1931.

1999. Kalamazoo's City Hall has been on this site since 1931.

c1900. The house had a variety of windows including the arched ones in the tower. The Lawrence House, now the Park Club, was just to the east.

1925. The City of Kalamazoo government moved into the Perrin-Milham house in 1925. It underwent extensive alterations amounting to $40,000.

McNair House
Northeast Corner, East Lovell and Henrietta Streets

It was logical that local physician Dr. Rush McNair would want his new house built on this corner, just across the street from the new Bronson Hospital building, an institution he helped organize. Dr. McNair began practicing medicine in Kalamazoo in 1887, continuing for the next fifty years.

Designed and completed in 1912 by well-known Kalamazoo architect Forrest Van Volkenburg, this Neoclassical house had a full-height, curved, semi-circular entry porch with Ionic columns. The front dormer had a Palladian window in addition to a returning cornice. The Adam-style doorway had an elliptical fanlight with sidelights. The stucco house also had pilasters, rectangular windows and a boxed eave with a dentiled molding at the cornice.

Tragically, Dr. McNair's son Noel had died just two years earlier at the age of seven. In his honor, Dr. McNair referred to this house as "Noel Place" and had a memorial window installed.

Joldersma and Gilman Funeral Home, subsequently renamed Joldersman and Klein, purchased the house in 1923, later building additional space. They sold it to the Upjohn Company in 1942, but continued to use it for a few more years. The Company took it over in 1949 for their medical division and later for the marketing research staff. This department moved to the new administration building on Portage Road in 1961, and shortly thereafter, the Upjohn Company demolished the house.

The site where the McNair house sat is currently vacant except for a small section that contains a rose garden.

> *"Mr. Van Volkenburg… has succeeded in creating work which is not only appropriate to its purpose but satisfactory to the eye as well."*
>
> The Ohio Architect, Engineer and Builder
> *August 1915*

1915. McNair's Neoclassical home had an elaborate front entryway complete with a second-story balcony.

c1925. Additions were added to both sides of the house after it became a funeral home.

1999. A small rose garden sits where the McNair house once was located.

1915. Wicker furniture was prevalent throughout the house, including the living room.

KALAMAZOO: LOST & FOUND

Cedar West Apartments
West Cedar Street, 200 Block, North Side

In 1889, Kalamazoo businessman Bradley Williams and son Malcom changed the name of the father's company to Williams Manufacturing and began producing windmills and agricultural implements. The company grew, and in 1891, did $70,000 of business.

The business prospered and so did the family. About 1890, Malcom moved into the west side of this enormous new Queen Anne apartment building. At the same time, another Williams Manufacturing partner, Homer Manvel, took up residence on its east side.

The stone foundation of the building held up solid brick walls that rose two stories high, the stories delineated by stone beltcourses. Typical of Queen Anne, gables of several styles punctuated the roofline. Each side had a two-story bay window, and the two-story front porch filled the space between twin towers, each capped with a "witch's hat" roof. The porch, towers, and perfectly matched stairways rising from the sidewalk in front added a grand presence to the house, as well as symmetry, unusual for Queen Anne design.

Malcom Williams left Williams Manufacturing in January 1902, and joined W.B. Cramer to form the Automatic Machine Company. Later that same year, Automatic Machine merged with Burtt Manufacturing and went into the automobile production business, with Williams as its vice president.

Malcom Williams remained in residence at 212 West Cedar until sometime shortly after 1915. After his departure, other members of the Williams family remained. As time passed, records indicate that the two large apartments were divided into multiple smaller units. The last known family member there was Mae Williams, who died about 1958. In 1959, the Williams' estate sold the building to the City of Kalamazoo, who razed it for a parking lot.

1959. This photo shows the still grand looking Cedar West Apartment building shortly before its demolition.

1999. A parking lot fills the former Cedar West Apartment building site.

Mansion Row
West Main Street [now Michigan Avenue], between Oakland Drive and South Park Street

Aptly nicknamed "Mansion Row," this stretch of Main Street, now Michigan Avenue, between Oakland Drive and South Park Street contained houses, many built between 1875 and 1890, that were larger and more grandiose than what were found anywhere else in Kalamazoo. Also enhancing their stature was their placement far back from the sidewalk. There were a wide variety of styles including Italianate, Queen Anne, and some of Kalamazoo's only residential examples of Chateauesque and Richardsonian Romanesque.

As the street changed from residential to commercial in the 1920s, so did these houses. Some were reused for a time as funeral homes, schools and a rectory. These and the rest gave way for car dealerships, grocery stores, offices, gas stations and parking lots. The last house came down as recently as 1986. Following are the stories of two of them.

Dewing House
North Side of West Main Street [Michigan Avenue], west of North Westnedge Avenue

Fortunately, William S. Dewing was one of the owners of a sash and door company, for it provided all the cherry woodwork in his and wife Carrie's new Queen Anne house. Completed five years earlier in 1882, it had a steeply-pitched roof with a central tower. Finials decorated not only the top of this tower, but also each gable. The paired windows had carved moldings with label stops.

Dewing invested in many Kalamazoo companies and also created the Lake Farm for Boys. This eventually merged with the Children's Home, an institution founded by his parents, William G. and Jane Dewing, to form what is now known as Lakeside Boys and Girls Residence.

c1900. The north side of "Mansion Row" just west of South West Street is dotted with five very elaborate houses. The Dewing House is second to the left.

1999. The site for the Dewing House is now part of St. Augustine Cathedral's parking lot.

c1885. The Dewing house had elaborate spindlework at the porch and a unique bracket shape at the cornice.

KALAMAZOO: LOST & FOUND

Casket Company, which was the first in the country to manufacture cloth-lined caskets.

In 1887, Allen and his wife Hannah built this twenty-five room Chateauesque house, hoping it would provide enough room for their seven children. This unique house had a steeply-pitched roof with ornamental cresting and a variety of vertical elements like towers, chimneys and spires. The windows had hood molds with label stops. The house also had multiple dormers, two balconies and an elaborate porte-cochere.

Ten years after the completion of the house, Allen developed Allen Boulevard behind his house where the first dwellings appeared two years later. After his death in 1910, the family continued to live here until 1932. Five years later, the house came down and the site became a used car lot. St. Augustine's Parish had begun purchasing land adjacent to this house for their new parish complex. The site of the Allen house became the location for their new church, now a cathedral, completed in 1951.

> *"There is no home in Kalamazoo that approaches it in size and none that encroaches on its design."*
>
> Kalamazoo Gazette, *November 24, 1928, describing the Allen House*

The Dewings lived in the home until 1924 when they sold it to St. Augustine's for their rectory. The church was in the process of planning a new high school to the northwest of this house. It remained a rectory for over fifty years until its demolition in 1975. The site remained green space until it was paved and incorporated into the church parking lot.

Allen House
Northeast Corner, West Main Street [Michigan Avenue] and Allen Boulevard

Oscar M. Allen came to Kalamazoo in 1853 at the age of twenty-five to establish a paint and decorating business. In 1868, he started the firm he became famous for, the Globe

◱ 1999. St. Augustine Cathedral sits on the site of the Allen House, directly on the corner of Allen Boulevard.

◰ 1890. The towers of the Allen House were topped with "candlesnuffer" roofs.

HOMES

Augustus and Caroline Bartlett Crane House
South Rose Street, 400 Block, West Side

Married in 1896, Augustus (A.W.) and Caroline Bartlett Crane lived in and around this block until they moved into this house in 1907. Mrs. Crane likely designed the house, and there is documentation that establishes its builder, William Shannon, as one of the principals of the Kalamazoo Interior Finish Company.

By the time the Cranes moved in, A.W. Crane had established himself as a well-known radiologist. Caroline Bartlett Crane involved herself in many activities, ranging from sanitation to divorce and beyond. One of her interests was housing for low and middle wage earners. Working with local architect Gilbert Worden and the City in the early 1920s, she also later designed the extant "Everyman's House" on Westnedge Avenue Hill.

The much larger 420 South Rose house was very modern for its time, and successfully combined Dr. Crane's office and the family's residence into one structure without sacrificing home comforts. It owes its looks in part to "Craftsman" designs that had begun to sweep the country—a slight flare at the building's base, the principal windows arranged in groupings, eaves set into deep gables, and a moderately sloped roof line.

The Cranes moved to 1429 Hillcrest Avenue in the middle 1920s, while Dr. Crane kept his office at 420 South Rose. Just years after the

c1928. The back of this photograph reads: "Residence designed by Mrs. Bartlett Crane, 420 S. Rose, the family home for years."

Cranes' deaths in 1935 and 1936, their son, Dr. Warren Bartlett Crane, established his own family residence and office there. The younger Cranes moved out in the 1940s, but Warren Bartlett Crane maintained his office at 420 South Rose until the late 1950s. His wife inherited the property after his death, and demolished the house in 1963 for a 20-car parking lot.

"O dearest, let us get our home-nest built! We need it and want it so."

Caroline Bartlett Crane, in a letter to her husband on February 17, 1906

1999. The former site of the Crane family home-office now provides automobile parking space.

c1923. Caroline Bartlett Crane, left, and daughter Julia enjoy the weather on the sleeping porch, likely on the west side second story of their home at 420 South Rose Street.

KALAMAZOO: LOST & FOUND

Alfred and Frances Connable House
South Prospect Street, 100 Block, East Side

Alfred Connable and Frances Peck met on a tennis court in Petoskey and married in 1896, soon after Connable received his law degree. Granddaughter of Kalamazoo County pioneer Horace M. Peck, Frances' roots ran deep in Kalamazoo, and it is here they made their home. For some years after they married, they lived in a duplex on South Street. As they started their family, Mrs. Connable carried on her family's philanthropy, and Connable began a career in business and local government.

Just after the arrival of their third child, the Connables moved into this new Neoclassical home in 1905. At the top of West Main Hill, slightly southwest of the Henderson Castle, the house faced south, towering over the slope toward Grand Avenue below. Contractor Frank Flaitz carried out the design flawlessly, from the rusticated stone foundation, to the denticulated cornice with its frieze band below, to the full-height Ionic-columned central entry. Interestingly, an almost identical, but slightly smaller version of the Connable House appeared that same year in the extant Boudeman House on South Street.

Soon the family had five children, and the large home became a gathering place for the neighborhood. Impromptu plays took place

c1905. Taken shortly after construction, the fine details of the Neoclassical home are clearly evident in this photograph. The presence of the people on the porch, right, provide evidence of its grand scale.

on the third floor stage, as did regular Sunday afternoon concerts in the music room. As the years passed, Mr. Connable involved himself in politics, hosting President Taft in 1909, and eventually serving two terms as mayor. Mrs. Connable died in 1929, leaving a young family behind.

Mr. Connable moved to Plainwell about 1940, where he died in 1951. Just before 1945, third child Alfred Jr. moved back to the family home. He stayed until about 1955, when he sold it to Kalamazoo College. The following year, the City approved the use of the building as a women's dormitory, but the College never carried out the use. Vandalized in 1958, the College razed the home the following year.

> *"There was a spirit of openness in the house. All the kids would play there, and there were lots of children's parties."*
>
> Alfred Connable, Jr.

1999. The Connable home sat at the top of this hill, above where the trees grow today.

Hubbard Homestead
Southwest Corner, Lovell and Rose Streets

Caroline Bartlett Crane's memorial to Silas Hubbard following his death indicates that he and wife Mary established this home shortly after their marriage in 1854.

Silas Hubbard arrived in Kalamazoo in 1838, and found a job teaching school. Mary Loomis arrived six years later, and became one of educator Lucinda Hinsdale Stone's first female students. By the time they met and married ten years later, Hubbard was making significant real estate investments, including this site, where he and his wife lived for more than four decades.

The house is Italianate, popular during the period between 1840 and 1880. Its low-pitched, hipped roof is common, as are its deep eaves and decorative brackets. Window hoods are also typical, but the square ones used here are less so than the round ones found on numerous other homes of the period. The two-story bay window on the east side is also less usual—when employed, they more often only rose one story. The home's front porch may or may not be original, as Italianates were designed both ways.

Silas Hubbard lived long enough to serve his community in a variety of ways: as township supervisor, co-founder of Kalamazoo's Republican Party, and as one of several organizers of the Kalamazoo Paper Company. He helped the Unitarian church by providing a $20,000 gift to erect a new church building. He died in 1894, followed by his wife in 1899. Several years later, Unitarian minister Caroline Bartlett Crane and her husband, Dr. Augustus Crane, lived in the house for several years.

In 1923, the Hubbard Homestead was demolished for a gas station. About 1959, the gas station was razed for the City's District Court-Public Safety Building.

c1902. This photograph of the Hubbard Homestead shows it narrow profile. It was clearly designed for an urban lot.

1999. The demolition of the later Sinclair gas station on the former Hubbard Homestead site made space available for a District Court-Public Safety Building in the International Style.

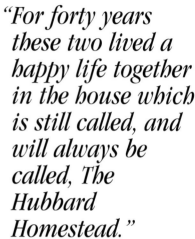

c1902. The Hubbard Homestead sitting room interior. Note the elaborate fireplace mantel at left and the bay window at right. Caroline Bartlett Crane plays the piano at the rear.

> *"For forty years these two lived a happy life together in the house which is still called, and will always be called, The Hubbard Homestead."*
>
> **Caroline Bartlett Crane,**
> *in her memorial to Mary Olivia Loomis Hubbard, 1899*

William and Harriette Stone House
Northwest Corner, Douglas Avenue and West Main Street

Dr. William Addison Stone came to Kalamazoo in 1891, to serve as assistant superintendent of the State Asylum. During his tenure there, he helped coordinate the establishment of both Brook and Colony Farms. Dr. Harriette McCalmont, educated at Women's Medical College in Philadelphia, joined the Asylum's staff in 1896. Two years later they married, and Mrs. Dr. Stone resigned her position. Her husband left the Asylum in 1910 to begin a private practice. That same year, they moved into this new home, one of Kalamazoo's finest examples of Prairie School architecture.

With a large footprint rising two stories, this monumental house was double the size of it neighbors. Its low-pitched roof and bands of casement windows gave it a horizontal, grounded orientation, and a slight flare at ground level anchored it firmly to its tree-lined site. Said to have been designed by a Fred Maher, no evidence of such a person was found. However, George W. Maher, who worked alongside Frank Lloyd Wright in architect Joseph Silsbee's studio in Chicago, designed Prairie homes for several decades, and Maher scholar Donald Aucutt recently confirmed George Maher as the Stone House architect. In a paper published in *The Inland Architect* in 1887, Maher said, "... a house should have massiveness and solidity to express the idea of substantiality." The Stone house clearly embodies this belief.

Dr. William Stone lived here until his death in 1924. Dr. Harriette Stone remained in the home until her own death in 1931. Their architect son lived here with his wife until the middle 1950s. In 1959, the house served as home to Western Michigan University's Theta Xi fraternity. It was demolished in 1965 to allow the implementation of a plan that converted Kalamazoo and Michigan Avenues into multi-lane, one-way streets, connecting Kalamazoo Avenue to West Main Street via Douglas Avenue.

c1937. Almost thirty years after construction, the Stone house still appeared well-married to its site — a hallmark of Prairie School design.

1999. The Stone House was demolished for this "corner-rounding" project.

Sill Terrace/Prange Building
Northwest Corner, Lovell and Rose Streets

Kalamazoo physician and medical historian Rush McNair called it "…the pretentious Sill Terrace." Regardless of the various adjectives applied to it, this 1870 building undoubtedly cast an impressive shadow at the time of its completion, and continues to do so despite its wrapping in a major addition during the middle 1920s.

The original building provided twelve apartments for Kalamazoo's wealthy and influential citizens, and was the result of a partnership between Dr. Joseph Sill and Andrew Fleming. Records indicate that Dr. Sill moved the extant Austin-Sill house from this site to a location one lot west, where it remains, and the 1873 maps of the *Combined Atlases of Kalamazoo, Michigan, 1873, 1890* show the real estate in Fleming's name. A 1907 *Kalamazoo Gazette* review reported that together, the men invested $39,000 in the land and building.

Built at the height of its period, this large Italianate closely followed the formula of a deep cornice with decorative brackets underneath the eaves of its flat roof. However, the most inviting aspects of this building were its doors and windows. A large, central double entrance sat at the top of a stairway that rose from the street, flanked halfway toward either end by smaller but equally impressive single entrances. Separated by sets of bay windows, each door received a crowning pediment, and the windows in-between and on either side rose the full height of the first floor rooms inside.

Fleming died in 1880, and Sill lived until 1905. Who owned the property immediately after Sill's death is unknown, but the April 30th, 1907, *Kalamazoo Evening Telegraph* reported that Fleming's daughter, Bertha Geilfuss, and Lucille Merrihew bought the building for $21,100; it had been put up for sale to settle a "partition suit."

↱c1880. This photograph, taken by well-known Kalamazoo photographer Schuyler C. Baldwin, shows Sill Terrace in all of its Italianate glory. Note the elaborate window hoods on the second and third stories.

↱1896. Augustus Crane courted the Reverend Caroline Bartlett during her residence at Sill Terrace, and she is shown here seated in her study. The back of the photograph reads: "Apartments, Sill Terrace, taken the day before my marriage."

"Dining rooms were in the basement and excellent meals were served by Mrs. N.H. Nicholson."

Undated newspaper clipping

About two years later, records indicate that optician Henry T. Prange owned Sill Terrace, but he maintained his offices on South Burdick Street until the middle 1920s. Before he moved his office to this building, he did two things. The first may have been Kalamazoo's first attempt at selling condominiums—he announced in 1920 that he had formed a company, Prange Apartments Incorporated. Prange's idea was to sell $25,000 of shares at $10 per share, and have the tenants take ownership of their apartments.

No reports of the outcome of that venture surfaced, but shortly thereafter, Prange hired local architects Billingham and Cobb to create an addition for the building that gave it more space and a brand-new character. The architects took a "Colonial" design approach for the newly renamed Prange Building, which accomplished several things at once. The addition first extended, and then wrapped the north, east and south sides in a new layer of brick. This created additional floor space at each level, new fenestration with four ground level entries, three for storefronts and one in the center for access to new offices above the storefronts, and the apartments now behind them.

The descendants of H.T. Prange retained ownership of the building for over eighty-five years, until the middle 1990s, when they sold it to Ryan Reedy.

> *"The building is of brick construction, four stories high including the basement. Three partitions extended from the basement to the roof and when opened provided practically four separate houses with twelve apartments."*
>
> Kalamazoo Gazette, *October 18, 1925, shortly after the building was remodeled*

◪ 1999. The Prange Building today, still in its middle-1920s wrappings.

◪ 1896. The interior of Reverend Caroline Bartlett's apartment at Sill Terrace shows off the amenities that residents there enjoyed—a frieze encircles the upper walls, picture molding, large pocket doors between rooms and large fireplaces.

Louis and Harriet McDuffee House
Northwest Corner, West Main Street and Stuart Avenue

Harriet and Louis McDuffee left Boston for Kalamazoo in 1878. McDuffee worked for a ceramics import firm and as his position improved, he rose to the position of partner in what became Jones, McDuffee and Stratton. Looking for a "western outpost" from which he could make his business trips, McDuffee found Kalamazoo an advantageous community between Detroit and Chicago.

The couple lived on Kalamazoo Avenue until their exquisitely detailed Queen Anne home was ready in 1890. Milwaukee's E. Townsend Mix executed the design, likely recruited because of Mrs. McDuffee's Wisconsin family connections. Raised in Ripon, her father was a bank president there.

Mix, well-known for his homes, commercial buildings and churches, is described in a recent Historic Milwaukee Incorporated's docent training guide: "…Mix…single-handedly molded the appearance of Milwaukee through the patronage of an entire generation of leading businessmen." And, "Mix was not an instigator of new fashions, but he quickly understood and assimilated new styles. He had a fine grasp of design and excellent control over the use of ornament."

Mix designed the McDuffee house just right. Its exterior reflected the appropriate details— its irregular roof, the shingled gables, bay windows, and its asymmetrical porch—which all worked together to avoid a "smooth-walled" appearance, a hallmark of the Queen Anne style. The interior also reflected the style, both in execution and design. For example its "growlery" provided a place for gentlemen to retire after dinner for discussion. Throughout the original building specifications, the terms "finest" and "best" are used when describing the craftsmanship and the finish materials.

Daughter Alice remained in the home after her parents died, until about 1946. Parsons Business School used the house for about five years, and moved out in 1954. The home was razed in 1958.

> *"…when in 1878 Mr. McDuffee decided to establish a western residence from which to take his trips…he eschewed Detroit and Chicago for less frantic Kalamazoo…."*
>
> Unidentified newspaper article, c1936, reporting how the McDuffee family came to Kalamazoo

1999. Bill and Andrea Casteel, former owners of the nearby Stuart Avenue Inn, created this garden on the former McDuffee home site in the early 1990s.

1890. Architect E. Townsend Mix's Queen Anne home for the McDuffees. Note the covered area at left, the porte-cochere, for receiving and discharging buggy, and later automobile, passengers.

Education

KALAMAZOO'S early settlers were much like others who migrated from the East to the land west of the Appalachians—they held education in high regard. The Federal government had done its part by implementing the Land Ordinance of 1785 which set aside a section in each township for the support of public schools. Many of our early pioneers came from the Northeast where they attended schools, so they logically wanted an education for their children as well. Local control was critical to the early successes of education, and the people decided what type and level of education they wanted to offer, as the Michigan Territory did not make any specific mandates.

Kalamazoo's first public school opened in 1833 on the southwest corner of East South and Henrietta Streets. Being the Village's first unofficial public building, it shared space with the courts and several churches, depending on the day of the week. In the evenings, it became the site for the community's Lyceum, a place where townspeople debated the issues of the day.

In the early years, most public education stopped at the end of grammar school, today's equivalent of the eighth grade. High school was considered unnecessary for most students. If a student continued after grammar school, that education came at an additional price.

One private institution that provided a high school curriculum was the Michigan and Huron Institute which also opened in 1833. In addition to high school, it also offered college-level courses and trained Baptist ministers, the religious denomination that provided the school's funding. In 1838, the University of Michigan chose Kalamazoo as a branch school site offering both high school and college courses, training teachers, and preparing students for the Ann Arbor campus. The citizens raised enough money for the Branch's two-story frame structure built on Academy Square, now part of Bronson Park. Eventually, the Institute and the Branch would merge in 1841 into what is now known as Kalamazoo College.

As the population grew, the need for more schools grew as well. When a new school was built, an additional district was created. By 1850, there were four different school districts in Kalamazoo, each with its own officers with the power to hire teachers, raise funds and establish curricula. To address the disparity that developed among the districts, the State acted in 1851 to give communities the power to combine districts into one system to be governed by a Board of Trustees, today known as a Board of Education. Later laws gave these boards the right to levy taxes to support all levels from primary to high school.

By 1859, the newly created Kalamazoo system had built Union School on the northwest corner of Vine and West Streets, now Westnedge Avenue, which served as the only school until individual elementary schools began sprouting up across the Village a decade later.

Public schools were not the only option available during the first half of the nineteenth century. In 1836, a Mr. Hall opened the first private elementary school, succeeded by Mrs. Lucia Eames in 1842. The first parochial

> *"Yet it is as an educational center our city will be best remembered by our visitors. We frankly claim as great a variety of educational institutions as is possessed by any city of the state."*
>
> Kalamazoo and Education
> October 1914

school opened in 1851, administered by the Catholic Church, followed by a Christian Reformed school in 1877. Nazareth Academy, operated by the Sisters of St. Joseph, began as a girls' private school and later grew into a college.

Kalamazoo also became home to several professional schools. Gregory Commercial College opened in 1858, followed by Parsons Business School in 1869. Maher's Business University opened in 1906 and later merged with Parsons.

Finally, another community fundraising effort took place just after the turn of the twentieth century, but on a much larger scale than its predecessor in the 1830s. This time it was to entice the State to locate its Western State Normal School in Kalamazoo. In October 1903, residents in Kalamazoo voted by a margin of eight-to-one in a special election to borrow $70,000 for the project. With this money, they provided twenty acres of land atop Prospect Hill west of town, a site selected by the Olmsted Brothers. The City also agreed to supply natural gas, electricity, streets and sidewalks. In addition, the community offered the Normal School use of their public school buildings until the training school was ready for occupancy. This level of support was unprecedented in Kalamazoo's history and showed keen foresight as Western State Normal School, now Western Michigan University, is the largest educational institution in the region and a major economic force.

Kalamazoo's pride in its educational institutions matched its pride in the buildings themselves. Publications written by State Superintendents and various national experts in the nineteenth century placed greater emphasis on the interior space rather than the exterior. Illumination, sanitation, ventilation, furniture and equipment were more important to them than architectural details. However, this did not stop Kalamazoo residents from employing good architectural design in these buildings. Almost all of the schools constructed reflected popular period styles. Union School was Italianate in style, Parsons a less exuberant Queen Anne. Some buildings were more sober, perhaps reflecting a particular philosophical approach or merely a limited budget.

Public schools were then, and still are, a matter of public record. Therefore, defining their history is a somewhat easier task than that of private and parochial schools whose records are either lost or hidden somewhere in an attic or basement. For public schools, determining an architect or contractor was relatively easy. For most of the others which were private ventures, written records were either sketchy or not kept at all.

School names were carefully chosen to reflect the parish, founder, purpose, or location. For practical reasons, Kalamazoo's public schools were for many years named after the streets they faced. A plan in 1901 called for the adoption of presidents' names as a lesson in patriotism and history. Implemented in Kalamazoo in the 1920s, Portage School became Washington, Frank Street became Lincoln, and East Avenue became Roosevelt. During that same period, new schools were added and named for Presidents Harding and McKinley.

The places featured here are gone now, but what has not disappeared is the value the community places on education. Many residents, past and present, found their way to Kalamazoo to attend or teach in one of these institutions, and many stayed. Our community is far richer for their presence and contributions.

Previous Page: c1880. Frank Street School. North side of Frank Street between North Burdick and Edwards Streets.
Courtesy Kalamazoo Valley Museum

This Page: c1910. Art Class, East Hall, Western State Normal School.
Courtesy Western Michigan University Archives and Regional History Collections

Barbour Hall
Nazareth, Michigan, Northwest Corner, Gull and Nazareth Roads

In 1889, the Sisters of Saint Joseph came to Kalamazoo to manage Father Frank O'Brien's Borgess Hospital, and are still here, more than a century later. For several years after their arrival, they lived at Borgess. Later, they moved to LeFevre Institute, and in 1897, to a new building on former Humphrey family farm acreage at Gull and Nazareth Roads. Once there, they immediately opened their new girls' school, Nazareth Academy. And just four years later, Father O'Brien presented Reverend Mother Anthony Nolan with plans for a boys' school, which were quickly approved.

O'Brien's childhood friend and Detroit attorney Levi L. Barbour assisted financially, and construction of the boys' building began. Completed in the fall of 1902, they dedicated it to Barbour's mother and moved in on October 24th. The simple, almost square structure showed little exterior decoration, excepting its hooded, Queen Anne style windows and a corbelled cornice. Inside, there were six or seven rooms that the burgeoning school soon outgrew. Father O'Brien raised more money, and in 1908 they made a large addition to the south, covering the front of the original building. Four years later, with the boys again crowded, the Sisters added Ryan Hall on the north, or rear, of the original building. Less than a decade later, almost 200 boys boarded at the school.

c1945. This 1908 addition to Barbour Hall was constructed in front of the original 1902 building, which peeks out from behind, just in front of the small wood shed. Ryan Hall, a 1912 addition, stands just behind the original building.

Originally serving boys aged six through ten, the administration later widened the age range to include eleven- and twelve-year-olds. The boys' curriculum included grammar and composition, arithmetic, reading, spelling, American history, geography, French and religion. Socially, using the words of a 1930s Barbour Hall brochure, the boys were: "…expected to be gentlemanly, courteous, neat in appearance, respectful…" and "…careful of their own property and the property of others."

Enrollment declined steadily during the 1970s, and the school closed in 1979. Its buildings were demolished the following year.

1902. Newly completed Barbour Hall faced south, just east and north of the Nazareth motherhouse.

"The school aims to awaken, develop and train in the boys all the physical, moral and intellectual instincts which will form in them the best possible kind of character…."

1930s Barbour Hall promotional brochure

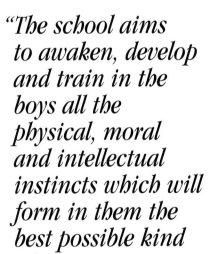

2000. This green space and parking area now occupy the former Barbour Hall buildings site.

Kalamazoo High School Building No. 2
South West Street (now South Westnedge Avenue), 700 Block, West Side

Although the building that sits here today is commonly referred to as "Old Central," few recognize that this is the site's fifth school building. The legacy began in 1859 with the first centrally located building, known as Union School. Constructed on a piece of land purchased from A.C. Balch for $6,500, its design was Italianate. Union stood three and one-half stories with multiple chimney pots and a cupola sprouting from its low-pitched roof.

Safety concerns had surfaced earlier, but in 1880, they arose again in earnest. School Board minutes indicate that the building underwent at least four major inspections by local and regional contractors and citizens. Ultimately, the Board voted that year to raise funds for a new building and to demolish Union.

That fall, while construction plans moved ahead, students attended school in other locations: Lovell Street School, Plymouth Church, the Unitarian church and Kalamazoo College. As 1880 ended and 1881 began, the Board approved Chicago architect E.S. Jennison's plans, which agreed to reuse as much of Union's original material as possible.

They paid Jennison $400 for his plans and specifications, which estimated the new building's cost at $31,000. They also awarded the construction contract to Frederick Miller of Battle Creek, and hired Kalamazooan Ulysses Wheaton to supervise construction at $3 a day, not including Sundays. By the end of July 1881, they re-laid the original cornerstone from Union school into the new building's wall.

Queen Anne in design, the new school sat close to the block's northeast corner, and presented a lively entrance, complete with a bell tower to house old Union's bell. A stone beltcourse separated the first half-story from that above, and a brick beltcourse did the same between the next two floors. The street facades were punctuated with decorative brickwork, indentions and protrusions, and the east wall offered a splendid bay window wall that rose from ground to gable. At each story, those windows received individual decorative treatments, and then were defined as a group by pilasters on either side and a capping hood of brick and stone.

Designed for 600 students, the arrangement of the building placed seventh and eighth grade pupils on the first floor, and high school students on the second. The *Kalamazoo Daily Telegraph* described part of its interior: "The double stairways leading to different floors are very handsome, broad flights up to half distance, then a return with side arches supported by cherry columns...."

Unfortunately, as this building neared completion, architect Martin Roberts and builder William Beeman again raised construction quality concerns. The Board once again called in experts who ultimately reported that while the building could be used, the floors and basement walls should be carefully monitored. Opened in 1882, it was joined in 1891 by the

c1895. This photograph, taken from the east, shows the complementary main facades of the second building, an 1881–82 Queen Anne, right; and the third building, the 1891 grammar school, left.

2000. The present school building, now known as the Community Education Center, fills the entire east side of the block.

1866. Union School, the first school on the site and home of "The Kalamazoo School Case," during which the U.S. Supreme court upheld a community's right to tax its citizens for the support of secondary school education.

"...you come away thoroughly delighted with the arrangement...."

Kalamazoo Daily Telegraph, *January 17, 1882, reviewing the 1881–82 High School Building*

◪c1900. The third and fourth buildings on this site are shown here. The 1891 grammar school on the left, and the fourth building, the 1898 high school on the right, built by Albert White.

third building on the site, a new grammar school to the south. The two were physically connected sometime before 1896.

On an early February morning in 1897, the 1881–82 building caught fire, and its remains later were demolished. The grammar school remained, but high school classes were shifted downtown to the YMCA. One year later, the fourth new building, again on the north corner, opened to receive students. These two buildings served until 1913, when the south portion of the fifth and current building was completed. Construction of the remaining complex was completed in stages, including the north half and auditorium in the middle 1920s. This entire complex is listed on both the National and Local Historic District registries.

EDUCATION

Kalamazoo College: Upper College/Williams Hall, Kalamazoo/Lower Hall, Bowen Hall and Mirror Lake
Bounded by Academy Street, Michigan Avenue, Monroe and South Streets

Founded in 1833, Kalamazoo College is the oldest private institute of higher learning in the State of Michigan. Originally named the Michigan and Huron Institute, it later merged with the local branch of the University of Michigan, and moved into the University's building on "Academy Square," now known as Bronson Park. In 1841, the University of Michigan left Kalamazoo, but the local institution remained and renamed itself the Kalamazoo Literary Institute.

In 1845, the school acquired acreage on a hill west of town and constructed its first building there. About ten years later, the State Legislature amended the school's charter. Now known as Kalamazoo College, the school began granting bachelor's degrees.

That first building, called "Upper College" and later known as Williams Hall, was erected between 1846 and 1855, just east of the extant Hoben Hall. The school sold nearby residential lots from the original parcel to finance its construction. Williams' brick and stucco exterior stretched 104 feet by 46 feet, and faced east. When finished, it rose four stories into the air, and perfectly concluded a splendid vista from South Street below. The interior layout included study rooms, sleeping rooms, a chapel and the library. Although a 1916 fire reduced its height to three stories, the fourth floor rose again in 1923.

In 1859, Kalamazoo Hall, also known as Lower Hall, cost approximately $10,000 to build, and sat near the present intersection of South Street, Oakland Drive and Michigan Avenue. Until then, female students used the old "Branch" building in what is now Bronson Park. Trustees had just announced a fundraising campaign for a new women's building when the ladies were evicted from the Branch. Local citizens relocated the Branch to the middle of a nearby road, believing that if it remained on its original site, the park they wanted there would never come to fruition. The female students moved into the basement of the Baptist Church while department head Lucinda Hinsdale Stone continued fundraising in earnest. In the end, most of the money came from Kalamazoo citizens. The College sold Kalamazoo Hall after the new Bowen Hall building was finished in 1902. Kalamazoo Hall was razed in 1912.

According to College reports, fundraising for Bowen Hall began before 1900 with a $2,500

1999. These apartment buildings and the houses behind them now fill the former Lower Hall site.

c1860. Built primarily to house male students and provide classrooms, the "Upper College" building was renamed Williams Hall in 1924, honoring Dean Clarke Benedict Williams. It served as a barracks during World War I, and was demolished in 1936 after Hoben Hall was completed.

1999. Williams Hall sat just about here, but overlooked the town below, instead of the campus quadrangle.

1999. Bowen Hall sat approximately here, where the east end of today's Hicks Center and its abutting parking lot come together.

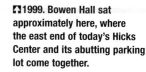

KALAMAZOO: LOST & FOUND

gift. Finished and equipped in 1902 at a cost of $60,000, it was designed in the shape of a "T," and sat where the east end of Hicks Center and the adjoining parking lot meet, facing north. It met multiple needs by providing classrooms, laboratories, lecture rooms, administrative offices, a new chapel and library. The College named the building after trustee and benefactor Charles Clark Bowen. Its 1969 demolition was brought about by the need to expand the dining hall and student center to the west.

Mirror Lake (really a small pond on Arcadia Creek) disappeared from the College landscape in 1924. It sat below Williams Hall, near today's Hoben Hall, occupying a small area from roughly just inside the east end of the current athletic center, Academy Street, and the railroad tracks, where parking is now located. Considered a nuisance for years, it was nonetheless the site of many and varied college activities. These included tugs of war, and as the 1933 College Annual reminisced: "Professor Praeger's biological specimens inhabited it. Many freshmen were led out to contemplate its beauty in the moonlight. College couples spent many evenings on its shores."

> *"It became a tradition to usher in spring on the campus with make-shift cloudbursts consisting of paper bags filled with water which were pelted on student passersby...."*
>
> Kalamazoo Gazette, December 1936, recounting the many pranks at Williams Hall over the years

c1860. Henry Coddington built Lower Hall. Lucinda Stone's students deserved the best, and Italianate design was the high style of the period. It speaks of grand elegance from its three stories of tall, narrow, elaborately crowned windows, to its deep overhang with supporting brackets, to its three-sided front and rear bays, each topped with unusual hexagonal towers.

c1920. Bowen Hall could be termed an Institutional Queen Anne. Multiple gables punctuate the parapetted roof line, and the heavy use of bay windows and a "T" shaped footprint break up its many facades. Cut stone formed the foundation and part of the first story, while the remaining walls were finished in brick and terra cotta.

1999. A maintenance building, the east end of the Anderson Athletic Center, and a parking area fill the former Mirror Lake site.

c1891–1904. "Tennis Courts, Mirror Lake, Athletic Field and Path to the Lower Building as seen from in front of the 'Dorm.' Time, between 1891 and 1904." — Inscription from back of photograph.

EDUCATION

Parsons Business College
North West Street [now Westnedge Avenue], 100 Block, West Side

Parsons Business College alumni include businessman and former mayor Frank Milham, attorney Dallas Boudeman and cereal king W.K. Kellogg. Founded in 1869 by New Hampshire native William Frederick Parsons, it was then known as the "Kalamazoo Business College and Telegraph Institute," and graduated nineteen students its first year.

Housed in several business district buildings over its life, Parsons started at the southeast corner of Burdick Street and Michigan Avenue, moving later to the extant Humphrey block on the southeast corner of Portage Street and Michigan Avenue, and then on to the Chase block at Michigan Avenue and Rose Street.

The history of this 1902 building, constructed by Albert White for the school, began when Parsons bought the land for $6,000. He moved the school and his family in that same year. According to one account, classrooms were on the third floor; the Parsons' three-bedroom apartment and administrative offices were on the second; and rooms for student activities occupied the main floor.

The Queen Anne style building had broken facades with a corner tower, although some other typical elements are missing, like a steeply-pitched roof and gable ornament. Still, its appearance conveyed that its owner was up with the times, but simply chose to take a sober approach in its design.

Inside, the school focused on serious business. By 1925, 10,000 students had graduated and the curriculum had evolved significantly. Classes then included business administration, accounting, salesmanship and advertising. Parsons' sons inherited the school, and when son W.W. died, the estate sold it to Edgar C. Stewart. In 1946, the Veterans Administration announced it would move into the building, staying until about 1952, when demolition plans were announced. The building was razed and the site is now partially occupied by a building that belongs to St. Augustine's Church School.

↗c1909. After the school moved from this building in 1946, it relocated several more times. Davenport College acquired it in 1956, and now operates from buildings several miles west of downtown.

> "... the Parsons Business College can no longer be accommodated in business blocks...."
>
> Kalamazoo Gazette, *quoting W.F. Parsons' 1892 announcement that a new building would be constructed*

↙2000. The former Parsons Business College building site today.

↗c1909. Parsons students learned contemporary banking practices at the College Bank, at the rear of this classroom scene.

William Street School
William Street, 500 Block, South Side

These two small adjoining buildings served the Christian school community for over fifty years. Part of the Christian Reformed parochial school system, they carried on an educational tradition that began in 1875 in a small building behind a church on Walnut Street. The Holland Reformed Church, on the southeast corner of Paterson and North West Streets (later North Westnedge Avenue), erected its own small North West Street Christian Reformed School for $500 in 1892. In 1893, the Second Reformed Church assumed responsibility for its operation.

North West Street School operated until 1905. The year before, church members laid the cornerstone for the front half of this school on William Street, a bit more than a block away. It cost $3,100 to complete, and the members dedicated the four-classroom building with a ceremony held on January 3, 1905.

The student population grew even larger, and three years later a second, nearly identical building was built directly behind the original. Slightly larger than the first, its builders connected the two edifices, doubling classroom space.

In 1912, the Church relinquished control of the school to its membership, ending its days as a parochial institution. A kindergarten opened there in 1938, but in 1940, reports of the buildings' deteriorated condition surfaced. Unstable ground had weakened the foundations and City officials warned of collapse. Somehow, they survived and remained in service for another decade until North Christian School on Cobb Street was finished in 1950. The school association sold the William Street School, which met with the wrecking ball in 1954. A parking lot now occupies the site.

1999. A parking lot occupies the former William Street School site.

c1915. The two adjoining buildings forming William Street School were simple, two-story brick rectangles. Well-lighted, the windows had both stone lintels and sills.

EDUCATION

Michigan Female Seminary
Southeast Corner, Gull Road and Riverview Drive

Organized in 1856, the Michigan Female Seminary provided a private secondary education for young women. The Presbyterian Church funded the school, and they purchased thirty-two acres of land on the east side of the Kalamazoo River. The school also raised the necessary capital through private contributions and subscriptions.

Progress on the building, designed by Chicago architects Bayles and Coleman and built by James Prince, proceeded over the next two years, but slowed primarily because of the Civil War. The school finally opened on January 30, 1867, with fifty-four pupils.

Modeled closely after Mount Holyoke in Massachusetts, the Michigan Female Seminary offered classes in all subjects to girls fifteen and older. Along with coursework, exercise and "domestic duties" were part of daily life. The school established strict rules to govern its students.

In 1874, Bush and Paterson built a two-story wooden wing to the south that provided more dormitory space. This wing made way in 1892 for Dodge Hall that more than doubled its size.

c1900. Queen Anne-styled Dodge Hall, with its gabled roof and towers and extended side porch, had several recitation and music rooms, additional living space, a gym and an elevator.

The Michigan Female Seminary closed in 1907. The enrollment never reached the level their board hoped it would. Also, the institution never was on a firm financial foundation, and with no endowment, tuition increased steadily each year.

O.M. Allen, Sr. purchased the property and over the next twenty-five years, his estate rented space in the building for apartments. In 1935, demolition of the building began to reduce the estate's tax burden. At the same time, the Allen estate sold three acres of the property to St. Mary's Roman Catholic Parish which spent the next three years salvaging materials from the Seminary building for their new church, that was completed in 1938.

While the Michigan Female Seminary is gone, it lives on in the bricks and wood of the original church building which is now part of St. Mary's School.

"Tuesday last was the opening of a new and important era in the history of our already notable village. On that day was laid the foundation cornerstone of one of the noblest edifices ever erected in a civilized country."

Kalamazoo Gazette
October 30, 1857

1890. The Italianate main building had long narrow windows with moldings, stone lintels and an elaborate front porch. It contained classrooms and living space.

2000. To the left, right and behind this parking lot, Seminary Hill now contains stores, restaurants, apartments, houses, medical offices and St. Mary's Roman Catholic Church.

St. Joseph Elementary School
Lake Street, 900 Block, South Side

Attempts were made in 1890 to establish a second Catholic parish and school in Kalamazoo. The Sisters of St. Joseph opened St. James Parish and school on the south side near the Kalamazoo Paper Mill in 1891, but it closed within a year, mostly due to its remote location.

A second try thirteen years later met with greater success, beginning with the purchase of the Parker homestead on Lake Street. A solemn ceremony in October 1904, laid the cornerstone, and the combined school and church for the newly renamed St. Joseph Roman Catholic Parish opened in October of 1905. The Sisters of St. Joseph continued to manage the school.

Built by local contractor A.D. Loughead, the simple building had a unique Dutch gable at the parapet. The double-hung windows originally had stone band moldings above them. Also at the top of the gable was one fanlight and two circular oculus windows.

Until 1915, St. Joseph Church occupied the first floor of this building. An additional two-story school structure, called the Rochford Building, was built to the southeast of the original school in 1955. The primary building continued to be used as a school until 1968, replaced by a new school building behind it named the Bennett Building. A parking lot is now on the site of the old St. Joseph School.

c1911. The stone moldings, bell tower and Dutch gable are evident in this photograph.

"The beauty of the new site appealed to the people and opened their imagination possibilities for a great future."

St. Joseph Church Dedication Booklet, 1915

1999. A parking lot now marks the site of the original building.

1967. The school's entrance was altered over the years. Just to the left of the building is the rectory, completed in 1947.

EDUCATION

Public Elementary Schools

As Kalamazoo's population expanded in the 1860s, the demand for more schools increased. During these years, separate elementary schools were built, and the Union School remained solely for high school education. The elementary buildings followed the population shifts, first located in the central Village area, and then spreading to the new neighborhoods beyond, including Stuart, Northside, Vine and Edison. Many of these schools are located on their original sites, although not in the same buildings. The following are a selection of the schools that are gone completely.

Lovell Street School
Southeast Corner, East Lovell and Pine Streets

Lovell Street School was the first separate elementary school, built in 1867. In June 1884, this Queen Anne structure replaced the original building which had been destroyed by fire six months earlier. Designed by local architect Martin Roberts and built by Myers and Sons, it boasted a prominent central bell tower and gabled roof. A shed dormer shielded the front door.

After the completion in 1926 of Harding School, located just behind this building, Lovell Street School became the Kalamazoo Public Schools' Administration Building. Bronson Methodist Hospital purchased both buildings in 1960. That year they tore down Lovell Street School, but integrated Harding School into their hospital facilities. A medical building now sits on the site of the Lovell Street School.

North Westnedge Elementary School
North West Street [now Westnedge Avenue] between Lawrence and Florence Streets, West Side

In 1888, architect Martin Roberts and builder John Campbell completed a new school house on Kalamazoo's north side. It resembled Roberts' Lovell Street School with a central tower, gabled roof and paired windows.

George Rickman & Sons built an addition to the rear in 1907. A petition from the parents of the school's students led to the construction of a much larger addition to the front of the building in 1926, designed by Billingham and Cobb and built by the DeRight Brothers.

In 1962, the school closed because it needed extensive repairs to comply with the State Fire Marshall's recommendations. Demolished in 1965, the site remained vacant until 1973

c1930. This photo shows the 1926 addition to the front of North Westnedge Elementary, in addition to the older sections to the rear.

2000. A series of townhouses facing Lawrence Street now sit on the site of the North Westnedge Elementary School.

1999. Although Roosevelt Elementary School is gone, the name lives on in the Roosevelt Apartments completed in 1990.

c1912. East Avenue Elementary School boasted a commanding view of Kalamazoo. Despite its multitude of windows, the building was fairly plain, its only decoration being the beltcourse at the top.

2000. The former Bronson Medical Center-East is now on the site of the Lovell Street school.

c1925. Windows in this Queen Anne building were grouped either in twos or threes, all topped with a unique series of moldings joined by beltcourses.

when a series of nineteen townhouses was built over a two-year period.

East Avenue Elementary School
Northeast Corner, East Main Street and Charlotte Avenue

In 1883, the Board of Education completed a new school for the City's east side. Overcrowding led to the construction of this building in 1909, at the top of the hill on the corner of East Main Street and Charlotte Avenue, just up from the original building. Designed by architect John Chubb and constructed by local builder Thomas Foy, it boasted twenty-one classrooms that more than doubled the school's original space.

Renamed Roosevelt Elementary in 1926, it remained a school until its closure in 1975. Borgess Hospital purchased it in 1978 for offices, but these plans never materialized. The Hospital demolished it in 1988. The Roosevelt Hill Apartments are now on this site, along with the Eastside Neighborhood Association.

McKinley Elementary School
Southeast Corner, South Burdick and West Emerson Streets

Growth on the south side of Kalamazoo led to the completion of South Burdick School in 1886. In 1924, Billingham and Cobb designed a new building which wrapped around the original one on two sides, adding classrooms, a gymnasium, and an auditorium along with a new name. Renamed McKinley Elementary, after the slain president, A.J. DeKoning built the new structure.

Sixteen years later in 1940, M.C.J. Billingham designed a new addition to the east with four classrooms and removed the nineteenth-century structure. Henry Vander Horst was the builder.

McKinley Elementary School closed in 1980 due to declining enrollment. Torn down in 1988, the Salvation Army replaced it with their new building three years later.

> *"Nationally famous for their excellence, the public schools of Kalamazoo offer the children of this community an educational opportunity seldom equaled, and still more seldom surpassed."*
>
> Kalamazoo Gazette
> *October 18, 1925*

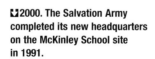

↗ 2000. The Salvation Army completed its new headquarters on the McKinley School site in 1991.

↗ 1945. McKinley School is a classic Billingham and Cobb design with a colonial entrance, large windows, stone coping at the roofline and a decorative band at the cornice.

EDUCATION

Western Michigan University

Western Michigan University was organized in 1903 as Western State Normal School, an institution created primarily for teacher education. Even though many of the original buildings on East Campus still stand, including East Hall, the oldest, completed between 1905 and 1909, there are some buildings and spaces that are gone or hidden.

Trolley
Northeast Side of Normal Hill west of Davis Street

One of the biggest challenges students faced daily in 1905 was how to climb up Normal Hill. Wooden stairs built by faculty members replaced a steep path. The State Legislature in 1907 added another solution by appropriating funds for a double track railway completed the next year. The trolley actually was a funicular operated by an electric motor in a small brick building at the top of the incline, winding and unwinding two cable drums which would lower and raise the two cars.

Running ten hours daily, each car contained four benches built with the passing side closed and the outer side open for boarding and exiting.

By 1948, the school ended the railway service due to its deteriorating condition and to campus expansion which spread to the west. The cars and rails were sold for scrap and in 1960, the school took down the brick control house.

Even after being gone for fifty years, the trolley still remains fresh in the memories of many alumni.

The Barracks
East Side of Michigan Avenue south of West Lovell Street

During World War I, the school became a site for the Student Army Training Corps — men who received basic training and academic classes on campus. Their barracks, built below Oakland Drive, was completed in October of 1918, just weeks before the Armistice. One year later, due to the school's increasing enrollment, the building was used for classrooms and offices for the Art, Home Economics, English and Education Departments. Besides being called the Barracks, it went by two other names over the years — the Temporary Building and Sprau Hall.

The school continued to use the Barracks until it came down in 1953. Currently an addition and parking lot for the physical plant, originally the Manual Arts Building, is on the site of the Barracks.

c1919. Western Michigan University was one of the few colleges in the nation with a funicular. It made travel up to East Hall from Davis Street much easier.

1999. The trolley ran alongside these cement steps, which replaced the wood originals.

1999. A physical plant addition and parking lot are on the site of the Barracks.

c1953. The Barracks was a simple wooden building with double-hung windows. North Hall can be seen at the top of the hill, upper right.

KALAMAZOO: LOST & FOUND

Library Reading Room
North Hall, East Campus

Initially housed in East Hall, the school's library found a new home in 1924 in North Hall, designed by Henry Turner and Victor Thebaud. Considered by many to be the best planned teachers' college library building in the nation, the jewel of the building was the two-story main reading room, 147 feet long and 38 feet wide, that could accommodate three hundred students. A large marble fireplace with an ornamental mantle decorated the interior that was filled with tables and chairs. Paintings donated to the college by local mint entrepreneur and art collector A.M. Todd hung on the walls.

Completion of Waldo Library in the late 1950s on the west campus led to North Hall being remodeled for the College of Business Library. The fall of 1958 saw the installation of a steel floor system which divided the main reading room into two levels.

North Hall is no longer used by the College of Business, but is utilized by a number of different departments, including book storage for the University Libraries. The main reading room is not lost but hidden, waiting for a time when this glorious space will be restored to its original splendor.

↙c1925. A.M. Todd's art gifts found a dramatic home in this arched reading room, including Thomas Hill's "Yosemite Valley" which hung over the fireplace. A multitude of windows drew a great deal of light into this magnificent space.

Trailer Village
Southwest Side of West Michigan Avenue near Oliver Street

Enrollment at the school more than doubled between 1945 and 1946. This sudden influx of students, many of them married veterans, led to the creation in 1946 of Trailer Village on part of the first nine holes of the former Arcadia Brook Golf Course, now owned by the college. Most of the trailers were from the Army and were furnished by the school. "Trailerville" had its own governing board with rules and social events. At one time the total population numbered over three hundred residents.

By 1951, more permanent apartment buildings were planned for both on and off campus. These trailers were slowly sold off and the village was gone by 1953. Read Fieldhouse and the Gary Center were built on this site three years later.

↖c1949. This site included a total of 133 trailers that were arranged on streets with a nearby central shower and laundry building. West Michigan Avenue is at the top of the photograph.

↙2000. The Student Recreation Building and Read Fieldhouse are now on the site of Trailer Village.

"During the course of a year hundreds of visitors find their way to this beauty spot or are piloted there by local citizens proud of their city's possession."

Kalamazoo Gazette, *October 18, 1925,* discussing the location of East Campus

↗2000. North Hall's main reading room has been divided and subdivided into many different spaces.

EDUCATION

Streetscapes

LIKE THE RINGS formed when drops hit the water's surface, Kalamazoo's homes and businesses radiated outward from its center in rings, the growth accompanying connecting arteries as they were laid.

As streetscapes developed, the streets were often named after a landscape feature or a person. Portage Street received its name from the creek, Burr Oak Street from a tree common to the area and Burdick Street after General Justus Burdick. Peeler Street, on a more humorous note, was named after City Assessor George Winslow's dog!

Main Street is an exception. The centers of many settlements, most Main Streets began as mixed-use areas — places where residences inter-mingled with commerce in a pattern that developed over several hundred years. Over time, Main Street's emphasis became more heavily commercial. As communities grew outward, two types of "reduced-size" Main Streets appeared in adjacent developing neighborhoods.

Smaller, neighborhood business districts met the day-to-day needs of "first ring" neighborhood residents, like those in Kalamazoo's Stuart and Vine neighborhoods. A druggist, meat market, grocer and perhaps a bakery filled a first ring neighborhood's needs. Ten or twelve blocks from the City's center, residents were close enough to still get downtown easily on foot or by streetcar to buy a new pair of knickers or make a bank deposit. The West End business district featured in this chapter is one example of a first ring neighborhood business district that served nearby Stuart and West Main residents.

True to form, many of the West End's businesses opened at ground level in the houses that first occupied the block. Later, the commercial spaces grew, often with "wrap-around" additions. In most cases, however, the floors above the businesses remained dedicated to residential use. Just prior to and in the early decades of 1900, most of these adapted houses were replaced with buildings that despite their commercial appearance, were specifically designed for both occupancies.

Kalamazoo's Edison, a "second ring" neighborhood was, and still is, the largest in the City. Beginning about twelve blocks southeast of the City's center, its Washington Square business district is larger and more diverse than the West End's — more of an "urban business district." Located further from downtown, urban districts provide more goods, services and housing choices than smaller neighborhood districts, but still lack the number of options available downtown.

Washington Square's businesses expanded over time to fill in most of several blocks on both sides of Portage Street. For many years, the Square had its own firehouse, dentists, physicians, the town's first chiropractor, at least one bank, several groceries, a department store and some light industry. Edison residents made fewer trips downtown because their own commercial district allowed them to conduct more business close to home.

Regardless of location, a number of common, clearly understood concepts went into creating center city and neighborhood commercial streetscapes. These concepts played a major role in defining each district's character. The

> *"The essential spine of this development was the street...."*
>
> **Richard Longstreth,** *author,*
> The Buildings of Main Street

most critical component was a pedestrian orientation. Using the street as an anchor, buildings stood close together, abutting the sidewalk and each other in a building-dense setting. When a business person or shopper arrived, they completed their business or shopping within this compact area. This pedestrian orientation, its importance forgotten in the post-World War II decades, is again recognized today as a major component of "livable" communities.

To honor the street and allow for individuality, architects and builders focused their attention on the street facades, a component that varied little over decades of growth in villages, towns and cities. Building size and architectural ornament allowed each business to establish its own identity on the street facade. Because the sides and rears of the buildings were mostly unseen, owners wisely invested in decorating their buildings' public faces.

A third concept in streetscape development was architectural compatibility. Beginning with a community's first building and for several decades after 1900, the design of most new buildings was at least partially influenced by what existed nearby, especially in terms of size and mass. As a result, commercial streetscapes developed a rhythm where most buildings had a rectangular footprint, presented a rectangular public facade, and took a generally box-like shape. It was understood that most buildings would rise to within several stories of one another. This last convention varied more widely beginning in the late nineteenth century, due to construction engineering developments and land valuation factors.

Residential neighborhood growth also followed a number of conventions. Housing options found in the center city were over the shops and businesses in commercial districts, major apartment buildings and row houses. However, middle nineteenth and early twentieth century homeowners called increasingly for single-family, free-standing houses.

Again, "understood" concepts were applied. Residential areas often included small, middle-sized and large domiciles, all within the confines of that single neighborhood, providing for diversity of both size and cost. These neighborhoods continue to be pleasant places to live. As with commercial districts, the vast majority of homes respected a similar setback from the sidewalk. Although greater than the setback applied to commercial districts, it was still close enough for residents sitting on their front porches to engage in conversation with passersby.

Although free-standing, these homes were also constructed in a somewhat dense arrangement. On more prominent streets, they sometimes were built on several lots which allowed for a larger home and yard. On some of the narrower and less traveled streets, they were built one per lot.

Regardless, when a resident stood on the sidewalk and looked toward the end of the block, he or she could see a row of houses whose straight setback line was visually relieved by porches, stoops, and an occasional fence. Between the sidewalk and street the curb lawn was punctuated with large trees that softened the transition from road to yard, and shaded both homes and street.

Kalamazoo streetscapes developed as the community was settled, beginning near Portage Street and Michigan Avenue. In his community history, printed in the 1867–68 *City Directory*, Kalamazooan Alex J. Sheldon said: "…and gradually, the Village grew into order." That is exactly how it happened. By 1835, the Village had eleven merchants. Between 1836 and 1840, land speculators rushed in, and by 1840, merchants had expanded west toward Rose Street. By the 1850s, much of the area between the two streets had filled with buildings. From there, new construction traveled in all directions, creating new streetscapes.

All of the streets described in this chapter still exist, but most of the streetscapes have changed dramatically in character.

Previous Page: c1880. Main Street (now Michigan Avenue) looking east from Rose Street.
Courtesy Kalamazoo Public Library Local History Collection

This Page: c1914. South Burdick Street looking north from South Street.
Courtesy Kalamazoo Public Library Local History Collection

Asbestos Row
North Burdick Street [Kalamazoo Mall], 100 Block, East Side

An 1853 map shows buildings at the north and south end of this block. At some point during the next 25 years, the middle filled in with small, one-story brick veneer buildings with shed roofs. Inside, grocers, butchers, barbers, jewelers, clothiers, tailors, shoe and glove makers, flour and feed purveyors and restaurateurs offered their goods and services to a bustling downtown clientele.

Thriving for decades, a review of businesses on the Row between the 1860s and 1920s shows few vacancies. But as time passed, these little buildings aged, and the newspapers and historians noted that although they caught fire a number of times, the fires were always easily subdued, as if the buildings were somewhat fireproof, like asbestos. The damage was usually patched, and the merchant resumed business.

According to one historian's notes, H.R. Rood from Detroit owned the buildings in the 1880s, and the public called them "Rood Row." Kalamazoo businessman William S. Dewing later bought them, but by that time, they were called Asbestos Row, due to their fire-resistant reputation. Their appearance eventually became the subject of public complaint. Finally, in September 1927, City Manager Albert Ten Busschen received reports on the buildings from his fire chief, building inspector and health officer. The health officer especially criticized the buildings' condition, indicating they were: "…unfit for human habitation or occupation for any kind of business."

The following April, Dewing contracted with builder Henry Vander Horst for the $165,000 Dewing Building, and Asbestos Row disappeared. Its replacement wraps the corner from Michigan Avenue, where, north of its pedestrian underpass, it deepens to create multiple full-depth retail and office spaces. At the time of its construction, the Dewing was the only building downtown to fill an entire block's streetscape.

> *"While firefighters fought to quell the flames, crowds would hoot and shout, yelling 'cut the hose, cut the hose. Let 'em burn….'"*
>
> Kalamazoo Gazette, *reporting on Asbestos Row in the 1950s*

↗2000. Designed by William Stone and constructed to accommodate fourteen stories, the Dewing Building remains much as it was built, despite a plan in the early 1980s to add five floors.

↖c1905. Under the awnings in the middle of this streetscape, Asbestos Row merchants provided a variety of goods and services to Kalamazoo residents.

STREETSCAPES

Lovers Lane
South, from Portage Street at Sheridan Drive

The origin of Lovers Lane appears to lie in the roadbed of the old Kalamazoo and Three Rivers Plank Road. According to a December 1850, entry in the "Incidents of the Early Settlement of Kalamazoo" printed in the 1867 *City Directory:* "The first five miles of the Kalamazoo and Three Rivers Plank Road [were] completed."

Plank roads sprang up all over the State in the middle of the nineteenth century, and construction increased when the State Legislature passed a general plank road law in 1848—the same year the Kalamazoo and Three Rivers Company was formed. The road began in the Village, proceeded southeast on Portage Road, turned south at today's Sheridan Drive, proceeded past the Milham farm (now Milham Park), turned west toward West Street, (now South Westnedge Avenue), and then south again. Although never completely planked, its finished portions were heavily used by farmers transporting their crops to market.

As the area's railroad system expanded, the high-maintenance plank roads lost favor. This fact may indirectly explain why this road was renamed Lovers Lane. With both Portage Road and Westnedge Avenue carrying more and more vehicular traffic, the old plank road likely became quiet and less used. *A Dictionary of Americanisms* defines lovers lane as:

c1920. Lovers Lane became a quiet place after the plank road to Three Rivers was pulled up.

"A road, street, etc., to which lovers resort to be alone," and this shady road probably worked well for trysts. The term was first used publicly in San Francisco's *Golden Gate Gazette* in October 1881: "Sunday afternoon as a young lady and gentleman were promenading through Lovers Lane they were attacked by a ferocious dog."

This scene provides a quiet departure from the urban streetscapes featured elsewhere in this chapter. Usually located in areas then considered rural, lovers lanes appeared all over the Michigan and American landscape.

2000. Lovers Lane is not quite as inviting to lovers as in days past. However, the Milham Park golf course, on the left, is a busy place year around, offering summer golf and winter sledding.

> "...a road, street, etc., to which lovers resort to be alone."
>
> *Definition of lovers lane, from* A Dictionary of Americanisms

KALAMAZOO: LOST & FOUND

West End Business District
West Main Street, 700—800 Blocks, South Side

Buildings probably appeared here before the 1850s. The Village was swelling outward, and its "first ring suburbs" were developing. In this case, it was the historic Stuart neighborhood.

The West End business district began life as a streetscape of primarily residential buildings. Over time, it evolved to mixed-use, where ground floor space provided goods and services for the neighborhood's immediate needs, and upper floors provided residential space. As time passed, the mix of businesses grew and stabilized. For more than six decades, a variety of establishments operated here, including at least one grocer, a meat market, and a drug store.

The longest-lived business was Dunwell's Drug Store. Opened in 1905 near the corner of what was then the intersection of Oakland Drive and Main Street, Mr. Dunwell later demolished his first building, replacing it with a two-bay brick building. The single-story corner building east of Dunwell's was also demolished and replaced with a filling station in the early 1920s. West of Dunwell's, another earlier building was replaced with a two-story brick, mixed-use building with apartments above and retail space below.

The corner filling station disappeared between 1950 and 1960, when the corner was rounded to gain a wider intersection. Like dominoes, Dunwell's fell next, around 1970, and the building to its west between 1975 and 1980. The building shown at the far right in the historical photo was the oldest of the group, and the only one that survives. Records indicate that it predates 1900 and housed a meat market for many years. It has served as home to Jones Gift Shop for about fifty years. The surrounding land is mostly dedicated to parking for a fast food restaurant on the south side of the block.

> *"For more than six decades, a variety of establishments operated here."*
> Pamela O'Connor

↗ 2000. The building at right, Jones Gift Shop, now stands alone.

↙ c1939. The West End business district bustled with activity in the late 1930s. The building standing at the far right, then known as Zormor's Market, is today's only survivor.

100 Block of West Main Street (now Michigan Avenue)
North Side

This is a block of "firsts" in the heart of the commercial district. Over a period of nearly 200 years, natural and man-made assaults have resulted in major streetscape changes. In 1831, Hosea Huston opened the community's first store at the west end of this block. The Village's first physician, Jonathan Abbott, moved in upstairs. The first post office opened in that same building the following year, and in 1834, a tornado ripped through the settlement, taking at least one roof in this block with it.

In 1850, the Village's first major fire occurred here, and inadvertently cleared space for the Italianate styled Cosmopolitan Hotel, soon renamed the Burdick House. From the time of its completion in 1854, the hotel acted as a magnet for the block. Over the 120-year life of this hotel and its successor, scores of businesses operated within steps of its entrance.

A second fire in 1855 leveled all buildings west of the hotel, and soon the entire block was filled with Italianate styled buildings, providing space for merchants Roberts and Hillhouse, druggists and stationers, and Lilienfeld &

c1917. The seven-story "New" Burdick Hotel, completed in 1911, was followed by the ten-story Hanselman Building next door on the right. In 1912, Frank D'Arcy remodeled the building near the other end for his "New Theatre." The storefront on its left is the former Roberts and Hillhouse location.

c1890. When this photograph was taken, the east half of the subject block, at left, had already been rebuilt once, beginning with the Burdick Hotel, whose awnings were then extended on all floors.

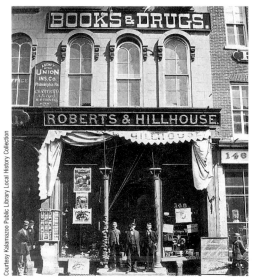

1882. This storefront originally stood alone. An identical storefront was later joined to its left, probably between 1857 and 1869, exactly where the "Union Ins. Co." sign is located, above the "R" in Roberts.

KALAMAZOO: LOST & FOUND

Brother, who sold liquor and manufactured cigars. In 1866, Main Street was one of the first laid with Nicholson pavement, another indicator of its commercial importance. As the remainder of the century passed, Kalamazoo City and Home Savings Banks located here, as did hatters, tailors, dressmakers, several drug stores, clothiers, a grocer and others.

In December 1909, in one of the Village's best documented disasters, a third fire laid waste to the hotel, and days later, indirectly brought about the collapse of the building to its east. Just four months after that, the next building to the east collapsed, and when it fell, it pulled the cornice off the corner bank and pushed a large crack up through its facade. In the end, the owners razed the bank, thereby vacating the remainder of the block to the east.

In 1911, the "New" Burdick Hotel filled the lots where Star Bargain and the old hotel had been. Inside, skylights provided natural light over an arcade that pushed north through the building from Main Street (now Michigan Avenue) to Water Street. The arcade provided space for about a dozen small businesses.

Noting all of this building activity, Frank D'Arcy moved his business across from the south side of the street, remodeled the storefront, and opened his New Theatre in 1912. Over time, most of the streetscape's remaining Italianates were replaced or redesigned as Art Deco and modern commercial block styles, culminating in the construction of the skyscraping Hanselman Building in 1913.

The mixed-use Hanselman offered retail space at street level with offices above. A "Three Part Vertical Block," its designer exploited its ten-story height by dividing up groups of floors similar to the parts of a column: base, shaft and capital. Its materials conveyed a sense of permanence: a glazed terra cotta exterior with marble inside.

During the late 1950s, 1960s and 1970s, the community undertook a number urban renewal measures it hoped would stem the movement of population and business to the suburbs. The construction of Kalamazoo's pedestrian mall was one of the earliest of these measures. In 1972, plans for a hotel and civic/convention center were announced for this block. By winter 1973, all of these buildings were gone, as well as those on the other three sides of the block. A single building replaced them.

> *"Kalamazoo Avenue, subsequently laid out ... was expected to be the principal street of the village. ... but its projectors were disappointed in their expectations, for business persistently clung to Main Street."*
>
> History of Kalamazoo County, Michigan 1880

2000. The two-story section of the development on this site today houses offices and retail, while the tower portion at left accommodates hotel guests.

c1950. This photo shows an early 1930s remodeling of the two buildings on the Burdick Hotel's left, from Italianate to Art Deco. Note also the former Roberts and Hillhouse storefront with its later twin, far left.

100 Block of West Main Street [now Michigan Avenue]
South Side

It is hard to imagine a dense growth of burr oak trees on this side of the street, but in 1839, they surrounded the house recently completed for Justus Burdick that faced Main Street. Built by E.R. Ball, who just had finished the new County Courthouse, this Greek Revival home sat far off the street on what is now Exchange Place. Called "handsome," "imposing" and "one of the most elegant private residences outside of Detroit," it was moved in 1855 to face South Rose Street, continuing as a boardinghouse.

The Burdick estate had begun selling the frontage on Main Street to meet the growing demand for more commercial buildings. The first brick building on the south side of West Main Street appeared a few years earlier on the southwest corner. By 1864, nine substantial brick and wood buildings filled the entire block from South Rose to South Burdick Streets. All were versions of Italianate, the first architectural style popular for both residential and commercial buildings.

For the next one hundred years, these structures accommodated a wide variety of goods and services from clothing, hardware, food, furniture, drugs and shoes, to lawyers, physicians, tailors and photographers. Certain buildings seemed to attract the same type of tenants. To this day, the east end of the block houses a banking institution, starting with First National Bank in 1863 to Keystone Community

1879–1882. Looking southeast. New ornate cornices were added to some of the buildings and one, the third from the right, even received a mansard roof which added a fourth floor of usable space.

c1875. Looking west from South Burdick Street. The first building completed on the block can be seen in this photograph, far left.

1869–1870. Parker's Mammoth Store at 137 and 139 West Main Street boasted a unique arcade on the second floor. Arches were prevalent everywhere from the doorways to the cornice. The building's facade had signage for all its tenants.

Bank today. Mannes Israel built a brick building on the west end in 1864 for his dry goods store, and for the next eighty years, three other similar businesses occupied the premises, including J.R. Jones Sons and Company. For a time, several lawyers had their offices located conveniently on the upper floors of this building just across from the County Courthouse.

Typically, the first floors of all these buildings were commercial establishments that sold goods while the upper floors contained people providing services, along with fraternal organizations that needed meeting rooms. One of these buildings even housed the Kalamazoo Public Library between 1885 and 1893.

The first major change on this block occurred in 1907 when two buildings on the east end came down to make way for Kalamazoo's first modern "skyscraper." Designed by Chicago architect Joseph Llewellyn and built by local resident Henry Vander Horst, the Kalamazoo Building boasted eight stories that towered over other structures and contained a wide variety of commercial tenants.

The other major changes to this block were accidental, rather than planned. Fire ravaged the J.R. Jones and Sons Store in 1945, destroying the two buildings on the west end. This space was then used for parking. Another larger fire in 1964 at the Lew Hubbard Store led to the demolition of the five buildings west of the Kalamazoo Building. One edifice remained in the middle of the block until 1971 when it was torn down, leaving just the Kalamazoo Building. The rest of the space has been used for parking ever since.

Ironically, the first building on this block, the Justus Burdick House, still exists on the southeast corner of Vine Street and South Westnedge Avenue, having been moved a second time in 1881. It still stands while the others only exist in photographs and memories.

c1935. A portion of the Kalamazoo Building is on the left. Most of the buildings had been changed over the years except for the Italianate with the rounded windows near the middle of this photograph.

2000. Plans were announced in the late 1980s to build an office building on this site but nothing has materialized. It remains a parking lot.

1965. For seven years the Bon Ton Beauty Salon was the last building on the block besides the Kalamazoo Building at left. Built in 1859, at one point in its life it housed Parker's Mammoth Store.

STREETSCAPES

West South and South Park Streets
Southwest Corner

Years ago, houses lined almost all of West South Street from South Rose Street to Oakland Drive, with the exception of Bronson Park. The three homes on South Park Street pictured in the photograph are a good example. They were built in the 1880s on land owned by Silas Trowbridge, an early settler.

In 1885, James Sebring and Leroy Cahill purchased two lots. Cahill, a manufacturer of agricultural implements, completed his Italianate house in 1886, and it can be seen in the distance in the photograph.

Sebring, owner of a grain elevator business, built his Queen Anne home on the corner the same year as Cahill. Typical of the style, it had a gabled roof, dormers, a variety of shingles, including fish-scale, a multitude of windows and a decorative porch.

Sebring sold half of his lot to Charles and Mary Peck who erected their Queen Anne house in 1887. Along with all the typical elements, this structure had an unusual onion domed tower topped by a decorative finial and with uniquely-shaped keyhole windows.

The Joseph Westnedge Post of the American Legion purchased the Peck house in 1926 for their headquarters. Fred Buckley purchased the Sebring house one year later and for reasons unknown, it was vacant for the next twenty years.

In 1947, the Kalamazoo Institute of Arts moved into the Peck house. The W.E. Upjohn Estate purchased the Sebring house the following year and tore it down. In 1956, after receiving funds from the Kalamazoo Foundation and Donald and Genevieve Gilmore, the Art Institute purchased the Cahill house and six others along South Park and West Lovell Streets. They leveled all of them, including the Peck house, for the new building they completed in 1961.

2000. In 1998, the Kalamazoo Institute of Arts completed a multi-million dollar renovation of this building, originally designed by the Chicago architectural firm of Skidmore, Owings and Merrill.

c1900. The Sebring and Peck homes were typical examples of the Queen Anne style, but the Peck had an unusual onion domed tower. It was very similar to the house built for Peck's brother, Horace B. Peck, that became the Kalamazoo Public Museum.

Washington Square
Portage Street and Washington Avenue

This intersection has a long history beginning in 1834 with the creation of Portage Street, a major north-south road through the county. A few hotels and boardinghouses were built here, but the first significant change occurred in 1858. In that year, the land east of Portage Street and south of Washington Avenue became the National Driving Park, a site for horse races, fairs and circuses.

Due to the park, initial development at this intersection was limited to the west side of Portage Street. By 1905, small buildings, filled with commercial tenants, began to spring up on the east side of the street. Local builder Thomas Foy completed a substantial three-story structure on the west side in 1908. Other buildings of similar size soon were completed.

The intersection grew tremendously over the next twenty years. Renamed Washington Square in the 1920s, the area contained a variety of businesses including department, grocery, drug, hardware and dime stores. In addition there were ice cream and beauty shops, bakeries, restaurants, cleaners, meat markets, a theater and a funeral home. The Kalamazoo Public Library established a branch in this block in 1919, and stayed until its new building was completed in 1927.

Washington Square had its own business association and weekly newspaper called the *South Side News*. The area had different types of sales and promotions, many of which still are used today.

Washington Square changed over the last thirty-five years, as many of the businesses could not compete with the national chains. In the early 1970s, the adult entertainment industry came to this area making a definite impact.

Although Washington Square is different from what it was fifty years ago, a number of businesses and institutions remain in its core helping to maintain its vitality.

2000. Although there are some vacant stores, Washington Square today still contains several businesses along this single-block area.

1938. In 1928, the Bank of Kalamazoo completed this distinctive corner building, at left, that later housed Lyons. Washington Square had many long-standing businesses including Barber's Department Store and Wise's Hardware.

1925. Looking south on Portage Street. Notice the streetcar tracks which reached this area in the 1880s.

South Burdick Street
East Side, South of Reed Street

Every neighborhood contained a small business district with grocery, drug and hardware stores, meat markets, barbers and shoemakers—all the services that residents needed on a daily basis. Before the era of one- or two-car families, these services needed to be within walking distance for residents. The east side of South Burdick Street at the intersection of Reed Street was such a place.

This area south of the City began to develop in the middle 1880s, first with houses, later with a school. A great majority of the residents in the area were Dutch, many of them operating small one- or two-acre celery farms adjacent to their homes. In fact, a nine-block stretch of South Burdick Street from Stockbridge Avenue to Alcott Street contained nearly fifteen different small farms.

In the late 1890s and early 1900s, commercial buildings appeared following the development of the residential neighborhoods. The most prominent structure on this side of the block is the two-story brick building at 1609 and 1611 South Burdick Street, now the 1800 block, completed between 1905 and 1906.

For years the building was home to Bushouse Hardware and to a meat market operated by a variety of owners, those with the longest tenure being Sam and Peter Luyendyk. The second floor contained residential space for a number of tenants.

Cornelius Grofvert, a cigar maker, had his business in the small building to the north, and Ralph Wolthuis, a long-time shoemaker, was next door.

As the years went by, the businesses in these buildings changed as both the neighborhood and people's buying habits altered. Small family-operated grocery stores and meat markets could not compete with larger chain stores elsewhere.

The activities inside these buildings has certainly changed over the years, but the structures remain as a reminder of a time when people could get what they needed within walking distance of their homes.

↱c1919–1922. Both stores and houses were interspersed along the street; also notice the streetcar tracks.

"Detroit has long been famed for her handsome avenues, but nowhere can she show more delightfully shaded and cleaner streets than Kalamazoo."

Kalamazoo Daily Telegraph Trade Edition, *1887*

↱2000. Several of the buildings remain, including the two-story brick structure which has housed a security service for over twenty years. There is a small grocery store on the corner.

Amusements & Entertainment

THIS CHAPTER touches only on a few of the ways that Kalamazooans have entertained themselves in the past. From amusement parks to zoos—Kalamazoo has had it all.

In the 1830s, the "early days," and for several decades after, much entertainment was enjoyed at home. Travel was more difficult then, so family, friends and neighbors played parlor games, told stories and held sing-alongs. The sing-alongs were often accompanied by a small reed organ called a melodeon, which was manufactured in downtown Kalamazoo on Main Street.

When people ventured out for entertainment, it was often combined with education. Students and adults attended "lyceums," which were held in the community's first public building, a school. Although the term lyceum actually refers to the venue, it was also used to describe the format of the lectures, concerts and other programs offered. In the late nineteenth and early twentieth century summers, chautauquas were popular, and used a format similar to the lyceum, only out-of-doors, under the protection of a tent.

Transportation became easier with the advent of streetcars, and live theater, musical performances and novelty acts appeared in communities across the United States. In the 1790s, American cities including New York, Boston and Philadelphia became major theater centers. But not every community could support a theater company, so traveling companies were formed that moved from village to village in the early and middle decades of the 19th century. When one arrived in Kalamazoo, it appeared in one of the new local venues. Some of the most popular were the 1853 Fire Hall on South Burdick Street, and the 1866 Union Hall on the southwest corner of Portage Street and today's East Michigan Avenue. Some of that building's framework remains, converted to office space.

Kalamazoo held grand community celebrations, including anniversaries of its founding and change of status from village to city. On these occasions, parades, concerts, contests and other events took place. They attracted huge crowds, like those gathered to see the "Human Fly" who in 1909, scaled the south facade of what is now known as the Haymarket Building on East Michigan Avenue. Community street fairs of the late 1890s and sporting events were planned and attended with the same enthusiasm as these anniversary parties.

One world event that resonated in Kalamazoo brought about a lasting change. The end of World War I gave birth to an organization that has since become a Kalamazoo institution: the Douglass Community Center.

The Frederick Douglass Community Association was created as a service club for black, off-duty military men stationed at Fort Custer in Battle Creek. Located in the 200 block of North Burdick Street on the upper floor of the now-demolished Turn Verein Hall, the Association offered entertainment and recreational programs. It grew in both mission and programs, evolving into a place where Kalamazoo's black residents could congregate legally and enjoy a social, recreational and intellectual life. Douglass' activities included

> *"The solution to the problem was to make the public get out and ride the streetcars on Saturdays and Sundays. How? By building an attraction at the end of the car line as a lure to the citizenry."*
>
> **Al Griffin,**
> *author of* Step Right Up, Folks!, *discussing the streetcar companies' solution for increasing weekend ridership on newly created lines*

dances, basketball teams, theater, scout groups, study groups and handicraft groups. The Association moved from its North Burdick home to West Ransom Street in 1941, and then again to Paterson Street in 1984, where it operates today.

During the decades on either side of 1900, entertainment moved from the primarily private to the public realm. New and often elegant buildings followed this trend, including the 1882 Academy of Music, chronicled in this chapter. Nickelodeons and vaudeville theaters appeared just before 1910, and shortly after that, the photoplay theaters, including the Elite, also in this chapter. Movie palaces soon followed, all locating in or near the central business district. Some opened and closed quickly, and some lasted, easily adapting to the next genre. The Majestic, later known as the Capitol Theatre on East South Street, was one of Kalamazoo's longest-lived, operating from 1907 until 1977.

Clubs and fraternal orders provided another means to engage in social discourse and entertainment. Although many of these had missions geared to the charitable and social needs of community residents, members also had lots of fun together at dances, banquets and other events.

The City built active and passive parks for its citizens. America's best known landscape architect, Frederick Law Olmsted, once said: "I have all my life been considering distant effect and always sacrificing immediate success and applause to that of the future." These words surely inspired the creators of Kalamazoo's parks, for they used enormous foresight in their decisions. By the time a Parks Commission was created in 1910, Kalamazooans had already long enjoyed their own village green, Bronson Park, and many others.

Kalamazoo had 27 parks by 1939, covering almost 600 acres. About two-thirds of that acreage was added under the supervision of William L. LaCrone. Milham Park, the largest in the system, saw major development during LaCrone's tenure, including its swimming pool, a tourist campsite, a zoo and a golf course. LaCrone initiated major improvements at other parks, often through Depression-era Federal work programs, which continued for a half-decade following his death in 1935.

The City's 1941 *Annual Report* indicates that this year brought a close to the use of the Depression-era, Federal Works Progress Administration "...as a construction agency in the building of our parks." By then Kalamazooans had 42 parks to enjoy. In 1940, almost 150,000 children had used the six neighborhood playground parks alone. At the same time, residents could choose from three golf courses, 11 tennis courts, 14 baseball diamonds, four different picnic grounds, an archery range, horseshoe pits and winter ice skating rinks all over the City.

Kalamazoo always kept pace with the nation, including the development of its own amusement park, Oakwood, in 1893. The surprising thing is that Oakwood's development, like that of many similar parks across the nation, was the means to another end, a fact that is further discussed in this chapter. If residents knew about this scheme, they chose to ignore it and had their fun anyway.

Since the 1950s, suburban development and the popularity of the automobile have dispersed Kalamazoo's population and the locations of its entertainment venues. Most movie theaters are now in the suburbs. As for home entertainment — it is still there, but is now often enjoyed not in small groups, but by a single person in front of a television or computer screen.

Previous Page: 1925. The early Douglass Community Center on North Burdick Street provided a service club for black military men from Fort Custer in Battle Creek, but eventually evolved into much more.

Courtesy Western Michigan University Archives and Regional History Collections

This Page: c1895. Architects Mason & Rice of Detroit designed this 1892 building as a home for the Young Men's Christian Association, bestowing it with an appropriate mix of reverence and Queen Anne exuberance. It burned down in 1911.

Courtesy Kalamazoo Valley Museum

Oakwood Park
Entrance formerly on North Side of Parkview Avenue, between Kent and Barnard Avenues

Then known as Lake View, this park opened in July 1893, followed by the completion of its pavilion and bandstand in August. Attendance increased significantly in 1894, when the Citizens Street Railway laid track to the site along Asylum Avenue, now Oakland Drive.

Streetcar companies across the nation often constructed amusement parks at the end of their lines as a means of building ridership. At the same time, the company owners bought property along the rights of way before its value inflated, and later sold it at a handsome profit. Hence, some of our nation's "streetcar suburbs" were born.

Soon after 1900, the Park regularly featured theater, opera, vaudeville and orchestra performances, in addition to other amusements such as roller skating, swimming and boating. In 1904, operators changed its name to Lake View Casino, and again in 1907, to Oakwood Park.

Edward Esterman managed the Park between 1909 and World War I, when streetcar ridership was high and the Park was busy. He kept its entertainment calendar crowded with activities, and provided a midway, as well as aquatic and other acts.

The advent of the automobile and the War's onset dealt the Park a double blow. It continued operating through the late 1910s and 1920s, but patron numbers dropped drastically and it died a slow death. The roller coaster was disassembled in 1925, and the main building's roller rink closed in 1937. Not long after, the Knights of Pythias bought the main building and remodeled it in 1941 for use as their lodge hall. A 1944 fire destroyed the structure.

Today, most of the park site is occupied with homes. A small access to the lake is owned and maintained here by the City.

c1905. The postcard view of Oakwood Park's Main Building provides the viewer with an idea of the building's size. The sign hanging from the lower right entry reads: "5¢ Vaudet." The concession stand, lower left, sold cold drinks and hot peanuts.

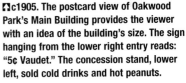

c1895. The Park's bandstand, graced here by three admirers, was constructed in 1893.

> *"After a 5 cent streetcar ride (preferably in an open car), one needed only money to complete the outing."*
>
> Ethel Perry Eaton,
> *talking about Oakwood Park,*
> *in* Glimpses of the Past, "City Pride" *1991.*

2000. Most of the former park site is now covered with homes just below this rail along Parkview Avenue, about one block west of Oakland Drive.

City Park Pools

The City of Kalamazoo created a Recreation Department in 1924. Its winter offerings included ice skating and "coasting." In the summer, baseball, basketball, tennis, and swimming were the popular sports.

Although initial swimming venues were located indoors at public schools, officials quickly appropriated $500 to create a "bathing place & boat lagoon" at Milham Park. They immediately dammed and dredged the creek, and began to build a bath house. In 1926, 4,000 people used this new pool. The Park, opened in 1911, was in part a gift to the City from former Kalamazoo Mayor Frank Milham.

In May 1933, President Roosevelt's Congress passed the Federal Emergency Relief Administration Act (ERA). The ERA provided Depression-era financial relief through state and local agencies. Congress soon followed with the National Industrial Recovery Act, providing an appropriation of $3.3 billion for public works projects. These programs, known by their acronyms such as WPA (Works Progress Administration), CCC (Civilian Conservation Corps) and others, put thousands of people to work across the country.

These projects, among other things, provided the nation with enhanced public parks, and Milham Park was one beneficiary. Work began immediately on a new stone bath house and concrete apron for the pool, for which the City paid only slightly over $3,000; the Federal government paid for the rest.

In 1924, the City purchased land on its north side from Althea Vande Walker Everard, who, along with husband, Herbert H., had lived in Kalamazoo for many years. Bounded

1936. "Water Fete" participants lined up along the edge of Milham's pool and shelter house for this group picture. Note the extensive stone masonry work, an identifying feature of many of the projects carried out during the Depression's work relief programs.

2000. The site of Milham Park's former pool and shelter house area is now mostly green space.

2000. A green area and basketball court now fill the former wading pool space at LaCrone Park, where thousands of children spent their summers playing in the water.

1935. LaCrone Park's pool, although more modest in size and design than others in the City, recorded attendance during the 1938–39 seasons of almost 8,000 swimmers.

by Paterson Street, Cobb Avenue and William Street, this park's nearby residential areas were rapidly developing. In 1935, the City unveiled a formal plan for the park, including baseball diamonds, playground equipment, and at the east end, a wading pool. This time, Federal public works programs paid for more than a third of the $32,000 cost.

The park was named in honor of former Parks Department superintendent William LaCrone. LaCrone's career achievements appeared everywhere in the City. He tripled the City's park acreage, undertook major improvements, landscaped the City's new Hall, acted as sexton at both cemeteries, and organized the City's forestry department.

In 1936, the City and the Red Cross co-sponsored a "Water Fete" at Milham Park to celebrate the completion of its enlarged pool. About that same time, ideas for a new east side park germinated. Covering two acres on either side of Trimble Avenue, Rockwell Park cost about $22,000 to build, and the Federal government absorbed almost two-thirds of the cost.

The park's namesake, Ethel Rockwell, taught public school in Kalamazoo and supervised the school system's physical education department. Her innovative programs earned her a national reputation. Rockwell died in 1936, and her new park featured a wading pool with a stone and wood comfort station.

For many years, the pools at these parks, and others at Southside, Verberg and Upjohn Parks, enjoyed great popularity. They were avidly used until 1963 when the State Health Department judged their sanitation systems deficient and ordered them drained. Sprinklers were set up in the pools after that, but Kalamazoo's youth apparently found no excitement in making a trip to the park to do something easily accomplished in their own back yards.

Proposals for full-sized, neighborhood parks pools fell to budget cuts in 1967. A single new community pool came to fruition in 1971, when the Nicholas Kik pool opened at Upjohn Park. Its predecessors, the little pools that served the community's youngsters for so many decades, were finally filled in during the early 1970s.

"The Department of Recreation seeks, through the utilization of leisure time, to build physique, develop character, and promote better citizenship among boys and girls of school age… and to provide such forms of recreation as will enlist their participation rather than mere observance."

Department of Recreation report,
1936 City Annual Report

⬈ 2000. Rockwell's former wading pool site now contains playground equipment. Note some of the old stone work in the background, to the right.

⬉ 1941. The cover of the City's 1941 *Annual Report* featured Rockwell's pool and comfort station. Rockwell Park had 5,400 square feet of stone masonry, a hallmark of Depression-era public works projects.

AMUSEMENTS & ENTERTAINMENT

Uptown Theater
Southwest Corner, North Burdick [Kalamazoo Mall] and Eleanor Streets

The opening of this theater in 1938 appears to have garnered more national attention than any of its Kalamazoo predecessors. Theater executives made appearances, and Hollywood stars telegrammed their good wishes, including Errol Flynn, Bette Davis, Fred Astaire, Ginger Rogers, Edward G. Robinson and Alice Faye.

The Uptown's opening was the featured event of the "North Burdick Street Progress Celebration" and many adjoining businesses participated with coordinated open houses and sales over a four-day period. Huge crowds gathered, and hundreds were turned away from the theater opening, which took place only a little over three months after construction began. That construction was actually a renovation of a half-century-old commercial Italianate building that had served for several decades as home to the Wheeler-Blaney Company.

In late December 1937, local theater mogul Peter Schram announced that his Mayfair Theater (later renamed the Uptown) would go into the building. He appointed Stewart-Kingscott Company as project architects, and Henry Vander Horst general contractor, who completed the work at an estimated $30,000. The *Kalamazoo Gazette,* in its review of the renovation, noted the theater's new Art Deco design, its sleek glass and stainless steel materials, and its many innovations. These included "magic eye" entry doors and drinking fountains — both of which would operate automatically as a patron approached. The theater also had a second floor soundproof "cry room" for parents and babies.

After a twenty-year life, the Uptown closed in 1959. In 1967, the Schram estate sold the building to Waber Development, who made alterations and leased the building for a number of years. In 1991, the City's Downtown Development Authority took title and razed the building for the Arcadia Creek Redevelopment Project.

1938. The Uptown's second floor lounge, fitted with sleek, modern furnishings. The signs over the left and right doors at the end of the lounge read: "Ladies" and "Cry Room."

1938. This photo shows the Uptown shortly after the building renovation.

2000. The former Uptown Theater site is now occupied by the rear of the Kalamazoo Valley Museum, completed in 1996.

"The front facade will be flood lighted, with the light in constantly changing colors."

Kalamazoo Gazette
December 26, 1937

KALAMAZOO: LOST & FOUND

Municipal Ice Rink
Lake Street, 400 Block

Before this ice rink became a reality, Kalamazooans skated in the old-fashioned way, waiting for the temperatures to drop enough to convert water to ice. Sometimes they skated on the rivers, and sometimes in the Vine and Stuart neighborhoods areas, which the City flooded for this purpose.

Kalamazooans were still skating in the middle of the twentieth century. In 1956, Commissioner Willis Dunbar asked the City to procure estimates on an artificial rink. Dunbar proposed that the City consider using a portion of the income derived from the sale of its lighting plant to finance the project.

Public and private conversation continued, and the following March, the City received a letter from resident Lloyd Yenner, sent on behalf of a group who supported the idea. Yenner sent a petition with signatures as proof of that interest. These documents obviously helped convince the City of the community's support, and by the following October, requests for bids went out for installation of the rink's refrigeration system.

During the 1958–59 season, almost 28,000 children and adults skated at the new rink. The 1959–60 season saw a significant increase, and attendance reached 44,000. In 1965, local architects Stone/Parent designed a roof for the rink, and the Kalamazoo Foundation made a grant to help cover its cost.

The rink enjoyed great popularity into the 1970s. However, in 1976, two issues combined to bring about its end. Were it to continue, the rink would need extensive maintenance. Further, the City's Water Department, whose site backed up to the rink, needed additional space. The City Commission voted in March 1976, to close the rink. Its "warming house" was demolished in 1999.

c1959. A City employee applies a spray of water to build up the ice on the new City rink.

"On Friday, the 18th of January, this year, a group of men were having lunch together and the subject of winter recreation facilities in Kalamazoo came under discussion."

Lloyd Yenner,
in a letter to the City Commission, March 11, 1957

c1967. The rink's 1966 roof allowed for its use during heavier snows, when an uncovered rink would have been closed.

2000. This drive and storage area cover the former ice rink site.

National Driving Park
Bounded North by Washington Avenue, South by Hays Park, West by Portage Street and East by Cameron Street

Horse racing and horse raising were important, early forms of entertainment for the residents of Kalamazoo, dating back to 1837 with the formation of the Kalamazoo Jockey Club. In 1856, a new organization named the Kalamazoo Town Agricultural Society organized and raised $10,000 that allowed the members to purchase in 1858, 64 acres at the intersection of Portage Avenue and Washington Street. They added fences, buildings and a one-mile track suitable for racing.

Nationally-known trotters such as Flora Temple, came here to compete. Thousands of spectators saw her break the world record for a one-mile course on October 12, 1859, an event immortalized in a Currier and Ives engraving. During the Civil War, the Park became the site for several local regiments, whose soldiers camped and drilled here before being sent into battle.

The Michigan State Agricultural Society held their annual fairs at the National Driving Park in 1863 and 1864. The Kalamazoo chapter of the Ladies Soldiers' Aid Society held a Sanitary Fair in conjunction with the 1864 fair, raising over $9,000 for soldiers. The Park also became the site for the Kalamazoo County Fair beginning in the middle 1860s. P.T. Barnum and the Ringling Brothers pitched their circus tents here for many years. Transportation to the National Driving Park was made easier in 1884 when the streetcar line extended this far. The last event held at the Park was a Fourth of July celebration in 1893. One week later, newspapers reported the dismantling of the grandstand and the sheds. Three years afterwards, local developer Charles Hays began to purchase the old National Driving Park, subdividing it into lots for the countless houses and commercial structures that became the core of the Edison neighborhood.

> *"The residents of the Big Village are much indebted to the promulgation of this beautiful park for these annual enjoyments and pleasures, for participating in which even as delightful spectators, the absorbing cares and anxieties of daily life are forgotten."*
>
> Kalamazoo Gazette
> *April 6, 1876*

c1885. The only known photograph of the National Driving Park shows the entrance, track and exhibition area in the middle of the field.

2000. The Washington Square business district and part of the Edison neighborhood are located on the site of the National Driving Park.

1873. This illustration from a Kalamazoo County Atlas shows the grandstand, sheds and other buildings west of the fairgrounds; built by Bush and Paterson in 1859.

KALAMAZOO: LOST & FOUND

Elite Theatre
South Burdick Street [Kalamazoo Mall], 300 Block, East Side

A better name for the Elite Theatre may have been the "Petite." Nearly all of its life, this lively little theater was dwarfed by its northern neighbor, the Browne/Peck building.

George Rickman and Sons built the Elite in 1912 for Harry Waterman of Chicago and local real estate developer Charles Palmer. Its Moorish principal facade carried out a popular theater theme, using cream terra cotta and marble accents. Its most engaging element was its loggia, with arches whose keystones mimicked the ancient Greek Comedy character masks. Fanlights over the mahogany doors echoed the arches. The land and finished building cost $40,000.

The Elite's apparent size was deceiving. Inside, it accommodated between 700 and 900 people,

c1918. The petite Elite, designed by Rockwell LeRoy.

1950. Fidelity Federal Savings & Loan, now Standard Federal Bank, bought the Elite, but retained its facade for many years.

1951. The building's 1951 remodeling gave it a very different and somber public face.

who were kept comfortable in the summer with a system of automatic ventilation ports and fans.

Originally devoted to "photo-plays," or silent pictures accompanied by live music, the Elite was ahead of its time. Until then, only large metropolitan areas had built theaters like it; smaller cities generally did not benefit until after World War I. When the Elite changed hands in November 1912, the new owners added vaudeville. In 1913, they began to use to "Kinemacolors," a process that added color to the film using filters.

In 1925, Fidelity Federal Savings and Loan bought the Elite for a reported $67,000. They remodeled the interior and added a basement. In the early 1950s, they remodeled again, giving the building a very different and somber look. In 1975, the Browne/Peck building next door was demolished above ground, and a new building, now Standard Federal Bank, went up on its foundation. At the same time, the former Elite underwent an $800,000 transformation that sought to better match its exterior with the new building next door.

"From the moment the moviegoers arrived to buy their tickets, there was a sense of something special, a feeling that to step inside was to enter another time and place."

Gene Kelly, *movie star and dancer, from* Great American Movie Theaters

2000. Part of the little theater still stands behind this solid brick and glass facade today, although it is impossible to detect.

Majestic/Capitol Theatre
East South Street, 100 Block, South Side

Excitement rang through the air on November 18, 1907, when the new Majestic Theatre opened on East South Street just east of South Burdick Street. Designed and built by Frank P. McClure of St. Louis for $45,000, the combination vaudeville and motion picture house could seat up to 1,100 people. It was nearly standing room only for both performances that day as tickets ranged from $0.10 to $0.25. The headline attraction that first night was the American Florence Troupe composed of six male and female acrobats. The newspapers reported that people came from Battle Creek, Jackson, Flint and even Grand Rapids for these first shows.

The Majestic was one of the first houses built by Walter S. Butterfield on his way to becoming one of the largest theater owners in the state. The major color scheme of the interior was red, white and gold. The theater boasted eight boxes that each seated six people in conversation chairs built so that the occupants could easily turn around and talk with the people behind them, but hopefully not during the show.

The theater was renamed the Majestic Gardens in 1918. Six years later it was extensively rebuilt, remodeled and reopened as the

c1910. The building had a dentiled cornice and stone moldings over the windows. As with most theaters, the storefronts and upper floors were filled with physicians, photographers, fraternal organizations and even music and dance schools.

Capitol Theatre. Some of the first sound pictures were shown here in 1929. Remodeled and redecorated twice more in 1940 and 1955, the theater suffered declining attendance in the 1960s and 1970s as did many other downtown theaters, due to television and new suburban theaters. The Capitol existed until 1976, when it was demolished to make way for a parking ramp.

> "If ample spaces, elegant proportions and handsome furnishings entitle a theatre to the name Majestic the new vaudeville theatre of that designation which was formally opened Monday night has been correctly classified."
>
> Kalamazoo Evening Telegraph
> *November 19, 1907*

1955. The last major renovation gave the Capitol a new marquee. The Bennett Photography Studio at right, was one of the longest tenants, there from 1953 until 1976.

2000. A municipal parking ramp replaced the Capitol Theatre in 1977.

KALAMAZOO: LOST & FOUND

Arcadia Brook Golf Course
Area Surrounding Western Michigan University's Recreation Center and Kalamazoo College's Angell Field

In 1927, local developer Charles Hays opened a riding club and private golf course adjacent to the Oaklands, now part of Western Michigan University. He opened it to the general public in May 1928, renaming it the Arcadia Brook Golf Course. The first nine holes ran east of the Oaklands and south of West Michigan Avenue. An additional nine holes opened six months later on the north side of the street.

In addition to the golf course and riding academy, the area contained a driving range, practice greens, tennis and shuffleboard courts, an archery range, a dining room, and a clubhouse with rooms to rent. Its advantageous location placed it close to downtown and the railroad depots. One paid $0.35 for nine holes of golf and $0.75 for an hour of horseback riding.

The course continued operating until 1943. The following year, Western Michigan University purchased the first nine holes, the clubhouse, the Oaklands and the riding academy along with Gateway, a municipal golf course adjacent to this one.

Trailer Village, providing homes for student veterans, opened on this site in 1946. The school began to use the old clubhouse in 1948 for meeting rooms, a dormitory and dining facility for the faculty. Completion of Read Fieldhouse and the Gary Center in 1956 considerably changed this area. Part of the clubhouse remained for many years as the University's Public Safety Department until the early 1990s. Interestingly enough, there continues to be a recreational center on this site, however only for students, faculty, staff, and alumni of Western Michigan University.

1934. Two of the back nine holes are now part of Kalamazoo College's football, baseball and soccer fields.

2000. Western Michigan University's Student Recreation Center and University Arena now sit on the first nine holes of the Arcadia Brook Golf Course.

1934. Number nine green with the clubhouse, originally a Greek Revival house. The former Oakland Gym and Science Building on Western Michigan University's East Campus can be seen in the distance.

"The course is certain to prove one of the most attractive in this part of the state."

Kalamazoo Gazette
May 18, 1928

AMUSEMENTS & ENTERTAINMENT

Academy of Music
South Rose Street, 100 Block, East Side

"There is no reason why Kalamazoo should cheat itself out of the finest things, out of the fruit and cream of modern civilization so to speak which brought so much to the place." Thus spoke local resident Charles May at a public meeting held at Corporation Hall on March 26, 1881, to discuss the need for an opera house in the Village. Up to this point, Union Hall on Portage Street was the venue for public entertainment, but many at the meeting had concerns about the building's conditions.

Twelve men, who formed the Kalamazoo Opera House Company, looked into potential sites and fundraising options. They chose a site on South Rose Street immediately across from the County Courthouse. They set a goal of $30,000 to be raised primarily by subscriptions. In May, Lyman Kendall and Frederick Bush went to Chicago to meet with potential architects, choosing Dankmar Adler who had a very talented staff member named Louis Sullivan who eventually became his partner and one of America's most influential architects.

Work quickly commenced, and within ten months the building was completed. The name changed in December from the Kalamazoo Opera House to the Academy of Music as the Committee reported the name had become so commonly used. What surely also motivated their decision was the owner of Union Hall, who now referred to his building as the Kalamazoo Opera House.

The Academy of Music opened on May 8, 1882, with a sold-out program of speeches, music and a performance of *Virginius the Roman Father* featuring John McCullough; tickets sold for up to $5.00 each. The newspapers reported that "…much exclamations of admiration" were given. This is understandable when one reads the description of the interior with its cherry woodwork, crimson velvet walls embossed

1887–1888. Made of Philadelphia brick trimmed with Berea stone, the Academy of Music had a mansard roof with a portholed dormer, corner pinnacles topped by finials, an ornamental cornice and horizontal stone beltcourses. The storefronts and upper offices were filled with a variety of tenants ranging from barbers and bakers to dentists and lawyers.

c1882. Above the proscenium arch was a life-size fresco of Guido's "Aurora." The drop curtain was crimson satin fringed with gold and white lace.

c1882. The house seated 1,200 and was lit with 400 gas jets and a main chandelier eleven feet high and nine feet wide.

KALAMAZOO: LOST & FOUND

with gold paper, and frescoed ceiling. The elaborate four side boxes were draped in peacock blue and maroon plush with plate glass mirrors along the walls.

The total cost of the theater was $65,000, over double the original estimate, as the Committee decided to select the best when it came to seating, lighting and decoration. Kalamazoo businesses supplied much of the building materials along with products from Chicago and New York.

For the next thirty-five years, the Academy was home to traveling companies performing classic plays such as *Hamlet* and contemporary pieces like *Under the Red Robe*. In addition, there were lectures, local and national orchestras, choirs and even boxing matches. One of the most unusual attractions occurred in 1888, when Bartholomew's Equine Paradox played the Academy for one week with eighteen horses, four ponies, a mule and a donkey. In 1897, the Academy of Music became the first local site for a demonstration of Edison's Vitascope, one of the first motion pictures.

The theater's name changed in 1916 to the Regent, now a vaudeville and silent movie house under the management of W.S. Butterfield. It continued to operate until a fire in June 1930, destroyed the entire theater leaving only the front portion of the building, which was remodeled three years later by M.C.J. Billingham. This front portion stood until 1967 when it and two other adjacent buildings were taken down for a new eight-story office building, which included the Industrial State Bank, now known as Comerica Bank.

2000. The Comerica Building has been on the site of the Academy of Music since 1968.

1946. The Academy of Music building here, on the right, minus its dormer. The Stevens Block is on the left.

> *"The long anticipated event has occurred and last evening, the Academy of Music, that temple of the muses, which since March 1881 has been before the people of Kalamazoo in one shape or another was thrown open to the public, and an intensely admiring throng it was that packed the house even to the abode of the heaven borne."*
>
> Kalamazoo Gazette
> *May 9, 1882*

Young Women's Christian Association (YWCA)
West Main Street [now Michigan Avenue], 400 Block, South Side

The first Young Women's Christian Association in Michigan was formed in Kalamazoo in 1885, with nine girls wanting to meet for Bible study. Soon this number tripled and the organization rented rooms in various downtown locations. Their first gift amounting to $500 arrived in 1893, which allowed them to purchase two years later this house on West Main Street, now West Michigan Avenue.

The Italianate structure had been built in 1861 by William House, a businessman and real estate investor. It was a classic example of an Italianate with a cubic shape, rounded paired windows, a two-story bay window and paired brackets at the cornice. A rounded cupola topped the structure.

By the 1890s, the YWCA had expanded into community and social work. Since 1888, it assisted women working in factories by feeding them regular lunches and dinners, and providing opportunities to further their education. Members met daily trains greeting new women who were coming to town for employment and offering them necessary information and direction. Out-of-town females, or women without a home, could

c1907. The small entry porch is very common for an Italianate. Notice also the pagoda style roof on the cupola and the paired windows at the cornice. The house was very symmetrical, but broader than ones built later.

rent rooms on a temporary basis at the YWCA for $3.50 a week including room and board.

By 1908, the home became inadequate to handle the YWCA's needs and they sold it for $10,000 to G.P. Truesdale for a funeral home. The YWCA once again rented rooms downtown, eventually moving into a new building on South Rose Street by 1919. Their first permanent home on West Main Street continued as the Truesdale Funeral Home until 1986, when it was demolished for a parking lot.

2000. A parking lot is on the site of the structure built by William House. It was the last of the mansions on Main Street to come down.

KALAMAZOO: LOST & FOUND

Young Men's Christian Association (YMCA)
Southeast Corner, West Main [now Michigan Avenue] and South Park Streets

Kalamazoo's Young Men's Christian Association dates from 1885. After renting various rooms downtown, the organization built its first building in 1892 on the southeast corner of West Main Street, now Michigan Avenue, and South Park Streets. This building served the YMCA until fire destroyed it in January 1911.

The Board of Directors immediately met to begin plans for a new building. A ten-day campaign in March raised $30,000, which added to the insurance money, gave the YMCA a total of $65,000. Work began in August and a grand community celebration occurred on September 23, 1911, when President William Howard Taft came to lay the cornerstone.

Forrest Van Volkenburg designed the new building, completed one year later in September 1912. The new YMCA, touted as fireproof, contained a gymnasium, swimming pool, parlors, and dormitory rooms that were rented to members who were moving to town or simply traveling through. Gifts towards the building ranged from $4,000 from Dr. William E. Upjohn, to $0.08 from a local

c1925. The building contained a dentiled cornice and a columned entrance. Notice the stone treatment on the first floor and the YMCA symbol at the roof.

newsboy. Membership by 1913 numbered 1,500 men and boys.

The need for more space led the YMCA in 1941 to build an addition that matched the older building in architectural style and materials. Twenty-five years later, plans were underway to build a new facility on West Maple Street, which opened in 1970. The First Congregational Church tore the old YMCA building down that same year for additional parking.

2000. A parking lot for the First Congregational Church has been here since 1970.

c1914. YMCA gymnasium also had a saucer running track. Of the 1,500 members in 1913, 500 were boys.

c1955. The 1941 addition, left, duplicated the original building almost perfectly. At this same time, the original cornice was removed and the entrance was redesigned.

"This building was started in the early fall, is rapidly nearing completion and will be one of the finest buildings in the city when it is completed."

Kalamazoo Telegraph-Press
April 30, 1912

AMUSEMENTS & ENTERTAINMENT

Elks Temple and Lodge Hall
East South Street, 100 Block, South Side

Although no longer a purely social organization, the Benevolent and Protective Order of Elks traces its origins to 1867, and a convivial group of English immigrants living in New York, the "Jolly Corks," whose name was derived from a popular drinking game of the day. By 1886, the group renamed itself, grew significantly, and begat new Lodges, including Kalamazoo's, whose members supported many charitable activities.

With a turn-of-the-century membership of over 600, Kalamazoo's Lodge needed a permanent home. In 1902, it bought land on West South Street and prepared building plans. However, it sold that site instead, making a $2,000 profit, and bought an East South Street Italianate house for $14,000. Originally home to financier Henry Brees, it was first known as Brees Terrace, and later as Drake Terrace, after Brees' stepdaughter and heir, Soledad Dela Vega Drake.

With another $12,000, the Elks hired Grand Rapids firm Osgood & Osgood to design an addition, and Kingsley & Stock from St. Joseph to complete construction. The addition included a mahogany meeting room, combined dining and banquet rooms, and two bowling alleys. Dedicated in May 1905, Lodge members met and socialized there for the next 23 years.

In June 1928, the organization again remodeled, with another rear addition and a new Art Deco facade, and considerable interior changes. The $100,000 cost was financed with $24,000 from the organization's treasury and a $75,000 mortgage. DeRight Brothers Construction carried out the work.

In 1941, the Elks leased the Maple Hills golf course west of the City, and bought that property three years later. In 1959, the membership sold the downtown Lodge. In 1962, LaFourche Realty razed the building. The site is now part of a parking ramp and office complex.

c1908. Elks gathered on the front porch of their home soon after it was remodeled to accommodate their needs. Note the large rear addition on the right.

1960. Just two years before the building was demolished, this photo shows its Art Deco facade, constructed during the 1928–29 remodeling. Note the original Italianate style windows that still overlook the alley above the fire escape.

c1908. With their 1905 addition, the Elks received an elegant, mahogany-trimmed lodge room.

2000. The former Elks site now contains a structure that combines a parking ramp with offices.

Redpath Chautauqua
Green Space on the East Side of East Hall, Western Michigan University

Before there was radio, television and the Internet, there were Chautauquas, annual events in many American cities around the turn of the 20th century. Communities in the summer would be entertained and educated by leading lecturers, politicians, musicians and performers. Kalamazoo's first Chautauqua was held at Oakwood Park in 1907, and a second one took place in 1909.

Four years later, Western State Normal School sponsored the Redpath Chautauqua run by the Redpath Lyceum Bureau of Boston that came here for one week in July at the end of the School's summer term. Over the next fourteen years, the Redpath Chautauqua returned, offering lectures on Asia, birds, Shakespeare, Bolshevism, the high cost of living, human nature, health and international relations, and debates on such issues as socialism and government ownership of the railroads. During World War I, aviators and medical personnel gave thrilling reports from the front. There were all types of musical performances ranging from soloists to quintets from all over the world, and presentations of Shakespeare dramas and Gilbert and Sullivan operettas.

The School offered discount tickets to students with prices for the general public just slightly higher. Every morning there would be a special children's program, like ventriloquist Edgar Bergen who came in 1923 and 1924.

Chautauquas declined in the middle 1920s due to new forms of entertainment like radio and motion pictures. The last Redpath Chautauqua occurred here in 1926. The tennis courts are long gone, but it would not be hard to stand in their general location and imagine the thousands of people gathered there on a summer day to learn and enjoy.

2000. The land where the Chautauqua tent was once erected is currently used by WMU's Athletic Department as a practice field.

c1920. Afternoon programs began at 3:00 and evening ones at 7:30 so as not to conflict with the students' classes.

c1920. So many people attended during the program one year that the tent needed to be enlarged.

"This year an unusually fine program has been offered. Lectures, entertainments, music all combine to make it a program of splendid diversity and interest."

Western Normal Herald
July 7, 1920

Milham Park Zoo
Milham Park, Northeast Corner, Lovers Lane and Kilgore Road

Following a lead set by Detroit students who bought an elephant for Belle Isle Zoo, students at Kalamazoo's Lake Street School each contributed a penny to buy monkeys for their new zoo at Milham Park. Soon, Jiggs and Maggie were entertaining the public with their antics. The zoo collection began in 1926, with the gifts of a bear cub and two fawn in addition to the monkeys.

The zoo benefited from Depression-era Works Progress Administration (WPA) programs when in 1936, workers constructed new stone animal enclosures in the park's northeast corner. Cave-like, their massing was above and below ground level, creating a more natural setting for the animals.

The public enjoyed the zoo for decades. A 1943 *Kalamazoo Gazette* article reported six bears in residence. In 1962, Blackie the bear gave birth to cubs, the first, and apparently the only, who were born and survived locally in captivity.

Over time, however, it was "captivity" that became a public issue, along with a 1970s series of human offenses against the animals, especially the bears. One bear's paw was maimed when someone threw a rock into an enclosure, and another injury occurred when someone tossed in glass.

A committee met in the early 1970s to determine the zoo's future, but could not find a solution. In 1976, the City unsuccessfully sought a new home for the remaining bears. Over the next fifteen months, one was put to sleep due to disease and a second died, leaving just one. The City put the last bear down out of compassion in October 1977, thereby closing the zoo. The stone enclosures were demolished in 1983.

c1936. Park workers gather in front of one of the new stone animal enclosures at Milham Park. Stone construction of this type was a hallmark of Depression-era, public works projects in Kalamazoo.

2000. The former zoo area is now open space.

> *"The City also received letters. Only one opposed putting the bear to sleep. That letter suggested closing the park to all humans and letting the bear live."*
>
> **Art Sills,**
> Kalamazoo Gazette, *October 20, 1977, writing about the zoo's remaining bear*

Odds & Ends

THE SUBJECTS of this chapter mostly represent "non-buildings." They are architectural "accessories" that helped to make places memorable. Whatever we choose to call them, most acted to enhance the appearance of our community, or simply helped to make it the community it was.

These are not places where people lived, worked, worshiped or manufactured things, but they are nonetheless important, for many added interesting and fine features to the collective landscape. One might call them "utilitarian," because while they had a purpose, it was usually not to enclose space and provide human shelter. Just as important as the *Lost* buildings covered in the first nine chapters of this book, these ancillary things and places are those that people came into contact with often, but only for brief periods of time.

Perhaps the major difference between most of these accessories, long gone, and those that have replaced them, is that appearance played a critical role in their creation.

For example, consider something seemingly as unimportant as a water tower. Kalamazoo had a number of brick towers at one time. The one on Westnedge Hill is featured in this chapter. If you look closely at that tower, and then look at the former water works on South Burdick Street in the Public Buildings chapter of this book, you recognize that design was important, and begin to make connections between the two. Kalamazoo's water towers did their job, and looked good doing it. While the inside was where the towers' work went on, the exterior, or "window dressing," made these structures visually pleasing. America's water towers of today seem to do one of two things quite apart from that earlier goal: they either attempt to disappear altogether or they cast giant smiley-faces across the landscape.

For another example of this point, compare the horse trolley shelter within this chapter and a contemporary bus shelter — a contrast which leaves us wishing we had more of the former. Although it is difficult to detect a single specific reason why this shift from the visually pleasing and functional to merely functional took place, it may be that Kalamazoo and other communities have suffered as a result.

"I commend to you and your associates this, the loveliest village in the West, with all its precious interests."

Village President Dwight May's exaugural address, 1875 Village Annual Report

c1948. Certainly an ancillary piece of our past, the former fence and gate that bordered Mountain Home Cemetery along West Main Street served its function in an attractive manner.

Courtesy Schafer's Flowers Family

East Michigan Avenue Bridges
East Main [now Michigan Avenue], between 600 and 700 Blocks

This site was a busy thoroughfare even before Kalamazooans constructed the first bridge here in 1835. Prior to that time, visitors and residents ferried across the river at approximately this same spot.

According to a *Kalamazoo Gazette* account, the first bridge here was a "corduroy" road. The citizens donated $200 and the State matched those funds. Constructed of logs, corduroy roads were used over low or swampy areas. Even though the depressions between logs were filled with smaller logs and gravel, corduroy roads were always rough and often dangerous.

About the middle 1880s, a new bridge spanned the river, delicate in appearance clear up to its finial-topped end sections. Accounts differ as to its composition, iron or steel, but it is nonetheless amazing that this unassuming structure carried traffic over the river for almost four decades.

In a report at the end of his term in 1925, City Manager Clarence L. Miller urged the community to replace the bridge on what is now East Michigan Avenue. A year later, Miller got his wish when construction of the City's most appealing bridge began here. The City's *Annual Reports* confirm its reported cost of $110,000.

The bridge's triple concrete spans began and ended at water level, arching upward to about six feet in between. The street level balustrade was regularly pierced to lighten its appearance and provide a view of the water. Lighting, provided by a series of stylized, tree-like pylons stretched twenty feet into the air, each with multiple globes nestled underneath abbreviated branches.

Completed in 1927, the bridge was almost seventy years old when it was replaced in 1996.

c1915. This middle-1880s metal bridge over what is now East Michigan Avenue looks lightweight when compared to its successor.

"The new bridge in East Avenue is said to be one of the prettiest spans along M-17....Wide walks skirt each side...."

Kalamazoo Gazette
May 1, 1927

c1927. The reinforced, cast concrete bridge completed in 1927 is the most graceful ever designed for this location.

2000. The 1996 bridge on this site is simple in its design.

KALAMAZOO: LOST & FOUND

Nicholson Pavement
Many Streets in the Center City

Wood blocks played a large role in the lives of many Kalamazooans. The blocks supported them as they traveled by road.

Confusion exists about the first use of Nicholson pavement in Kalamazoo, but no one questions that it was a vast improvement over dirt. The 1880 *History of Kalamazoo County* refers to it by name, claims it appeared in 1866, and reported that the first section was laid on Main Street, now Michigan Avenue, between Rose and Portage Streets. Another section covered Burdick Street between Fireman's Hall and the Michigan Central Railroad tracks.

Records of wood block roads exist from Washington, DC to Chicago to Dallas. Although a wide variety of woods were used, including oak, hemlock, cottonwood, tamarack, and blackgum, cedar was the local favorite. The *Kalamazoo Gazette* published an article on January 28, 1951, describing the then historic process: "...the street to be paved was leveled off and a bed of gravel laid, the blocks were jammed in between the two curbstones so tightly it was impossible for one of them to work loose. Gravel was poured into the cracks remaining between the blocks and the road was complete." A scholarly paper on wood block streets in Dallas indicates that the procedure worked much the same way there.

That same *Gazette* article profiles a local paver, Jahai (or Gahy, as indicated in the *City Directories*) Peters, whose skills were in great demand for a number of years. The *Gazette* wrote: "It took a keen ax and about 4,200 feet of cedar logs six inches in diameter to pave one block of a Kalamazoo street in 1890." However, wood block did have its problems, including swelling, shrinking and fungus. A decade later, Village Council minutes indicate that brick had replaced wood as the preferred paving material.

c1884. A Nicholson street paving crew stopped to pose for the camera near the intersection of Edwards and Water Streets. Note the cobblestone gutters on either side of the wood block.

2000. Although some City streets retain their brick, which followed Nicholson wood-block pavement, most are now topped with asphalt.

"It also took the skill that only one man in the city could provide — a husky Dutchman with the energy of a Mexican jumping bean named Jahai Peters."

Kalamazoo Gazette
January 28, 1951

ODDS & ENDS

Streetcars

There have been a variety of ways to get around in Kalamazoo. By 1882, the *Kalamazoo Daily Telegraph* promoted a streetcar system that would provide cheap and rapid transportation within the Village. Organized by businessman Jeremith Boynton, the Kalamazoo Street Railway Company received the franchise in March 1884. Eight lines were proposed, but only six were completed. These stretched to the east, north and south sides of the City. The longest route went from downtown to the National Driving Park. Next to this park were the barns for the cars and horses. The streetcars officially began on June 8, 1884, which happened to coincide with the start of Race Week at the Driving Park. Fares everywhere were five cents.

Over the next few years, old routes were expanded and new routes begun. In 1893, the Michigan Electric Railway Company took over operations. They moved quickly early that year to electrify the system which they completed by July 3, 1893.

Twenty-five new yellow and red motor cars arrived from St. Louis, Missouri, each sixteen feet long with a capacity of twenty-two passengers. As opposed to the horse-drawn streetcars that were operated by only a driver, the electric ones had both a conductor and motorman. An extensive article appeared in the *Kalamazoo Gazette* describing the rules and regulations for these two employees, discussing everything from their uniforms to what the various bells meant.

The electric cars now had the ability to master the hills surrounding downtown Kalamazoo.

1889. John Wall drove this car on route #2 which ran down Burdick Street from Frank to Burr Oak Streets.

c1920. The Oakland route ended at Parkview Avenue. Perry Holden is standing on the right.

2000. The City of Kalamazoo has operated the Metro Transit Bus System since 1967.

KALAMAZOO: LOST & FOUND

Service usually ran from 6:00 in the morning until 11:30 at night.

The National Driving Park ceased to exist by 1893, but soon thereafter the streetcars had a new attraction to take residents to, namely Oakwood Park at the intersection of Oakland Drive and Parkview Avenue. In fact, the Michigan Electric Railway Company was one of the investors in this recreation area. During the summer a special street car with open sides and canvas curtains traveled this route. Some older residents still recall riding these cars in an effort to cool down on hot summer days.

The streetcars in Kalamazoo continued to operate until 1932, already feeling the impact of the automobile. An employee strike that year over wage cuts ended streetcar service in the City. A new, privately operated bus system gave people more mobility, and the City assumed responsibility for its operation in 1967.

"The street car lines will be completed early this morning and the public will be afforded ample accommodation in getting to the track."

Kalamazoo Gazette
June 9, 1884

Lines traveled up West Main Street, South West Street, now Westnedge Avenue, East Main Street and Oakland Drive, opening those areas for development. The newly created Edison neighborhood had a streetcar line circling it.

↱2000. The approximate location of the West Main Street streetcar stop.

↰c1890. This Queen Anne stop sat on West Main Street in front of Mountain Home Cemetery. It had a gabled roof decorated with circular shingles and a wide overhang, perfect for protecting waiting riders. Newspaper articles state it was built by cemetery employees.

City Market
Southwest Corner, Mills Street and East Michigan Avenue

In October 1910, Mayor Charles Farrell appointed a committee with members from the City Council to investigate creating a market place in the City to sell fruits and vegetables. They were motivated by the congestion and excessive noise caused by the number of farmers and peddlers selling their produce at various locations in the City and on public streets.

After careful study and visits to other communities, the committee recommended in January 1911, to create a market to operate from May 1 until November 1. They also suggested beginning with a temporary market before creating a permanent one. The first site chosen was North Rose Street north of Water Street. However, the construction of the Masonic Temple delayed the opening of the market until 1913, when it moved to the east side of North Rose Street between Kalamazoo Avenue and the Michigan Central Railroad Depot. A market master, aided by a policeman, managed the operation and kept track of the licensed and unlicensed peddlers.

Through the years, the market, later renamed the City Market, moved to five other locations.

c1935. Every week the market master would report to the City Commission the number of people who came and the amounts of produce sold. Overcrowding and inaccessibility were problems at this location.

The above photograph of the market was taken at the southwest corner of Mills Street and East Michigan Avenue across from the Municipal Power and Light Plant where the market was located between 1932 and 1947. That year it moved to its present location west of Bank Street between Lake Street and Stockbridge Avenue, where the City of Kalamazoo continues to operate it to this day.

2000. The property where the City Market once stood is vacant, but the Michigan Bakeries building still stands.

> *"We believe such a market is not only a necessity but that its establishment would result in the mutual interest of all of the citizens of the city."*
>
> City Council Minutes
> January 23, 1911

KALAMAZOO: LOST & FOUND

South West Standpipe
Northwest Corner, Inkster Avenue and South West Street (now South Westnedge Avenue)

The need to have a supply of water available for fire fighting led the City of Kalamazoo in 1910 to build a standpipe at West Main and Hilbert Streets. They followed this three years later with one more on East Main Street and this one, on the northwest corner of South West Street, now known as South Westnedge Avenue, and Inkster Avenue.

All three were very similar in design with some minor variations. The major difference was their capacity. The last two built held 500,000 gallons, the first one 350,000. The three standpipes were composed of steel tanks on concrete foundations enclosed by brick structures. All had crenelated tops very similar to the Kalamazoo State Hospital water tower completed earlier in 1895.

Plans were underway in 1912 to build this standpipe on Inkster Avenue and South West Street. The City appropriated $55,000 for this standpipe and the one on East Main Street. Kalamazoo resident Richard Heystek built both concrete foundations. The Reeves Brothers Company from Alliance, Ohio, received the contract for the two steel tanks and local contractor David Little built both brick enclosures. The City even paid for landscaping both sites with trees, shrubs and vines.

Twenty-five years later, all three standpipes came down as they were considered ineffective due to their low elevations. The one on Inkster and South Westnedge Avenues stood until 1939, replaced by an elevated tank in the 1200 block of Edgemoor Avenue. Houses now fill the former standpipe site.

◤2000. Several houses were built on this site after 1940.

◤c1935. Cylindrical in shape, the standpipe had a crenelated top and stone moldings and sills at the windows, and a stone molding over the door.

Mountain Home Cemetery Receiving Vault
1402 West Main Street

This pared-down, chapel-like building is not quite gone, but it is literally disappearing before our eyes. A familiar site to many, it sits in Kalamazoo's 1849 Mountain Home Cemetery, centrally located within, quietly awaiting its fate. It may not have much time left.

Constructed of limestone a century and a quarter ago, it served for years as a burial "receiving vault," or place for the recently departed to rest for a short time before they were committed to the ground. If a person died of a contagious disease, their body could not go into the vault. If they died and owned a burial lot in Mountain Home, flat rate vault "accommodations" were $3.00 for up to thirty days, with written permission required for stays of more than a week. The vault today has not held bodies for decades, serving instead as a rather fancy "garage" for landscape maintenance equipment.

Mountain Home's vault is clearly one of the most visually pleasing cemetery buildings in the City. Its 1878 Gothic design is fitting, both for its intended use, and for the Victorian period in which it was built. Its roof is steeply pitched and its pointed arch door appropriate. Simplified pinnacles flank each front corner and a foliated design atop the parapeted gable takes the place of a similarly designed vergeboard that might have appeared on another Gothic-inspired building.

The building *can* be rehabilitated. A study conducted in the late 1990s indicates that it is not beyond repair.

> *"One looks and admires, till he wonders why so much of beauty is bestowed upon the resting place of those who cannot see."*
>
> Kalamazoo Telegraph, 1887
> special edition of the newspaper titled
> "Kalamazoo Leads The World"

2000. At over 120 years old, the vault's finial has disappeared, the pinnacles have toppled, and the buttresses are cracked and pulling away.

2000. Erosion has taken a serious toll on the vault's exterior.

1963. Not quite forty years ago, the almost 100-year-old vault was beginning to show signs of deterioration.

*There are places
    I remember
All my life,
    though some have changed
Some forever not for better
Some have gone
    and some remain...*

In My Life, John Lennon and Paul McCartney. 1965

2001. This building in downtown Kalamazoo's Haymarket Historic District is one example of the contributions that rehabilitated commercial buildings can make to the overall character of a community.

John A. Lacko

Kalamazoo: Found

WHEN ONE USES THE WORD "FOUND," it is usually in reference to something that is missing. Although none of the places that follow were ever lost in a strictly-defined sense, some *were* endangered. So, for the purposes of this publication, we employed an altered definition for "found," which better describes them. It reads: "Buildings whose original character has been actively or passively preserved or restored, or new construction designed in a historically and architecturally compatible manner, respectful of significant nearby buildings."

> *"In the end, the character of a civilization is encased in its structures."*
>
> **Frank O. Gehry,** *architect, from an interview with* Time, *June 17, 1996*

In the past forty years the nation has "found" a change of attitude toward its built environment, due in particular to the nation's historic preservation movement. Even though preservation efforts began much earlier (in this country the effort dates to before the Civil War), the movement intensified in the last half-century, gaining a popularity that is now demonstrated in many communities as a valuable planning and rehabilitation tool.

In Kalamazoo, no major tragedy or turning point boosted our historic preservation movement, as was the case in other communities. Rather, it was a series of events on the local, State and national scene that blended together, propelling the thrust.

Kalamazoo joined the nation enthusiastically when it began to change physically in the 1920s in a slow, automobile-driven metamorphosis. The State renamed Kalamazoo's Main Street and made it a secondary highway, and traditional urban centers everywhere faced and eagerly met the challenge of catering to the car. Over time, parking lots replaced buildings and road improvements took precedence over historic buildings and other public works projects.

> *But rather than design a transportation system to get the most out of America's cities, American redesigned its cities to get the most out of the automobile.*
>
> Richard Moe and Carter Wilkie, from *Changing Places: Rebuilding Community in the Age of Sprawl*

More and more, citizens created lucrative new businesses supporting the car culture, and Victorian-era and early twentieth-century buildings did not accommodate those new businesses well. In 1929, the City of Kalamazoo hired Jacob Crane to develop its first City plan. In his report, Crane remarked that Kalamazoo had some good architecture in its old buildings, but in its rush to accommodate four-wheeled vehicles, the community largely ignored his comments. So for the next thirty years, these historic buildings, considered old-fashioned and unmanageable, gave way to low-rise, modern utilitarian structures and parking lots.

Beginning in the 1950s, and almost every week for years, the *Kalamazoo Gazette* reported on visits of wrecking balls to buildings. At about that time, serious concern arose in Kalamazoo about what we were losing — and losing fast.

2001. Little Rose Place is an exceptional example of late nineteenth and early twentieth century community planning. It is comprised of well-built, period homes, the earliest constructed by middle-class families connected to the building trades.

John A. Lacko

Finally, in 1965, leading State historian and then chair of Western Michigan University's History Department, Dr. Willis Dunbar, recommended that the Kalamazoo City Commission establish a six-member historical commission charged with identifying important historic resources in the City and preserving historical materials. The City acted on Dunbar's recommendation that June, and created a city advisory board known as the Kalamazoo Historical Commission.

On the national level, things were also moving. In 1966, Congress signed into law the most significant piece of Federal historic preservation legislation ever created. The National Historic Preservation Act, passed during the "Great Society" years, established an enhanced National Register of Historic Places. Part of that legislation, the earlier-established 1935 National Register of Historic Places, now includes thousands of resources deemed significant in American history on a local, State and national scale. The new 1966 legislation also established a national Advisory Council on Historic Preservation and authorized preservation matching grants to the states and to the National Trust for Historic Preservation, the nation's largest non-profit preservation organization.

Michigan already had a State Register of Historic Places, and now its Federal counterpart had some influence to discourage and sometimes halt demolition of listed resources. "Protection" was exactly what the Kalamazoo Ladies' Library Association had in mind. The organization had built and still owned the first building dedicated to a woman's organization in the United States, and pursued listing it on the State Register in 1962. Expansion plans for the Civic Theater directly next door called for the demolition of the Association's building, and ultimately, the Ladies' Library became the first Kalamazoo building listed on both the State and National Registers of Historic Places.

Since then, hundreds of Kalamazoo buildings have been listed on the National Register, either individually or as part of a historic district. The majority of these were listed after 1971, as a direct result of surveys conducted by the City's Historical Commission.

> *I'll make you this challenge. You name me one community that is noted for its shopping malls and parking lots, and I'll name you ten that are noted for something of historical importance.*
>
> Al Seiler, Pike County (Illinois) Board Member,
> from the *Jacksonville Journal-Courier*

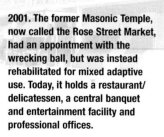

2001. The former Masonic Temple, now called the Rose Street Market, had an appointment with the wrecking ball, but was instead rehabilitated for mixed adaptive use. Today, it holds a restaurant/ delicatessen, a central banquet and entertainment facility and professional offices.

John A. Lacko

As of 2001, Kalamazoo's eight National Register Historic Districts include those on South Street, and in the Stuart, Vine, Rose Place and West Main Hill neighborhoods, as well as the three comprised of Bronson Park and its surrounding buildings, downtown's Haymarket area, and Western Michigan University's East Campus. Another twenty-five individual sites are also listed.

While listing resources on the National Register is primarily honorific, in some cases, incentives and protection are available. Federal tax credits, accessible for appropriate rehabilitation of income-producing buildings, can help cut rehabilitation costs. The work must follow the Federal Secretary of Interior's Standards for Rehabilitation, and is reviewed by the Federal government's agent, the State Historic Preservation Office. The owner of the building receives a tax break for appropriate work and the entire community enjoys the associative benefits including preserving the community's character and stabilized or increased property values.

Protection for National Register resources is limited. If a project includes or is near a National Historic resource and the project receives Federal funding or requires Federal licenses, the law requires undertaking a "Section 106" review process to help avoid or mitigate potential adverse impacts on the resource.

In 1971, the City's Historical Commission hired Dr. Peter Schmitt from Western Michigan University's Department of History to conduct the community's first formal historic resources survey. Five months later, the Commission created a committee to study the feasibility of creating a "Local" historic district in Kalamazoo in accordance with new State legislation, Public Act 169.

Public Act 169 gave local communities the ability to create Local historic districts and attendant commissions to create standards and guidelines, and the power to regulate certain exterior work on resources within those districts. Other states approved similar legislation in the 1970s and 1980s.

Kalamazoo's first Historic District Study Committee presented its recommendation to the City in July 1972. The recommendation included a two-block section of South Street between Westnedge Avenue and Oakland Drive, as well as the aforementioned Ladies' Library Association building on South Park Street. After Local listing of these resources, the City Commission also created the attending [Local] Historic District Commission (HDC), following the State legislation. Beginning in 1973, the City created five additional Local districts in the Stuart, Vine and Rose Place neighborhoods, as well as the Haymarket and South Burdick Street areas. These Local districts' boundaries often mimic those of the National Register districts.

Resources in Kalamazoo's Local districts now number close to 1,800, and while Local district property owners are regulated, they can also take advantage of tax credits for approved work.

Throughout these years, the value of our architectural and historical heritage became even more important to our community. That same era, the middle 1970s, also saw Kalamazoo's largest and longest community-wide campaign to save a single resource. About 1974, the State announced plans to demolish the Kalamazoo State Hospital Water Tower on Oakland Drive. A "Save the Tower Committee" launched a fund drive that raised $208,000 in twenty-two months from fifteen foundations, local and Federal governments, and nearly 4,000 individuals. Residents had clearly identified the water tower as an integral component of their community—a part they did *not* want to lose.

Coincidentally aiding the campaign was the 1976 United States Bicentennial. Many communities, like Kalamazoo, planned several years in advance for the year-long celebration. The national event piqued almost everyone's interest in history, genealogy and preservation, and the Kalamazoo Historical Commission carried out many activities. It produced brochures, erected signs, reprinted historic maps, held a homes tour, and published its first book, *Kalamazoo: Nineteenth-century Homes in a Midwestern Village* authored by Dr. Peter Schmitt. Schmitt used his earlier-conducted historic resources survey as a nucleus for this publication, while internationally-known architectural photographer Balthazar Korab took the photographs. The publication of this book helped to raise needed funds to support the Commission's projects, and at the same time, heightened awareness of the City's architectural heritage.

2001. This house, erected by Catholic Family Services in 1995 at the corner of Den Adel Court and South Westnedge Avenue, provides an excellent example of sensitive "infill" construction that seeks to blend in with nearby buildings.

John A. Lacko

The Historical Commission, today known as the Kalamazoo Historic Preservation Commission (KHPC), continued its educational mission by producing another book in 1981, *Walking Through Time* by Brendan Henehan. Based on the work of subsequent historic resources surveys, the book is still used today as a reference guide. The KHPC continues to publish informational brochures and calendars, sponsor conferences, tours, and special events, and brings in nationally-known speakers to address the public on preservation issues. During National Historic Preservation Week, it also annually recognizes property owners and others for their role in preserving Kalamazoo's character through its historic resources.

Preservation played an important role with the Arcadia Creek/Arcadia Commons development, which runs north and then east and west of the Kalamazoo Radisson Hotel complex. When this project intensified in the middle 1980s, preservationists became concerned about plans to demolish almost all of the buildings in the area. Two were subsequently placed on the National Register of Historic Places. The first was the 1872 Lawrence and Chapin Iron Works which then housed Vermeulen's Furniture Store. The other, the 1913 Masonic Temple, is now known as the Rose Street Market. Despite attempts by Kalamazoo County government to demolish the Temple for parking, its later owners renovated the building for offices and commercial space.

The State Historic Preservation Office declared the entire Arcadia Creek project area eligible for the National Register of Historic Places in 1989. It contained many fine late 19th century and early 20th century brick buildings, and because the City would receive Federal funds to carry out the project, the area was afforded the earlier-described Federal Section 106 review. This review insured that the project would be scrutinized for possible negative impacts on the historic buildings, and attempts made to remove or mitigate those impacts.

Seven months and many meetings later, developers, the City and its Preservation Commission, with public input, came up with a plan. This group approved a Memorandum of Agreement in 1990 that allowed the demolition of some buildings and at the same time created a design review commission. The commission established guidelines for new construction and rehabilitation of the historic resources remaining in the project area. The Memorandum also required the City to hire a Historic Preservation Coordinator, who currently coordinates its preservation activities.

The local preservation community was again involved with a Section 106 review in the early 1990s, when the Michigan Department of Transportation announced plans to use Federal money to improve West Main Street through the West Main and Stuart National Register Historic Districts. This Memorandum of Agreement, along with the one concerning Arcadia Commons, are now used as models to illustrate how these reviews can positively impact a project's outcome.

The Kalamazoo Historic Preservation and District Commissions continue to fulfill their charges. The City demonstrates its commitment and sets a rare local government example in maintaining both commissions, and charges each with different responsibilities. While the Preservation Commission educates and advises on general preservation matters, the District Commission regulates work in the Local historic districts. Most communities throughout the nation have but one commission overseeing both tasks.

2001. The Haymarket Building, one of the largest in the District by the same name, was one of the earliest and widely-recognized adaptive use projects that took place there. The building now houses mixed uses including retail, a restaurant and professional offices.

John A. Lacko

Aiding these Commissions are several non-governmental, non-profit organizations. Neighborhood associations, including the Stuart, Vine and Gateway Coalition Associations, represent property owners, conduct home tours and workshops, and offer informational meetings. These groups also publish brochures about their neighborhoods, erect signs, and raise funds for neighborhood amenities like period street lighting and other improvements. Other organizations, including the City's Downtown Development Authority and Kalamazoo Neighborhood Housing Services, cooperate by providing both funding and actual rehabilitation services for historic residential and commercial buildings.

Kalamazoo's Downtown Development Authority promotes preservation through rehabilitation grant programs and cooperates with several neighborhood organizations to sponsor tours of houses, condominiums and apartments in their respective areas. The Kalamazoo County Historical Society, organized in 1948, has also held tours and regularly sponsors meetings and lectures on history and preservation. All of these groups are composed of people who give of their time and talent because they believe that Kalamazoo's architectural heritage is one of its most important resources.

Historic preservation has changed in Kalamazoo as elsewhere, especially in recent decades. For well over a hundred years after the movement began in early 20th century, and as recently as the 1970s, its emphasis was firmly rooted in preserving only the biggest and best resources. But more recently, as the nation recognized its disinvestment in core communities, the focus has widened. As National Trust President Richard Moe stated in the preface of his recent book, *Changing Places*:

> *Communities can be shaped by choice or they can be shaped by chance.*
> *We can keep on accepting the kind of communities we get, or we can insist*
> *on getting the kind of communities we want.*

In the late 1970s and 1980s, the nation's traditional towns and cities were clearly threatened, and it was this realization that propelled the preservation movement into a broader context. Groups of good buildings create good places, and good places form good communities that work well for people. Kalamazoo had lost many good buildings, and in some cases was losing entire blocks, especially in the central business district. What to do?

> *... if we had left our downtowns intact, they might once again have fitted*
> *our needs, as City Centers in Europe have traditionally done.*
> Bettina Drew, from *Crossing the Expendable Landscape*

By slowly but steadily moving to a "planning" focus, preservationists in the last twenty years have not only exposed threats to our remaining urban resources, but also the costs of our past actions — in our cities *and* our countrysides. It is not a pretty picture. The outward movement from cities has devastated agricultural land and business, open space and other areas necessary to sustain nature that, in turn, sustains people. As a result, many preservationists now also consider themselves environmentalists.

2001. In the late 1980s, the W.E. Upjohn Institute for Employment Research converted the 1905 former Boudeman home in the South Street Historic District for adaptive use as office space.

John A. Lacko

By moving more into the planning arena, preservationists have again heightened the public's awareness — this time to the beauty of traditional urban planning. Intense use of urban infrastructure by people who live and work in close proximity helps everyone realize more for their tax dollar and increases livability. Reduced automobile use as a result of dense placement of homes and businesses and greater use of public transit means less fuel burned and transportation dollars spent more effectively.

This planning awareness has again carried through to government. In 1999, Kalamazoo completed its new Comprehensive Plan and for the first time it contained a historic preservation element. An increasing number of states now mandate that local governments consider historic resources in the planning process. At this writing, such legislation is being discussed at the Federal level as well.

Where are we now? Preservation at the beginning of the 21st century is about much, much more than bricks and mortar, although materials and design remain a critical part of the equation. Today, preservation has everything to do with successful community revitalization — traditional town and city centers and neighborhoods brought back to life and along with it, a back-to-the-city movement that is gaining momentum.

Revitalization is about preserving place, and a growing appreciation for traditional urban environments. It is about renovating old buildings and using them for new or original purposes. It is about living over the shop and small business and identity development. It is about putting people to work in building trades that pay far more than a chain-store minimum wage. It is about redeveloping neighborhoods for people of all income levels. It is about buying materials from local suppliers that better supports the local economy. It is about high-quality new urban design that complements what already exists. The underlying point is this: reusing old buildings and insuring high-quality new architecture is good for people, business and property. Thriving businesses and increasing property values are hallmarks of a vital community.

... the history of architecture must not be confined to masterpieces... Unknown

Not always the biggest or best, the buildings, objects and places included in *Kalamazoo: Found* represent the depth and breath of preservation activity in Kalamazoo. Many have received meticulous care throughout their lives, like Stetson Chapel at Kalamazoo College or the Ladies' Library Association building on South Park Street.

Some, like the Portage Street Fire Station, hovered perilously near demolition more than once, only to be rescued at the eleventh hour. One, the multi-storied Gibson building on Parsons Street, was dying the slow death of disinvestment, but recently has had a change of fortune.

We have classified the resources in this section into three categories. If its original use has not changed throughout its life, and it received appropriate physical attention and maintenance, we have classified it as an example of "preservation." Kalamazoo's City Hall, Vander Salm's Flower Shop on South Burdick Street, and Loy Norrix High School all illustrate this classification.

2001. Now O'Duffy's Pub and Cosmos Restaurant, this small commercial building in the Vine Historic District has been home to many different businesses. Until about a decade ago, it was accompanied by two other, similar-sized buildings, offering a small, central location for neighborhood goods and services.
John A. Lacko

If a resource's original use was changed and it was rehabilitated, it falls into the "adaptive use" category. Grace Christian Reformed Church on South Park Street, now offices for Diekema Hamann Architecture + Construction, and the former gas station now enjoying life as the Water Street Coffee Joint are just two examples.

When a new or old building is located on a previously empty site, it is considered "infill." Examples of this category include the relatively new Public Safety Station No. 7 on Parkview Avenue, and the turn-of-the-century houses relocated several years ago to the southeast corner of South Westnedge Avenue and Academy Street. In fact, moving buildings is once again becoming popular in Kalamazoo after a half-century hiatus as witnessed by the "rescue" of the above houses, as well as one that found a new home on the southwest corner of South Park and Cedar Streets in 1999.

However these activities are described, they fall under the broader category of preservation because ultimately, when accomplished sensitively, they have everything to do with placing a high value on community character and a sense of place.

Who does this work? Most are not supermen or superwomen, nor are they professional developers. But rather, many who engage in preservation are entrepreneurs who often learned on the job when they could not find tradespeople with appropriate skills. However, while many are self-taught, others *are* professional craftspeople, contractors and developers with most of their previous primary experience in new construction. Their one common experience is this: they all digested and learned to use a new lexicon when they delved into the world of preservation.

What motivates them? Sometimes, they fall in love with a building, or a building is for sale at a bargain price. Often, they simply get swept up in a flurry of preservation activity. But in all instances, they share the ability to see what their buildings had been in the past and their potential for the future.

As an example of how these things happen, in the early 1990s a little renaissance began along Kalamazoo Avenue. First, two buildings that sided the 100 east block were rehabilitated. A few years later, one that sides the 200 west block was started. In 1998, new owners began renovations on two more buildings in the middle of that same block, which are being completed at this writing.

In closing, we regret one thing: that we could not include every good example of preservation in Kalamazoo. Do not assume that because a building, object or place is not included here, it is not a good building or project. There may be ten to twenty times as many "good ones" as we could afford to include. Unfortunately, the size of this book was tied to a publication budget.

So, this is a sampling of what is out there. Read this book and as you do, go out and walk the community. You will be rewarded by what you see and energized by the potential of what is to come. Kalamazoo has accomplished a great deal, but future opportunities abound and we are not done yet. Through the lens of preservation many have and will rediscover one of the beauties of life in Kalamazoo.

2001. These buildings are just a part of an ongoing rehabilitation renaissance along Kalamazoo Avenue, including both residential and commercial spaces.

John A. Lacko

Ladies' Library Association
333 South Park Street

This is a building of "firsts," including the first building to be built by and for a woman's organization in the United States, and the first building in Kalamazoo to be listed on the National Register of Historic Places.

The Ladies' Library Association began in 1852 and gave women of the community an opportunity to gather and discuss the literature of the day. They also held lectures, concerts and created the first library in the Village. The Association fulfilled its dream to have its own home in 1878, with the completion of this Victorian Gothic structure, designed by Chicago architect Henry Gay and built by Bush and Paterson. This style became the frequent choice during the 19th century for art and educational institutions.

There were no major changes to the building until 1931, when the O.F. Miller Company added a kitchen and several rooms. Concern about the overall condition of the structure led the Association to hire Ann Arbor architect Richard Frank in 1975 to develop a plan of action. The work, that took four years to complete, included repairing the roof and the brick, rebuilding the front entrance and restoring the interior. Contractor Donald B. Smith Company and restoration experts Conti Building and Restoration were two of the firms who participated. Total cost of the work amounted to over $150,000 that came from local foundations, government grants and Association fund-raisers. Members also participated by helping to clean paintings and books.

Ten years later, the exterior needed additional repair. The Association received a Michigan Bureau of History grant along with support from five local foundations and the members themselves. In 1991, it hired Quinn Evans/Architects from Ann Arbor to direct the project, and Kalleward-Bergerson as the contractor. They replaced the original slate roof with a new one guaranteed to last another one hundred years.

The members of the Ladies' Library Association have a deep and profound dedication to this building. While this is not their only activity, it certainly gives them a great sense of pride and accomplishment.

↗2000. The trefoil window in the middle of the tower and the gargoyle at the top of the porch column are later additions.

↙c1880. The building has arched windows on the side and limestone banding, typical of Victorian Gothic. Notice also the shed dormers at the tower and the cresting on the roof.

"I can't stress enough the togetherness of everyone working to restore that building. If women can do that for one building look what they can do for the community."

Mrs. Barbara Dussette, *past Library president from* Women With a Vision

Parker House
1546 Spruce Drive

Most people believe that finding a house on a large piece of land is nearly impossible in an urban setting. Not so with this structure, that sits on two and one-half acres in the Oakland Drive neighborhood. Harry B. Parker completed the house in 1923 for his wife Pearl and their seven children. Parker had been in the newspaper business for fifteen years before organizing the first Kalamazoo automobile dealership in 1911. He also played the flute with several orchestras, including the Kalamazoo Symphony.

The present owners, Jeff and Honore Lee, purchased the home in 1998. Both the house and the grounds had been neglected for several years. The front steps were gone and both the back and front yards were overgrown. The Lees spent much time in the beginning clearing and opening up the land and the house.

The owners upgraded the electrical system so they could improve the interior lighting, and removed the carpets to refinish the oak floors. They restored the original copper window screens, repainted the rooms and renovated the basement. The original steam heating system is in good condition and continues to heat the house. The Lees gutted the kitchen and installed new flooring, cupboards and appliances. At the same time, they opened up the back entrance and improved the landing to the basement. The house has two stacked sunrooms on its south side. The first is Honore's art studio, and the other will eventually become Jeff's home realty office.

The Lees discovered a landscape plan for this house from thirty years ago that gave them some ideas. Rather than place the front stairs in a straight pattern, they decided to curve them to resemble a river. They also unearthed a foundation from a stable or barn near their garage, where the Parkers kept horses. Work on the grounds is an ongoing process that will continue for many years to come.

Neighbors supplied the Lees with stories and anecdotes about the house. It is no surprise, as Mrs. Lee commented, "Everyone who has lived here has loved both the house and the land."

> *"I like the layout of the rooms, how they transition from one to another. This looks like a dark house, but it is not."*
>
> **Honore Lee,** *owner*

2001. This Craftsman house has a hipped, front-gabled roof with deep eaves. The exterior is both brick and stucco decorated with half-timbers, and situated at the top of a hill with a long front entrance.

100 North Edwards Street Block

From about 1895, when the first two brick bays in this block were constructed, until 1994, at least one business here catered to the horse, the buggy, or the automobile. Newton Carriage Company was the first occupant, taking up residence in the southern-most two bays. Blacksmiths, carriage trimmers, repairers and painters soon followed.

The third bay, which went up quickly after the first two, served briefly as headquarters to Blood Brothers Automobile and Machine Company. The last, single-story building was constructed about 1924. Other businesses that eventually established themselves in the block include two hotels, apartments, a laundry, a furnace installer and a store fixtures company.

Collectively, the buildings make up a "Two-Part Commercial Block," an architectural form generally characterized by a lower, street-level zone, and an upper, above-the-street zone that consists of one to three additional stories. These zones are visually separated by a horizontal element which divides them physically, like the cornice on these buildings' center bays, just below the second-story windows.

The Two-Part Block was the most prevalent commercial building form during the 100 years between 1850 and 1950. Typically, the main floors were used for public or commercial purposes, like banks, hotel lobbies and retail shops. The upper floors served more private functions such as offices, meeting halls and residences. Double-duty or "shophouse" buildings date back to antiquity, with commerce at street level and homes above.

The longest tenant here was Auto Parts Distributors, who remained 47 years. When the last tenant vacated in 1993, the renaissance began. Local businessman and preservationist Rodger Parzyck heard the buildings might be for sale. Parzyck and Kalamazoo architect

↗ 2001. After more than two years of rehabilitation, this recent photo demonstrates a dramatic return of the buildings' early character.

Nelson Nave took a closer look and saw potential. Eventually partnering with five others, they bought the buildings and began the rehabilitation in 1994.

Nave's offices now occupy the south bay. The next two are home to Kalamazoo Antiques. The large, center bays house Parzyck's Heritage Company Architectural Salvage business, and part of the north end is occupied by Viavi, a garden and gift shop. The partner-owners received a 1996 Merit Award from the Kalamazoo Historic Preservation Commission for returning the buildings to productive uses and helping to revitalize Kalamazoo's downtown. The buildings were added to the Haymarket Local Historic District in 1998.

↙ 1994. This photograph documents the buildings' appearance prior to rehabilitation, including the enclosed bays.

"The best buildings are not those that are cut, like a tailored suit, to fit only one set of functions, but rather those that are strong enough to retain their character as they accommodate different functions over time."

Robert Campbell, *author*
Cityscapes of Boston

Vander Salm's Flower Shop & Greenhouses
1120 South Burdick Street

Marking a half-century in the business of plant growing, Jacob Vander Salm, second-generation head of the family business, opened this new store literally just around the corner from the old one.

Jacobus Vander Salm (Jacob's father), began commercial gardening on Kalamazoo's mucky south side in the early 1890s. Beginning literally up the hill from the present business site, Jacobus grew celery and pansies, soon doing well enough to build a small greenhouse behind his home at 123 Wall Street.

Son Jacob took over the Wall Street business in 1910. Expanding, he added delivery service, additional greenhouse space and other buildings. By the early 1930s, this construction filled a good share of the large block's interior. In 1936, the family opened a shop downtown in the McNair Building. But even then, Jacob was making bigger plans.

Vander Salm collaborated with architect M.C.J. Billingham on this 1940 building. More than anything, it is the use of materials, not its size, that makes the building impressive. The sales building, which is shaped like an "L," uses dressed, multi-colored stone from Ohio, Illinois, Michigan, Indiana and Tennessee, to draw the eye. The two arched gable windows at the front and side, complete with their own dressed-stone voussiors, or wedged-shaped blocks, further establish the building's distinctive street presence.

The attached, rectangular conservatory has one rounded end—its style similar to one Vander Salm had seen in New Orleans. However, the design for the conservatory's glass roof, graceful and well-balanced, was Vander Salm's alone. In 1970, the original conservatory was replaced with a replica, built in New York and then shipped to Kalamazoo where it was re-assembled on site.

Vander Salm's is still family-owned and operated—more than a century and three generations later. This long-time home to the venture provides a perfect example of how a building can assist a business in cultivating its identity over decades by imprinting its image in the minds of passersby using nothing more than its uncomplicated, handsome appearance.

"The stone for the store building is in many hues of red, gray, white and tan…"

Kalamazoo Gazette, *May 24, 1940, describing the recently-completed Vander Salm's building*

2001. Vander Salm's Flower Shop, a century-old, family-operated business on South Burdick Street, has made this attractive building its home since 1940.

Northside Neighborhood

Even though every day hundreds of people drive through this neighborhood, very few actually see it. There are many myths and misperceptions about the Northside neighborhood that have persisted for years. If one takes the time to really get to know the neighborhood, one will find it contains many surprises.

The Northside neighborhood, covering approximately two square miles, is one of the City's three largest neighborhoods. The boundaries include Dunkley Street to the north, Willard Street to the south, Gull Street to the east and Douglas Avenue to the west. The neighborhood also encompasses over a mile of industrial property, along with Lincoln International Studies School, Northglade Montessori Magnet Elementary School, the Douglass Community Association, the YMCA, the Alma Powell branch of the Kalamazoo Public Library, several churches and a number of parks.

Over 1,700 homes and three apartment complexes are in the neighborhood. According to the 1990 census, over 51 percent of the homes are owner-occupied, a statistic that has grown over the last ten years. The neighborhood is not as transient as one might imagine, and a number of the homes have been owned by the same residents for over fifty years.

The crime rate has decreased due to the Neighborhood Watch program and the City's Public Safety Department. The overall housing stock has improved because of the work done by the City of Kalamazoo and several local agencies including the Kalamazoo Northside Non-Profit Housing Corporation and Kalamazoo Neighborhood Housing Services. These organizations are not only renovating older existing structures, but also are building new infill houses throughout the neighborhood.

Another very important organization involved with neighborhood improvement is the Northside Association for Community Development, incorporated in 1981. It is actively involved in helping people find housing along with coordinating other programs like Neighborhood Watch and educates residents on pertinent issues. The organization currently is

2001. The Kalamazoo Northside Non-Profit Housing Corporation donated this house at 711 North Elizabeth Street to the City of Kalamazoo after its recent rehabilitation.

2001. This house at 814 Mabel Street contains simple double-hung windows throughout the house.

developing a grocery store and retail complex, and their office on North Burdick Street is a very active community center.

As with all the Kalamazoo neighborhoods, the Northside contains a variety of architectural styles. Many still remain from the late 19th century, like the 1897 Queen Anne at 801 North Church Street. This brick house has a gabled roof and decorative moldings over the windows.

The wooden-sided bungalow at 711 North Elizabeth Street, built in 1919, is now a Kalamazoo Public Safety mini-station. It has a very simple front porch and gabled roof.

The 1931 house at 814 Mabel Street has several Colonial Revival features including a portico with simple columns and a pediment, a hipped roof and a shed dormer.

The house at 802 West Paterson Street is called a Minimal Traditional and reflects several different styles. Completed in 1943, it has a front gable and stone facing.

The Northside neighborhood is filled with residents who care deeply about their community and the people who live here. They are working hard to improve the quality of life for one and all.

2001. This Queen Anne at 801 North Church Street has fish-scale shingles at the top of the gabled roof and a very simple side front porch.

"When I think of the [Northside] neighborhood, I just think of family."

Mattie Jordan, *executive director, Northside Association for Community Development*

2001. Many houses like this one at 802 West Paterson Street were built across the City during and after World War II.

Young Women's Christian Association, now the Richard F. Chormann Building
211 South Rose Street

The Young Women's Christian Association (YWCA) operated in multiple Kalamazoo locations for almost forty years before it completed this building. It first bought an empty lot here, and then the former Cornell residence next door. While cafeteria and clubroom construction commenced on the lot in 1918, the organization used the residence as their offices.

Three years later, it took down the house and added to the new building, using a design by well-established Grand Rapids architects Fred Robinson and Antoine Campau. This 1922–1923 addition provided the organization with a substantial street presence. Robinson and Campau decorated the symmetrical main facade with conservative Colonial Revival details befitting the YWCA's image.

Years passed and the organization's mission changed with the times. It closed the cafeteria in 1980, a move that was quickly followed by shutting its swimming pool. After years of consideration, in May 1983, the organization put 211 South Rose Street on the market so they could build a new facility. Over the next two years, several proposals appeared, but none resulted in a sale until 1985, with Parkstone Properties' offer.

Using an Eckert Wordell Architects design, Parkstone contracted with Kalleward-Bergerson for the 1986–1987 renovation and addition. It demolished the 1918 building and the northeast portion of the 1923 building, and then cleaned the remaining 1923 building, giving the front facade a new entry canopy and windows. For the rear addition, the architects employed the same fenestration, brick and cornice design of the 1923 building, but gave its massing a divergent approach. Thrusting itself east in a series of steps, it successfully distinguishes new from old, and provides a second main entry that beautifully terminates a vista from the Kalamazoo Mall.

First of America Bank later bought the YWCA building, and its successor, National City Bank, now owns 211 South Rose Street, which is part of the Bronson Park National Register Historic District.

c1987. Eckert Wordell's design for the rear addition was sensitive to the 1923 YWCA building, while clearly establishing the addition as new architecture.

"The 1923 building was in wonderful condition."

Rick Wordell, *talking about Eckert Wordell's 1986 renovation-addition plan for 211 South Rose*

c1925. Grand Rapids architects Robinson and Campau decorated their design for Kalamazoo's YWCA with terra cotta — both in the cornice and shell-motif ornaments over the main floor windows on the building's South Rose Street facade.

Stockbridge-Everard House
821 West South Street

Lumberman and investor George Stockbridge chose the popular Queen Anne style for his new house completed in 1895. It contained many of the typical characteristics including a gabled roof, decorative shingles, multiple chimneys, numerous window styles and sizes, and an elaborate front porch. Local legend holds that the New York architectural firm of McKim, Mead and White designed the structure. It later became home to the H.H. Everard family who lived there off and on until after World War I. During the influenza epidemic of 1917, the Everard family, by then living in Detroit, gave permission for the house to be used as a hospital. Divided into apartments and retail space after being sold at the beginning of the 1920s, it also had a long life as a fraternity house. By the early 1980s, it contained eleven apartments.

During this time, architect David Pyle and engineer James Thorne began looking for new offices. This home fit all their requirements including a downtown location, sufficient parking and most importantly, architectural character. They purchased the property in 1982 and began the work. Pyle, who directed the project, had a great deal of previous experience, having worked as the project architect at the Wood-Upjohn House and the Michigan Central Railroad Depot, among others.

It took close to three years to complete the work at the Stockbridge-Everard House. Pyle and Thorne created seven offices on the first floor and a total of five apartments on the first and second floors. They were able to restore the oak woodwork and replace it when necessary. The main lobby of the office section is decorated with hand stenciling by artist Judith Ziobron. They solved a challenge when they found a supplier in Alabama for the cresting on the roof. Pyle developed the exterior color scheme and found the original sunburst decoration on the top of the front porch gable, hidden under fifteen coats of paint. Despite many challenges, the owners feel they brought the house back close to its original condition.

> *"We created something that hopefully will live beyond us."*
> David Pyle

c1895. Members of the Everard family sit on the front porch. Notice the original porch once wrapped around the front and the east side (left).

2001. The Stockbridge-Everard House is an excellent example of adaptive use.

Fire Station No. 5, now Public Safety Station No. 5
619 Douglas Avenue

In operation since 1908, this station is the oldest active public building in the City of Kalamazoo. Forrest Van Volkenburg designed this and two other neighborhood stations between 1907 and 1910, to meet the needs of the town's growing population. He chose Tudor Revival for this structure in the midst of the Stuart, West Douglas and Northside neighborhoods. Its typical characteristics include a gabled roof, stucco and half-timbered walls, and large arches with keystones. The columns are decorated with imposts.

The station now houses a fire engine and several public safety officers, three of whom are neighborhood liaison officers. Some of the building's features that reflect its age remain, including the hayloft door at the back, trapdoor for the fire pole, original lockers, and a great deal of original woodwork. Also, it is still possible to see where the horses who pulled the old equipment chewed on the inside bricks.

To withstand the weight of a new fire engine, concrete replaced much of the wooden first floor. In the past fifteen years, the City installed a new front door and a ventilation system for truck exhaust.

In 1982, the City of Kalamazoo seriously considered closing this station, but decided to keep it open. There may come a time when this discussion takes place again. However, this building, whether or not it functions as a public safety station, always will play a role within the neighborhoods surrounding it.

"This station is rich in tradition."

Sergeant Pat Hall, *retired*

↗ 2000. This recent photo shows the enlarged, single vehicle entrance, at left.

↙ c1910. This early photo shows two separate vehicle entrances, at left.

KALAMAZOO: LOST & FOUND

Academy Street Brick
Kalamazoo College

In 1991, an idea presented itself that led to the restoration of much of the 1200 block of Academy Street. Kalamazoo College flanks the street here on the north and south sides — a place long appreciated for its siting and architecture. Jeff Sherman, a College employee and mason, approached the school's facilities management department with the idea of restoring the street, using as much original brick as possible.

The idea eventually made its way to the City's Public Works Department where it received a positive response. An agreement was struck: the College would provide the labor for the restoration project, and the City would assist by laying new substrate, curbs, gutters and provide additional salvaged brick as required.

The project began in 1992, and has followed the same course since. Each summer, Sherman trains a small crew of students to work with him on the project, and the College makes a modest investment in hammers and saw blades for brick cutting. The students learn on the job while Sherman supervises and works along side of them.

In the years since, the successive crews of masons-in-training have restored almost four blocks of Academy Street, beginning at Monroe Street at the west end, and working east down the hill toward the Anderson Athletic Center. The crew is restricted to a six-week timetable each summer, working around major campus events, making the project's results even more impressive.

Although the restoration is not finished, what is completed sends a potent message to visitors and those who travel the street regularly: this place takes pride in its physical presence as an expression of what it is — a place that has a history and expects to be here for a long time. The Kalamazoo College campus would not be the same without this street.

Thanks to Sherman's plan and the commitment of the College and the City, Academy Street will long live to help define and preserve the character of the College and the surrounding neighborhood for decades to come. The project won a Merit Award from Kalamazoo's Historic Preservation Commission in 1999.

"The Kalamazoo College campus would not be the same without this street."

Pamela O'Connor

2001. Ongoing each summer since 1992, the restoration of Academy Street at Kalamazoo College is a joint effort of the College and the City.

National City Arcadia South and Arcadia North
West Side of North Rose Street between Water and Eleanor Streets

This complex in Arcadia Commons combined the rehabilitation of an older building along with the construction of a new one. In 1988, First of America Bank announced plans to bring several of their corporate offices that were scattered throughout the downtown area together under one roof. It chose this site on the west side of North Rose Street between Water and Eleanor Streets.

The site contained one of the most unusual industrial buildings in Kalamazoo. The Lawrence and Chapin Iron Works, completed in 1872, originally housed an iron foundry that used pig iron mined along the banks of the Kalamazoo River. The company built its structure here to use Arcadia Creek to power the machinery. It supplied iron for many of the agricultural implements firms in the area.

Local architect L.D. Grosvenor chose the Second Empire style with its long, narrow windows topped with moldings, paired brackets, and a distinctive mansard roof decorated with dormers. Constructed by local builders Bush and Paterson, the building received an addition in 1881. By the middle 1890s, the Iron Works closed. The City studied the building in 1897 to see if it might be a suitable city hall. Instead, it became, among many things, a rescue mission, interurban railway station, skating rink and for over fifty years, home to the Vermeulen Furniture Company which built a warehouse to the north of the main building in 1949. It was listed on the National Register of Historic Places in 1983.

Next to the Lawrence and Chapin Iron Works, on the southwest corner of North Rose and Eleanor Streets, sat the Kalamazoo Laundry Building complex, consisting of several buildings from the late 19th to the early 20th centuries. Vacant for some time, the Downtown Development Authority purchased the buildings in 1983.

One of the biggest stumbling blocks for the Arcadia Commons partners was the challenge of cleaning up ground and water contaminants, including asbestos, lead, gasoline and cleaning fluids. After the City paid for the initial clean-up, concerns about future liability led to several of the partners, including First of America, to sign a ground lease with the City. In short, the company owned the buildings, but the City assumed responsibility for any further clean-up costs.

To design its new 110,000-square-foot complex, First of America chose Hobbs+Black Associates, Inc. of Ann Arbor. It renovated all three buildings, now referred to as Arcadia South. The exterior bricks were cleaned, windows repaired, the original vaulted first floor exposed and a new slate roof installed. At the same time, the Downtown Development Authority paid to resurface the front of the parking deck next door with matching brick.

1996. Arcadia North is an example of infill, which blends together both historic and modern architectural elements.

It also removed a twenty-foot section of the ramp west over Water Street to expose the Ironwork's ornate south facade.

An enclosed walkway links Arcadia South to the new building, Arcadia North, built on the Laundry building site. This new building contains elements inspired from the Ironworks structure such as the long narrow windows with moldings and lintels, and a decorative cornice with paired brackets. Its rounded glass entrance adds a modern element. A.J. Etkins Construction Company was the contractor for this $12 million project. First of America merged with National City Bank in 1998.

> *"We were able to preserve what turned out to be a jewel of the community."*
>
> **Michael McMahon,**
> Kalamazoo Gazette
> *July 31, 1994*

c1881. Notice the ornate slate roof with the cresting at the top of the middle tower in this photograph, taken not long after the completion of the 1881 addition to the rear.

2000. Currently, National City Bank, which merged with First of America in 1998, occupies approximately 75 percent of both buildings. It leases space in Arcadia North to a law firm and in Arcadia South to a software company.

The Harvey-Macleod House
204 Monroe Street

Shortly after Dr. Leroy Harvey moved to Kalamazoo to chair Western State Normal School's Biology Department, he found a picture of a home just like this in a magazine. Soon after, Harvey contracted with architect Forrest Van Volkenburg to design a copy for his lot at the top of Academy Street. Contractor Edward Hartman did the major work, while other Kalamazoo contractors completed the detail work. L.F. Bremer graded the lot, William Little handled the masonry, and decorator Martin Larsen did the painting, wallpapering and canvassing. Materials came from local suppliers, including Edwards and Chamberlain, Star Bargain House, Gilmore Brothers and Johnson & Howard.

A Dutch Colonial Revival, the house has a "gambrel" or barn-style roof, thereby giving it the "Dutch" prefix. Americans built thousands of homes in this style between 1880 and 1940. However, while its shape and mass are Colonial Revival, several elements of the popular Craftsman style were added: the front entry pergola and large stucco piers, the matching piers anchoring the corners of the sunroom, and the knee braces under the second story eaves. Adding interest to the roof's long slope, an eyebrow dormer looks over the street.

The Harveys moved into their new, $8,000 house in 1911, and lived there until 1926 when the Schaberg family bought it. The Schabergs sold the house to A. Garrard Macleod, M.D. in 1945, and in the half-century since, members of the Macleod family have lived there.

In the Macleods, the house found its finest stewards. The family made no significant changes to the home, and for good reason — the floorplan is convenient and the best materials were used. Dr. Harvey's daughter, Caroline Harvey Sleep, presented the original plans and specifications, documenting the construction and costs, to the Macleods. They include comments from Van Volkenburg, including the type of wood used on each of the floors. For example, the attic floors were to be: "…pine…free of sap and knots."

One of Dr. Macleod's sons, George, and his wife Linda moved into the house in the early 1980s, and continue to care for this exceptional home in the West Main Hill-Henderson Park National Register Historic District.

2001. The Harvey/Macleod House at Monroe and Academy Streets represents the most interesting aspects of two different architectural styles, Dutch Colonial Revival and Craftsman.

"…it's so solidly built, and it's a convenient house — I can't think of any way I'd change it."

George Macleod, *owner*

J.W. Bosman Building
Northeast Corner, South Burdick and Dutton Streets

The J.W. Bosman Building has anchored the northeast corner of South Burdick and Dutton Streets for almost a century. Dr. John W. Bosman and his family lived in a house on this same corner prior to 1906, when they moved up the street to 427 South Burdick Street — now known as the Isaac Brown House, a National Register Historic site.

Soon after their move, the Bosmans razed their house on this corner and undertook construction of this combination commercial-residential space. Started in 1909, the building forms a Two-Part Commercial Block, with its lower, street-level zone physically separated from the second floor by the restrained cornice just below the second-story windows. While conservative in its overall design, the building's strong suit reveals itself in the use and placement of brick, well-captured in a beltcourse above the second-story windows, and its window hoods, each punctuated with an oversized keystone.

The building's uses have remained strictly commercial at street level, with residential above. Susan and Albert Trombley bought the building in 1989, believing it was a good value. The main floor had been vacant for two to three years and the apartments needed major work. City records indicate that the building had accumulated an impressive list of code violations over the previous years, mostly on the second floor.

The Trombleys had a plan: spending more than a year, they moved into each apartment, renovating while in residence, and then moved out again. They did the vast majority of the work themselves, and only when the apartments were finished did they begin work at street level. When the job was completed, they had stripped multiple coats of paint from floors, woodwork and stairs throughout the 8,000-square-foot building, and exposed and restored its original tin ceilings.

The Trombleys opened their hair salon in 1992, and lived in the Bosman Building until about 1995, when they outgrew their space and moved into a house. However, their salon still operates from the main floor, and the Bosman Building's second floor remains residential, just as it has always been.

"It's amazing how much change has taken place around us."

Albert Trombley,
talking about the change in the area since he and wife Susan purchased the J.W. Bosman Building in 1989

2000. The J.W. Bosman Building was rehabilitated in the early 1990s by Albert and Susan Trombley, who now operate their hair salon, Tromblay, on the main floor.

Kalamazoo City Hall
241 West South Street

In the midst of the Great Depression, the City of Kalamazoo accomplished an amazing feat. It completed its new City Hall in September of 1931, without any need for a bond issue or a tax hike, having set aside the necessary funds for seven years.

The Art Deco structure, designed by Weary and Alford of Chicago, replaced two houses on this site that had served as City offices since 1925. Previously, City Hall was located in Corporation Hall on South Burdick Street. Kalamazoo's voters approved the construction of a new building in 1930, having been reassured that taxes would not be increased and local labor would be used. The City spent a total of $524,000 on the project.

It took nine months for the O.F. Miller Company to complete the four-story reinforced concrete building which is decorated on the exterior with granite and limestone. The building's flagpoles, lights and railings to the garage on the south side are decorated with a floral motif, a prevalent theme on Art Deco structures. The City Commission selected the Studio of Architectural Sculpture to design the limestone relief scenes at the top of the building. An Inscription Committee selected twelve local historical events that were carved at each corner.

One of the most striking portions of the interior is the central lobby, covered with travetine, an Italian marble. The lights, elevator, clock, drinking fountain and mailbox all carry out the Art Deco theme. Local artist Otto Stauffenberg painted the walls and ceiling of the combined Commission Chambers and Municipal Courtroom.

The only major exterior change to this building occurred in 1978, when Tower-Pinkster Associates made the south entrance barrier free by adding a lift and extending the vestibule.

2000. City hall is a typical Art Deco building, with its vertical massing and multiple applied decoration. It is located within the Bronson Park National Register Historic District.

The building's interior has experienced two major multi-year renovations between 1966 and 1970 and between 1991 and 1995, due to the changing spatial needs of City departments. Most recently in 1999, Conservation and Museum Services of Detroit cleaned the Commission Chambers mural, removing over seventy years of dust and smoke.

City Hall continues to serve not only as the day-to-day center of City government, but also as a symbol of the City itself.

"New City Hall Impressive in Its Simplicity, Dignity, Spaciousness, Practicality and Utility Combined."

Kalamazoo Gazette *headline*
August 30, 1931

KALAMAZOO: LOST & FOUND

423 and 425 South Westnedge Avenue

This compact, well-proportioned duplex was constructed of brick and stucco about 1910. It rests on the site of an earlier, single-family residence in the section of the City still referred to as "Bronson's Addition." Its simple architectural elements echo several also used to embellish Italian, Spanish and Mission "Eclectic" designs employed in the United States for four decades, beginning just before 1900. Its roof line is low-pitched and may have displayed red clay tiles in its earlier days, the eaves are a bit deeper than earlier period designs, and its dual front entries are each ornamented with a receded archway.

Above those entries, the main facade becomes even more interesting, with second-story indentations appearing on the upper corners. A cornice line begins here, and travels down each side, providing definition between the stories. With a rectangular footprint at ground level, the building falls deeply into its lot, allowing just enough room at the rear for a two-car garage.

Over its first six decades of life, the duplex served residential tenants, some of whom also owned the building, including Homer Den Adel and Adrienne Hybels. Residents who lived here must have led stylish and comfortable lives. Divided into upper and main floor flats with almost identical floor plans, the apartments remain mostly intact. Dual, public and private entries were designed for residents at the rear, and for visitors at each front corner.

A small sun room in each flat overlooks Westnedge Avenue. From there, the living room, sitting or dining area and kitchen line up along the south side and the bedrooms and bath along the north, creating a simple and efficient floor plan with relatively spacious rooms. Picture frame molding and rails grace the living area walls, and each living room has a fireplace. Hardwood stairs and floors complement the overall scheme.

Current owners and attorneys William Schlee and Thomas Thorne follow in the footsteps of several other attorneys who have used the building as office space for about 20 years. In 1997, 423 and 425 South Westnedge Avenue was fittingly added to the Vine Local Historic District.

◊ **2000. This former residential duplex at 423 and 425 South Westnedge Avenue is a pleasing part of the Vine neighborhood's streetscape.**

"Buildings have lives in time, and those lives are intimately connected with the lives of the people who use them… They change and perhaps grow as the lives of their users change."

Patricia Waddy, *architectural historian, from* How Buildings Learn, What Happens After They're Built

The New Bronson Methodist Hospital
601 John Street, bounded by John, South Burdick, Vine, Jasper and Walnut Streets

Beginning in the 1950s, small residential and commercial buildings began to disappear from this former neighborhood, an area that was early occupied by Dutch settlers. Overall, between the middle nineteenth century and groundbreaking for this new hospital, over 100 mostly residential buildings vanished from the landscape.

The Hospital conceived the new project in the early 1990s, as the former compound was judged both obsolete for future medical services and too expensive to renovate for that purpose. It eventually acquired about 14 acres of land to the south, demolishing or moving remaining buildings. For the new complex design, the Hospital turned to one of the nation's oldest, continually-operated architectural firms, Boston's Shepley Bulfinch Richardson and Abbott (SBRA).

SBRA, established in 1874 by master architect Henry Hobson Richardson, is responsible for both old and new landmarks nationwide, including The Art Institute of Chicago, Boston's Trinity Church, and more recently, Yale University's Irving S. Gilmore Music Library.

The new complex holds significant urban appeal — especially on its Vine Street facade, that is pushed up to meet the street. At about 750,000 square feet, the complex appears less imposing than it otherwise might, as its designers divided the facades into visually-manageable pieces. A series of joined pavilions, these sections house physicians' offices, ambulatory care and in-patient facilities.

The complex's fenestration is liberal and well-placed, with multiple entrances, generous window area, and a large, southeast-facing atrium. The exterior of the main level is dressed in stone, while upper stories feature brick, accented with cast decorative elements set into vertical pilasters and columns. As a finishing touch, soft green trim adorns the windows, doors and rooflines. Contractors Barton Malow Company of Southfield, Michigan, and Kalamazoo's CSM Group completed construction in late 2000.

"This $181 million project reflects not only an investment in state-of-the-art health care facilities, but also a reinvestment in southwest Michigan [and] in downtown Kalamazoo…"

Frank Sardone, *president and CEO, Bronson Methodist Hospital*

2001. The Vine Street facade of the new Bronson Methodist Hospital holds significant urban appeal with its closeness to the street, its warm materials and well-placed fenestration.

2001. The new Bronson Hospital's main entrance, which faces northwest, is signaled by a large green space and porte-cochere.

Doubleday House
214 Woodward Avenue

Had one been in the Stuart neighborhood on April 7, 1999, one might have been shocked to see this house slowly moving down the middle of Douglas and Kalamazoo Avenues before coming to rest at its new location on Woodward Avenue. Completed in 1910 by Fred Doubleday, co-founder of the office supply company Doubleday Brothers and Sons, it originally sat on the north side of Jefferson Avenue just west of Douglas Avenue in the West Douglas neighborhood. After Doubleday's death in 1963, the home had a series of owners and residents, including the Harper Funeral Home. Harper's plans in 1998 for a new facility called for the removal of this home through demolition or relocation.

Local property owner Brian Spalding acquired the house in 1999, and moved it that April to a piece of property four blocks away, on the east side of Woodward Avenue between West Main Street and Kalamazoo Avenue. The lot had been vacant since a fire in 1997 destroyed an 1880 Queen Anne home.

The house is an example of a foursquare, a style popular during the early years of the 20th century. These homes typically have two stories with a box-like shape, wide overhanging eaves, multiple dormers and front porches with Tuscan columns.

This house, which currently contains two apartments, maintains the setback of the other homes on the block. After its move, the house received a new exterior color scheme. The above-grade, stone-faced foundation and stone piers for the porch columns are modern, but match the home's originals. The basement windows are new.

This house, an example of both rehabilitation and infill, matches the other ones around it so well that one would be hard pressed to identify it as a recent addition to the neighborhood. Mr. Spalding received an Award of Merit in 2000 from the Kalamazoo Historic Preservation Commission for this project.

"...one might have been shocked to see this house slowly moving down the middle of Douglas and Kalamazoo Avenues..."

Lynn Houghton

2001. The foursquare is known for having little ornamentation with the exception of a variety of windows. This house has a very typical bay window at the side.

Kalamazoo County's Usonian Homes
Parkwyn Village, Kalamazoo
Galesburg Country Homes, Galesburg

Frank Lloyd Wright is undeniably "America's architect." His better-known buildings are spread across the United States and include Fallingwater in Pennsylvania, New York City's Solomon R. Guggenheim Museum, and Hollyhock House in Hollywood. However, the Midwest is where Wright worked for much of his life and it claims the majority of his work—including that in Kalamazoo County, which holds the largest concentration of his "Usonian" style buildings anywhere.

Using some of the elements of his earlier-established Prairie style, Wright designed the Usonian as his response to what he considered a lack of good, small house design, and diminished post-Depression financial resources. Wright designed his first Usonian in 1936, for a suburban Madison, Wisconsin lot. A little more than ten years later, a local group, comprised of men who were employed by the Upjohn Company (now Pharmacia) and their families, banded together with the objective of building a new type of residential community.

1999. The McCartney's Frank Lloyd Wright Usonian home in Parkwyn Village, Kalamazoo. Following the home's triangular floor plan, its roofline forms points in several different directions.

First finding a 72-acre parcel near Galesburg, part of the group decided it was too rural. They separated and soon found a smaller tract in the City of Kalamazoo's southwest corner. Naming it Parkwyn Village, Eric and Ann Brown, Robert and Winifred Winn, Ward and Helen McCartney and Robert and Rae Levin each built a Frank Lloyd Wright Usonian of their own. At the same time, the Galesburg group, who nicknamed their development "The Acres," moved ahead as well. Eventually, they built four Wright-designed homes, beginning with David and Christine Weisblat's 1948 Usonian.

Back in Parkwyn Village, Helen and Ward McCartney finished their Usonian in 1950. Well-married to its site, it sits low and moves from its center in three different directions. And like many Usonians, it has seen its share of alterations. Some owners decided that their homes were too small soon after completion, and in the McCartney's case, bedrooms, bathrooms, a dining area and other space were added over the home's half-century life.

1999. The Brown home's living room with its soaring ceiling. The large hearth, a common Usonian feature, is in the left foreground.

1999. The McCartney's Frank Lloyd Wright Usonian home in Parkwyn Village, Kalamazoo. Note the use of concrete block as both a building and design component.

In most instances, additions are sensitive to Wright's original. More than one, including Galesburg's Weisblat Usonian, has an addition designed by former Wright apprentice John Howe, who had visited when the homes were going up in the late 1940s and early 1950s.

The homes express diverse exterior shapes, although their earth-bound settings make this variety difficult to appreciate. The McCartney

home is best described as a series of connected triangles. The Brown home, also in Parkwyn Village, uses rectangular modules as does Galesburg's Weisblat house. The Galesburg Meyer Usonian employs Wright's "solar-hemicycle" design. Facing east in a not-quite half circle, it is the architect's attempt at energy conservation. Each home utilizes unique, individually designed, sometimes perforated, concrete block for both interior and exterior walls. Most also feature Wright's signature deep, cantilevered eaves.

In general, these homes have intimate entries like Wright's larger Prairie designs. As one moves from entry to common living area, the space expands into the core with larger rooms and higher ceilings. The focal point of these areas is the hearth—another feature in keeping with Prairie design. The "large" space is then reduced as one moves from the core outward to private areas, including bedrooms, that were, in the words of Wright biographer and scholar Brendan Gill, "…as small and snug as ship's cabins."

As a result of the homes' smaller and distinct designs, day-to-day living can be challenging. However, most inhabitants of these Usonians, some of whom are original owners at this writing, recognize that each of them has chosen a once-in-a-lifetime opportunity to live in the physical manifestation of one important artist's expression.

> *"However, when Helen McCartney saw the completed Levin house, she decided that she did not want to build any house if she could not have a Wright house."*
>
> **Laura Chamberlain,** *from* Frank Lloyd Wright's Usonian Communities in Kalamazoo, Michigan

1999. The Weisblat home in Galesburg is sited and designed in harmony with its landscape, like the other Usonians in Kalamazoo County.

1602 Grand Avenue

Homeowner Doreen Brinson loves her house and neighborhood on West Main Hill. "There are young families, and several other generations living here, and my neighbors are incredibly supportive, while being unobtrusive." Although small in size, Brinson's house sits well above the confluence of three streets, Grand, Prairie and Grove, giving it a rather regal appearance.

The West Main Hill neighborhood was initially settled, though sparsely, before the turn of the 20th century. However, it was not until about the time Brinson's house was built shortly after the turn of the century, that the streets began to fill with homes. This phenomenon took place mostly over the next thirty years, resulting in an agreeable mix of large, medium, and small-sized homes — a model for everyone.

Research indicates that Ralph and Charlotte Richardson lived here between 1942 and 1962, and were possibly the home's longest-term occupants. Mr. Richardson served as secretary-treasurer and general manager for his family-owned Richardson Garment Company, that had moved to Kalamazoo from Vicksburg in 1915. Among other items, his company produced "…ladies afternoon, street and porch dresses…"

A home for about ten families in its nearly 100 years of life, this little bungalow's exterior has changed little over that period with the exception of its 1995 vinyl siding. Originally constructed in stone, wood and stucco, its materials are similar to those used on hundreds of thousands of other bungalows across the United States during this same period. In its many variations, the bungalow became one of the most popular small house forms constructed until about 1930.

On the inside, the house has changed with the times to accommodate the needs of different

2000. This little bungalow in the West Main Hill neighborhood has provided a snug home to about ten families in its almost 100 years.

owners. A wood burning stove was installed and subsequently removed, a patio was laid and the porch screened. Kalamazoo craftsman Brett Grinwis stripped and refinished the floors. More recent interior work includes a new custom kitchen outfitted by cabinet-maker Ian Nielsen, and a 1999 half-bath remodel, undertaken by Brinson herself with help from friends.

1602 Grand Avenue sits within the northwestern boundary of the 1995 West Main Hill-Henderson Park National Register Historic District.

"I love my house! They'll probably have to carry me out in a box!"

Doreen Brinson, *homeowner*

KM Industrial Machinery
530 West Kalamazoo Avenue

Erected in the late 1920s, likely for the International Harvester Company, this building was sited in this specific location for good reason. The Michigan Central Railway ran directly behind it, making Harvester's receipt of large farm implements possible. Sears Roebuck and Company's farm business followed Harvester here in the late 1940s, staying about a decade. When Sears left in 1958, Goodwill Industries moved in and stayed until a July 1980 fire forced its departure.

At the same time, Walter Byers' company started looking for a new home. A rail consolidation project appeared as though it would demolish the company's then home on East Michigan Avenue, and it was Byers' wife, Doris, who spotted the former Goodwill site. After careful consideration, Byers decided to take a chance. The site fit his company's physical needs and the structure appeared sound, making renovation an economically sensible approach. For three months, the Byerses and their children gutted the building's interior and readied it for remodeling.

The building had potential. Its Mission-influenced, stepped parapet disguises its sloped roof, dressing up the building for the street, and its geometric front masonry enhances its personality. Working initially with contractor Jim Schelb's assistance, Byers remodeled the interior. And while he blocked in previously-boarded window openings on the building's sides (not a strictly-preservationist approach), at the same time he uncovered the large front display windows, that once again greet passersby. Paint and steel siding cover an earlier failed exterior coating.

Byers' investment allows the building to once more make a positive contribution to the neighborhood and the City's tax roles, while giving KM Industrial Machinery the visibility it needs. The building sits in the Stuart Neighborhood Local and National Register Historic Districts.

1981. This snapshot shows 530 West Kalamazoo Avenue just before its c1981 renovation began.

> *"People respect property if it is properly maintained."*
>
> **Walter Byers,**
> *from an interview with the* Kalamazoo Gazette *in 1981*

2001. Constructed as a farm implements showroom, this late-1920s, Mission-influenced building is once again used for displaying the large apparatus that KM Industrial Machinery sells.

A.M. Todd Company
1717 Douglas Avenue

Albert M. "Mint King" Todd conceived his empire in the 1860s in St. Joseph, Michigan. In 1891, he moved to Kalamazoo and erected his first commercial building at Rose Street and Kalamazoo Avenue. This building below, the second and current home of Todd's agricultural and manufacturing legacy constructed in 1929, stands as a testament to the "age of industry" in Kalamazoo's northwest corner.

As the construction trades developed new structural materials, the more traditional brick and stone moved into the realm of adornment. Kalamazoo architects Billingham and Cobb used those older materials here, decorating this building's concrete skeleton in a restrained but artful manner. From the basket weave brick bond underneath the windows, to the carved limestone surrounding the entry and the shell forms topping the pilasters, the use and placement of these materials add depth and visual interest to an otherwise plain facade.

The building's original front extended five windows' distance on either side of its entry. Dubbed a "twentieth-century Gothic Revival," it also seems to embody Prairie and Moderne influences. The low copper roofs capping the entry and original front corners, and the beltcourse that travels between the window tops, work together to give the building a strong horizontal emphasis.

Multiple rear annexes now stretch the edifice deep into its lot, while the front additions add office space and maintain the building's character. In 1964, the north front corner was added by Miller-Davis. Tower, Pinkster, Titus designed the 1991 south side addition. Kalleward-Bergerson handled that construction, and Statler Ready Mixed Concrete cast the matching decorative elements with a mold taken from the stone originals.

"The man who builds a factory builds a temple."

Henry Ford

c1941. Miller-Davis Company constructed A.M. Todd's 1929 building, as well as multiple later additions. This photo show shows the first addition, far left, at the rear of the original.

2001. The Todd building's additions on the right front corner, completed in 1964, and the left side, in 1991, faithfully replicate the refined elements and overall feeling of the original.

Rickman House
511 Woodward Avenue

The quest to find a single-family home in the Stuart neighborhood led Fred and Leslie Decker to purchase this house in 1977. Local builder George Rickman originally completed the Italianate structure in 1878 for his family. Despite a series of owners over the years, miraculously it was never divided into apartments like most of the houses in this historic district.

The house is an example of an asymmetrical Italianate, L-shaped with a cross-gabled roof and side wing. It features wooden clapboard siding with corner pilasters. The original front bay window was later replaced with a box window topped with a shed dormer. Previous owners added the present kitchen and second-floor sun porch around World War I.

The Deckers estimate that they have renovated every room, some even twice, especially the kitchen and bathrooms. Having no previous home repair skills or renovation experience, they learned quickly. Their first major projects were rebuilding the carriage house and re-roofing the house. Fred Decker developed the present four-color scheme for the exterior. Fortunately, all of the interior oak woodwork was never painted and simply needed to have its old varnish stripped.

The Deckers always wondered how their two children felt growing up in an older home. Both now live in the Stuart neighborhood—one owns her own historic house and the other plans eventually to buy one himself. Apparently, the preservation experience of the last twenty-four years has been a positive one for the entire family.

c1879. George and Jane Rickman stand in front of the house with their ten children. Notice the original front bay window and decorative vergeboard and finial at the gable end.

2001. This modest four-bedroom Italianate has remained a single-family home since its completion.

"These houses exist independently of us. All that we are doing is keeping this house a little while until we pass it to the next caretaker."

Leslie Decker, *owner*

Kalamazoo's Bed & Breakfast Inns

106 Thompson Street, now Hall House Bed & Breakfast

Constructed by contractor Henry Vander Horst as a home for his family and business in 1923, this building stands guard at the corner of West Main and Thompson Streets, a gateway to the West Main Hill neighborhood and Kalamazoo College.

As a commercial contractor, Vander Horst's concrete-reinforced steel construction technique was probably entirely normal for him, but remains altogether unusual for residences of any type or period. Inside, Vander Horst specified exceptional materials for the Colonial Revival, selecting oak, Italian marble, Honduran mahogany and tile from Detroit's famed Pewabic Pottery. He installed modern, upscale amenities, including an intercom system, several bathrooms with multiple-head showers and large closets. Finally, drawing from the painter within, Vander Horst himself embellished the library ceiling with a mural depicting the rural Netherlands, replete with windmill, and stenciled the entryway ceiling.

Used as a residence until the early 1980s, its owner moved to Illinois and put it up for sale. Three years later, still unoccupied, Pamela and Terry O'Connor purchased it. With the necessary permits and plans in hand, they worked with local contractor Tom Nie to convert it for use as a bed and breakfast inn.

Believing that less is more, the O'Connors made no substantial changes to the building's floorplan, except a conversion of the former attic into living space. Nie also remodeled the kitchen, while Mrs. O'Connor supervised the repair and refinishing of almost all of the building's interior surfaces. Five months later, in February 1986, Hall House Bed & Breakfast opened for business. The inn, now owned by innkeepers Terri and Scott Fox, is in the West Main Hill-Henderson Park National Register Historic District.

447 West South Street The David Lilienfeld House, now Kalamazoo House

This house has seen thousands of visitors during its one-and-a-quarter centuries. Constructed in 1878 for wealthy German immigrant David Lilienfeld and his family, it served as a private residence for its first half-century, including a decade as home to Kalamazoo industrialist and artist Frank D'Arcy. Beginning in 1932, its use was converted, and for its second half-century served the community as the Donovan Funeral Home, later the Betzler-Donovan Funeral Home.

In 1985, with demolition scheduled, Louis Conti, Annette Conti and several partners rescued it, and made plans to rehabilitate and use the Queen Anne as a bed and breakfast. In early 1986, they began work, moving from attic to basement, converting the building's use for overnight guests. With a history of good maintenance they were not faced with structural repairs, but focused on the building's detail, inside and out.

After much research, the partners carried out some of the work themselves, and contracted with experienced professionals for the remainder. In the end, they converted the attic for guest accommodations, restored original

↖2000. Hall House Bed & Breakfast became the perfect adaptive reuse for the large former Vander Horst family residence on a small city lot.

> *"Polished cherry floors, wainscoting and doors lend the room a timeless beauty…"*
>
> Kalamazoo Gazette, *May 15, 1986, discussing the Bartlett-Upjohn House's interior*

↙2000. The Kalamazoo House, formerly the Lilienfeld home, was saved from the wrecking ball and rehabilitated for use as a bed and breakfast.

plaster walls, stripped and re-grained many square feet of interior woodwork, hung yards of hand-printed, period wallpaper, and glazed and stenciled walls, including some executed by local artist Judith Ziobron.

On the outside, a 1930s-era stucco covering hid the building's brick. It could not be removed without damaging the structure, so the stucco was painted using a period, multiple-color scheme. A new cast-concrete balustrade completes the building's welcoming, central-city landscape plan.

The Lilienfeld/Kalamazoo House was named to the National Register of Historic Places in 1986, and is now owned and operated by Louis Conti.

229 and 237 Stuart Avenue, now The Stuart Avenue Inn

The Stuart Avenue Inn operates primarily from two buildings near the southern boundary of the Stuart neighborhood, one of Kalamazoo's earliest "streetcar suburbs." The Inn's early roots are at 405 Stuart Avenue, where Andrea and Bill Casteel opened Kalamazoo's first bed and breakfast in 1983.

In 1985, they bought the 1886 Bartlett-Upjohn House at 229 Stuart Avenue, a block south of the original inn. Named after Kalamazoo publisher Edgar Bartlett and Dr. James Upjohn, one of the founders of The Upjohn Company,

the house was earlier converted to apartments. The Casteels rehabilitated and redecorated, returning the first and second floors to a plan closely resembling the original. Removing multiple kitchens, stripping and refinishing walls, floors and trim, they transformed the inside and outside of this enormous Queen Anne from a white elephant to a polychromed charmer. Just as they finished, they took on two more projects—they bought the Chappell house next door on the north, and began a major garden project on the south.

The construction date of the Chappell House is in question—its shape and detail offer elements from several periods. Named for the family who lived there for over six decades, it, too, was converted to apartments. Over the next year, the Casteels worked to convert this building for overnight guests as well, including a sitting room, kitchen, and innkeepers' quarters on the main floor.

As they worked on the Chappell House, they laid out the "McDuffee" garden on the former McDuffee family home site. The garden now welcomes visitors and residents to the neighborhood. Mary Lou and Tom Baker bought the Inn in 1996, becoming its new proprietors.

All Stuart Avenue Inn buildings lie within the Stuart Area National Register and Local Historic Districts.

> *"Vander Horst himself embellished the library ceiling with a mural depicting the rural Netherlands, replete with windmill, and stenciled the entryway ceiling."*
>
> Pamela O'Connor,
> *regarding the history of the Hall House Bed & Breakfast*

2001. The Bartlett-Upjohn (left) and Chappell (right) Houses of the Stuart Avenue Inn had earlier been divided into apartments; they now create an inviting entry to the historic Stuart neighborhood.

203 and 219 South Westnedge Avenue, now Patricia White Interiors and The Basket Case

In this case, endangered buildings found new homes and empty lots found new buildings. Building-mover and preservationist Annette Conti is no novice, and she proved it. Friend Rodger Parzyck made the initial observation: Bronson Methodist Hospital needed more space for their new complex, and these houses were in the way. With the counsel of others, including Kim Cummings and former City Commissioner Nicolette Hahn, Conti waded into the organizational maze.

"There were many times when the project felt overwhelming…" Conti remarked afterward. It is no surprise, given the permits and scheduling changes that occupied the early phase. Bronson Hospital also owned the relocation lots, and Conti cites the Hospital's assistance and flexibility as a key element of the project's success.

During the second week of October 1996, the buildings took an 11-block journey from 133 and 134 East Dutton and 611 South Rose Streets, northeast to the 200 block of South Westnedge Avenue. During phase two, new foundations were built for the two foursquare-styled homes nearest Academy Street, who were then joined by a connecting addition.

Conti worked and supervised as the crew rebuilt porches and restored windows, and then turned its attention to the interiors.

The third house, now located near the center of the block, was in poor condition and required greater time and attention. Conti especially enjoyed this challenge, using period "Stick-Style" pattern books as one rehabilitation guide.

Both buildings are now occupied by locally-owned businesses. The joined houses are home to Patricia White Interiors, whose parent business was originally located downtown. In November 1997, the business returned from the suburbs to its roots. Patricia White, who took her first look at the buildings earlier that year, envisioned what could be and made her decision within a month. Next door, Trish Smith liked the visibility and ambiance, and moved her Basket Case gift business there about a year later.

The project, nominated for a national preservation award in 1998, received a Merit Award from the City's Historic Preservation Commission that same year.

"The most important criteria was that my project fit within the surrounding neighborhood… I felt the scale should be compatible with surrounding homes…"

Annette Conti, *project developer*

↖2000. This South Westnedge streetscape once again expresses a character it missed for decades.

Walwood Hall
East Campus, Western Michigan University

Completed in 1938, this Gothic Revival building located in East Campus is actually two connected buildings: Walwood Hall, Western Michigan University's first dormitory originally for women, and Walwood Union, the student union that contained dining and recreational rooms, a cafeteria, ballroom and offices for both the Women's and Men's Leagues. Named for Dwight B. Waldo, the University's first president and Leslie Wood, a long-time professor, Malcolm, Calder and Hammond designed the building, that continued to be used as a dormitory and later as a fraternity house into the 1980s.

A major fire in 1989 seriously damaged the kitchen and other areas of the building. Need for new office space led the University in 1991 to undertake a major renovation project at Walwood, creating offices for various departments including the University's Foundation, Alumni Relations, Development, Research, Medieval Institute, Cistercian Studies, New Issues Press and the School of Public Affairs and Administration.

Hobbs+Black Associates of Ann Arbor directed the renovation with work done by Kalleward-Bergerson of Kalamazoo. The redesign maintained the general open feeling of the building, its public spaces, such as the front lobby, and its overall architectural integrity. Hobbs+Black used original plans and photographs as a resource. Offices were divided into workstations using landscape furniture. Architectural features such as beamed ceilings, wood paneling, wainscoting, and original lights were maintained as much as possible, although some paneling was duplicated. The University installed new mechanical, electrical and fire suppression systems. In the middle 1990s, the Kalamazoo Historic Preservation Commission presented Western Michigan University with an Award of Merit for the work on this building. The success of this project, an example of adaptive use, illustrates the wonderful possibilities that exist with the University's older structures.

"We attempted to change the function of the building without changing the character."

Patrick Halpin, *former construction administrator, Western Michigan University*

2000. Walwood Hall is just one of the buildings included in Western Michigan University's East Campus, which is listed on the National Register of Historic Places.

KALAMAZOO: FOUND

Noble House
505 Woodward Avenue

Kim and Dave Williams saw potential when they decided to purchase this Queen Anne house in the Stuart neighborhood in 1992. Completed by James and Hattie Noble in 1889, it remained a single-family home until its middle-1950s owner created four apartments. By the time the Williamses bought it, the house was in poor repair. Despite its condition, they managed to find clues that the house was something special. For Kim Williams, overlooking the painted woodwork and three layers of linoleum covering the original oak floor, it was the foyer with its two sets of double doors.

The Williamses wanted to return the house to a single-family home, so to raise needed income, they continued to rent the other three units while living on the main floor. They improved the apartments to attract good tenants. They have done most of the work themselves, engaging friends and relatives to teach them such skills as installing drywall, finishing floors, painting and papering walls, and basic plumbing and electrical work.

There have been some surprises. As the Williamses have incorporated the apartments, they have found stairways and even stained glass hidden behind walls and closets. Kim Williams recommends that everyone have at least one crowbar in their toolbox.

The Williamses now own fourteen additional properties in the Stuart and West Douglas neighborhoods. Renting and maintaining close to sixty units is now their full-time job.

2001. The Noble House is a typical Queen Anne with a gabled roof, a variety of windows, large front porch and use of texture on the exterior.

As far as their original house goes, by the middle of 2001 and after nine years of labor, the last apartment disappeared and the Williamses reached their initial goal of owning a single-family home in a neighborhood they love.

"I learned you can do anything yourself. I also learned patience and the true value of neighbors."

Dave Williams, *owner*

The Style Shop
217 South Burdick Street [Kalamazoo Mall]

Over its years, this 1880s-era building's main floor was home to Kalamazoo Heating and Plumbing, a commercial laundry, a drug store and other businesses, always with offices and furnished rooms upstairs. The Style Shop women's apparel store opened here in the middle 1920s.

For five decades, a large marquee hung over its entry, eventually becoming part of Kalamazoo's downtown landscape. It was probably at this same time that its owners "modernized" the building, by adding large upper-story windows and Art Deco-influenced masonry.

When The Style Shop closed, Jacobson's Home Store, its next door neighbor, bought the building and used it for storage until it, too, closed in 1993. By then, with its marquee gone and storefront neglected, The Style Shop building sat unused for the remainder of the decade.

Enter Patrick Halpin and Peter Wiegand of Southwest Builders Incorporated. Having carried out successful renovation work for others, they bought this old building to develop and re-sell. Initially, their engineers discouraged them — rehabilitation was too risky, they said. However, when they looked more closely, they discovered a second, later footing laid just inside the original, giving Halpin and Wiegand the go-ahead.

Nelson Nave worked as consulting architect. Southwest began work as soon as they devised a plan to move old and new materials in and out of the building, which is locked in by other structures on three sides. They designed a rear egress from the third floor down that would eventually hold a circular stair. But before the stair was installed, they used this "chase" to transport materials in and out.

As the crew worked, it further reinforced the building, replaced its windows with some of similar profile, and finished the interior for mixed use. Just before completing construction, Southwest replaced the building's signature marquee — a respectful gesture to its history.

A specialty store, Ripe, bought the main floor, and the upper floors offer residential condominiums of approximately 1,700 square feet each. With an investment of $426,000, including assistance from the Downtown Development Authority's Building Revitalization Program, Wiegand and Halpin have created new/old space in a building that again makes a contribution to the downtown economy and its visual landscape.

2001. This 1880s building was "modernized" after the turn of the century, giving it a different look from others of that period. In 2000 and 2001, Southwest Builders rehabilitated its facade and interior.

> *"We're thrilled by the response this [rehabilitation] project has received."*
>
> **Patrick Halpin,** *vice president, Southwest Builders*

1572 Spruce Drive

Spruce Drive consists of a horseshoe of homes that moves west from 2000 Oakland Drive, then arcs south and again east, returning to 2100 Oakland Drive. Collectively, they form the Spruce Park development.

In 1911, 190 building lots were carved from the Waite family farm. By 1913, builder-developer Orley Haas was marketing the 35 or so Spruce Park lots to Kalamazooans, offering "Allotments DeLuxe." Among the Park's assets were a streetcar line, and, as Haas phrased it, location: "…on the southwestern skyline of Kalamazoo."

With a booming population, four Spruce Park homes were finished by 1914. Evidence suggests that architect Ernest Batterson designed this house at 1572. The architect incorporated elements of two popular period styles. The roof's steeper slope, rolled eaves and front chimney signal a Tudor Revival. The knee braces under the eaves, entry piers and pergola reflect the period's Craftsman craze. The stucco finish, common to both styles, perfectly suited this suburban architectural hybrid.

Banker and businessman C. Hubbard Kleinstuck and family were the home's longest tenants, moving there in the early 1920s. Kleinstuck's grandfather, Silas Hubbard, had long owned the estate opposite on Oakland Drive, some of which was also under development, eventually becoming the Hillcrest neighborhood. The Kleinstucks made one major alteration to their Spruce Drive house — a large rear addition that approximately doubled the floor space. Smaller changes include enclosing the front entry and widening its pergola cover.

The Kleinstucks lived here until the late 1980s, and were good caretakers — a tradition carried on by the home's subsequent and current owners.

> *"We love this house. We'd heard that Caroline Kleinstuck bought it for her son, Carl [C. Hubbard Kleinstuck] when he got married."*
>
> **William Brennan**, *owner*

◤c1915. 1572 Spruce Drive shortly after it was completed. Notice in the foreground, the "Artistic Street Lighting" promoted by developer Orley Haas.

◤2001. This stucco cottage appears little changed from the street, despite the large c1925 addition at the rear (far left).

Loy Norrix High School
Southeast Corner, Lovers Lane and Kilgore Road

A new design theory brewed for several generations before this school appeared on Kalamazoo's rural landscape. Architecture that served America for over a century was cast aside as outmoded. "Modernists" declared that buildings, densely packed on small blocks within a larger grid, had become passé thinking. New architecture would fit the building to its purpose, not the other way around, and these new buildings, free-standing or clustered, would be surrounded by open space.

Americans, with post-World War II encouragement, left the city; schools soon followed. After a battle with Portage educators over this site, the Circuit Court ruled in November 1957, in favor of the Kalamazoo Board, and planning proceeded. Dr. Loy Norrix, Kalamazoo's twenty-year Superintendent, died less than two months later, and immediately afterward, Kalamazooans decided for the first time in their history to name a school after a local educator.

A committee worked with Chicago architects Perkins & Will. The *Kalamazoo Gazette* reported the school would be: "...constructed around...'educational concepts' instead of simply an arrangement of walls and rooms to which educational programs are adjusted." In keeping with Modernist theory, the approach garnered a national award for this new school in the International Style.

The plan included four, free-standing, clustered buildings with the center building housing the "study-resources" area. The designers joined this cluster, via a walkway, to a second, tighter cluster of three additional buildings, housing auditorium and physical education spaces.

Students arrived in November 1960, when contractors Herlihy Mid-Continent substantially completed the classrooms. It finished the second cluster last, and the community dedicated the almost $5 million, 200,000-plus-square-foot facility in September 1961.

Just years later, the education demands of the baby-boom generation burst the new school's seams. In 1967, the school system added portable classroom buildings, and by 1969, began planning for remodeling and additions. By 1971, architects Richard Prince and Associates had faithfully instilled the new work with the look and feel of the original, at a cost of about $3.6 million, while roughly doubling the floorspace.

Single- and double-storied, the complex uses glass extensively to define space, giving the facility an uncompromised openness. This element is counter-balanced by the buildings' significantly higher energy use—a challenge that, school officials hope, will be addressed as technology innovations occur.

"The committee first determined educational needs. Then it recommended a structure designed to meet those needs."

From the 1961 Loy Norrix School dedication program

2001. With its 1971 renovation and additions, Loy Norrix High School now serves about 1,300 students.

Brown House Carriage Steps
427 South Burdick Street

There is more to the Italianate home on the east side of South Burdick Street between Lovell and Cedar Streets than the house itself. Just a few yards from its front door near the curb are the only known carriage steps remaining in Kalamazoo. People walk by them every day not realizing what they are or who owns them.

Loan agent Isaac Brown completed the house in 1867, living here with his family until his death in 1904. It is a classic Italianate with its cubic shape, front bay window, hipped roof, wide cornice and decorative molding over the long, narrow windows. Brown installed the plain, stone carriage step in front of the main entrance to the house.

In 1906, Dr. John W. Bosman purchased the home, adding an office on the south side of the house for his practice. He then located another carriage step across from the office's front door. This one, more decorative than the other, is in the shape of a serpent. Dr. Bosman's name is carved into the side facing the street.

The house was just one of several on both sides of South Burdick Street that were used by physicians, due to the close proximity of Bronson Hospital, just one block to the east. In fact, this section of the street had the nickname "Doctors' Row." Dr. Bosman continued to practice here until 1914. It later became the residence and office for Dr. William C. Huyser for almost sixty years, until 1976. It then became a home for Harold and Patricia Van Werden who continued to rent the side office. The law firm of Levine and Levine, which had their practice in that location, purchased the entire house in 1998.

Work on South Burdick Street in 2000 led to the removal of the carriage steps. When the City completed the work, they returned the steps to their original places, reminding people of a time before parking meters and blaring horns, when horse-drawn carriages used the steps to deliver their occupants to their destinations.

↗ 2001. Dr. Bosman chose a serpent style for this carriage step. His name is engraved on the opposite side.

> *"People walk by them every day not realizing what they are or who owns them."*
>
> Lynn Houghton

↖ 2001. This is the oldest set of the carriage steps, installed by Isaac Brown.

Public Safety Station No. 7
2331 Parkview Avenue

In 1983, the need to reduce response time on the south side of the community, especially in the Oakwood neighborhood, led the City of Kalamazoo to construct this Public Safety Station on the south side of Parkview Avenue between Laird and Barnard Avenues. The City hired architect Michael J. Dunn to design the building and Shannon-Kline, Inc. to build it. The site had been vacant since the demolition of the old Oakwood Elementary School in 1963. In fact, contractors needed to remove part of the school's foundation to construct some of the load-bearing walls.

Designed during the years when the City created the Public Safety Department, it became important for the building to create a bond, not a fortress, between the Department and the neighborhood. The older homes on the street inspired the architect to integrate compatible details such as a gabled roof and clapboard siding. To prevent the station from overpowering the streetscape, Dunn set the building back, providing turn-around space for the fire equipment. To make the building low maintenance, vinyl, rather than wood siding was used, with the exception of the wood fish-scale shingles in the two gables that were stained. On the side of the building is a park-like setting, complete with gazebo and barbecue, where officers can enjoy being part of the neighborhood.

Dedicated in June 1984, this infill building blends in nicely with the surrounding structures. It is a practical and sensitive addition to the neighborhood.

> *"This was much more than designing a building, it was designing a relationship more than anything else."*
>
> Michael J. Dunn, *architect*

◊2000. The tower not only reflects what one might find on older fire stations, but also serves a very practical purpose as a place to dry fire hoses.

KALAMAZOO: FOUND

Gibson Mandolin-Guitar Company, now Kalamazoo Enterprise Center
225 Parsons Street

Orville Gibson found his way to Kalamazoo in the 1870s, and over the next three decades, his string instrument building techniques put Kalamazoo on the musical map of the world.

After clerking for several local businesses and working in his home shop, Gibson opened his own manufactory in the middle 1890s. By that time, his talents were already widely recognized. In 1902, Gibson entered into an agreement with five other Kalamazoo men to form the Gibson Mandolin-Guitar Manufacturing Company Limited. The group paid Gibson a lump sum plus two years' salary to share his knowledge, and he allowed his name to be used on the company and its products. Gibson left the company in 1909 and returned to his home state of New York.

Until the 1920s, the company specialized in mandolins, and its 1917 headquarters on Parsons Street focused on that activity. Builder Gerard Van Eck began construction the previous year, using a design by Kalamazooan G. Gilbert Worden, who estimated the building's cost at just over $51,000. An April 1917 edition of Gibson's sales newsletter, *The Sounding Board Salesman,* described the building: "The Gibson factory is of day-light construction and is one of the show places in Kalamazoo. It is of steel and concrete construction, making it absolutely fireproof but the artistic was not overlooked..." The building's design allowed for two future stories to be added, and the newsletter further reported that the plans called for "twin plants of five stories each."

The design has merit. A rectangle with projecting front (south) and side (west) entries and stair towers are rimmed with a simple decorative parapet.

Gibson's owners had clearly planned for growth, but the firm's expansion exceeded their wildest dreams. It quickly became the world's most widely-respected stringed instrument manufacturer. As early as the 1920s, it marketed to and received testimonials from "Gibsonites" as far away as Australia. By 1925, there were 2,000 Gibson sales representatives on the road.

In 1944, Chicago Musical Instruments acquired Gibson, and the company's most explosive growth began under the direction of Ted McCarty, who became president in 1950. The factory grew outward, rather than upward, and added more new, shorter buildings in 1950, 1960 and 1964 to accommodate increased production. By the 1960s, it produced 1,000 guitars daily. Increasingly, these were its popular electric guitars, including the solid-body "Les Paul" and "Flying V" models.

Norlin Corporation bought Gibson in 1968, and in 1981, moved its headquarters to Nashville, Tennessee. Kalamazoo production was gradually phased out and Norlin closed the Kalamazoo plant altogether in 1984.

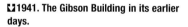
1941. The Gibson Building in its earlier days.

⬅ 2001. The Gibson Building experienced substantial rehabilitation work in 2000 and 2001.

"Judge J.W. Adams, president of the Company, during an address, told the assemblage that Gibson was the largest company of its kind in the world."

The Sounding Board Salesman, *Volume 6, August 1917, No. 2,*
Excerpt from a report of the Gibson Company's housewarming for their new building at 225 Parsons Street

About 1986, Kalamazoo Enterprise Incorporated bought the 1917 and adjoining buildings, renaming the complex the Kalamazoo Enterprise Center. The Center leases floor space to a variety of businesses, including Heritage Guitar Incorporated — a high-end guitar manufacturing company formed by several former Gibson employees. In 2000, the 1917 building was judged eligible for the National Register of Historic Places. Further, the area in which the building complex lies was designated a State Renaissance Zone, which encourages reinvestment by freeing property and business owners of most State and local taxes for fifteen years.

At this writing, the 1917 building is undergoing rehabilitation. In 2000, its reinforced steel bled rust onto the building's concrete skin. Now, its exterior has been patched and painted, its smokestack stabilized, and a new elevator, boilers and air handling units installed for current and future tenants. Perhaps the building's own renaissance has begun.

⬅ 1936. This interior photo shows the gluing department, with the large "day-light" windows in the background.

Woodward School, now the Woodward School for Technology and Research
606 Stuart Avenue

During the 1920s and 1930s, the local architectural firm of Billingham and Cobb designed a number of public elementary schools in Kalamazoo, several of which still stand. Woodward Elementary School, completed in 1930, was one of their most striking designs. It replaced the original 1880 school and addition, both demolished for a playground.

The Georgian Colonial Revival building is symmetrical overall, with a central portico supported by six metal Corinthian columns, each twenty-six feet high. The three doors at the entrance are topped with fanlights. Balanced by two wings decorated with pediments, the structure also contains a central tower with a working four-sided clock, repaired in 1986. The main lobby and classrooms contain oak woodwork. The original lockers, which line the main hallways, remain in use.

Woodward, a magnet school since 1997, is now called the Woodward School for Technology and Research. Over the last four years, a great deal of work was done on the interior of not only this building, but also on the adjacent building to the north, completed in 1921 and presently referred to as the "annex," and on the one-story addition to the south completed in 1961. Between 1997 and 1998, walls were removed to create larger classrooms allowing for multi-age teaching. The architectural firm of Eckert Wordell directed this project. In addition, an elevator, video production studio and science laboratory were installed in 1999. Diekema Hamann Architecture, a local firm, handled this phase. Most recently, the school's parents' organization funded a new playground at the rear of the main building and a garden on the corner of Stuart Avenue and North Street.

Anyone visiting this building soon realizes that they are in a quality school structure built with style.

"The feel of this building is wonderful."
Christie Enstrom-West, *principal, Woodward School for Technology and Research*

2001. This building is a classic example of Georgian Colonial Revival with columned entrances on the east and west sides. It also has a number of fanlights, a dentiled cornice, pilasters and quoins.

The Oaklands
Western Michigan University, West Michigan Avenue

It is difficult to imagine this house, now in the center of a major university, as part of a 600-acre estate, but it was indeed. Built for $15,000 in 1869 by local merchant Robert Babcock, this twenty-three room Italianate was nicknamed "The Oaklands" for the many oak trees surrounding it. It has all the distinctive characteristics of the style, including bracketed eaves, hooded windows, cubic shape, paired front doorway and a cupola. It also has a stunning circular staircase made of walnut.

The house had a series of owners, including local entrepreneur Benjamin Austin and his son-in-law, railroad contractor Daniel Streeter, who raised horses on the estate. Their most famous horse was Peter the Great, the finest trotter of his day. Dr. Charles Boys purchased the estate in 1920, living in the house, but selling off most of the land for both the Arcadia Brook and Gateway Golf Courses and a riding academy.

Western Michigan University purchased the house in 1944 to serve as the president's residence. It continued to fulfill that responsibility until 1974. Some time later, the University replaced electric wiring, plaster, flooring, and repaired windows. Following that work, in 1982, the Oaklands was used as the first Designer's Showcase house, a fund-raiser that benefited the Kalamazoo Symphony Orchestra and Kalamazoo Institute of Arts. At the end of the event, a private campaign raised funds from various sources and groups associated with Western Michigan University to support the house. In 1988, the house, painted white for many years, received a new color scheme more appropriate to its architectural style. The Kalamazoo Historic Preservation Commission presented an Award of Merit to the University for its work here.

The Oaklands continues to be used by the University as a reception center and overnight accommodations for staff, visiting alumni and University guests. The house is listed individually on the National Register of Historic Places and is part of the Stuart Local Historic District.

> *"Its [Western Michigan University's] historic homes link pioneers and bustling present, providing continuity in a changing world."*
>
> Preservation & Progress: Historic Homes of Western Michigan University, *c1990*

2000. The Oaklands is an island of calm in the center of a very active campus.

c1920. The house appears basically the same except for the exterior color and front entrance. Notice the stairs off the side porch.

Kalamazoo State Hospital Water Tower
Oakland Drive, Kalamazoo Regional Psychiatric Hospital

Rising over the treetops, the Kalamazoo State Hospital Water Tower has served as a landmark for this community for over a century. A need to improve both the Hospital's water supply and fire protection led the State of Michigan in 1892 to appropriate $18,000 for a water tower. Detroit architect William B. Stratton designed the Queen Anne brick structure that complemented the original hospital buildings.

Completed in 1895, the 175-foot tower, then Kalamazoo's tallest structure, is actually a tower within a tower. The brick outer walls conceal a second inner tower containing a large steel tank and two smaller ones. Hand-cut stone blocks are at the first five feet, followed by a red brick cylinder, then a yellow brick crenelated curtain wall supported by brackets and topped with a high-pitched roof with four dormer windows. Local mason Benjamin Roe supervised the project. The tower provided needed water during a disastrous downtown fire in December 1909.

In 1971, a section of the curtain wall needed to be stabilized due to a bulge discovered years earlier. Plans to restore the tower in 1968 stopped due to a lack of State funds. In January 1974, the State announced the tower would be demolished due to its condition.

This declaration led to an unprecedented community campaign to save the structure. A group formed, called "Save the Tower Committee," set a goal of $200,000. They hoped to raise this amount with speakers, buttons, photography contests, and other events. Many schools integrated the tower into their curriculum. By October 1975, the Committee raised $208,000 from fifteen foundations, from both Federal and local governments and from 4,000 individuals.

Architect Richard Frank directed the restoration project, that was carried out by the Miller-Davis Company. Constructing a scaffold completely around the tower, it took the structure apart brick by brick to repair it, and installed new steel beams along with a new masonry wall, completing the work by the fall of 1976. The Water Tower is on the National Register of Historic Places and designated an American Water Landmark.

1997. The Michigan History Division, Department of State now operates the tower.

c1894. This photograph, taken during construction, shows the inner tank, that was exposed again during its restoration in 1976.

"It is quite simply, a landmark that the people of Kalamazoo wanted to preserve — and did."

Preservation News, *January 1976*

710 and 716 Charlotte Avenue

These homes on Kalamazoo's east side are two examples of how appropriate "infill" development can help restore an entire neighborhood.

Research shows that homes existed earlier on these sites, which share a common property line. At 710 Charlotte Avenue, the original house may have been close in design to its replacement. In the years following the turn of the last century, many bungalows like this were constructed in the United States. They were an excellent choice for a middle-class family—belying their petite exterior appearance with spacious rooms inside.

The original home at 716 Charlotte was older, from before 1895, and was probably two stories, much like several that still exist across the street.

Both homes deteriorated, perhaps as they reverted from owner-occupied to rental. This phenomenon took hold in Kalamazoo as it did elsewhere—many families moved to the suburbs following World War II, enabled by easily-obtainable mortgages for then-rural housing developments, and freedom for those who could afford a car.

Homes in all cities were harder to sell, and many became rentals. As their owners now often lived out of town, normal repairs were delayed or neglected altogether. The City of Kalamazoo ordered the original homes at 710 and 716 Charlotte Avenue demolished in 1973 and 1989, respectively, as a result of neglect.

At this point, non-profit Kalamazoo Neighborhood Housing Services (KNHS), got involved. The organization has worked since 1981 to revitalize neighborhoods by improving housing stock. In 1999, KNHS embarked on a new venture. Recognizing that streets filled with homes make better neighborhoods than streets with empty lots, KNHS is filling those lots with new, sympathetically-designed "infill" homes constructed of modern materials. The Charlotte Avenue homes represent two of six projects that KNHS scheduled for 2000.

KNHS Construction Manager Roger Eriksen supervises the work, using new stock plans created from earlier Sears kit homes. He adapts the plans as needed, including 716 Charlotte, which was altered for barrier-free use. As a result, KNHS is helping new homeowners stake their claims and helping reinvigorate Kalamazoo's wonderful neighborhoods. This work earned KNHS a 2001 Merit Award from the Kalamazoo Historic Preservation Commission.

> *"From its beginning in 1981, neighborhood revitalization has always been our common thread."*
>
> **Bonnie Garbrecht,**
> *Kalamazoo Neighborhood Housing Services*

2001. These two homes on Charlotte Avenue on Kalamazoo's east side represent Kalamazoo Neighborhood Housing Service's successful venture into "infill" construction to help restore neighborhoods.

Humphrey Block
Southeast Corner, East Michigan Avenue and Portage Street

This building likely holds the title for longest-held incorrect name in the City of Kalamazoo. People have called it the Peninsula Building since the 1980s—after research determined an 1874 construction date, and indicated it once housed a restaurant called the "Peninsular." Later information eclipsed that theory, but the "Peninsula" name stuck.

The building's correct name, the Humphrey Block, was actually awarded in 1855, before it was finished, when General Bissel Humphrey died. Humphrey had been civic-minded and was well-liked by his fellow Kalamazooans, so the building's owners named it in his memory. It was still called the Humphrey Block at the turn of the last century.

Over its long life, the building provided space for multiple uses, including home to Parsons Business College, the Starkey and Gilbert Furniture Company, Sam Folz' clothing store, the Kalamazoo Stove Company and many others. Upholsterers, jewelers, tailors and dentists occupied its second and third floors.

Remodeled multiple times, the change that most affected the building's exterior took place likely after 1915, when its slender Italianate windows were traded for horizontal "Chicago-style" fenestration. At the same time, owners pulled down the ornate cornice and replaced it

with a dentiled beltcourse. Later, in the 1980s, owners once again replaced the windows.

Tom and Gitti Huff began their careers as urban renovators in the 1970s. They bought this building in the middle 1990s, and partnered with another couple to create the Olde Peninsula Brewpub & Restaurant on the main floor. When contractor Peter Wiegand was finished there, he had built the restaurant, offices on the second floor, and three third-floor apartments.

Today, the Huffs own about thirteen downtown Kalamazoo buildings, and continue their work to give each a new life, further stimulating the City's renaissance.

◤2001. Contractor Peter Wiegand collaborated with architects Slocum Associates to help create a main-floor restaurant and brewpub, with offices and apartments above in a middle 1990s renovation for owners Tom and Gitti Huff.

"After all, preservation and saving cities are really fraternal twins."

Arthur Cotton Moore, *architect and planner*

◤1894. The Humphrey Block's original tall and slender windows gave the building a lofty look.

Triangle Service Station, now The Water Street Coffee Joint
315 E. Water Street

This architecture might be termed "1930s Gas Station," but "1990s Coffee House" works just as well. The second life of this little cottage clearly demonstrates how adaptable old buildings can be.

Kalamazooan Lester Rice helped pump about 35,000 gallons of gas weekly when he worked here in the 1940s. He was eventually promoted to manager, and later bought the franchise on this little "golden triangle" on the point between Kalamazoo Avenue and Water Street. By the time current occupant Mark Smutek secured a lease on the building in 1993, 60 years had passed.

Once on the scene, it took Smutek seven months to work his wizardry. On a shoestring budget, he worked at night after his regular daytime job. Inside, he enclosed the two-bay service area to create indoor seating. Salvaged woodwork from Western Michigan University's Walwood Hall found a second home as built-in benches — seating that beckons patrons to relax and read a morning paper or carry on the cerebral or mundane kinds of conversations that people have in coffee shops.

On the other side, Smutek installed the coffee bar's very compact counter and work area. And everywhere indoors, starbursts of copper erupt from a celestial blue "sky" on flush-mounted lighting fixtures. These were created by Smutek and his friends, inspired in part by the Kalamazoo State Theatre's "atmospheric sky" feature. Smutek also removed paint from the brick exterior and added awnings to fend off the early morning sunshine. In 2000, he designed a novel all-weather addition that took the place of the earlier awnings. Constructed by Kalamazoo builder Scott Spink, it can be opened on three sides in warm weather for *al fresco* coffee quaffing, and enclosed and heated in cooler months.

2001. The shape of the building has changed slightly, with an additional seating area at left that is enclosed and heated in cold weather.

The golden triangle is golden once again. The building's treatment and use, with its whimsical yet comfortable interior and its eye-catching exterior, demonstrate what a big imagination can do on a small budget. A popular place both day and night, the Water Street Coffee Joint may be of the most often-visited little buildings in downtown Kalamazoo. Its rehabilitation garnered a 1995 Award of Merit from the Kalamazoo Historic Preservation Commission.

1945. Lester Rice earned about $25 a week when he worked at the Triangle Service station at 315 East Water Street with its trim, cottage-like appearance.

"The building already has a story; all you do is add the next interesting chapter."

Stewart Brand, *author,*
How Buildings Learn:
What Happens after They're Built

262 and 264 East Michigan Avenue

This simple, three-story brick building began life about 1885 as a harness shop. Although its original facade most likely featured an Italianate design, former owners removed the cornice in 1951.

The story here, though, is not about the building's facade, but rather what has happened inside. As have many downtown buildings, this one experienced multiple, usually retail, main floor uses, including a grocery, a used furniture outlet and a sporting goods shop. And up until about 1950, it appears that its second and third floors served as offices and residences. After that time, like many other urban buildings, its upper floors were left vacant and decaying.

In 1990, Nancy Troff and Michael Harrell were in the market for downtown living space. Troff had earlier experimented with converting upper-story footage in a South Street building for the residential rental market, while Harrell had some design experience. They pooled their collective resources, bought this building, and Harrell assembled a draft floorplan for their future abode.

Designer Don Chapman prepared finished plans from Harrell's draft, and contractor Peter Wiegand turned them into reality in 1991. The rear and middle of the third floor now accommodate the master bedroom, bath and a large den, that, loft-style, looks down on to the living-dining area below. The second floor features a large living-dining area, a kitchen, bath and guest room. The building's main floor continues to be used for retail.

Part of the Haymarket Local and National Register Historic Districts, 262 and 264 East Michigan Avenue sit within a block that has seen dramatic restoration work in the past two decades, reestablishing the street's distinctive character and attracting additional investment.

↗1992. During the building's 1991 renovation, its second and third floors were converted to living space. This view looks down from the third floor study into the second floor living area.

> *"I love living downtown for a million reasons."*
>
> Nancy Troff, Welcome Home, *May/June 1992*

↗2001. This dressed-down facade covers a building with an exciting recent interior history.

West Douglas Neighborhood

Kalamazoo's hilly terrain is well illustrated in the West Douglas neighborhood on the City's northwest side. Almost the entire area is elevated. Its highest point, the highest in the City, is here on the site of the former Southwest Michigan Tuberculosis Sanatorium, later known as the Northwest Unit of the Kalamazoo Regional Psychiatric Hospital. Fairview Park, former site of the Fairview Hospital, is also found here. The neighborhood takes its name from Douglas Avenue on its eastern boundary. The name itself came from politician Stephen Douglas who visited Kalamazoo in 1860. A small section of Douglas Avenue and Mountain Home Cemetery are listed on the National Register of Historic Places and are part of the Stuart Local Historic District.

The neighborhood possesses many fine homes, the majority built between 1880 and 1918. The houses themselves, for the most part, are modest in size and reflect a variety of architectural styles — especially those popular during the last half of the 19th and early 20th centuries. In addition, there are several tract houses built after World War II.

The house at 631 Summer Street is a Queen Anne completed around 1890. It has a gabled roof, decorative clapboard and an unique porch with sets of columns and a simple railing. This street also has several other Queen Anne houses of various sizes.

2001. This Queen Anne house on Summer Street is one of many of this type found on this avenue.

American foursquares and bungalows also prevail here. The house at 1303 West North Street, built in 1921, is a classic bungalow, having a gabled roof with a wide, bracketed overhang, double-hung windows and a front porch with a stoop framed by wing walls.

Through the years, largely through efforts by the West Douglas Neighborhood Association organized in 1980, the neighborhood has seen a decrease in crime and a stabilization of the housing stock. Even though the majority of the houses are not owner-occupied, the owners, for the most part, are taking better care of their properties and making a significant contribution to the neighborhood's renaissance.

"I see it [the West Douglas neighborhood] going in an uphill direction."

Sandy Groat,
West Douglas Neighborhood Administrator

2001. This bungalow on West North Street is very horizontal, spreading low and long.

St. Luke's Episcopal Church
247 West Lovell Street

This church is striking not only for the building, but also for its setback. Although it is on a major thoroughfare, it easily could fit in the center of an English country village.

Organized in 1837, the first two of St. Luke's early churches were located on Church Square at the southeast corner of South Park Street and West Main Street, now Michigan Avenue. In 1884, this congregation merged with St. John's Episcopal Church, which had its building on this West Lovell Street site.

Detroit architect Gordon Lloyd designed this English Gothic structure covered with Amherst stone. The building contains a high central tower, decorated with narrow louvered windows, and flanked by the main sanctuary to the west and a chapel to the east. All the interior woodwork is oak. Local builder Henry Coddington received the construction contract. Members attended services in the new church for the first time on January 10, 1886. The *Kalamazoo Gazette* commented that day, "Externally it is a pleasing specimen of grace and picturesqueness, harmony and symmetry…"

In 1893, parishioners Edwin and Cynthia Van Deusen financed the construction of a new parish house next door on the east side. Designed by the Chicago firm of Patton and Fisher, it also was built by Henry Coddington.

Over the years on numerous occasions, the main sanctuary and chapel have been repainted and redecorated, some of these alterations prompted by liturgical changes. The most recent redecoration occurred between 1989 and 1990. Additional stained glass was installed in the last fifty years throughout the chapel, sanctuary and narthex.

Architect William Stone designed a new parish house, built by Roy Stevens, in 1956, in front

2001 The steeply-pitched, gabled roof and pointed-arch windows are evident characteristics of the English Gothic style. The church also has a porte-cochere on its west side, on the right front in this photo.

of the older one, adding classrooms, offices, kitchen and dining space. The original parish house came down in 1977, replaced with an addition designed by Dick Slocum and built by the Miller-Davis Company, giving the church a choir room, library and additional space. The parish saved some of the stained glass and woodwork from the older building and incorporated it into this newer structure.

Now one hundred and fifteen years old, St. Luke's Episcopal Church has served its congregation well, and has become a beloved landmark of the community.

"The fabric [congregation] of the church is preserving it for the next generation."

Del Farnsworth, *archivist, St. Luke's Episcopal Church*

Wood-Upjohn House
530 West South Street

Words such as "statuesque" and "dignified" are two that can be used when discussing this classic, nineteen-room Italian villa located in the South Street Historic District. It took fifteen months and a total of $25,000 for builders Bush and Paterson to complete this house in 1878, for banker William Wood and his family.

Dr. William E. Upjohn, then president of the Upjohn Pill and Granule Company, purchased the house in 1905. His family remained there until 1968, when his stepson, Irving S. Gilmore, donated it to the City of Kalamazoo for an adult community center. The Center housed senior citizen programs and the Parks and Recreation Department. Gilmore's gift also stipulated that the house would eventually revert to Kalamazoo College.

Fourteen years later in 1982, the deed for the house went to the Kalamazoo Chapter of the American Red Cross. The organization had previously located next door, in the Gilmore house at 516 West South Street, and installed their health, wellness and nursing programs there. A private campaign raised over $200,000 to renovate the structure. Architect David Pyle and Conti Building and Restoration Company worked on the project for the next two years. They installed a new slate roof, rafters, gutters, and rebuilt the chimneys and front steps.

Designer Annette Conti oversaw the interior work, including stripping the mahogany woodwork and the walnut stairway, and installing new carpeting and wallpaper. Artist Judith Ziobron repainted the dining room ceiling medallion and stenciled various rooms.

The American Red Cross remained at both homes until 1999, when it moved to its new location in Oshtemo Township. The two homes then reverted to Kalamazoo College. The College sold this one to Bill and Sandy Shauman, who have returned it to a single-family residence. After over thirty years without a kitchen or laundry area, the Shaumans spent their first year returning these facilities to the house, as well as renovating the three and one-half baths. The projects for the Shaumans will continue, but they quickly have restored this structure back to its original purpose—a family home.

2000. Never altered in any way, the house has kept its basic style. All elements remain except for the finial at the top of the tower.

c1925. The central tower makes this an Italian villa. It also has bracketed eaves, long narrow windows with moldings up above, a bay window, occulus windows, decorative quoins and a porte-cochere. Notice the finial at the top of the tower.

"The house does not live like its size. It lives like a regular house."

Bill Shauman, *owner*

Garrett-Shell House
828 South Rose Street

Bobby Joe Shell saw something in this house back in February 1994, when he and his wife Barbara walked through it. He liked its overall lines. Mrs. Shell fell in love with the front doors and the foyer. They certainly were viewing a diamond in the rough as the structure had been abandoned for close to a decade.

Built sometime before 1890, the house was a long-time home for the family of Charles H. Garrett, founder of the Garrett Insurance Agency. In 1957, it became the church, school and parsonage for the Evangelical Lutheran Latvian Church, headed by Reverend Arturs Piebalgs.

The Shells encountered glass, garbage and other debris scattered throughout the interior. Many of the rooms lacked electricity. Holes in the roof allowed rain and snow to seep into all areas of the house, resulting in major water and mold damage.

Finding no financial assistance at local lending institutions, corporate or government housing programs, the Shells funded the entire rehabilitation project themselves — some of it with credit cards.

Between March 1994 and November 1995, the Shells, with help from family and friends, cleaned up the house, starting with the six inches of ice throughout the basement. Mr. Shell then constructed four bedrooms, a kitchen and other living space in the basement where he, his wife and their five children lived for the next four years while they worked throughout the rest of the house.

In addition to their full-time jobs, the Shells have done almost all of the work themselves, except for the new roof, exterior painting and furnace installation. Their older children

◼ c1900. Members of the Garrett family stand in the front of the house. The original front porch was remodeled later.

they installed. Both owners worked to replace all of the window glass. Mrs. Shell loves wood and has stripped, sanded and refinished just about every piece in the house. It took two years for her to complete the doors. She also chose the interior decorations including paint colors, wallpaper and furniture for all the rooms.

With the exception of the front foyer, two closets and some miscellaneous woodwork, the house is finished. The Shells have since purchased the house next door and two on Rose Parkway on the other side. Their original house now is valued at eight times its initial cost, illustrating that sometimes having a single vision can pay off in many ways.

> *"As we worked on the house, I could feel it coming back to life."*
> **Bobby Joe Shell,** *owner*

◘1994. This photograph was taken shortly after the Shells purchased the house. It had been boarded up for almost four years and every window was broken.

◘2001. The house is an example of Queen Anne, with a front gable decorated with fish-scale shingles. There also is decorative trim at the corners and below some of the windows.

became very involved, learning valuable skills they have taken away with them.

Prior to the Shells' occupancy, the double-brick constructed home was painted beige and gray. Mrs. Shell developed a new color scheme, very close to the original of deep red, green and white, by scraping paint off the bricks.

Every inch of this house has been touched. Mr. Shell still can recall how many sheets of drywall and how many boxes of electrical wire

Lustron Houses
3032 Broadway Avenue, 2022 Lakeway Avenue, 1009 Clover Street, 1228 Miles Avenue, 2922 Ferdon Road, 1002 Westfall Avenue

Built inside and out with steel, Lustron houses represent one of America's most unique housing types. The need to develop inexpensive homes after World War II led the Lustron Corporation of Columbus, Ohio, to produce prefabricated, rectangular houses between 1948 and 1950. Founder Carl Strandlund convinced the Federal government to provide not only the steel, still rationed, but also millions of dollars in loans and a surplus aircraft factory.

The company produced three basic models with two or three bedrooms. Porcelain-enameled panels, two feet square, covered the exterior and a steel roof topped each home. Available in five basic colors, all of which were permanent, buyers were advised to choose wisely. Each house arrived in 3,000 parts, ready for assembly.

Almost all of the models came with built-in metal features like cupboards, shelves and vanities. The company advertised the houses as maintenance free, and touted them as fireproof, insect-proof and decay-proof.

Kalamazoo has six Lustron houses, each with two bedrooms, found in the Milwood, Winchell, Arcadia and South Westnedge neighborhoods. Some of the subsequent owners chose to enclose front entrances and build additions to the side or rear. Three are blue, two are yellow and one is blue-green. Many have their original windows and all have their original steel roofs.

The Lustron Corporation, unfortunately, had several things working against it. Many financial institutions would not issue mortgages for such an unusual home, and often, local building codes restricted their construction. Finally, the distribution system created by the company was too cumbersome. The Lustron Corporation had hoped to produce one hundred houses a day, but at its height, could only reach that goal by one-quarter.

In the end, only 2,498 Lustron houses were built and assembled in thirty-six states. Many continue to be maintained in excellent shape and could potentially qualify for the National Register of Historic Places, as they have surpassed their golden anniversaries.

"A New Standard For Living"
Lustron Corporation slogan, 1947

2001. This yellow Lustron at 1002 Westfall Avenue in the Arcadia neighborhood is in pristine condition.

2001. The Milwood neighborhood boasts two Lustrons, including this blue one at 1228 Miles Avenue. Its front porch was enclosed.

The Marlborough
471 West South Street

This gem has reigned over South Street since 1923. Built of 230 tons of steel, concrete, and over 200,000 bricks, it took shape under the supervision of contractor Henry Vander Horst, after a Mediterranean-influenced design by Billingham and Cobb. Built at an estimated cost of $400,000, the Marlborough offered 75 apartments, ranging from two to six rooms. Each had a folding bed and a complete kitchen. Monthly rent covered utilities, ice, laundry, maid and janitorial services.

The gem's brilliance dimmed mid-century. City residents were fleeing to the suburbs, and the Marlborough's owner deferred maintenance. In the late 1970s, new owner William T. "Ted" Little decided to take a risk that would turn the building's fate. Little referred to this revival as a tribute to his step-grandmother who had lived there. That may be true, but Little also believed that people would stay or move downtown to live in a condominium.

Over the next fifteen years as buyers purchased floor space from Little, his team of craftspeople converted the building from rentals to individually-owned units. Beginning on the fifth floor, clients worked with Bob Shannon, whom Little calls "the most important man of all." Shannon helped new owners translate their needs into custom urban homes. The crew eventually worked their way down, floor by floor, until the last residential unit sold in 1995. During the renovation, artist Bill Scudella re-used stained-glass windows from a church in the Marlborough's units, offering owners both light and privacy.

Today's Marlborough residents are enthusiastic about living there. John Schmitt and his family bought their condominium in 1994. Schmitt, who lived in downtown Kalamazoo many years earlier and then in Richland, Michigan, says, "I love it! It's hard to remember life before…"

2000. The Marlborough. A faded gem, made to shine again.

Resident Patricia Bluman left Kalamazoo in the early 1980s — just as the Marlborough began to shine again. She returned to Kalamazoo in 1998 and visited the building during a historic homes tour. Bluman moved into her 1,400-square-foot unit, which features 22 windows, about six months later and plans to stay.

The Marlborough is a 1983 inductee to the National Register of Historic Places.

"I absolutely fell in love with the building's character, history and substance."

Patricia Bluman, *Marlborough resident*

Orrin B. Hayes, Incorporated
543 West Michigan Avenue

This building is not the first on its site — it replaced a large house as Kalamazoo's growing commercial area spread west from the City's center in the early 1920s. Erected as a Packard automobile dealership by Detroit investors, this distinguished-looking building has remained in service to the automobile since it was constructed. Designed by Kalamazoo architect and engineer G. Gilbert Worden, and constructed by Henry L. Vander Horst at a cost of about $33,000, the building's design was likely based on a standard used by other Packard dealerships. Mason James Shirlaw set the limestone that is used extensively on the building's principal facade.

When Packard departed, Kalamazoo Buick Sales moved into the building. During the early 1930s, Kalamazoo Motor Coach Company was there, headed by former Mayor Alfred B. Connable. In 1938, Orrin B. "Pug" Hayes moved his own dealership here from East Water Street. Since then his son, Robert O. Hayes, Senior, and grandson Robert O. Hayes II, have succeeded him at the helm. "Pug" Hayes' great-granddaughter, Amy Krone, has also joined the family business, making it a four-generation operation.

The building design is an "Enframed Window Wall" that was popular between 1900 and 1950. The arrangement gives the facades of small and moderately-sized buildings a visual order, incorporating major glassed-in areas surrounded by simple, almost continual decorative elements. In this case, the facade is broken into two window walls divided by the central entry. Then, simple elements like the engaged Ionic columns are connected at the top by a reserved cornice, keeping the facade relatively flat in appearance. This allows the observer to focus on what is displayed behind the glass.

Builder Vander Horst's name plaque was re-set at the building's base in 1985 when architect Arno Yurk prepared a sensitive rehabilitation design. With this work completed, most of the building's best elements are still present. Exterior awnings now function in place of the earlier interior shades.

"When we did the showroom (in 1985), we had people stopping by all the time and telling us that they were related to the architect and the builder, or that one of their relatives had worked here."

Robert O. Hayes II

↑2001. The building's best elements were retained through a sensitive 1985 rehabilitation.

↑c1945. This distinguished-looking building is graced by engaged Ionic columns, a delicate dentiled cornice, and a classical pediment high over its central entry.

Hoben House, now the L. Lee Stryker Center
Kalamazoo College, Academy Street

Dr. Allan Hoben completed this classic, Colonial Revival home in 1925, financing the $16,500 project himself. Evidence exists to indicate that Kalamazoo architect Forrest Van Volkenburg designed it, and the building carries the major hallmarks of the style: a balanced facade with a centrally-located front entry accentuated with sidelights and a covered porch.

Kalamazoo College purchased the home from Dr. Hoben several years after its construction, and Hoben remained there until his retirement in 1935. He used the house primarily as his residence, but frequently entertained on behalf of the College: senior students had Sunday morning breakfast with the president, resident College trustees had a standing invitation to visit, and prominent College guests found overnight accommodations there.

In 1939, New York architect Aymar Embury designed an addition for the west end of the house. However, it was not constructed until after 1963, and when it happened, Embury's plans were scaled back. Dr. Weimer Hicks was the last head administrator to live in Hoben House, moving out shortly after he retired in 1972. For the next five or six years, the house was sometimes used to accommodate campus visitors.

Toward the end of the 1970s, the College found a new, full-time use for Hoben House. As a memorial to their son, L. Lee Stryker, Kalamazooans Dr. Homer and Mrs. Mary Jane Stryker established a memorial grant at the College to provide permanent funding for a business program that had located on campus in 1955. An affiliate of the Industrial Relations Center of the University of Chicago, it had matured and needed a home of its own. Hoben House was renovated in 1978 for that purpose, becoming home to the L. Lee Stryker Center. The Center now houses a number of programs including business development consulting and community enrichment courses.

In 1985, local architect Richard Schramm designed a large, two-story addition at the rear of the original building. Named after Kalamazooan Burton H. Upjohn, it provides additional classroom and meeting space.

> *"The house is designed to serve the College socially and educationally."*
>
> **Allan Hoben,** *former president, Kalamazoo College*

2001. The Stryker Center's 1985 Upjohn wing, right, is large, and is easily seen from the east or west, but barely visible from directly in front of the original house.

601 South Burdick Street

Almost everyone has heard the saying: "…history repeats itself…" and the story of this Tudor Revival "shop-house" is proof. Constructed by then-young contractor Henry Vander Horst as his office and family residence about 1909, the half-timbered stucco and brick building occupies a prominent corner on the southern border of Kalamazoo's central business district.

The building served the Vander Horst family as office and home until 1923. Its shop-house use continued several years later, when physician John B. Burns moved in with his own family, using some rooms for his practice and the others as residence. The Burnses remained until the middle 1950s. Following their departure, a succession of businesses and residential occupants moved in and out over the next three-and-a-half decades.

In the early 1990s, Josephine and Roy Ellison bought the property, and after significant rehabilitation, opened their restaurant, Josephine's European Dining, on the main floor. Imitating a pattern established by earlier occupants, they reserved the second floor for themselves. They chose this particular building for three reasons: it was well-priced, it was in the downtown area, and it provided them an opportunity to live and work on the same premises.

When the Ellisons bought the building, its most recent use had been as an office downstairs with two apartments above. "It was trashed," said Roy Ellison. "There had been cheap remodeling on top of cheap remodeling, and then to fix that, they did some more cheap remodeling."

The Ellisons spent an estimated $90,000 on the rehabilitation. They gutted the main floor, going down to the original plaster and in some places, the studs, eventually restoring much of the house's original floorplan. When they finished, two rooms were filled with tables and chairs for diners on the west and north sides, while the south and east sides held their compact commercial kitchen and restroom.

The Ellisons closed Josephine's in September 2000 to return to their northern Michigan home. At this writing, the building was recently sold. The new owner, Nicholas Fedesna, plans a tavern and grill for the main floor with living quarters upstairs.

2001. This Tudor Revival "shop-house" has been used almost continuously as a combination home-business since Henry Vander Horst built it around 1909.

> *"There were fake Styrofoam ceiling beams, Z-Brick, and paneling everywhere."*
>
> **Josephine Ellison,**
> *talking about the building, before its early 1990s rehabilitation*

Michigan Central Railroad Station, now the Intermodal Transportation Center
459 North Burdick Street

New York architect Cyrus Eidlitz designed this Richardsonian Romanesque station for the Michigan Central Railroad in 1887. The local contracting firm of Bush and Paterson built it. Eventually, the Michigan Central Railroad became part of the New York Central, still later Pennsylvania Central systems, and finally Amtrak in 1971.

In 1974, Kalamazoo was the first Michigan city to proceed with plans for an intermodal transportation center where trains, buses and taxis would be under one roof. After purchasing this station in 1975, the City received a grant from the Michigan Department of State Highways and Transportation to acquire more land, employ an architect, and pay for construction costs. Kingscott Associates, Inc. provided architectural services and the Miller-Davis Company served as contractor.

Work began during the winter of 1977. A major challenge was to repair the exterior red sandstone blocks, approximately two feet high, three feet long and eighteen inches deep. A mason at Miller-Davis developed a special tool that allowed workers to pull the sandstone blocks out, turn them over and then place them back, thereby exposing the inside face on the exterior. Indoors, new offices, ticket counters, restrooms and a restaurant were constructed.

The building reopened on November 21, 1977. One year later, the City received a grant to install a new heating and cooling system, add outdoor lighting and renovate the east end for rental space. Kingscott Associates, Inc. also carried out this project. In 1986, the City received an additional grant from the State of Michigan to replace the original slate roof with concrete tiles and renovate the copper gutters. Shannon-Kline, Inc. completed the work.

The building has basically remained the same since 1977, with the exception of the restaurant, which gave way to a public safety station. After so many decades, this station still provides a welcome site to the weary traveler returning home.

◪2000. Added in 1977 was a covering for bus patrons. The building is listed on the National Register of Historic Places and the Haymarket Local Historic District.

"Center Is Hailed As Prototype."

Kalamazoo Gazette *headline*
December 22, 1977

◪1890. The station has a distinctive Syrian arch that was a part of the porte-cochere at the main entrance. It also has a hipped roof with wide eaves and an eight-sided tower.

Seth Thomas Clock
200 Block, East Michigan Avenue

Over its more than 130 years, this clock has appeared in at least five different locations within Kalamazoo's central business district.

Seth Thomas began making clocks for Eli Terry's company about 1807, after completing his carpenter's apprenticeship. Over his career, his work became legendary. Thomas died in 1859, and by the time Kalamazoo's Seth Thomas clock was manufactured, his sons were operating the company.

When Kalamazoo's clock arrived about 1868, it was installed in the 200 block of what is now East Michigan Avenue. About 1890, retailer Sam Folz bought it and moved it a short distance to the front of his store, on the southeast corner of East Michigan Avenue and Portage Street. In 1924, jeweler Miron D. Ellis bought it and is believed to have moved it twice—once to a site one-half block west, between what was then First National and American National Banks, and then again in 1934, to the front of his own store in the 200 block of West Michigan Avenue.

1956. Jeweler Miron Ellis stands next to the Seth Thomas clock, outside his jewelry store in the 200 block of West Michigan Avenue.

The timekeeper moved again to the 200 block of the South Kalamazoo Mall in 1969, about the same time it was donated to the City of Kalamazoo. It stayed until the street reconstruction began on the mall in 1998. The clock turned up a year later in the City Yards, laying on its side, exposed to the elements and partially covered with snow.

The City, with encouragement from its Historic Preservation Commission, promised to resurrect the Seth Thomas clock. In 2000, Kalamazoo Custom Metal Works completed its restoration and the City reinstalled the clock that September near its original home, in the 200 block of East Michigan Avenue.

2001. The Seth Thomas clock in its current home, near its original location, was restored and re-erected in September 2000.

1969. The Seth Thomas clock, standing in its South Kalamazoo Mall location.

> *"It's not just an old-time clock, it's part of us and our community."*
>
> **Pamela Hall O'Connor,**
> *Chair of the Kalamazoo Historic Preservation Commission, talking with the* Kalamazoo Gazette *in September 2000*

527 West South Street, now Hospital Hospitality House

Although this house is no longer a single-family residence, it still maintains that feel in its current incarnation. Furniture merchant Edwin Carder built this classic Italianate in 1866. Dr. Edwin and Cynthia Van Deusen later bought the home when the Neoclassical style was popular, and added the paired-column portico.

The house had a series of owners and residents until 1985, when the Junior League of Kalamazoo purchased it for the Hospital Hospitality House. The home provides overnight accommodations for needy, out-of-town families of critically-ill or injured patients at Borgess Medical Center and Bronson Methodist Hospital.

The house was never divided into apartments, so little work was required to ready it for its new purpose. Minor alterations were carried out to meet City code, including the installation of smoke detectors and fire exits. Maintaining the interior woodwork in the house was a high priority.

The house provides beds for twenty-one people every night with five bedrooms upstairs and one down, created by using the parlor. An average stay is three to seven days. It is staffed at all times by full- and part-time employees and is governed by a board of directors. Most of the building's current income is used for basic maintenance. Financial support comes not only from the two hospitals, but also from churches, businesses, foundations and former guests, many of whom remember how staying in this house gave them such comfort during a very difficult time.

> *"They [the guests] feel as if they are enveloped in love and this house brings that out."*
>
> **Jean Forrest,** *executive director, Hospitality House*

2000. This house has the typical cubic shape of the Italianate style. The windows and porte-cochere are also hallmarks. The Neoclassical portico was added later.

KALAMAZOO: FOUND

Borgess Medical Center
1521 Gull Road

In 1917, the need for space propelled Borgess Hospital to build a new facility on Gull Road, northeast of their original downtown location. M.C.J. Billingham designed and Henry Vander Horst built the new four-story brick structure, and just ten years later, the Hospital began another two-year construction project. The original building, called the east wing, received a fifth floor, a gabled roof and a new layer of bricks on the facade in addition to a rear wing. Built to the west was a matching five-story structure called the west wing. A central main building connected these two. Also constructed at this time, just to the west of the hospital, was St. Camillus Nurses' Home. D.A. Bohlen and Son from Indianapolis chose Victorian Gothic for the entire complex. Kalamazoo's DeRight Brothers handled the construction.

Over the next sixty years, Borgess added new floors and new buildings. By far, the most extensive work occurred between 1984 and 1993.

Kingscott Associates and architect Nelson Nave directed the project. The north wing, originally built in 1971, received three more floors and a green metal roof complementing the older buildings. The rear of the 1929 east wing came down for the Lawrence Education Center, and the older buildings received new windows, eavestroughs and downspouts. D.C. Byers Company cleaned and repointed the brick, and cleaned and repaired the building's exterior stone.

2001. The new entrance was a major challenge and an accomplishment. The modern additions, like the copper canopy, complements the older elements.

The most complicated part of this project was rebuilding the entrance that was lowered to ground level. To stabilize its port-cochere, contractors sunk a series of piers underneath and added concrete on top. The new front entrance led to a new lobby, chapel, restrooms and gift shop.

Medical complexes are often in a continual state of planning and building. Borgess announced in 2001 a renovation and construction project that doubles the amount of money spent less than twenty years ago. Unfortunately, these plans call for the demolition, rather than the renovation, of St. Camillus, the former nurses' home built in 1927, for a 900-car parking ramp that will forever alter the unified front facade of the complex.

> *"Medical complexes are often in a continual state of planning and building."*
>
> Lynn Houghton

2001. The hospital complex blends well together. The east wing almost came down during the late 1980s renovation, but budget constraints prevented it.

491 West South Street

Like a cat, this house has had almost nine lives, and is the only building in the City of Kalamazoo that has garnered two awards for rehabilitation work.

Constructed as a single-family residence sometime during the 1860s or 1870s, this Italianate-styled building served as home for the Wyckoff family for more than twenty years. Joseph Wyckoff's granddaughters, Blanche and Evelyn Hull, were also descendants of Latham Hull, the first president of Kalamazoo's First National Bank, now National City Bank.

The house was converted to apartments after the Wyckoffs left and, during the 1920s, was converted again for a funeral home. Still later, it served as home to Kalamazoo Musical Instruments, and after that, an antiques shop and a bridal salon. The antiques shop's rehabilitation earned a 1982 award from the City of Kalamazoo's Historic Preservation Commission.

Greenleaf Capital, Inc. bought the building in 1998. The following year, Van Dam & Krusinga contractors carried out Kalamazoo architect Jon Stryker's rehabilitation design. Jeff Smith supervised the work.

The result is an eye-catching return to an exterior close to the building's original architectural roots. The contractors removed most earlier additions, including a full-width front porch, a series of rear additions and a porte-cochere. They repaired the foundation and straightened the structure after years of settling and compromising alterations.

Inside, they restored the main stairway, replaced missing moldings and scoured a local architectural salvage firm for replacement doors and other interior elements. Outside, they constructed a new front entry and a rear addition that accommodates an elevator, stairwell and additional office space.

2000. 491 West South Street, now home to Greenleaf Trust's Retirement Division.

In May 2000, Greenleaf Capital, Inc. received a merit award for its work on 491 West South Street from the City's Historic Preservation Commission. This was not the first time the company had been involved in award-winning rehabilitation work. When its Trust division needed a new home in the downtown area earlier in the 1990s, Greenleaf bought and renovated the building directly across the street at 490 West South Street. That earlier work also earned a rehabilitation merit award.

"…the owner and architect wanted to retain as much of the building's integrity as possible."

Dan Schefers, *partner, Van Dam & Krusinga, rehabilitation contractors*

Johnson House
211 Woodward Avenue

Dr. William Johnson had this classic Italianate house located in the Stuart neighborhood built for his family, that included stepdaughter Madeleon Stockwell who, in 1870, was the first woman to enter the University of Michigan. She returned to Kalamazoo in 1873 with her husband Charles Turner to live with her parents at this house. She remained here until her death in 1924, surviving both her parents and husband.

The house sold to architect M.C.J. Billingham and his family, who lived there for the next thirty-five years. Subsequently it was a fraternity, sorority and apartment house.

Current owners Angie and Herm Van Hamersveld have lived here for the past twenty years. The previous owner, Fred Royce, had rebuilt the front fence and installed a brick walkway. At this same time, the front foyer received a new marble floor and stenciling by artist Judith Ziobron.

The Van Hamersvelds maintained the apartments for a few years until recently when they returned it to a single-family residence. Almost all of their work was spent on the interior of the house. Five layers of linoleum were peeled away from the kitchen floor to reveal termite damaged floor joists. They were repaired and covered with a new wood floor. Removing carpet in the library and dining room exposed the original wood floors. Mrs. Van Hamersveld discovered a small section of a floor stencil in the library that she replicated around the perimeter. A life-long artist, many of her paintings decorate the dining room walls.

The house contains four rooms on the second floor and a third floor attic that leads to the cupola, one of only a few left in the City. It had to be completely rebuilt with new railings and a stairway, and is a very popular place for their grandchildren.

Living in an older house was the farthest thing from the Van Hamersvelds' minds. Mrs. Van Hamersveld finds it exciting that Madeleon Stockwell Turner lived there—not only a scholar and writer, but an artist as well. She finds it a real inspiration to live in Mrs. Turner's house.

1997. The house has all the traditional elements of an Italianate, including a low-pitched roof, cubic shape, paired cornice brackets, long narrow windows with decorative moldings and a cupola topped by a finial.

"This is a very livable house. It's a fun place to be."

Angie Van Hamersveld, *owner*

c1868. Dr. and Mrs. Johnson stand outside the house that has changed little in over 135 years.

Schmidt House
315 Creston Avenue

Julie and Peter Schmidt were looking for sidewalks, trees and a school within walking distance when buying their first house in 1983. The Westnedge Hill neighborhood had what they wanted and they purchased this 1916, two-bedroom bungalow. Initially the couple spent their time stripping woodwork and redecorating rooms. Mr. Schmidt, who received on-the-job training, also remodeled two bathrooms.

By the early 1990s, the couple, now with two children, required more space. Rather than sell and move to the suburbs, they decided to stay and enlarge the house. The Schmidts had experienced water damage near the shed dormers on the front and back. To correct this problem and add more room, they raised the roof, lifting its peak and creating additional second-floor space.

Work started in June 1994. Pulver Construction opened the rear of the house, lifted the roof, and extended the kitchen three feet. It took two weeks to frame the new structure. The former attic space on the second floor now had the height for the two new rooms, a bedroom and another bathroom.

At the same time, Mr. Schmidt removed the cedar shakes which covered the original clapboard and replaced about two-thirds of the old clapboard with new. He rebuilt the front porch opening it with a new railing, columns and wing walls. The Schmidts finished the exterior with a new paint color scheme.

Inside, Mr. Schmidt did almost all of the finishing work, including the drywall, flooring, plastering and much of the electrical and plumbing. Cabinet maker Dennis Dahl crafted cabinets, chests and bookcases. The owners finished the interior with bungalow-period colors, furnishings, light fixtures, carpeting and wall decorations, completing the work in December 1997.

There was a great deal of interest from neighbors during this project, and not coincidentally, several other homeowners have since decided to enlarge their houses rather than leave the neighborhood and the City.

2001. The remodeled house now has a gabled dormer at the front. Peter Schmidt constructed many of the eave brackets and had new half-round gutters installed.

"This wasn't what the house looked like originally, but it was appropriate."

Julie Schmidt, *owner*

1993. Originally, the house had a shed dormer at the front and back, and cedar shakes covered a combination of clapboard and stucco.

Grace Christian Reformed Church, now Diekema Hamann Architecture + Construction
612 South Park Street

Because its members left the First Christian Reformed Church, this building was named for the "Protesting" Christian Reformed congregation in 1926, on property formerly owned by Arthur Prentice. The *Kalamazoo Gazette* reported that contractors Schipper and Dykstra erected the building of buff brick and stone, using a plan by Dutch church-design specialists Daverman Associates of Grand Rapids. Reminiscent of Italian architect Andrea Palladio's sixteenth-century designs, the main facade features a raised, giant order of columns that support a full entablature and pediment, giving it a larger-than-life appearance.

The congregation met here until a fire ravaged the building's interior in December 1935. Like other past homeless Kalamazoo congregations, it took temporary refuge at People's Church. Less than a year and $75,000 later, it returned. The assembly later changed its name to Grace Christian, and remained here until 1988.

The building sat empty for more than a decade, despite several potential renovation plans, and demolition plans were rumored. In 1999 a local firm decided to investigate. Then housed in an office park in Portage, Diekema Hamann Architecture + Construction decided it needed a building that better expressed its identity. It took a look at the church, but was discouraged by the apparent renovation costs.

It soon learned, however, that as the building sat empty, the building had become part of the Vine Neighborhood Local Historic District, qualifying it for potential Federal and State rehabilitation tax credits. When the company calculated the figures again, coupled with assistance from the City's Economic Development Corporation, it decided to proceed.

2001. This Diekema Hamann Architecture + Construction renovation for its own offices not only saved a threatened building, but did it with great respect and considerable style.

In order to qualify for rehabilitation credits, Diekema Hamann's renovation plans required approval at the local, State and Federal levels, with the State and Federal level approvals regulating the interior as well as the exterior. The plans were approved with few changes. As a result, the building's exterior looks much the same, and the interior space still expresses the openness of a church sanctuary. Some interior fittings were removed, including a false ceiling and a balcony, and replaced with an imaginative but respectful interior plan that includes a bridge across the open space. The firm completed the renovation in the spring of 2001—an effort that truly "saved Grace."

"This project exemplifies how a challenging re-use project can be addressed through preservation, vision and creativity."

Robbert McKay, *historical architect, Michigan State Historic Preservation Office*

Kalamazoo Institute of Arts
314 South Park Street

The Kalamazoo Institute of Arts' early locations were only two blocks east of its present site. Beginning in 1924, the Institute enjoyed its first home in the then new YWCA at the east end of Bronson Park. It moved about a block south soon after, taking space in the Kalamazoo Public Library annex—the former Horace Peck home. Later, it moved right next door to the former Kauffer family home where it stayed for almost two decades.

In 1947, the Institute purchased, renovated and moved into the Charles Peck house in the 400 block of West South Street, that for some time had housed an American Legion post. Ten years later, the Institute received a grant for a new building from the Kalamazoo Foundation that included assistance from philanthropists Donald and Genevieve Gilmore and the Upjohn Estate. It acquired adjoining real estate on West South and Lovell Streets, took up temporary residence in a former church, demolished the buildings on the site, and began construction.

The Institute moved into a new, one-million-dollar, Skidmore, Owings and Merrill (SOM)-designed building in September 1961. SOM's parent firm, established in Chicago in 1939, is known world-wide for its work. Based on a sketch by "Modern" architecture pioneer Ludwig Miës van der Rohe, SOM's new Institute bore a general resemblance to Miës' and Lilly Reich's German Pavilion for Barcelona, Spain's, 1929 International Exhibition.

Constantly expanding its programs and collections, the Institute was cramped for space in the early 1990s and launched a search for a firm to redesign the interior of the 1961 building and create an addition. It selected Ann Beha Associates, a Boston firm that ultimately respected the original in its redesign. Contractors Kalleward-Bergerson completed the work in 1998, which provides an enlarged gift shop, improved gallery space, renovated classrooms, and a new Community Cultural Center auditorium. Welcoming students and visitors, a spectacular glass chandelier executed by glass artist Dale Chihuly hangs high inside the new two-story entry.

The renovated result is a symbiosis of "Modern" and contemporary designs.

↳2000. The clerestory windows of the new Kalamazoo Institute of Arts lobby add to the light entering from the north, window-wall entry. The original building is left of the entry.

> *"It's a very important building, a type that's not built anymore, so it was exciting to have an opportunity to work with it and respond to it."*
>
> **Ann Beha,** *Institute re-design architect, from an interview with* Encore *magazine, September 1997*

309 East Water Street, formerly the National Storage Building

This edifice, taking nearly an entire block with its oddly-shaped footprint, has been a part of downtown's east end landscape for almost 100 years. Shortly after the turn of the last century, builder Henry Vander Horst, tobacconist Edgar Raseman, Sr. and trucking company owner T. William Hastings formed the National Storage Company.

The Company finished the first building next to the rail line in 1912. Constructed of concrete with brick curtain walls, it provided about 30,000 square feet of space. Within the next decade, the owners contracted with builder Gerard Van Eck to construct an addition which mimicked the original's details on the west side, roughly doubling the square footage.

Starting with a horse-drawn truck, National Storage offered a host of services to its individual and business clients: garment and fur storage; climate-controlled piano storage; vault rental for personal belongings and household goods; packing and crating shipments; and moving services.

Over the next twenty-five years, National Storage re-invented itself. The company continued to offer storage services, but added sales of household furniture and appliances in what was then a very avant-garde venue: the "discount" house. Using the same methods as chain retailers of today, it bought railroad carloads of goods at a larger discount than those offered to traditional main street retailers. This in turn, allowed it to sell the goods for less. By 1938, its advertisements claimed it was "The Big Warehouse Furniture Store" and offered living, dining and bedroom suites, washing machines, electric ranges, carpets and rugs.

National Storage sold the building in the middle 1970s and moved its business to another part of town. Current owners John Garside and James Woodruff bought the building in 1978. Parts are still used for storage, but it also now houses offices and a commercial kitchen. In 1999, the building's exterior received a facelift with the assistance of Kalamazoo's Downtown Development Authority's Building Revitalization Program. The building's masonry was cleaned, repaired, and re-pointed, allowing it to make a positive contribution to the area's renaissance.

2001. At almost 100 years old, and originally constructed for the National Storage Company, 309 East Water Street towers above other buildings in downtown's east end.

*We Ship—
We Store—
We Pack—
We Sell New
Furniture*

National Storage Company advertisement, from 1937 Kalamazoo Gazette

Doyle House
725 West Kalamazoo Avenue

It is easy to drive down Kalamazoo Avenue and completely miss this Queen Anne brick house that sits on the south side east of Elm Street in the Stuart Historic District. Local stone mason and builder James Doyle completed it in 1889. Doyle and his family only lived here for eight years. Subsequently, the home had several other residents. It became a two-unit apartment around 1915 and remained that way for nearly seventy-five years.

The present owners, Jim Cavender and Steve Sattem, purchased the property in 1979. For the next ten years they continued to rent the upstairs apartment for income while living downstairs. Currently, it is once again a single-family home.

One of the initial house projects was to replace the furnace. The owners have had others do the major structural work, for example in the kitchen and bathrooms, while they have focused their efforts on decorating. At first Cavender and Sattem chose to paint the walls, but later wallpapered each room. The white pine floors traditionally would have been carpeted, but they pulled up several layers of carpet before installing a more appropriate pattern. Much of the oak and pine woodwork was intact, requiring only varnish stripping.

Traffic noise from Kalamazoo Avenue is muffled by the twofold brick construction of the house and double storm windows, also installed for energy conservation. Brick homes and buildings of Chicago brick, including this one, were meant to be painted due to the bricks' porous nature. When the owners bought the house, the exterior was fire engine red with silver and black trim. They developed a more muted color scheme of darker reds and browns.

Wishing to improve the vicinity around them led Cavender and Sattem to purchase fourteen additional houses and one apartment building. Even though their main motivation for doing this has been for investment purposes, they have at the same time improved their neighborhood.

"His [Doyle's] residence… is built in the latest style of architecture and furnished and finished in a manner which indicates the culture and good taste of its inmates."

Portrait and Biographical Record of Kalamazoo, Allegan and Van Buren Counties, Michigan, *1892*

2001. The Doyle House has several typical Queen Anne elements, including an asymmetrical shape, side tower, gabled roof and fish-scale shingles. The finial is a replica of the original, still in owners' possession.

Appeldoorn House
532 Village Street

Situated on a double lot on the north side of Village Street just past South Westnedge Avenue in the Vine neighborhood, this house attracts a great deal of attention for its unique shape and very prominent roofline. Peter B. Appeldoorn, Jr., owner of a company that manufactured novelties, completed the house in 1895. It also became a long-time home for the Meinert family.

Records indicate that the wooden house is a mail-order catalog home from Tennessee's George F. Barber and Company. It is a simple Queen Anne with a gabled roof, small porches, dormers and fish-scale shingles. Its size and massing indicate some influence from the emerging bungalow style.

John Murphy and Pegg Osowski purchased the home in 1992. They wanted to live in the City and be close to where Osowski worked. Their initial task was to replace the leaking roof and repair both the chimney and foundation. Annette Conti had developed the exterior color scheme several years earlier, before the owners took possession of the structure.

Years ago, a small one-bedroom apartment had been created on the first floor of the house. Murphy and Osowski decided to dismantle it to create more living space. The inside of the house is very simple with fir woodwork throughout. The upstairs remained unfinished until the Meinerts moved in during the early 1940s. Murphy, who did almost all the recent work at the house himself except for the roof, created an upstairs bathroom and laundry room. The owners repainted and recarpeted nearly all the rooms.

Remodeling the kitchen presented a challenge because it has very little solid wall space. Murphy also remodeled the bathrooms downstairs. Overall, the house is quite open, with doorways and windows all around.

2001. Each side of this house presents the viewer with a different image.

The couple has an extensive back yard, much larger than normal for the Vine neighborhood. They have spent a great deal of time landscaping, and their advice to new property owners is not to dig anything up until spring.

Murphy and Osowski subsequently purchased two additional properties next door and across the street, preserving their investment and helping maintain the quality of the neighborhood.

> *"It was the outside [of the house] that attracted us the most."*
>
> John Murphy, *owner*

Henderson Castle
100 Monroe Street

Regalia manufacturer Frank Henderson did not set out in 1890 to build a house that would forever be known in Kalamazoo as "The Castle." He hired Milwaukee architect Charles A. Gombert to design a home for him and his family, building it on the highest point in Henderson's new development on the west side of the City. It took five years and $72,000 to complete the twenty-five-room sandstone and brick Queen Anne structure. The exterior is decorated with a multitude of gables, dormers, windows, finials, turrets and a three-story tower. Inside there is a variety of woodwork including mahogany, birch, bird's-eye maple, oak and sycamore, and a stunning ten-foot-square stained glass window at the front stairway designed for the building by Third Street Studio of Cincinnati.

The house remained a single-family home until 1945 when it was divided up into five apartments. In 1957, the property became a potential site for the Kalamazoo Institute of Arts, but instead came under the ownership of Kalamazoo College who continued to rent the apartments until 1975. Jess and Jane Walker purchased the house that year, converting it back into a single-family home.

The present owner, Fred Royce, purchased the Castle in 1981. Over the last twenty years, he has completed an endless amount of work. The woodwork has been stripped, walls replastered, the plumbing and electrical systems repaired,

↗2000. It is not known exactly when this house became known as a "castle," obviously aided by its commanding location atop West Main Hill.

chimneys rebuilt, and new light fixtures installed. Royce brought back the original exterior colors. Artist Judith Ziobron stenciled the second-floor walls. Royce now has a regular crew of craftspeople working on the house including full-time carpenter, Leonard Yonkman, who has been with him for twelve years.

Royce always has maintained his law office in the home and opened the Henderson Castle as an eight-room bed and breakfast establishment in 2001.

↖1894. This photo, taken during the home's construction when it was one of the few buildings around; note the window glass in Henderson Castle was not yet installed.

> *"What you do, you try to do right so you're not going to be back in 100 years. I don't want in fifty years to be mad that I saved a nickel."*
>
> **Fred Royce,**
> Kalamazoo Gazette
> *September 26, 1990*

Bronson Park
Bounded by Academy, Rose, South and Park Streets

The scene of political speeches and rallies, archaeological excavations, symphony performances, and itself the front yard of some of Kalamazoo's early residences, Bronson Park is as old as the community, about 170 years.

Two years after Village founder Titus Bronson arrived in 1829, he and partner Stephen Richardson agreed to set aside four squares of land for public use as an inducement to locate the county seat here. Two of these squares were first used for a jail and an academy. In the middle nineteenth century, those squares were vacated and ownership conveyed to the County, who subsequently gave the Village a ten-year lease. The Village renewed the lease in 1864 for a public park, this time for 99 years.

Since then, the park has experienced development and redevelopment. From 1864 to 1876, it was leveled, fenced, and planted with trees. In 1879, the Village implemented landscape designer Adam Oliver's park plan, including lighting, drinking fountains and the park's first display fountain. Over the next two decades, workers completed perimeter sidewalks, added seating, and graveled the interior walkways.

A band pavilion went up in 1899, and down again in 1908. Workers planted more trees, again added seating, and stocked the fountain basin with fish. In 1926, a new fountain replaced the original, and just years later, hard-surface walks and curbs appeared.

Throughout its first century and since, this place has fulfilled the role as the heart of the community. In 1856, Abraham Lincoln spoke here, followed by many others. And when, on different occasions in the 1960s, brothers Robert and John Kennedy spoke from the County Courthouse and City Hall steps, Bronson Park held the throngs who gathered.

The last sixty years have witnessed the park's greatest changes, the seeds of which were sown in 1936, with a fountain design competition held by the Kalamazoo Business and Professional Women's Club. University of Illinois Art Instructor Marceline Gougler developed the winning design in artist Alfonso Iannelli's Chicago workshop. Iannelli later visited Kalamazoo to consult on the design, and was ultimately paid for creating yet another new design, his own this time— the *Fountain of the Pioneers*.

The concrete and aggregate work, whose complete footprint is comprised of two matching pools in the east and west park center, is geometric in massing and line, and recounts an important event. Exactly 100 years before its construction, Native Americans were relocated from Kalamazoo to land in the west.

The *Fountain* itself stands in the east pool, its major sculptural elements consisting of a pair of figures and stylized landscape. A pioneer stands tall, gun raised, facing west. Face pressed into the pioneer's chest, a Native American resists, attempting to stand his ground. The west pool, with the same footprint as the east, brings balance to the overall design. Construction was

2001. This photograph shows the present-day park layout and its major components: the east pool and the *Fountain of the Pioneers*, the west pool with bronze sculpture, and the performance stage.

c1940. This post-construction image from the City's collection of historical photographs shows the *Fountain of the Pioneers* and is marked "Todd & Hall Syndicate Press, Kalamazoo, Mich."

KALAMAZOO: LOST & FOUND

> "The tower of the fountain showed, in stylized form, the pioneers' advance and the Indians' stalwart resistance."
>
> Sharon Rubin Goldman, *author,*
> *describing the* Fountain of the Pioneers *design*

c1939. Construction of the *Fountain of the Pioneers,* designed by artist Alfonso Iannelli and financed by the Works Progress Administration (WPA).

accompanied by a complete park redesign, financed by America's Depression-era Federal Works Progress Administration.

In 1976, the west pool became home to a group of bronze sculpture—a bicentennial gift from members of the Kalamazoo religious community and individuals. Inspired by the biblical verse: "When justice and mercy prevail, children may safely play," local sculptor Kirk Newman created cavorting, life-sized children, each upon a pedestal, so they rise above water's surface.

In 1998, the Kalamazoo Rotary Club held another design competition, this time for a performance stage at the park's west end. They selected architects Eckert Wordell's design, which incorporates materials and themes from its environment, including the rear support, whose geometric shape mimics the pioneer and Native American figures from the *Fountain*.

Contractor Miller-Davis Company completed the stage in 1999—work that was accompanied by new park walkways, seating and lighting. The *Fountain of the Pioneers* is set to be restored in 2002.

With the longest history of any "place" in the area, its famous and more mundane events, and its well-conceived public art and architecture, it is no surprise that Bronson Park, the center of Kalamazoo's center, continues as the heart of the community.

2001. The performance stage at the park's west end takes it materials and themes from the surrounding architectural environment.

American National Bank and Trust, now Fifth Third Bank
136 East Michigan Avenue

In 1833, Kalamazoo settler Theodore P. Sheldon founded a small loan business. Almost 100 years later in 1928, its successor, Kalamazoo Trust and Savings Bank, announced that they would soon build a new home on East Michigan Avenue at a cost of $1,250,000.

Chicago architects Weary & Alford offered evidence of their cutting edge Art Deco design in a *Kalamazoo Gazette* article: "We have designed this building in the soaring perpendicular style of architecture modern. There will not be one vestige of the time-honored Classic or Renaissance architecture..." In this declaration, they restated Art Deco design principles for the populace — to totally abandon the "Revival" styles of the previous decades.

The architects employed the full design repertoire, from the geometric, stylized floral medallions that move across the building's facade, to the colossal arched entry, to the ziggurat-styled uppermost floors that accentuate the building's upward momentum.

Contractor Henry Vander Horst completed the foundation, and O.F. Miller carried out the above-ground work in black granite, Indiana limestone, cast lead and steel. Otto Stauffenberg, a Hamburg, Germany-to-Chicago émigré, spent 600 hours hand-painting the bank lobby's vaulted ceiling.

Banking offices and general purpose floors were fitted with marble and terrazzo, and trimmed with black walnut. Floors eight, nine and ten were readied for medical use, providing tenants with compressed air, gas, and specialized electrical service for medical equipment.

A list of the building's occupants in 1931 indicates a healthy tenancy. Approximately thirty physicians and dentists, ten insurance companies, attorneys, and a variety of small businesses were in residence, including an optician, a jeweler, the Fuller Brush Company, and private offices for Kalamazooans Stephen Monroe, Mayor Rudolf Light, Chapin Dewing and Lewis Kirby.

Since then, occupants have come and gone, and the building's interior has changed to suit them. However, the exterior has remained essentially the same except for the additions of a front canopy and rear elevator. In early 1985, American National commissioned a restoration of the bank lobby ceiling. The following year, American National merged with Old Kent Bank. In 2001, Old Kent merged with Cincinnati's Fifth Third Bank.

The U.S. Department of Interior has determined the building eligible for the National Register of Historic Places.

> c1942. American National Bank and Trust Company Building, over ten years after its construction.

> 1997. Old Kent Bank-Southwest merged with Fifth Third Bank in 2001.

"It is at once a fine banking house and office building combined..."

Kalamazoo Gazette
May 7, 1930

Brown-Clapp House
711 West Lovell Street

For over 120 years, this house, built between 1867 and 1868, sat on the north side of the 400 block of West Lovell Street at the intersection of Potter Street between South Westnedge Avenue and South Park Street. Over the years, a series of middle-class residents lived here. It later was divided into apartments upstairs and retail space below.

Built originally as an Italianate with a hipped roof, geometric shape and long narrow windows, it burned in the 1890s. This led to its remodeling as a modified Queen Anne with a front picture window, gabled roof, decorative shingles and a large wrap-around porch.

In 1987, local preservationists Annette Conti and Lou Conti of Conti Building and Restoration, learned of plans to demolish the structure to make room for a series of parking garages directly behind the Marlborough building. The Contis decided to attempt something that had not been done in Kalamazoo for over twenty-five years, namely to move the structure. They were able to purchase a piece of vacant property next to another house they owned only three blocks away.

The Contis received a tremendous amount of cooperation from the City of Kalamazoo. When the previous house on the new site burned, the owners simply had all the debris, furniture and other items thrown into the basement and covered with the cheapest fill possible. The problem the Contis encountered excavating the new basement resulted in a new City ordinance regarding the placement of debris and the type of fill allowed.

In May 1987, amidst much fanfare and publicity, Dietz Movers from Muskegon relocated the house three blocks west on West Lovell Street. Eventually the Contis created three apartments and rebuilt the wrap-around porch. Mr. Conti was able to use many pieces he had salvaged from other structures. Having a sewer and water connection at the new site helped tremendously.

After the completion of the work, the Contis held an open house that attracted nearly a thousand people, who saw that there are alternatives to demolition. Since 1987, nine other houses have been moved within the City of Kalamazoo.

"It opened up the possibility that there are different ways of saving places.... This event was an absolute mind-opener for historic preservation."

Lou Conti

2000. The Brown-Clapp House, a modified Queen Anne, is an example of both adaptive use and infill.

Washington Square Branch, Kalamazoo Public Library
1244 Portage Street

Libraries are magical places, and the architects who design them want to make sure they use an appropriate style. Billingham and Cobb succeeded when they chose Tudor Revival for this building completed in 1927. The Kalamazoo Public Library had maintained a branch in the Edison neighborhood since 1910 and, after using several other locations, wanted a building of its own.

The building contains many typical Tudor Revival elements, including a steeply-pitched roof with side and front gables, a distinctive arched entryway, a prominent chimney, a front bay, and tall, narrow multi-paned windows set in stone. The rooms are decorated with oak woodwork, plastered ceilings and stone fireplaces. O. F. Miller Company built the structure.

A leaking roof led to its replacement in 1994 with asphalt shingles. Building Restoration Inc. also rebuilt the dormers and eaves. Two years later, the original metal casement windows were replaced with aluminum models with divided lights. Also, the Library solved a continual flooding problem by re-grading the land around the building and adding a pump.

By far the most extensive work done to the interior of the building took place during the winter and spring of 1997, under the direction of the architectural firm David Milling & Associates. Kalleward-Bergerson was the contractor. The work included cleaning woodwork, painting the ceiling, installing a lift to the basement, and new carpeting, furniture, lighting and shelving. New Bradbury and Bradbury wallpaper borders were added to all three rooms. Artist Michael Hayden designed new luminous shades for the fifty-two original wrought iron light fixtures fashioned by Billingham and Cobb.

The building has a long list of loyal patrons who are thrilled with the commitment the Kalamazoo Public Library has made to this building. The work completed has assured many that the Library will be around for a long time, offering its magic to generations of readers to come.

> *"Builders in Kalamazoo generally agree that the board of education got its money's worth in good taste in the erection of the Washington Square Library..."*
>
> Kalamazoo Gazette
> *November 19, 1927*

2000. Each side of the building contains a large prominent window, like this one, at right.

Stetson Chapel
Kalamazoo College, Academy Street

Former Chapel Dean Robert Dewey wrote: "The chapel is a stately building...calling for the best from its occupants, whether speakers, musicians, or a congregation...." He was right—this building seems to summon a sensibility from people that they usually hold in reserve.

At their semi-annual meeting in 1928, Kalamazoo College trustees acted on president Dr. Allan Hoben's dream for a chapel building. They also named it: "All who have known Dr. Stetson...will agree that this crowning feature of our quadrangle should be named for him." Dr. Herbert Lee Stetson had served the College for almost 30 years as a faculty member and administrator.

New York architect Aymar Embury II designed the Chapel. Preliminary drawings were complete when Hoben wrote to Embury on December 16, 1930, and asked: "With building costs being as they now are, don't you think that we could get an adequate chapel for $100,000?" In his return letter, Embury agreed. Then he addressed what he felt was a critical interior element: "...I wish you would give this careful consideration, and that is the row of columns on each side of the side aisle.... This will improve the appearance of the building tremendously, decrease the construction cost, permit added height in the center of the building and in every way give it a better architectural effect."

Hoben apparently concurred. Those columns truly enhance the Chapel's soaring interior space and contribute to the overall design that Embury dubbed "New England Meeting House." Outside, on its principal facade, six colossal Ionic columns support a dentiled pediment above. Below, its entry doors are capped with fanlights. Contractor O.F. Miller carried out Embury's design in brick and Indiana limestone. Completed in 1932, and referred to as the "Soul of the Campus," the Chapel has witnessed thousands of College and community ceremonies and events beyond its regular services, including theater, weddings, music, and addresses by local and world-wide scholars, dignitaries, celebrities and others.

Despite the inclusion of a tower in the Chapel's construction, bells did not ring there until 1984. Cast at the Whitechapel Bell Foundry in London, the bells' installation preceded an extensive 1986–1987 rehabilitation of the entire building, thereby guaranteeing Stetson Chapel a place in the College's future, and in the hearts and minds of all who visit.

> *"I can hear the echo of important voices...Alistair Cooke of the BBC...composer Aaron Copeland...novelist James Baldwin..."*
>
> **Dr. Lloyd Averill,** *dean (1954–1967), Stetson Chapel, remembering past Chapel events*

◄ July 1932. Stetson Chapel just after construction.

◄ 2000. Called the "Soul of the Campus," Stetson Chapel was listed on the National Register of Historic Places in 1982.

The Henry Gilbert House, now Scott Tribby Violins
415 West Lovell Street

This petite Queen Anne house has delighted passersby for well over a century. Its sophisticated placement of period elements perfectly suits its scale and location just three blocks west of the central business district. The arrangement of its gables and corbelled chimney bring balance to its roofline, while the porch balances the cut-away half of the facade, underneath the largest gable.

Sunbursts in the front gables, zig-zag and angular siding, and bull's-eye corner block gable trim combine to reward this building's serious observers. Pioneer and former *Kalamazoo Gazette* publisher and furniture manufacturer Henry Gilbert and his family must have been pleased to move here in 1888. Gilbert and his second wife, Myra, finished their lives in the home as well, dying on the same day in 1897.

Other well-known Kalamazooans also called this house home. Dimmen den Bleyker, son of another pioneer, Paulus den Bleyker, took up residence shortly after the Gilberts died. William Shakespeare, Jr. followed den Bleyker, remaining until mid-century.

Kalamazoo milliner Ethol Hotelling bought the house from Shakespeare in the late 1940s, remodeled its interior, and moved her business there from South Burdick Street. Over the next quarter century, the business grew to include accessories and women's wear. Hotelling closed her business when she retired, and a hair salon and offices for interior designer Armond Travis moved into the space.

An artist in his own right, the house's present owner has a great appreciation for the craftsmanship employed in the building's construction. Violin maker Scott Tribby made no major structural changes to the home, that he occupied with his family for a period after he opened his business there. Tribby returned the second floor to family use, and "reconverted" the main floor kitchen and bathroom to their original uses.

↰2000. The 119-year-old Queen Anne styled Gilbert House offers visual surprises for serious spectators.

Tribby now spends his days there, creating his own small works of art. "Looking at this beautiful building..." he says, "...people were more concerned with artistry, geometry and proportion then... it's an inspiring place."

The Gilbert House was named to the National Register of Historic Places in 1983.

> *"The atmosphere inspires my work."*
>
> **Scott Tribby,** *violin maker and current Gilbert House owner*

Salvation Army, now Scott, Doerschler, Messner and Gauntlett
244 North Rose Street

Standing like a fortress on the southeast corner of North Rose and Eleanor Streets in Arcadia Commons, this English Tudor Revival building was the Kalamazoo headquarters for the Salvation Army between 1927 and 1991. Kalamazoo architect Ernest Batterson executed the design, and local company George Lather & Sons constructed the building. It became known as the Citadel, which reflected the organization's military emphasis.

In the early 1990s, the Salvation Partners purchased the building to house Scott, Doerschler, Messner and Gauntlett, a long-time local investment, insurance and financial planning firm. Work began on the structure in June 1992. Kingscott Associates, Inc. of Kalamazoo oversaw the general design work with Superior Building Company as the contractor. In addition, Kingscott hired architect Michael J. Dunn to work on the exterior.

As the building next door came down, the parties involved with this project discovered, much to their surprise, that the two buildings shared a wall. The first step was to brace the building and construct a new south wall. The architect was able to match the brick and integrate key elements like brick pilasters, the position of the windows and the crenelations at the top. Poor condition made window replacement necessary, and new metal windows with true divided lights took their place. The contractor replaced the roof and front door, needing to comply with new rules concerning barrier-free access.

The designers totally gutted the interior to create three floors of office space within the two-story building. Taking down the back wall exposed a large, full-height window in the sanctuary that had been blocked for years. Including it in the design added a tremendous amount of light to the overall space. All three floors have offices situated around the perimeter and meeting space in the center, referred to as a "town-square effect." Deep jewel tones of burgundy and green color the interior to match the windows.

Completed in February 1993, just eight months after the work began, the building is not only home for Scott, Doerschler, Messner and Gauntlett, but also Parish Associates and Owen Group, Ltd.

♢ 2001. The Salvation Partners received an Award of Merit from the Kalamazoo Historic Preservation Commission for its work on this structure. The building is an example of adaptive use.

> *"The real challenge was not to come up with something that would duplicate the historic facility, but to find something compatible and in harmony."*
>
> **Michael J. Dunn,** *architect*

747 Wheaton Avenue

Benjamin Roe and his wife, Jeannie, are believed to have been this building's first occupants, beginning around 1883. A mason by trade, Benjamin Roe had emigrated from England in 1848. Local buildings that benefited from his craft include the former Post Office Building at West South and South Burdick Streets, the community's first purpose-built public library on West South Street, the former Academy of Music on South Rose Street, the extant Water Tower on the State Hospital grounds on Oakland Drive, and a number of railroad depots in southwest and south central Michigan.

This is undoubtedly a mason's house. Built of brick with a cut stone foundation, its shape is Queen Anne, with asymmetrical facades and an irregular, steeply-pitched roof with ornamented gables. However, its windows and hoods are from the earlier Italianate period. Tall and narrow, they are sometimes presented in groups and crowned with stone lintels. Given the time during which the house was built, at the end of one clearly-defined period and the beginning of the next, it is a visually satisfying marriage of the best elements of each.

Between its construction and the late 1980s, this house was home to a number of long-term residents. Records indicate that unrelated adults lived there beginning about 1910, and continued to do so for the better part of the next seven decades. Just before 1990, Tim and Janine Meulenberg moved in and began the home's rehabilitation, reversing many earlier "remodels."

Tim Meulenberg had inspected the building well before they bought it, and commented that it had been built: "...to stay there, and to move a little bit...with expansion in the summer.... Somebody who knew exactly what they were doing built that house." Working through a long interior project list, the Meulenbergs cleaned and refinished walls, replicated and replaced moldings, repaired ceilings, secured sagging plaster medallions, and updated the kitchen and bathrooms for contemporary use. Outside, they replaced front and side porch decking, repaired the foundation and repointed the brick.

The Meulenbergs received a 1995 Merit Award from the Kalamazoo Historic Preservation Commission for their rehabilitation work. Located within the Vine Neighborhood Local Historic District and a National Register Historic District, the house now has a new owner.

2000. 747 Wheaton Avenue offers elements of two period styles in the Vine Historic District.

"I had never seen this design before, I felt that the lines and designs were pretty well defined..."

Tim Meulenberg, *former owner*

Central Corners
Southwest Corner, West Vine Street and South Westnedge Avenue

Thousands of people pass by this intersection daily, many not realizing that a little over ten years ago these buildings were vacant and boarded up. It took the efforts of one community organization along with assistance from several others to bring this corner back to life.

The buildings that comprise Central Corners were constructed for the most part during the years 1922, 1926 and 1935. As with most neighborhood business districts, a variety of establishments filled the spaces including a drug store, bakery, barbershop, grocery store, dry cleaners, shoe repair and meat market. The upstairs space contained several apartments.

By the middle 1980s, only Jon's Barbershop at 507 West Vine Street remained. All other spaces were vacant. Private developers were not able to market the property. In 1991, Kalamazoo Neighborhood Housing Services (KNHS), a nonprofit community revitalization organization, stepped in and acquired the structures. This was the first time the organization ventured into developing commercial property, having concentrated previously on residential.

KNHS was able to raise funds from conventional lenders, community foundations and the City of Kalamazoo. This also became its first historic preservation tax credit project as the buildings are a part of the Vine Local Historic District.

The agency hired the local architectural firm of Eckert Wordell and as contractors, The CSM Group. Local contractor and neighborhood resident Kevin McCall assisted KNHS with the project.

A building on the east side that housed a grocery store was demolished to open up space, increase off-street parking and eliminate unnecessary square footage.

The building received a new roof, several new mechanical systems and new windows. Exterior brick was cleaned and repointed. All of the seven, second-floor apartments were gutted and rehabilitated, and they continue to be occupied. The work took about a year to complete.

With the exception of Klein's Bagels and the present-day Jim's Barbershop, the rest of the commercial space in these buildings is filled by nonprofit community groups, many of which service the neighborhood, including the Vine Neighborhood Association and Kalamazoo Neighborhood Housing Services. This rehabilitation has prompted a renaissance around this intersection with restaurants and other establishments moving here, adding vitality to the area.

2001. These buildings are very simple examples of both One-Part and Two-Part Commercial blocks. The only decorative element on the second story is the tile work near the cornice.

> *"We [the neighborhood] wouldn't have had the success elsewhere in the neighborhood if we hadn't revitalized that corner."*
>
> **Kevin McCall,** *Vine neighborhood resident*

Portage Street Fire Station
1249 Portage Street

Built in 1900, this building served Kalamazoo as Fire Station House No. 2 for over fifty years. Local architect Robert Gallup borrowed elements from two different architectural styles for this building. The masonry moldings over the windows and the two arched entrances with keystones are typical of Richardsonian Romanesque, whereas the fanlight windows are representative of the Colonial Revival style.

The building became a fruit market and general store between 1956 and 1958. For the next twenty years, until 1978, it housed a laundromat. Just one year earlier, the City had condemned the structure because of its condition. After years of raze orders and extensions, the City Commission finally ordered the building's demolition in November 1982.

Local contractor Donald Verbecke of Kal-West Contracting stepped in and bought the building just before the wrecking crew arrived. He wanted to renovate the space for offices and storage. Verbecke had developed a continuing interest in acquiring structures that needed recovery and this one did not disappoint him.

Displacing not only three hundred live pigeons that were living in the building, but also the debris they left behind, was a major challenge. It took close to a year to remove all the washers, dryers and tanks still in place from the laundromat days, and to replace close to 80 percent of the rotten tongue-and-groove maple floor. Verbecke also removed, stripped and refinished all the woodwork on the second floor where the firemen had slept.

The second story is supported by a unique design of cables, still in place, suspended from the attic that left the first floor column-free, allowing the fire equipment to come and go easily. The exterior bricks were cleaned, the fake facade removed, and the roof received new asphalt shingles.

Originally, Kal-West Contracting had an office on the first floor and an architectural firm rented the second. Currently, the building houses Carr-Ciadella Photography, Magic Maid and two large studio apartments. The Portage Street Fire Station, an example of adaptive use, is on the National Register of Historic Places, and received an Award of Merit from the Kalamazoo Historic Preservation Commission in 1984.

> *"Every time I drive by I like to look at it [the building]."*
> **Donald Verbecke,** *owner*

1909. The fire station's modest size and scale fit in well with the growing business district around it.

2000. The original front doors could not be replicated, but were replaced with ones that can open.

Westnedge Hill Apartments
2000 Block, South Westnedge Avenue

The *Kalamazoo Gazette* wrote in May 1885: "Apartment Houses are becoming very popular in Kalamazoo… A suite of rooms sufficient for an ordinary family can be rented… for from $8 to $15 a month." Apartment living has remained popular in Kalamazoo ever since, although rents increased substantially between 1885 and 1948, the year Kalamazoo's first apartment "complex" was begun on the north slope of Westnedge Hill.

In 1948, the City of Kalamazoo issued construction permits totalling nearly $3 million, with the $200,000 Westnedge Hill Apartments project among them. Situated on a large, partially-wooded hillside, the project was the brainchild of several local businessmen, including attorneys Garrett Troff and Gerald McKessy, developer Alfred DeBoer and others. Its success was as good as guaranteed—with World War II veterans coming home and settling in, the nation experienced an unprecedented need for housing.

Kalamazoo architect William Stone designed the complex in four sets of sixteen connected buildings. By shaping the sets in large "H" and "U" patterns, and connecting some at their corners, Stone provided living spaces with daylight on a minimum of two, and often three sides—a rare commodity in apartment living. He dressed the buildings in stucco and gave them simple, graceful details including the wrought-iron elements that support and surround the covered entries.

The one- and two-bedroom apartments range in size from about 750 to 900 square feet. Grand Rapids engineer Vernon Dean prepared some of the specifications, including the radiant, in-the-floor heating system that is still in use today. Local builder and partner Alfred Newbold handled the construction.

The Federal Housing Administration insured the mortgage, and required that rents for the 72 units be frozen at specific levels until the mortgage was paid, thus keeping them affordable for tenants.

Ross Stancati, one partner in the company that now owns the apartments, says that after five decades, the central location remains the biggest factor in the buildings' average 99 percent occupancy rate. The location is convenient, but it is also picturesque. Indeed, these and the pleasing design elements likely combine to draw new dwellers and keep the old—approximately ten of the complex's original, 1950s-era tenants still live here.

2001. This Westnedge Hill Apartment building is one of several on South Westnedge Avenue. There are three other sets of connected buildings in the City's first apartment "complex."

"I like my apartment a lot—with its layout, hardwood floors and plaster walls."

Westnedge Hill Apartment resident

Edison Neighborhood

Of the twenty-two neighborhoods in Kalamazoo, Edison, on the southeast side, has one of the most interesting histories. In the 1830s, Portage Avenue extended from downtown Kalamazoo to the south. In 1858, the National Driving Park opened on 64 acres at the intersection of Portage Avenue and Washington Street and for the next thirty-five years it was the site for horse races, fairs and circuses. Later, several paper companies erected mills here and their workers purchased homes nearby. A number of families in the area also kept celery farms adjacent to their homes.

Three years after the National Driving Park closed in 1893, local developer Charles Hays purchased the land and subdivided it into lots. For the next thirty-five years, Hays platted streets, alleys and boulevards, and soon they began to fill with many different styled houses. The Edison neighborhood grew tremendously between 1900 and 1930, alongside a nearby business district called Washington Square.

Currently, Edison is the largest neighborhood in Kalamazoo, with over 3,000 residential and

2001. In the Sears catalogs from 1921 through 1929, this bungalow at 1502 Egleston Avenue is referred to as the "Walton."

124 commercial buildings. The 1990 Federal census reported that over half of the houses are owner occupied, and their residents enjoy many traditional neighborhood amenities. These include the Washington Square branch of the Kalamazoo Public Library, Washington Writer's Academy, Edison Environmental Science Academy, St. Joseph Catholic School, the Bank Street Farmer's Market, Upjohn Park, and several churches and manufacturers.

Nearly every type of early 20th century architectural style is represented in Edison. The bungalow at 1502 Egleston Avenue is a Sears catalog house built in 1921. It has a long, low roof and a wraparound front porch with wooden piers and notched brackets. Egleston is one of Edison's three boulevards, along with Lane and Lay.

The Tudor Revival house at 728 Clinton Street, built in 1916, contains several characteristics found in this style including stucco cladding, defining half-timbering, and double-hung

2001. The cross-gambrel roof makes this Tudor Revival at 728 Clinton Street unique.

KALAMAZOO: LOST & FOUND

windows with small panes at the top. Atypical is the front porch and the cross-gambrel roof.

There are several duplexes in the Edison neighborhood including one completed in 1921, at 1903 and 1905 Elgin Street in the Linden Park development on the west side of Portage Street. Charles Hays' Kalamazoo Land Company built fifty-six houses on four square

◨2001. This duplex at 1903 and 1905 Elgin Street at one time had matching side arches and porches. One has been enclosed.

◨2001. This simple front-gabled Tudor Revival with a front portico is at 917 Lane Boulevard.

blocks offering affordable family homes. This duplex is finished in stucco with half-timbering at the top of the high-pitched gabled roof.

Built in 1931, the house at 917 Lane Boulevard is another example of a Tudor Revival. It has a high-pitched front-gabled roof with a simple front entryway.

These are just four examples of the variety of homes that can be found in this district. The Edison Neighborhood Association, organized in 1968, plays a crucial role in encouraging home ownership and improvement. The area is involved with several programs including Main Street, sponsored by the National Trust for Historic Preservation, that seeks to help revitalize historic commercial areas, and Partners Building Community, a local initiative. These combined efforts are all sharing significant success in Edison and Washington Square's revitalization endeavors.

"To empower the Edison neighborhood to maximize the quality of life and sense of community."

Edison Neighborhood Association
Mission Statement

Sarkozy Bakery
335 and 339 North Burdick Street

Since 1978, over two million loaves of bread have been baked behind the doors of this modest-looking brick building, the home of Sarkozy Bakery, a Kalamazoo institution. Coincidentally, Nicholas Lutten, a baker, completed the structure in 1892. Over the years it housed a bakery, a drug store and even a pool hall. The second floor contained apartments.

Wanting to go into business for themselves, Judy and Ken Sarkozy, who moved to Kalamazoo from the Detroit area, decided to open a bakery. They purchased equipment in June 1977, from the recently closed Reisch Bakery, located on the same side of the street.

The Sarkozys spent the next eight months getting the south side of this building ready, including installing the new electrical wiring and plumbing themselves. Mrs. Sarkozy even painted the first logos on the front windows. The ninety-year-old, nine-by-twelve-foot oven posed a daunting challenge as they dismantled it, with help, at its old location and reassembled it at its new home. Sarkozy Bakery opened for business on February 28, 1978.

The need for expansion led the Sarkozys to purchase the entire building in 1981. They hired local architect Arno Yurk to design the space. A new wide brick arch joined the two sides of the building together, and they filled the new north area with tables and chairs. They exposed the interior brick, laid new flooring tile and installed a new tin ceiling that matched the original. They then relocated the two entrances from the center to each side, using new custom-made doors adorned with brass, French-bread handles from Paris. The work, completed in 1983, more than doubled the size of the establishment. The second floor contains an office, employee lounge and storage.

2001. Sarkozy Bakery's Two-Part Commercial block has a bracketed cornice, stone lintels and sills.

Currently, Judy Sarkozy and her four employees bake six hundred loaves of bread daily, in addition to pastries and other delicacies. The Sarkozys have helped to start a renaissance along North Burdick Street and West Kalamazoo Avenue, and now almost every building there is renovated. Sarkozy Bakery received one of the first Awards of Merit from the Kalamazoo Historic Preservation Commission in 1985.

"This building matches the character of the business."

Judy Sarkozy

Architects, Builders, Contractors, Craftspeople & Artisans

Adler, Dankmar — architect (Chicago, IL)
- Academy of Music, 1882

Ann Beha Associates — architect (Cambridge, MA)
- Kalamazoo Institute of Arts renovation and addition, 1998

Ball, E.R. — architect and builder/contractor
- First County Courthouse, 1838

Barton, Paul & Associates — contractors (Kalamazoo)
- City Hall renovation, 1966–1967

Barton Malow — contractors (Southfield, MI)
- The New Bronson Hospital, 2000

Batterson, Ernest — architect (Kalamazoo)
- 1572 Spruce Drive, c1914
- Fairmount Hospital additions, c1920
- Comfort Station, 1921
- Salvation Army (now Scott Doerschler Messner and Gauntlett), 1927

Bayles & Coleman — architects (Chicago, IL)
- Michigan Female Seminary, 1857–1860

Billingham, M.C.J. — architect (Kalamazoo)
- Borgess Hospital (now Borgess Medical Center), 1917
- Third County Courthouse, 1937
- Kalamazoo Radiology (South Street), 1939
- McKinley Elementary School addition, 1940
- Vander Salm's Flower Shop and Greenhouses, 1940

Billingham & Cobb — architects (Kalamazoo)
- McKinley Elementary School, 1924
- Sill Terrace/Prange Building addition and renovation, 1925
- North Westnedge Elementary School addition, 1926
- Washington Square Branch, Kalamazoo Public Library, 1927
- A.M. Todd Company, 1929
- Fairmount Hospital addition, c1930
- Woodward Elementary new construction, 1930

Blok & Sheridan — builders/contractors
- Kalamazoo Radiology renovation, 1971

Bohlen, D.A. & Son — architects (Indianapolis, IN)
- Borgess Hospital (now Borgess Medical Center) remodel and addition, 1927–1929

Bonfield & Cumming — architects (Cleveland, OH)
- Greyhound Bus Station, 1941

Bremer, L.F. — excavator
- Harvey-Macleod House, 1911

Broeker, Erwin — architect
- First National Bank (now National City Bank) renovation, 1974

Building Restoration Inc. — contractors (Kalamazoo)
- Washington Square Branch, Kalamazoo Public Library roof rehabilitation, 1994
- Gibson Building exterior rehabilitation, 2001

Bush & Paterson — builders/contractors (Kalamazoo)
- National Driving Park buildings, 1859
- First County Courthouse renovation and expansion, 1866
- Corporation Hall, 1867
- Third County Jail, 1869
- Lawrence & Chapin Iron Works (now National City Arcadia South), 1872
- Michigan Female Seminary addition, 1874
- Wood-Upjohn House, 1878
- Ladies' Library Association, 1878
- Academy of Music, 1882
- Michigan Central Railroad Station (now Intermodal Transportation Center), 1887
- Post Office, 1892

The CSM Group — contractors (Climax, MI)
- Central Corners rehabilitation, 1991–1992
- The New Bronson Hospital, 2000

Campbell, John — builder/contractor (Kalamazoo)
- North Westnedge Elementary School, 1888

Case, William — builder/contractor
- Park Street Church of Christ, 1905

Casteel, Andrea and Bill — innkeepers/contractors (Kalamazoo)
- Stuart Avenue Bed & Breakfast renovations, 1985–1986

Chapman, Don — designer
- 262 and 264 East Michigan Avenue interior redesign, 1991

Chihuly, Dale — artist (Seattle, WA)
- Kalamazoo Institute of Arts entry chandelier, 1998

Chubb, John — architect
- East Avenue Elementary School, 1909

Coddington, Henry W. — architect/builder (Kalamazoo)
- Ladies Hall (a.k.a. Lower Hall) Kalamazoo College, 1859
- Michigan Female Seminary, 1867
- Methodist Episcopal Church, 1867–1869
- St. Luke's Episcopal Church, 1886
- Post Office, 1892
- St. Luke's Episcopal Church parish house, 1893

Conservation & Museum Services — conservators (Detroit)
- City Hall Commission Chambers ceiling restoration, 1999

Conti, Annette — designer/contractor (Kalamazoo)
- Wood-Upjohn House restoration, 1982–1984
- 203 and 219 South Westnedge moves and rehabilitation, 1997

Conti Building & Restoration (Kalamazoo)
- Ladies' Library Association restoration and rehabilitation, 1977
- Wood-Upjohn House restoration, 1982–1984
- Kalamazoo House rehabilitation, 1986
- Brown-Clapp House move and rehabilitation, 1987

Dahl, Dennis — cabinetmaker
- Schmidt House, 1994

Daverman & Associates — architects (Grand Rapids, MI)
- Grace Christian Reformed Church (now Diekema Hamann Architects), 1926

Dean, Vernon — engineer (Grand Rapids, MI)
- Westnedge Hill Apartments, 1948–1950

DeKoning, A.J. — builder/contractor (Kalamazoo)
- McKinley Elementary School, 1924

DeRight Brothers — builders/contractors (Kalamazoo)
- Armory, 1913
- Comfort Station, 1921
- North Westnedge Elementary School addition, 1926
- Borgess Hospital (now Borgess Medical Center) remodel and addition, 1927–1929
- Elks Temple remodel, 1929

Diekema Hamann Architecture — architects (Kalamazoo)
- Woodward Elementary interior renovation, 1999
- Grace Christian Reformed Church (now Diekema Hamann Architecture) rehabilitation, 2001

Diekema Hamann Construction — contractors (Kalamazoo)
- Grace Christian Reformed Church (now Diekema Hamann Architecture) rehabilitation, 2001

Doyle, James — mason/builder/contractor (Kalamazoo)
- Doyle House, 1889

Dunn, Michael J. — architect (Kalamazoo)
- Public Safety Station #7, 1984
- Salvation Army (now Scott Doerschler Messner and Gauntlett) rehabilitation, 1993

Eckert Wordell Architects (Kalamazoo)
- YWCA (now the Richard F. Chormann Building) rehabilitation and addition, 1987–1988
- Central Corners rehabilitation, 1991–1992
- Woodward Elementary interior renovation, 1997–1998
- Rotary Stage, Bronson Park, 1999

Eidlitz, Cyrus — architect (New York, NY)
- Michigan Central Railroad (now Intermodal Transportation Center), 1887

Embury, Aymar II — architect (New York, NY)
- Stetson Chapel, 1932
- Hoben House (now Stryker Center) addition, 1963

Eriksen, Roger — construction supervisor (Kalamazoo)
- 710 and 716 Charlotte Avenue, 2000

Etkins, A.J. Construction Company — contractors
- National City Arcadia North, 1993
- Lawrence & Chapin Ironworks (now National City Arcadia South) rehabilitation, 1993

Fairchild, Charles — architect (Kalamazoo)
- Kalamazoo Sled Company, 1895
- Armory, 1913

Fallis, Edward O. — architect
- Second County Courthouse, 1885

Flaitz, Frank — builder/contractor (Kalamazoo)
- Connable House, 1905
- B'nai Israel Temple building (E. South St.) renovation, 1910–1911

Foy, Thomas — builder/contractor (Kalamazoo)
- Foy Block, 1908
- East Avenue Elementary School, 1909
- Police Station, 1913

Frank, Richard — architect (Ann Arbor, MI)
- Ladies' Library Association restoration and rehabilitation, 1975
- Kalamazoo State Hospital Water Tower restoration, 1976

Frobenius & Huwiler — builders/contractors (Kalamazoo)
- People's Church, 1894

Gallup, Robert — architect (Kalamazoo)
- Portage Street Fire Station, 1900
- B'nai Israel/Congregation of Moses (S. Park St.), 1910

Gay, Henry — architect (Chicago, IL)
- Ladies' Library Association, 1878

Gombert, Charles A. — architect (Chicago, IL)
- People's Church, 1894
- Henderson Castle, 1895

Grinwis, Brett — craftsman (Kalamazoo)
- 1602 Grand Avenue renovation, 1997

Grosvenor, L.D. — architect
- Severens House, 1871
- Lawrence & Chapin Iron Works (now National City Arcadia South), 1872

Harrell, Michael — designer
- 262 and 264 East Michigan Avenue interior redesign, 1991

Hartman, Edward — contractor
- Harvey-Macleod House, 1911

Haughey, Black & Associates — architects
- Kalamazoo Radiology addition, 1971

Hayden, Michael — artist
- Washington Square Branch, Kalamazoo Public Library light fixture redesign, 1997

Heneika, James — builder/contractor
- Female Department central building and south wings, Kalamazoo State Hospital, 1859

Herlihy Mid-Continent — contractor
- Loy Norrix High School, 1960–1961

Heysteck, Richard — builder/contractor
- South West Street Standpipe, 1913

Hobbs+Black Associates — architects (Ann Arbor, MI)
- Walwood Hall rehabilitation, 1992
- Lawrence & Chapin Ironworks (now National City Arcadia South) rehabilitation, 1993
- National City Arcadia North, 1993

Holabird & Roche — architects (Chicago, IL)
- Fletcher Hospital, Kalamazoo State Hospital, 1897

Hopkins, David — architect (Kalamazoo)
- Methodist Episcopal Church, 1867–1869
- St. Augustine Roman Catholic Church, 1869

Howe, John (Jack) — architect (Spring Green, WI)
- Weisblat Usonian addition, 1961

Iannelli, Alfonso — artist (Chicago, IL)
- *Fountain of the Pioneers,* Bronson Park, 1940

Jennison, E.S. — architect
- Second Kalamazoo Central High School, 1880

Johnson, Tobias — mason (Kalamazoo)
- Kalamazoo State Hospital Female Department north wings, 1869

Kal-West Contracting — contractors (Kalamazoo)
- Portage Street Fire Station rehabilitation, 1983–1984

Kalamazoo Custom Metal Works — metalworkers (Kalamazoo)
- Seth Thomas Clock rehabilitation, 2000

Kalamazoo Neighborhood Housing Services — housing agency (Kalamazoo)
- 710 Charlotte, 2001
- 716 Charlotte, 2001

Kalleward-Bergerson — contractors (Kalamazoo)
- YWCA, (now the Richard F. Chormann Building) rehabilitation and addition, 1987–1988
- Ladies' Library Association restoration and rehabilitation, 1991
- A.M. Todd addition, 1991
- Walwood Hall rehabilitation, 1992
- Washington Square Branch, Kalamazoo Public Library rehabilitation, 1997
- Kalamazoo Institute of Arts renovation and addition, 1998

Kehoe & Nicols — plasterers
- Fletcher Hospital, Kalamazoo State Hospital, 1897

Kingscott & Associates Inc. — architects (Kalamazoo)
- Michigan Central Railroad Station (now Intermodal Transportation Center) rehabilitation, 1977–1978
- Borgess Hospital (now Borgess Medical Center) renovation, 1984–1993
- Salvation Army (now Scott Doerschler Messner & Gauntlett) renovation, 1993

Kingsley & Stock — builders/contractors (St. Joseph, MI)
- Elks Temple, 1904

Kinney, O.S. — consulting architect (Chicago, IL)
- Methodist Episcopal Church, 1867–1869

Larson, Martin — decorator
- Harvey-Macleod House, 1911

Lather, George and Sons — contractors
- Salvation Army (now Scott Doerschler Messner & Gauntlett), 1927

LeRoy, Rockwell — architect (Kalamazoo)
- Elite Theater, 1912
- Police Station, 1913

Little, David — builder/contractor (Kalamazoo)
- South West Street Standpipe, 1913
- Bronson Methodist Hospital addition, 1928

Little, William — mason
- Harvey-Macleod House, 1911

Lloyd, Gordon — architect (Detroit, MI)
- St. Luke's Episcopal Church, 1886

Loughead, A.D. — builder/ contractor (Kalamazoo)
- St. Joseph Elementary School, 1904

Maher, George W. — architect (Kenilworth, IL)
- Stone House, 1910

Malcolm, Calder & Hammond — architects
- Walwood Hall, 1938

Maxwell & Associates — architects
- City Hall renovation, 1995

McCall, Kevin — contractor (Kalamazoo)
- Central Corners rehabilitation, 1991–1992

McClure, Frank — architect
- Majestic Theater, 1907

Meulenberg, Tim and Janine — owners/contractors (Kalamazoo)
- 747 Wheaton Avenue rehabilitation, c1989

Miller-Davis Company — contractors (Kalamazoo)
- A.M. Todd addition, 1964
- Kalamazoo State Hospital Water Tower restoration, 1976
- Michigan Central Railroad Station (now Intermodal Transportation Center) rehabilitation, 1977
- St. Luke's Episcopal Church parish house addition, 1978
- Rotary Stage, Bronson Park, 1999

Miller, Frederick — builder/contractor
- Second Kalamazoo Central High School, 1880

Miller, O.F. — builder/contractor (Kalamazoo)
- Bryant Paper Mill office building, 1920
- Washington Square Branch, Kalamazoo Public Library, 1927
- A.M. Todd Company, 1929
- American National Bank (now Fifth Third Bank), 1930
- Fairmount Hospital additions, c1930
- City Hall, 1931
- Ladies' Library Association addition, 1931
- Stetson Chapel, 1932

Milling, David & Associates — architects (Ann Arbor, MI)
- Washington Square Branch, Kalamazoo Public Library rehabilitation, 1997

Mills, Joseph E. — architect (Detroit, MI)
- Edwards Hospital, Kalamazoo State Hospital, 1905

Mix, E. Townsend — architect (Milwaukee, WI)
- McDuffee House, 1890

Myers & Sons — builders/contractors
- Lovell Street Elementary School, 1884

Nave, Nelson — architect (Kalamazoo)
- Borgess Hospital (now Borgess Medical Center) renovation, 1984–1993
- 100 North Edwards rehabilitation, 1994–2000
- The Style Shop rehabilitation, 2001

Newbold, Alfred — contractor (Kalamazoo)
- Westnedge Hill Apartments, 1948–1950

Newman, Kirk — sculptor (Kalamazoo)
- Children at Play sculpture, Bronson Park reflecting pool, 1976

Nie, Tom — contractor (Kalamazoo)
- Hall House rehabilitation, 1986

Nielsen, Ian — cabinetmaker (Kalamazoo)
- 1602 Grand Avenue renovation, 1997

Oliver, Adam — landscape designer
- Bronson Park, c1879

Osgood & Osgood — architects (St. Joseph, MI)
- Elks Temple, 1904

Parzyck, Rodger — owner/developer (Kalamazoo)
- 100 North Edwards Street rehabilitation, 1994–2000

Patton & Fisher — architects (Chicago, IL)
- Kalamazoo Public Library, 1893
- St. Luke's Episcopal Church parish house, 1893

Pearson Construction Company — builders/contractors
- Greyhound Bus Station, 1941

Perkins & Will — architects (Chicago, IL)
- Loy Norrix High School, 1960–1961

Peters, Gahy — paver (Kalamazoo)
- Nicholson pavement

Pewabic Pottery (Detroit, MI)
- Hall House tile, 1923

Pratt, Herman — architects
- City Hall renovation, 1967

Prince, James — builder/contractor (Chicago, IL)
- Michigan Female Seminary, 1857–1860

Prince, Richard & Associates — architects (Kalamazoo)
- Loy Norrix High School remodel and additions, 1971

Pulver Construction — contractors (Kalamazoo)
- Schmidt House, 1994

Pyle, David — architect (Kalamazoo)
- Wood-Upjohn House restoration and rehabilitation, 1982–1984
- Stockbridge-Everard House rehabilitation, 1985

Quinn Evans/Architects — architects (Ann Arbor, MI)
- Ladies' Library Association restoration and rehabilitation, 1991

Reeves Brothers Company — builders/contractors
- South West Street Standpipe, 1913

Rickman & Atkins — contractors (Kalamazoo)
- Featherbone Corset Company, 1894

Rickman, George — builder/contractor (Kalamazoo)
- Rickman Hotel (now Rickman House), 1878
- People's Church, 1894

Rickman, George and Sons — builders/contractors (Kalamazoo)
- Kalamazoo Loose Leaf Binder Company, 1906
- North Westnedge Elementary School addition, 1907
- Elite Theater, 1912

Ritchie, William — builder/contractor (Kalamazoo)
- Waterworks, 1884
- Borgess Hospital (Portage Street) wing, 1889

Roberts, Martin W. — architect (Kalamazoo)
- Lovell Street Elementary School, 1884
- Waterworks, 1884
- Second Reformed Church, 1887
- North Westnedge Elementary School, 1888
- Borgess Hospital (Portage Street) addition, 1889

Robinson & Campau — architects (Grand Rapids, MI)
- Former YWCA (now the Richard F. Chormann Building), 1923

Roe, Benjamin — mason (Kalamazoo)
- 747 Wheaton, 1883
- Post Office, 1892
- Kalamazoo State Hospital Water Tower, 1895
- Potter Hospital, Kalamazoo State Hospital, 1898
- Burns Hospital, Kalamazoo State Hospital, 1900

Scheid & Herder — builders/contractors (Kalamazoo)
- Third Christian Reformed Church, 1907

Schelb, Jim — contractor
- KM Industrial Machinery rehabilitation, c1981

Schipper & Dykstra — contractors
- Grace Christian Reformed Church, 1926

Schramm, Richard — architect (Kalamazoo)
- Hoben House (now Stryker Center), 1985

Schuring, Tom — builder/contractor (Kalamazoo)
- Little Michigan, 1948

Scudella, Bill — stained glass artist
- Marlborough rehabilitation, 1980s–1990s

Seth Thomas Clock Company — manufacturer (Thomaston, CT)
- Seth Thomas Clock, c1868

Shannon, William — builder (Kalamazoo)
- Caroline Bartlett Crane House, 1907

Shannon-Kline, Inc. — contractors (Kalamazoo)
- Public Safety Station #7, 1984
- Michigan Central Railroad Station (now Intermodal Transportation Center) rehabilitation, 1986

Shepley, Bulfinch, Richardson & Abbott — architects (Boston, MA)
- The New Bronson Hospital, 2000

Sherman, Jeff — mason (Kalamazoo)
- Academy Street brick restoration, 1992–present

Shirlaw, James — mason
- Orrin B. Hayes, 1920

Simons, V.D. — engineer (Chicago, IL)
- Bryant Paper Mill power plant, c1920

Skidmore, Owings & Merrill — architects (Chicago, IL)
- Kalamazoo Institute of Arts, 1961

Sloan, Samuel — architect (Philadelphia, PA)
- Female Department Kalamazoo State Hospital, 1859

Slocum Associates — architects
- Humphrey Block rehabilitation, c1995

Slocum, Dick — architect
- St. Luke's Episcopal Church parish house addition, 1978

Smith, Jeff — construction supervisor
- 491 W. South Street rehabilitation, 1999

Smith, Donald B. Company — contractors (Kalamazoo)
- Ladies' Library Association restoration and rehabilitation, 1975

Smutek, Mark — owner/craftsman (Kalamazoo)
- Triangle Service Station (now Water Street Coffee Joint) rehabilitation, 1994

Southwest Builders, Inc. — contractors (Kalamazoo)
- The Style Shop rehabilitation, 2001

Spiers & Rhone — architects (Detroit, MI)
- Third Christian Reformed Church, 1907

Spink, Scott — builder (Kalamazoo)
- Triangle Service Station (now Water Street Coffee Joint) addition, 2000

Sprouge & McGoff — builders
- Bassett House, 1860

Stapert-Pratt-Bulthuis & Sprau — architects (Kalamazoo)
- City Hall renovations, 1966–1967

Statler Ready Mix Concrete — concrete contractors (Kalamazoo)
- A.M. Todd addition, 1991

Stauffenberg, Otto — decorative painter (Kalamazoo)
- American National Bank (now Fifth Third Bank) banking lobby ceiling, 1930
- City Hall Commission Chambers mural, 1931

Stevens, Roy — contractor
- St. Luke's Episcopal Church parish house, 1956

Stewart-Kingscott Company — architects (Kalamazoo)
- Uptown Theater, 1938

Stone/Parent — architects (Kalamazoo)
- Municipal Ice Rink Shed Roof, 1965

Stone, Smith & Parent — architects (Kalamazoo)
- People's Church annex, 1963

Stone, William — architect (Kalamazoo)
- Dewing Building, 1928
- Westnedge Hill Apartments, 1948–1950
- St. Luke's Episcopal Church parish house, 1956

Stratton, William B. — architect (Detroit, MI)
- Kalamazoo State Hospital Water Tower, 1895

Stryker, Jon — architect (Kalamazoo)
- 491 W. South Street rehabilitation, 1999

Studio of Architectural Sculpture — sculptors
- City Hall cornice reliefs, 1931

Sullivan, Louis — architect (Chicago, IL)
- Academy of Music, 1882

Thielbar & Fugard — architects
- Bronson Methodist Hospital addition, 1927

Third Street Studio — stained glass (Chicago, IL)
- Henderson Castle, 1895

Tower-Pinkster Associates — architects (Kalamazoo)
- City Hall renovation, 1978

Tower, Pinkster, Titus — architects (Kalamazoo)
- A.M. Todd addition, 1991

Trombley, Susan and Albert — owners/developers (Kalamazoo)
- J.W. Bosman Building rehabilitation, 1989–1992

Turner, Henry & Thebaud, Victor — architects
- North Hall, Western State Normal School (now Western Michigan University's "Western State Normal School National Register Historic District"), 1924

Van Dam & Krusinga — contractors (Kalamazoo)
- 491 W. South Street rehabilitation, 1999

Vander Horst, Henry — builder/contractor (Kalamazoo)
- Park-American Hotel addition, 1905
- Browne Block/Peck Building, 1906
- Kalamazoo Building, 1907
- 601 South Burdick, c1909
- Borgess Hospital (now Borgess Medical Center), 1917
- First National Bank (now National City Bank), 1917
- Orrin B. Hayes, 1920
- Hall House Bed & Breakfast, 1923
- Dewing Building, 1928
- American National Bank (now Fifth Third Bank), 1930
- Uptown Theater, 1938

Vander Salm, Jacob — conservatory designer (Kalamazoo)
- Vander Salm's Flower Shop and Greenhouses conservatory, 1940

Van Eck, Gerald — contractor (Kalamazoo)
- National Storage Building (now 309 East Water Street) addition, c1915
- Gibson Mandolin-Guitar Company, 1917

Van Leyen, E.C. — architect
- Park Street Church of Christ, 1905

Van Volkenburg, Forrest D. — architect (Kalamazoo)
- Central Fire Station, 1908
- Fire Station No. 5 (now Public Safety Station No. 5), 1908
- Harvey-Macleod House, 1911
- YMCA, 1912
- Fairmount Hospital, 1914
- McNair House, 1915
- Hoben House (now Stryker Center), 1925

Weary & Alford — architects (Chicago, IL)
- First National Bank (now National City Bank), 1917
- American National Bank (now Fifth Third Bank), 1930
- City Hall, 1931

Welsh, William — builder/contractor (Kalamazoo)
- Second Reformed Church, 1887

Wheaton, Ulysses — builder/contractor (Kalamazoo)
- Kalamazoo Public Library, 1893

White, Albert — builder/contractor (Kalamazoo)
- Borgess Hospital (Portage Street) additions, 1896–1902
- Fourth Central High School Building, 1898
- Parsons Business College, 1902
- B'nai Israel/Congregation of Moses (South Park Street), 1910

Whitechapel Bell Foundry — bell founders (London, England)
- Stetson Chapel bells, 1984

Wiegand, Peter — contractor (Kalamazoo)
- Humphrey Block renovation, c1995
- 262 and 264 East Michigan Avenue rehabilitation, 1991

Worden, G. Gilbert — architect (Kalamazoo)
- Gibson Mandolin-Guitar Company, 1917
- Orrin B. Hayes, 1920

Wright, Frank Lloyd — architect (Spring Green, WI)
- Kalamazoo County Usonian Homes, 1940s–1950s

Yonkman, Leonard — carpenter (Kalamazoo)
- Henderson Castle renovations, 1988–present

Young, Ammi — architect (Vermont)
- First County Courthouse, 1838

Yurk, Arno — architect (Kalamazoo)
- Sarkozy Bakery rehabilitation, 1983
- Orrin B. Hayes rehabilitation, 1985

Ziobron, Judith — artist and decorative painter (Kalamazoo)
- Johnson House stenciling, 1980
- Henderson Castle stenciling, 1983
- Stockbridge-Everard House stenciling, 1984
- Wood-Upjohn House stenciling and decorative painting, 1984
- Kalamazoo House wall glazing and stenciling, 1986

Sources Consulted

Books

Brand, Stewart. *How Buildings Learn: What Happens After They're Built.* New York: Viking, 1994.

Burgh, Robert. *The Region of Three Oaks.* Three Oaks, MI: The Edward Warren Foundation, 1939.

Cooledge, Harold N. *Samuel Sloan, Architect of Philadelphia, 1815–1884.* Philadelphia: University of Pennsylvania Press, 1986.

Dayton, Frank and Louis Allardt. *Kalamazoo Illustrated.* Kalamazoo, MI: Ihling Bros. & Everard, 1892.

Dewey, Robert, Conrad Hilberry, Lawrence Barrett, and Gail Griffin. *Kalamazoo College: A Sesquicentennial Portrait.* Kalamazoo, MI: Kalamazoo College, 1982.

Dobson, Raymond. *History of the Order of Elks.* Rev. ed. Chicago: Grand Secretary's Office of The Benevolent and Protective Order of Elks of U.S.A., 1978.

Drew, Bettina. *Crossing the Expendable Landscape.* St. Paul, MN: Graywolf Press, 1998.

Dunbar, Willis F. *Kalamazoo and How it Grew...and Grew.* Kalamazoo, MI: Western Michigan University, 1969.

_____. *Michigan, A History of the Wolverine State,* revised by George S. May. Grand Rapids, MI: William B. Eerdmans Publishing Company, 1980.

_____. *Michigan, A History Of the Wolverine State.* 3rd rev. ed. by George S. May. Grand Rapids, MI: W.B. Eerdmans Pub. Co., 1995.

Durant, Samuel W. *History of Kalamazoo County, Michigan, with Illustrations and Biographical Sketches of its Prominent Men and Pioneers.* Philadelphia: Everts and Abbott, 1880. Reprint, Evansville, IN: Whipporwill, 1985.

Dwight, Pamela, ed. *Landmark Yellow Pages.* Washington, D.C.: Preservation Press, 1993.

Eckert, Kathryn Bishop. *Buildings of Michigan.* New York: Oxford University Press, 1993.

Fisher, David. *Portrait and Biographical Record of Kalamazoo, Allegan and VanBuren Counties, Michigan.* Chicago: Chapman Brothers, 1892.

Fisher, David, and Frank Little, eds. *Compendium of History and Biography of Kalamazoo County, Michigan.* Chicago: A.W. Bowen and Company, [1906].

Flexner, Stuart, and Anne Soukhanov. *Speaking Freely: A Guided Tour of American English from Plymouth Rock to Silicon Valley.* New York: Oxford University Press, 1997.

Fogelson, Robert M. *America's Armories: Architecture, Society & Public Order.* Cambridge, MA: Harvard University Press, 1989.

Fuller, George, ed. *Historic Michigan, Land of Great Lakes: Its Life, Resources, Industries, People, Politics, Government, Wars, Institutions, Achievements, the Press, Schools, Churches, Legendary and Prehistoric Lore.* Dayton, OH: National Historical Association, Inc., 1924.

Gill, Brendan. *Many Masks: A Life of Frank Lloyd Wright.* New York: Da Capo Press, 1998.

Goodsell, Charles T., and Willis F. Dunbar. *Centennial History of Kalamazoo College.* Kalamazoo, MI: Kalamazoo College, 1933.

Griffin, Gail, Josephine Csete, Ruth Ann Moerdyk, and Cheryl Limer. *Emancipated Spirits: Portraits of Kalamazoo College Women.* N.p.: n.p., 1983.

Hager, David C. *Next Stop Kalamazoo!: A History of Railroading in Kalamazoo County.* Kalamazoo, MI: Kalamazoo Public Museum, [1976].

Henehan, Brendan. *Walking Through Time.* Kalamazoo, MI: Kalamazoo Historical Commission, 1981.

Hendry, Fay. *Outdoor Sculpture in Kalamazoo.* Okemos, MI: Iota Press, 1980.

Henry, Patricia. *The History of Oakwood, a Community of Kalamazoo, Michigan.* Bear Lake, MI: Pioneer Press, 1999.

Holly Manufacturing Company. *B. Holly's System Of Fire Protection and Water Supply for Cities and Villages.* Buffalo, NY: Thomas, Howard and Johnson, 1868.

Hughes, Robert. *The Shock of the New.* Rev. ed. New York: Alfred A. Knopf, 1991.

Hurd, Henry. *The Institutional Care of The Insane in The United States and Canada.* Baltimore: Johns Hopkins Press, 1916.

Huxtable, Ada Louise. *Kicked a Building Lately?* Berkeley, CA: University of California Press, 1988.

Jacobs, Jane. *The Death and Life of Great American Cities.* New York: Random House, 1961; Vintage Books, 1992.

Knauss, James O. *The First Fifty Years: A History of Western Michigan College of Education, 1903–1953.* Kalamazoo, MI: Western Michigan College of Education, 1953.

Kunstler, James Howard. *Home From Nowhere: The Rise and Decline of America's Man-Made Landscape.* New York: Simon & Schuster, 1998.

Liebs, Chester. *Main Street to Miracle Mile: American Roadside Architecture.* Boston: Little, Brown and Company, 1985.

Longstreth Richard. *The Buildings of Main Street: A Guide to American Commercial Architecture.* Washington, D.C.: Preservation Press, 1987.

_____. *History On The Line: Testimony in The Cause of Preservation.* Ithaca, NY: Historic Urban Plans, Inc., 1998.

Maddex, Diane, ed. *Built in the U.S.A.: American Buildings from Airports to Zoos.* Washington, D.C.: Preservation Press, 1985.

Massie, Larry B., and Peter Schmitt. *Kalamazoo: The Place Behind the Products.* Windsor, CA: Windsor Publications, 1981.

McAlester, Virginia, and Lee McAlester. *A Field Guide to American Houses.* New York: Alfred A. Knopf, 1984.

McCarthy, Sister M. Barbara. *A Covenant with Stones.* Nazareth, MI: Sisters of St. Joseph, 1939.

McKee, Harley, ed. *Historic American Buildings Survey—Michigan.* Detroit: Historical Society of Michigan & Michigan Society of Architects, 1967.

McLellan, David, and Bill Warrick. *The Lake Shore and Michigan Southern Railway.* Polo, IL: Transportation Trails, 1989.

McNair, Rush. *Medical Memoirs of 50 Years in Kalamazoo.* Kalamazoo, MI: n.p., 1938.

Meints, Graydon. *Michigan Railroads and Railroad Companies.* East Lansing, MI: Michigan State University Press, 1992.

Michigan, State Hospital, Kalamazoo. *Reports of the Board of Trustees of the Michigan Asylum for the Insane.* Lansing, MI: W.S. George & Co., 1857–1910.

Moe, Richard, and Carter Wilkie. *Changing Places: Rebuilding Community in the Age of Sprawl.* New York: Henry Holt and Company, 1997.

Moore, Arthur Cotton. *The Powers of Preservation: New Life for Historic Structures.* New York: McGraw Hill, 1998.

Mulder, Arthur. *The Kalamazoo College Story.* Kalamazoo, MI: Kalamazoo College, 1958.

Murtagh, William. *Keeping Time: The History and Theory of Preservation in America.* Pittstown, NJ: Main Street Press, 1988.

Naylor, David. *Great American Movie Theaters.* Washington, D.C.: Preservation Press, 1987.

Phillips, Steven. *Old-House Dictionary.* New York: John Wiley & Sons, 1994.

Picturesque Kalamazoo. Kalamazoo, MI: E.E. Labadie, 1909.

Picturesque Kalamazoo. Chicago: James P. Craig, [1890]. Reprint, Evansville, IN: Whipporwill Publications, 1984.

Pioneer Collections. *Report of the Pioneer Society of the State of Michigan Together with Reports of County, Town, and District Pioneer Societies.* 40 vols. Lansing, MI: W.S. George & Company, 1877–1929.

Potts, Grace, and Cheryl Lyon-Jenness. *Women With a Vision.* Kalamazoo, MI: Ladies' Library Association, 1997.

Putnam, Daniel. *Twenty-five Years with the Insane.* Detroit: John McFarlane, 1885.

Rickard, O'Ryan. *A Just Verdict: The Life of Caroline Bartlett Crane.* Kalamazoo, MI: Western Michigan University New Issues Press, 1994.

Rifkind, Carole. *A Field Guide to American Architecture.* New York: New American Library, 1980.

Rybczynski, Witold. *The Look of Architecture.* New York: Oxford University Press, 2001.

St. Luke's Episcopal Church. *A Chronological Souvenir of St. Luke's Church.* Kalamazoo, MI: St. Luke's Episcopal Church, 1903.

Schmitt, Peter J. *Nineteenth-century Homes in a Midwestern Village.* Kalamazoo, MI: Kalamazoo Historical Commission, 1976.

Stevenson, Katherine, and H. Ward Jandl. *Houses by Mail: A Guide to Houses from Sears, Roebuck and Company.* Washington, D.C.: Preservation Press, 1986.

Swantek, Sister Wanda. *Nazareth: Sisters of St. Joseph, Nazareth, Michigan, 1889–1929.* Kalamazoo, MI: Borgess Hospital, n.d.

Thomas, James, comp. *Kalamazoo County Directory With a History of the County.* Kalamazoo, MI: Stone Brothers, 1869.

Thomas, James M., comp. *Thomas's Kalamazoo Directory and Business Advertiser for 1867 and 1868 Together With a History of Kalamazoo From its Earliest Settlement to the Present Time.* Kalamazoo, MI: Stone Brothers, 1867.

Tomes, Nancy. *The Art of Asylum-Keeping, Thomas Story Kirkbride and The Origins of American Psychiatry.* Philadelphia: University of Pennsylvania Press, 1994.

Twombly, Robert. *Louis Sullivan, His Life and Work.* Chicago: University of Chicago Press, 1986.

VanBuren, Maurie. *House Styles at a Glance.* Atlanta, GA: Longstreet Press, 1991.

Vieyra, Daniel I. *"Fill 'er Up": An Architectural History of America's Gas Stations.* New York: Macmillan, 1979.

Warren, Francis H., ed. *Michigan Manual of Freedmen's Progress.* Detroit: The Commission, 1915.

Whiffen, Marcus, and Frederick Koeper. *American Architecture, 1607–1976.* Cambridge, MA: MIT Press, 1981.

Whyte, William H. *City: Rediscovering the Center.* New York: Doubleday, 1988.

Periodicals

Ambrose, Brian. "The Kalamazoo Guitar Heritage Continues," *Business Digest,* November 1989, 4–8.

Briscoe, Penny. "Her Business Was Tops in Kalamazoo," *Encore,* November 1998, 34–41.

Brooks, H. Allen. "The Early Work of the Prairie Architects," *Journal of the Society of Architectural Historians* 19 (1960): 2–10.

"Buildings Show Steady Growth," *Western Michigan College News Magazine* 4 (Winter 1954): 11.

Butler, Laura, and Thea Rozetta Lapham. "Stylin' in Downtown Kalamazoo," *Business Insight,* February 2001, 4–7.

"Classroom Crisis," *Western Michigan College News Magazine* 13 (Winter 1955): n.p.

Cohen, Zolton. "Living Downtown," *Welcome Home,* May/June 1992, 27–33.

"College Acquires More Property," *Western Michigan College News Magazine* 3 (Fall 1944): 8–13.

Crane, Caroline Bartlett. "The Story of an Institutional Church in a Small City," *Charities,* May 6, 1905, 1–8.

[Directories]. Village & City of Kalamazoo, MI. Publishers vary, 1860–present.

Garrison, Anne C. "It's a Paper World," *Business Topics,* January 1956.

Gregerson, Charles. "Early Adler and Sullivan Work in Kalamazoo," *Prairie School Review* 2 (1974): 5–15.

"History of Kalamazoo State Hospital," *Public Employee Press* 2 (March 21, 1958).

Hurd, Henry. "A History of the Asylums for the Insane in Michigan," *Michigan Pioneer and Historical Collections* 13 (1888): 292–307.

Jones, Ben. "The Steel's in Place: KIA's $8.8 Million Project Nearly on Schedule," *Encore,* September 1997, 34–35.

Kalamazoo Chamber of Commerce. *Gateway,* January 1, 1929.

Kalamazoo Gazette, 1837–present.

Kalamazoo Magazine, 1963–1966.

Kalamazoo Telegraph, 1849–1916.

Kalamazoo Telegraph-Press, 1911–1916.

Kalamazoo Weekly Telegraph, 1845–1913.

Keister, Kim. "Showing its Metal," *Historic Preservation* 47 (January/February 1995): 36–43+.

Kleinschmidt, Earl. "Major Problems in Sanitation and Hygiene in Michigan, 1850–1900," *Michigan History* 28 (July–September 1944): 420–445.

Lapham, Thea Rozetta. "Kalamazoo's 'Bob Villa', Thomas Huff, Helps Entrepreneurs While Rescuing Historic Buildings," *Business Insight,* (June 1996): 14–15.

Larkin, Kelle. "Amazing Grace: The Resurrection of a Church," *Business Insight,* February 2001, 32–35.

Lenderink, A. Rodney. "Western's Trolley Cars," *Western Michigan University Magazine* 23 (Winter 1964): 6–7.

Mason, Philip P. "The Plank Road Craze: A Chapter in the History of Michigan's Highways," *Great Lakes Informant,* Series 2, Number 1: 1–4.

McCarville, Jeanne. "From Celery to Roses: 48 Years and Growing," *Business Digest,* September 1988, 12–14.

Meints, Graydon. "The Kalamazoo Seven," *The Inside Track,* November–December 1979, 13+.

"New Gibson Factory Formally Opened with 'House Warming'," *The Sounding Board Salesman* 6 (August 1917): 5–7.

Rowe, Winifred, and Stanley Calfas, eds. *The Boiling Pot,* 1933. Kalamazoo, MI: Kalamazoo College, 1933.

"St. Augustine Cathedral: A Time Line," *The Augustinian* 88 (July 1989).

Schopbach, Richard. "A Michigan Landmark Passes," *Michigan History* 20 (Winter 1936): 59–68.

Sorensen, Christine. "The Jews," *Kalamazoo Magazine,* October 1965, 2–15.

———, "The Unitarians," *Kalamazoo Magazine,* Summer 1965, 2–7.

"Stryker Addition Named For Burton H. Upjohn," *Kalamazoo College Quarterly* 47 (Fall 1985): 11.

Thinnes, Tom. "A History of Creativity—But C-mon! A Welding Shop Wedding?" *Encore,* September 1998, 8.

———. "Judy, Judy, She's Never Moody," *Encore,* February 1993, 10.

———. "The Vander Salms—a Growing Family…and a Family Growing Business," *Encore,* April 1998, 10–14.

Vander Weyden, Jane. "How to Make a Kalamazoo Violin," *Encore,* January 1997, 50–55.

Waldmeister, D. Presley. "An Innside View of Hall House," *Encore,* September–October 1988, 54–59.

"Work of Forrest D. Van Volkenburg, Kalamazoo, Mich," *The Ohio Architect Engineer and Builder* 26 (August 1915): 12.

Weeks, Linton, "Leaving the Armories Unguarded," *Preservation* 50 (March–April 1998): 24–25.

Western Normal Herald, Western State Normal School, Kalamazoo, Michigan, 1916–1927.

Unpublished Research/Memoirs/Diaries

Alstrom, Eric. "First Methodist Church." Unpublished research paper, May 1986. Kalamazoo Public Library Local History Collection.

"An Art Center Grows in the Midwest." Unpublished historical research, 1966. Kalamazoo Public Library Local History Collection.

Averill, Lloyd. Seattle, to Pamela O'Connor, Kalamazoo, July 15, 1997. Typescript letter. Author's collection.

Bellson, Julius. "The Gibson Story." Unpublished history, 1973. Western Michigan University Archives and Regional History Collections.

Chamberlain, Laura. "Frank Lloyd Wright's Unsonian Communities in Kalamazoo County, Michigan." Unpublished research paper, 1999. Author's original.

Clark, Betty. "Scaling Prospect Hill." Unpublished memoirs, October 1959. Western Michigan University Archives and Regional History Collections.

Crossley, Carolyn. "Michigan Female Seminary." Unpublished research, June 1956. Kalamazoo Public Library Local History Collection.

Eaton, Ethel. "Glimpses of the Past." Unpublished memoirs, n.d. Author's collection.

Farnsworth, Del. "The Stained Glass Windows of St. Luke's Episcopal Church." Unpublished history, 1977. St. Luke's Episcopal Church collection.

Ferraro, Sharon. "Kalamazoo Reconnaissance Level Historic Resources Survey." Unpublished historic resources survey, 2001. Author's collection.

Frazee, Pearl. "The Plank Roads of Michigan." Unpublished research paper, n.d., Western Michigan University Archives and Regional History Collections.

Gernant, Harry. Unpublished autobiography, n.d. Loaned by family.

Henehan, Brendan. "History Through the Eyes of a Neighborhood: The Hillcrest Area up to 1930." Unpublished research paper, June 6, 1978. Western Michigan University Archives and Regional History Collections.

"History of the Kalamazoo State Hospital." Unpublished research, 1964. Western Michigan University Archives and Regional History Collections.

[History of Stetson Chapel]. Brochure, n.d. Kalamazoo College Archives.

Hoben, Allan, Kalamazoo, and Amar Embury II, New York, on December 16, 24, and 31, 1930. Typescript letters. Kalamazoo College Archives.

Houghton, Lynn. "The History of the Buildings Now Housing Biggs/Gilmore Associates." Unpublished research paper, 1986. Kalamazoo Public Library Local History Collection.

Kalamazoo Historical Commission. "Arcadia Creek Historic District: National Register of Historic Places Inventory." Nomination Form to federal government, 1989. Author's collection.

[Kalamazoo Public Library]. Annual Report, 1926–27. Kalamazoo Public Library Local History Collection.

Knauss, Carol. "A History of Bronson Park, Kalamazoo, Michigan, from 1829 to 1940." Unpublished master's thesis, 1982. Kalamazoo Public Library Local History Collection.

Light, Richard U. "History of the Senior Citizen Fund of Kalamazoo, Michigan." Unpublished history, 1955. Western Michigan University Archives and Regional History Collections.

Massie, Larry B. "A Report On The History and Significance of Fletcher Hospital, Burns Cottage and Edwards Hospital, Kalamazoo Regional Psychiatric Hospital, Kalamazoo, Michigan." Unpublished research, 1987. Western Michigan University Archives and Regional History Collections.

Meader, Robert, ed. "Historical Directory." Unpublished biographical collection, 1945. Kalamazoo Public Library Local History Collection.

Millar, Chris. "Mountain Home Cemetery Project." Unpublished research paper, 1999. Author's original.

Roe, Benjamin. [Personal Diary, 1901]. Western Michigan University Archives and Regional History Collections.

Ross, Viola. "A History of Theaters In Kalamazoo." Unpublished research paper, 1926. Western Michigan University Archives and Regional History Collections.

Rubin, Sharon Goldman. "Alfonso Iannelli: The Career of An Artist In The American Social Context, 1906–1965." Ph.D. dissertation, University of Minnesota, 1973.

Siedschlag, Lydia. Unpublished memoirs, April 1980. Western Michigan University Archives and Regional History Collections.

South Side Literary Club. "Washington Square, Kalamazoo, Michigan." Unpublished memoirs, 1966. South Side Literary Club. Kalamazoo Public Library Local History Collection.

Siemson, Walter. "A History of the Kalamazoo Public Library." Unpublished manuscript, 1972. Kalamazoo Public Library Local History Collection.

Swantek, Sister Wanda. [Abstract on Life of Levi L. Barbour, 1840–1924]. Unpublished research, 1981. Sisters of St. Joseph Historical Collections, Nazareth, Michigan.

Pamphlets/Brochures/Promotional Pieces

Allen, Ruth. "The Kalamazoo Water System, A Centennial Survey," 1976. Kalamazoo Public Library Local History Collection.

Christian Church (Disciples of Christ). Centennial Celebration Booklet, May 2, 1993. Kalamazoo, May 2, 1993. Christian Church (Disciples of Christ), Kalamazoo, archives.

Craft, Seth O. "History of The Kalamazoo State Hospital," Department information sheet, 1964. Western Michigan University Archives and Regional History Collections.

[Dedication Program], Loy Norrix High School, 1961. Kalamazoo Public Library Local History Collection.

Dunbar, Willis. "Financial Progress in Kalamazoo County Since 1834," Pamphlet, n.d. Kalamazoo Public Library Local History Collection.

[First Methodist Church]. Minutes of the Board of Trustees, 1868–1915. First United Methodist Church, Kalamazoo, archives.

Ford, Henry. "One Hundred-Fifty Years, First United Methodist Church of Kalamazoo, Michigan." Pamphlet, 1983. First United Methodist Church, Kalamazoo, archives.

Horvath, Betty. "The First 150 Years of St. Luke's Episcopal Church." Pamphlet, 1987. Kalamazoo Public Library Local History Collection.

[Intermodal Transportation Center]. Dedication Booklet, 1977. Kalamazoo Public Library Local History Collection.

"Kalamazoo and Education M.S.T.A." Pamphlet, 1914. Kalamazoo Public Library Local History Collection.

[Kalamazoo Chautauqua Assembly]. Program, 1907. Kalamazoo Public Library Local History Collection.

Kalamazoo, City. "Opening of the Kalamazoo City Hall." Program, September 1, 1931. Western Michigan University Archives and Regional History Collections.

Kalamazoo, City. Council Meeting Minutes, 1884–1918. City of Kalamazoo Records Center, Kalamazoo.

Kalamazoo, City. Commission Meeting Minutes, dates vary. City of Kalamazoo Records Center, Kalamazoo.

Kalamazoo, City. Annual Reports, 1884–present. City of Kalamazoo Records Center, Kalamazoo.

Kalamazoo, City. Assessor's Records, addresses and dates vary. City of Kalamazoo Records Center, Kalamazoo; City of Kalamazoo Assessor's Office, Kalamazoo.

Kalamazoo, City. Wrecking Permits, addresses and dates vary. City of Kalamazoo Records Center, Kalamazoo.

Kalamazoo, County. Tax Rolls, addresses and dates vary. Western Michigan University Archives and Regional History Collections.

Kalamazoo Public Schools. "Official Proceedings of the Board of Education of the City and Township of Kalamazoo, Michigan," 1864–present. Kalamazoo Public Library Local History Collection.

Kalamazoo, Village. Annual Reports, 1874–1884. City of Kalamazoo Records Center, Kalamazoo.

Kalamazoo, Village. Board of Trustees/Council Meeting Minutes, 1843–1884. City of Kalamazoo Records Center, Kalamazoo.

"The Marion R. Spear Story." Pamphlet, 1975. Western Michigan University Archives and Regional History Collections.

[McDuffy, L.P., Esq.]. Architectural Plans for Residence in Kalamazoo, Michigan, 1890. (Prepared by E.T. Mix & Co. Architects, Milwaukee, WI.) Kalamazoo Valley Museum Collections.

_____. Architectural Specifications for Residence in Kalamazoo, Michigan, 1890. (Prepared by E.T. Mix & Co. Architects, Milwaukee, WI.) Kalamazoo Valley Museum Collections.

"The New Bronson." Promotional newsletter, February 2000. Kalamazoo Public Library Local History Collection.

"The New Bronson." Promotional newsletter, August 2000. Kalamazoo Public Library Local History Collection.

"Pictorial Souvenir of the Police Department and Kalamazoo, Michigan." Promotional booklet, 1914. Kalamazoo Public Library Local History Collection.

Riopel, Anne M. "The Distinguished History of Kalamazoo Radiology on the Occasion of its Centennial Celebration." Pamphlet, 1997. Author's collection.

[St. Augustine Church]. Dedication Booklet. December 4, 1951. Kalamazoo Public Library Local History Collection.

[St. Joseph Catholic Church]. Dedication Souvenir. August 15, 1915. Kalamazoo Public Library Local History Collection.

Second Reformed Church. "One Hundred Years of Caring, A History of the Second Reformed Church." Pamphlet, 1985. Kalamazoo Public Library Local History Collection.

"Seventy-Five Years of Methodism—1833–1908." Pamphlet, 1908. First United Methodist Church, Kalamazoo, archives.

"Special Elk Souvenir and Minstrel Program." Pamphlet, n.d. Elks Lodge #50, Kalamazoo, archives.

[Stetson Chapel]. Rededication Brochure, 1987. Kalamazoo College Archives.

"Temple B'nai Israel, Proud Past Promising Future." Pamphlet, 1991. Personal Collection of Raye Ziring, Kalamazoo.

Yzenbaard, John. "A Goodly Heritage: Third Church A Christian Reformed Congregation, the First 75 Years." Pamphlet, 1982. Kalamazoo Public Library Local History Collection.

"100 Year of Christian Education." Pamphlet, 1977. Western Michigan University Archives and Regional History Collections.

"100 Years of Elkdom in Kalamazoo, 1887–1987." Pamphlet, n.d. Elks Lodge #50, Kalamazoo, archives.

[Historic Homes]. Tour Booklet, 1988. Kalamazoo Public Library Local History Collection.

Reference Materials

Atlas of Kalamazoo County, Michigan. New York : F.W. Beers & Co., 1873.

Buchner, Ward, ed. *Dictionary of Building Preservation.* New York: John Wiley & Sons, Inc., 1996.

Combined Atlases of Kalamazoo Michigan, 1873, 1890. Kalamazoo, MI: Kalamazoo County Historical Society, 1873, 1890. Reprint, Evansville, IN: Whipporwill Publications, 1984.

Illustrated Atlas of Kalamazoo County, Michigan. Detroit: William C. Sauer, 1890.

Mathews, Mitford M., ed. *A Dictionary of Americanisms on Historic Principles.* Vol. II. Chicago: University of Chicago Press, 1966.

"Redpath, James." *Dictionary of American Biography.* New York: Scribners, 1935, v. 8, 443–444.

"Redpath, James." *National Cyclopaedia of American Biography.* New York: James T. White Company, 1906, v.13, 118.

Sanborn Map Co. Insurance Maps of Kalamazoo. New York: Sanborn Map Co., 1887, 1891, 1896, 1902, 1908, 1932, 1958.

[Schematic Maps of Kalamazoo State Hospital]. 1961, 1975. Kalamazoo Public Library Local History Collection.

Who Was Who in America. Volume 1, 1897–1942. Chicago: A.N. Marquis Co., 1943.

Electronic Sources

Hazel, Michael. "They Called it Chautauqua." Available from: www.Star.Telegram.com/interact/chautauq.html. Internet; accessed April 8, 2000.

"Inaugural Address of (Chicago) Mayor Carter H. Harrison, Sr. May 9, 1881." Available from: www.chipuplib.org/004chicago/mayors/speeches/harrison81/html. Internet; accessed March 30, 2000.

Jurney, David H. "Wooden Street Paving." Available from: Anthropology Department Web site, Southern Methodist University at: www.smu.edu/~anthrop/woodstreets.html. Internet; accessed March 30, 2000.

"Lustron Facts and Links." Available from: www.piranhagraphix.com/Lustron/FactsandLinks/facts. Internet; accessed May 7, 2001.

Mackey, R. [Seth Thomas History]. Available from: www.ruralnet.org/clocks/seth.htm. Internet; accessed June 1, 2001.

Nabors, Jean. "A New Standard for Living: The Lustron Home." Available from: www.indianahistory.org/put/traces/lustron.html. Internet; accessed May 7, 2001.

Polson, Mary Ellen. "Steel Houses," *Old House Journal.* Available from: www.oldhousejournal.com/magazine/1999/december/steel/index.asp. Internet; accessed March 15, 2001.

Shepley, Bulfinch Richardson and Abbott. 1998 & 1999 & 2000. "Case Study: 2001, Bronson Hospital." Available from: www.sbra.com/html/kc/healthcare/hea__case. Internet; accessed April 16, 2001.

"Sullivan, Louis." *Britannica.com.* Available from: www.britannica.com/bcom/eb/article/html. Internet; accessed April 2, 2000.

Song Lyrics

Hupfeld, Herman. "As Time Goes By." Burbank, CA: Warner Bros. Music Corp., 1931.

Lennon, John, and Paul McCartney. "In My Life." London: Northern Songs, Ltd./Maclen Music Inc., 1965.

The authors thank the following individuals and others who gave their time in personal, telephone, written and electronic mail interviews.

Tammy Barnard	Alice Gernant	Don Rice
Patricia Bluman	Doris Graybiel	Ann Rohrbaugh
William Brennan	Sandy Groat	Fred Royce
Doreen Brinson	Patrick Hall	Stefan Sarenius
Walter Byers	Roger Hall	Judy Sarkozy
Andrea Casteel	Patrick Halpin	Steve Sattem
Jim Cavender	Robert O. Hayes II	Dan Schefers
Laura Chamberlain	Scott Hoeft	Peter and Julie Schmidt
Alfred Connable II	Brenda Hughes	John Schmitt
Annette Conti	Karen Jackson	Bill Shauman
Louis Conti	David Jarl	Bobby Joe and Barbara Shell
Nancy Davis-Smith	Mattie Jordan	Jeff Sherman
Fred and Leslie Decker	Art Kidney	Mark Smutek
Michael Dunn	Betsey Klepper	Ross Stancati
Susan Einspahr	Dave Kuitert	Marian Starbuck
Roy and Josephine Ellison	Honore and Jeff Lee	Mary Burdick Thorne
Christine Enstrom-West	Ted Little	Thomas Thorne
Del Farnsworth	Kevin McCall	Scott Tribby
Nicholas Fedesna	George Macleod	Susan and Albert Trombley
Margrete Flynn	Michael McMahon	Angelyn Van Hamersveld
Jean Forrest	Robbert McKay	Donald Verbeke
Earl Frazier	Tim Meulenberg	Chuck Vliek
Joe Fugate	John Murphy	Peter Wiegand
Bonnie Garbrecht	Nelson Nave	Dave and Kim Williams
John Garside	Pegg Osowski	Rick Wordell
	David Pyle	

Subject Index

Note: Included here are subjects of quotes, not persons quoted (*see* Sources Consulted, pp.264-272). Find individual or firm names of architects, builders, and contractors only under group headings beginning "architects" or "builders/contractors," unless noted in other contexts. Excluded are place names outside of Kalamazoo County.

Boldface page numbers refer to **definitions**. *Italic page numbers* indicate *drawings* or *photographs,* most often in addition to subject text on those pages. *Parenthetical italics* total the drawings and photos on their preceding page or range of page numbers. Maps are indicated by the letter m following a page number.

A

Abbott, Jonathon, 128
academies, 43, 240
    Catholic, 70, 108, 109*(3)*
    medical, 28
    public school, 252
Academy of Music, 138, 148–149*(5)*, 248, 257, 262
Academy Square, 107, 112
Academy Street, 54, 173
    1200 block, Kalamazoo College, 112, *183*, 225, 245*(2)*
    churches on, 59, *60*, 64
"Acres, The," Galesburg, 192, *193*
Adam-style entryway, *94*
adaptive use, as "found" category, **173**, 181*(2)*, *200*, 215*(2)*, *234*, *243*, *247*, *250*
adult entertainment industry, 133
advertisements
    photographic records as, 74, 87
    promotional campaigns as, 2, 44, 48, 87, 107
    signs as, *24*, *130*, *133*, *139*, *142*, 214–215*(2)*, 228*(3)*, *254*
African Methodist Episcopal Church, Kalamazoo. *See* Allen Chapel, A.M.E.
agricultural businesses, 83, 90, 95, 132, 162*(2)*, *195*, 196
Alamo Avenue, 30
Alano Club, *63*
Alcott Street, 80, 134
Allen, O.M., Sr., 116
Allen, Oscar M., and Hannah, 97
Allen Boulevard, 97
Allen Chapel, A.M.E., 59–60, 69*(2)*
Allen House, site, 97*(2)*
Allied Paper Co., 81

aluminum use, 74, 77, 244
A.M. Todd Co., *xvi*, 196*(2)*, 257, 260, 262, 263
American House (hotel), 17*(2)*
American Legion, Joseph Westnedge Post, 132, 235
American National Bank and Trust, 242*(2)*, 260, 262, 263
American Red Cross, Kalamazoo Chapter, 219
American Water Landmark, 212*(2)*
Ameritech (firm), *64*
Amherst stone, *218*
Anderson Athletic Center, Kalamazoo College, *113*, 183
Angell Field, Kalamazoo College, 147
Anthony Nolan, Rev. Mother, 109
antiques shops, 83, 176, 231
apartment buildings
    adaptive use and, 116, 181, *232*
    intentional, 32, 90*(2)*, *95*, 102–103*(4)*, *189*, 223, *251*
    school sites for, *112*, *118*, 121
apartments, 199, 202, 231, 237, 238, 239, 243, 250, 251
Appeldoorn House, Peter B., site, *238*, 258
Arcaded Block form, 9, 14*(2)*–15*(2)*
arcades, 129, 130
Arcadia Brook Golf Course, 121, 211
Arcadia Commons, 170, 184–185*(3)*, *247*, 259
Arcadia Creek, 73, *113*, 142, 170, 184
Arcadia neighborhood, Lustron house, 222
arches
    architectural styles with, sampled, *14*, *25*, *39(3)*, 44–45*(3)*, *49*, 130*(3)*, 164*(2)*, 182*(2)*, *218*, 242
    entryways and, *25*, 44–45*(3)*, *49*, *75*, *85*, 164*(2)*, 227*(2)*, 242, *244*, 252–253
    interiors with, *61*, 70–71, 110, 121*(2)*, *148*
    keystones in, *145*, 182*(2)*, 250*(2)*

arches *(continued)*
    materials used for, *46*, *49*, 110, 158*(2)*
    moldings and, 38*(2)*, 39*(3)*, *61*
    positions of, *61*, 110, 253
    sacred places and, *61*, 68*(2)*, 70–71, *218*, 240, 264*(2)*
    shapes of, 45*(2)*, 59, *64*, 68*(2)*, 80, *81*, *218*
    windows with, *36*, 38*(2)*, 39*(3)*, *49*, *56*, 80, *81*, 174*(2)*, *177*
architects, 73–74
    D. Adler, 148, 257
    E.R. Ball, 50, 130, 257
    E. Batterson, 30, 54, 204, 247, 257
    M.C.J. Billingham, 32, 119, 149, 177, 230, 257
    E. Broeker, 14, 257
    J. Chubb, 119, 258
    H.W. Coddington, 64, 116, 218, 258
    M.J. Dunn, 207, 247, 258
    C. Eidlitz, 227, 258
    A. Embury II, 225, 245, 258
    C. Fairchild, 43, 52, 77, 259
    E.O. Fallis, 43, 51, 259
    R. Frank, 174, 212, 259
    R. Gallup, 67, 250, 259
    H. Gay, 174, 259
    C.A. Gombert, 62, 239, 259
    L.D. Grosvenor, 91, 184, 259
    D. Hopkins, 64, 70, 259
    J. Howe, 193, 259
    E.S. Jennison, 110
    O.S. Kinney, 64, 260
    R.A. LeRoy, 6, 53, 145, 260
    J. Llewellyn, 131
    G. Lloyd, 218, 260
    G.W. Maher, 101, 260
    F. McClure, 260
    L. Miës van der Rohe, 235

architects *(continued)*
  J.E. Mills, 36, 260
  E.T. Mix, 104, 260
  N. Nave, 176, 203, 230, 261
  A. Palladio, 234
  J. Parent, 62, 263
  H. Pratt, 188, 261
  R. Prince, 205, 261
  D. Pyle, 181, 219, 261
  L. Reich, 235
  M.W. Roberts, 29, 56, 65, 110, 261
  R. Schramm, 225, 262
  J. Silsbee, 101
  S. Sloan, 27, 34, 262
  D. Slocum, 218, 262
  W. Stone, 125, 218, 251, 262
  W.B. Stratton, 212, 262
  J. Stryker, 231, 262
  L. Sullivan, 148, 262
  V. Thebaud, 121, 263
  H. Turner, 121, 263
  E.C. Van Leyen, 68, 263
  F.D. Van Volkenburg, 6, 49, 94, 151, 182, 186, 225, 263
  G.G. Worden, 98, 208–209, 224, 263
  F.L. Wright, 101, 192–193, 263
  A.B. Young, 50, 263
  A. Yurk, 224, 254, 263
architects, firms of
  Ann Beha Associates, 235, 257
  Bayles & Coleman, 116, 257
  Billingham & Cobb, 30, 103, 118, 119, 196, 210, 223, 244, 257
  Bonfield & Cumming, 20, 257
  D.A. Bohlen & Son, 230, 257
  David Milling & Associates, 45, 244, 260
  Haughey, Black & Associates, 32, 259
  Hobbs+Black Associates, 184, 259
  Holabird & Roche, 36, 259
  Kingscott & Associates, 45, 227, 230, 247, 260
  Malcolm, Calder & Hammond, 200, 260
  Mason & Rice, 138
  Maxwell & Associates, 261
  McKim, Mead & White, 181
  Osgood & Osgood, 152, 261
  Patton & Fisher, 45, 218, 261
  Perkins & Will, 205, 262
  Richard Prince & Associates, 205, 261
  Robinson & Campau, 180, 261

architects, firms of *(continued)*
  Shepley Bulfinch Richardson & Abbott, 190, 262
  Skidmore, Owings and Merrill, 132, 235, 262
  Slocum Associates, 214, 262
  Spiers & Rhone, 61, 262
  Stapert-Pratt-Bulthuis & Sprau, 262
  Stewart-Kingscott Company, 142, 262
  Stone, Smith & Parent, 62, 263
  Stone/Parent, 143, 262
  Thielbar & Fugard, 33, 262
  Tower, Pinkster, Titus, 196, 263
  Tower-Pinkster Associates, 188, 262
  Weary & Alford, 14, 188, 242, 263
architectural design, 2–4, 18, 124
  accessories and, 157–164*(18)*
  elements of, xiv, 9, 43, 51, 101, 176, 201
  entrepreneurs and, 177, 202, 220–221
  horizontal emphasis in, 176, *189*, 196*(2)*
  influences on, *103*, 119*(2)*, *145*, *189*, 193, *195*, 223, 238
  Modernist theory and, 205, 235, 242
architectural design, types of
  classic, 9, 80, *81*, 94, 99, 217, 242
  eclectic, 189
  foursquare, *191*, *200*, 217, 258
  linear plans for, 34–36*(9)*
  prefabricated buildings and, 19, 213, 222*(2)*, 238, 252
  solar-hemicycle, **193**
architectural styles
  Gothic *(see specifics that begin with English Gothic; Gothic; Gothic Revival; Victorian Gothic)*
  hybrids of, *32*, 59, 64, *178–179*, 184–185*(2)*, *186*, *196*, 199, 204*(2)*, 238, *248*, 250
  modern *(see Art Deco Style; International Style; Streamline Moderne Style)*
  renaissance *(see Italian Renaissance Style; Renaissance Revival Style)*
  revival *(see specifics that begin with Classical Revival; Colonial Revival; Dutch Colonial Revival; Georgian Colonial Revival; Gothic Revival; Greek Revival; Renaissance Revival; Romanesque Revival; Tudor Revival)*
  Tudor *(see English Tudor Style; Tudor Revival Style)*

architectural styles *(continued)*
  Victorian period, 56, 68, 164
  See also specifics that begin with, i.e., Chateauesque; Craftsman; Greco-Roman; Italianate; Minimal Traditional; Neoclassical; Prairie School; Queen Anne; Roman; Romanesque; Second Empire; Usonian
architecture
  formula, 10
  Functionalism in, 9, 18, 23, 40, 49, **52**, 53
  functions obscured by, *47*, 56, *62*
  historic, in Kalamazoo, xiii–xvi, **xv**, 1–255
  professionals active in Kalamazoo, 5–6, 257–263
armories, National Guard, 43, *52*
Art Deco Style, 20, *51*, *93*, *129*, 142*(2)*, *152*, *188*, 242*(2)*
arts facilities, 32, 49, 76, *91*, *108*, 148–149*(5)*, 175, 235
  See also theaters
Asbestos Row, *125*
Asylum Avenue, 139
Asylum Lake, *40*, 41
atriums, 190
attics, 32*(2)*, 186, 198, 232, 250
auditoriums, 45, 52, 111, 119, 148*(2)*, 235
"Aurora" (fresco), *148*
Austin, Benjamin, 211
Austin-Sill House, site, 87, 102
Auto Parts Distributors (firm), 176
Automatic Machine Co., merger, 95
automobiles, 16, 23, 227
  businesses associated with, *12*, 82, 176 *(see also* gas stations*)*
  church locations affected by, 61–62, 65, 68
  dealerships and sales, 18, 96, 175, 224
  effect on cities, 18, 60, 138, 139, 167, 172, 213
  garages for, *189*, 243
  predecessors of *(see* carriages*)*
  production of, *2*, 95
  See also parking lots
awnings, 11*(2)*, *13*, 21, 24–25*(3)*, 128–129*(4)*, 215, *224*

B

Babcock, Robert, 211
Balch, A.C., 110

balconies, 61, *64, 97,* 234
Baldwin, Schuyler C., photographer, 102
balustrades, 3, *37,* 158*(2), 198,* 199
Bank of Kalamazoo, 133
Bank Street, Farmer's Market, 162, 252
bankruptcies, 84
banks, 114
   branches, 16, 20, *56,* 133
   commercial district, 9, *11,* 14*(3)*–15*(2),*
     20, *21,* 130–131, 145, 149, 180,
     184–185*(2)*
   mergers and, 14, 15, 185, 242
   razed, 21, 129
   symbolism in design of, 9, 14, *15,* 242
   See also specifics, e.g., National City Bank
     (NCB)
Baptist churches, 107, 112
Barber, George F., 238
Barber's Department Store, *133*
barbershops, 249
Barbour, Levi L., 109
Barbour Hall, site, 109*(3)*
bargeboards, *91,* 197
Barley, Albert, *2*
Barnard Avenue, 139, 207
Barnum, P.T., circus, 144
barracks, World War I, 112, *120*
barrier-free access, 188, 247
Bartlett, Rev. Caroline, 62, *102,* 102–103*(2)*
   after marriage, 28, 88, *98,* 100
Bartlett, Edgar, publisher, 199
Bartlett-Upjohn House, site, *199,* 257
basements, 102–103, 110
Basket Case, The (firm), 200
Bassett, John C., and family, 89
Bassett House, site, 89*(2),* 262
battlements. *See* crenelations
beams, 3, 201, 226
bed and breakfast inns, 104, 198–199*(3),*
   239
bell towers
   chapel/church, *69,* 218, 245*(2)*
   school, 110, *111,* 117*(2), 118*
beltcourses, 196*(2)*
   brick, *79(3),* 110–111*(2), 187*
   dentiled, 21, *214*
   on schools, 110–111*(2), 118–119*
   stone, *36,* 95, 110–111*(2),* 148–149*(2)*
Benevolent and Protective Order of Elks
   (BPOE), 152*(3),* 258, 260, 261

Bennett Building, St. Joseph Parish, 117
Berea stone, 148–149*(2)*
Betzler-Donovan Funeral Home, 198
Bilbo's Pizza-in-a-Pan, *12*
Billingham, M.C.J., family home, 232
Binder Co., 74, 76*(3),* 261
Bissell, Dr. Helen, 27
Blakeslee Street, 30
block buildings. *See* commercial blocks
block materials
   cement, 12
   concrete, 16, 192–193*(2)* (*see also*
     concrete)
   sandstone, 227
   wedge-shaped stone, *177*
   wood, 129, 159*(2)*
Blodgett, Mr. & Mrs. Royal E., 54
Blood Brothers Automobile and Machine Co.,
   176
Bluman, Patricia, 223
boarding schools, *109*
boardinghouses, 89, 130, 133, 150
Bon Ton Beauty Salon, 131
Borgess, Bish. Casper, 29
Borgess Hospital, 27, *28,* 29*(3),* 109, 119
   building professionals and, 5, 29, 258,
     261, 263
   new Borgess Medical Center as, 229,
     230*(2),* 257, 258, 260, 261, 263
Bosman, Dr. John W., and family homes, *187,*
   206
Boudeman, Dallas, 89, 114
Boudeman, Donald, 48
Boudeman House, site, *92,* 99, *171*
Bowen, Charles Clarke, 113
Bowen Hall, Kalamazoo College, 112–113*(2)*
Boylan, Helen, 92
Boynton, Jeremith, 160
Boys, Dr. Charles, 211
boys schools, 38, 96, 109
brackets, *96,* 212*(2), 254*
   bungalows and, *217,* 252
   eaves with, *54, 98, 217,* 219*(2), 233*
   paired, *29,* 39*(3), 47,* 50–51*(2),* 89*(2),*
     100, 150, 184–185*(3),* 232*(2)*
   style, Craftsman, *54, 98*
   style, Italian Villa, *39(3),* 219*(2)*
   style, Italianate, *29,* 89*(2), 100,* 113, 150,
     232*(2)*
   style, Second Empire, 184, *185*

Brees, Henry, 21, 33, 152
Bremer, L.F., excavator, 186, 257
Brennan, William, 204
bricklayers. *See* masons
bricks, 3, *148,* 226, 237
   decorative, *79(3), 82,* 110–111*(2),*
     148–149*(2), 187,* 247
   exterior design and, *175, 182, 190, 198,* 199
   named types of, *148,* 237
   paths, streets, and walks, 159, 183,
     184–185, 232, 262
   restoration and, 183, 230
   stone (unspecified) and, 29, 51, 56, 234,
     245*(2)*
   structural uses (*see specifics*)
   technology and, 78, 220–221*(3),* 237
   See also masonry
bridges, 158*(3),* 234
Brinson, Doreen, home, *194,* 259, 261
Broadway Avenue, Lustron house on, 222
Broadway Street, 61
Bronson, Sally, home, 87
Bronson, Titus, 9, 43, 87, 240
Bronson, Village of, 43, 240
   churches, 59, 64
   commerce, 128, 242
   homes, 87, 137
   schools and colleges, 107, 137
Bronson Methodist Hospital, 27, 28, 33*(3),*
   94, 206, 229, 260, 262
   The New Bronson, 190*(2),* 257, 262
   property owned by, *118,* 190, 200
Bronson Park
   Academy Square and, 107, 112
   perimeter buildings, 28, 44–45*(5),*
     50–51*(3),* 54, 93, *93,* 180, *188*
   structures in, 240–241*(4),* 258, 259, 260,
     261
Bronson Park Historic District, National
   Register, 168, 169, 180, 188
Bronson's Addition, 189
Brook Farm, KSH, *27,* 40, 41, 101
Brown, Eric and Ann, Usonian home, *192*
Brown-Clapp House, site, *243,* 258
Brown House, Isaac, site, 187, 206*(2)*
Brown Paper Co., 82
Browne, Andrew, 23
Browne, Ella Drake, 21
Browne Block, 21*(2),* 263
Browne Building, 145

Bryant, Noah, 80, 93
Bryant Paper Co., 80–81*(4)*, 93, 260, 262
Bryant Paper Mill, 5, 81
Bryant Street, 80
Buckley, Fred, 132
builders/contractors, 60, 69, 70–71, 73–74
  B. Austin, 39
  E.R. Ball, 50, 130, 257
  W. Beeman, 110
  N. Blok, 32
  J. Campbell, 118, 257
  W. Case, 68, 257
  H.W. Coddington, 6, 46, 64, 116, 218, 258
  A.J. DeKoning, 119, 258
  F. Flaitz, 67, 99, 259
  T. Foy, 53, 119, 133, 259
  P. Halpin, 203, 262
  E. Hartman, 186, 259
  J. Heneika, 34, 259
  R. Heystek, 163, 259
  D. Little, 33, 163, 260
  A.D. Loughead, 117, 260
  K. McCall, 249, 260
  T. & J. Meulenberg, 248, 260
  F. Miller, 110, 260
  O.F. Miller, 30, 80, 174, 188, 242, 244, 245, 260
  A. Newbold, 251, 261
  T. Nie, 198, 261
  J. Prince, 116, 261
  G. Rickman, 6, 197, 261
  W. Ritchie, 29, 56, 261
  J. Schelb, 195, 261
  T. Schuring, 16, 262
  W. Shannon, 98, 262
  R. Sheridan, 32
  J. Smith, 231, 262
  S. Spink, 215, 262
  R. Stevens, 218, 262
  G. Van Eck, 208–209, 236, 263
  H.L. Vander Horst, 5, 14, 17, 21, 119, 125, 131, 142, 224, 226, 230, 242, 263
  D. Verbecke, 250
  W. Welsh, 65, 263
  U.D. Wheaton, 45, 110, 263
  A.J. White, *5,* 29, 67, 111, 114, 263
  P. Wiegand, 203, 214, 216, 262, 263
builders/contractors, firms of
  A.J. Etkins Construction Company, 185, 259
  Barton Malow Company, 190, 257

builders/contractors, firms of *(continued)*
  Blok & Sheridan, 32, 257
  Building Restoration Inc., 209, 244, 257
  Bush & Paterson, 6, 43, 46, 47, 50, 55, 116, 144, 148, 174, 184, 219, 227, 257
  Conti Building & Restoration, 174, 219, 258
  CSM Group, 190, 249, 257
  Daverman Associates, 234
  David Little Construction Company, 33
  DeRight Brothers, **6,** 43, 52, 54, 118, 152, 230, 258
  Diekema Hamann Construction, 173, 234, 258
  Donald B. Smith Company, 174, 262
  Frobenius & Huwiler, 62, 259
  George Lather & Sons, 247, 260
  George Rickman & Sons, **6,** 76, 118, 145, 261
  Herlihy Mid-Continent, 205, 259
  Hobbs+Black Associates, 200, 259
  Kal-West Contracting, 250, 259
  Kalleward-Bergerson, 174, 180, 200, 235, 244, 260
  Kingsley & Stock, 152, 260
  Miller-Davis Company, 196, 212, 218, 227, 241, 260
  Myers & Sons, 118, 260
  Paul Barton & Associates, 188, 257
  Pearson Construction Company, 20, 261
  Pulver Construction, 233, 261
  Reeves Brothers Company, 163, 261
  Rickman & Atkins, 62, 84, 261
  Scheid & Herder, 61, 261
  Schipper & Dykstra, 234, 261
  Shannon-Kline Incorporated, 207, 227, 262
  Southwest Builders Incorporated, 203, 262
  Sprouge & McGoff, 89, 262
  Superior Building Company, 247
  Van Dam & Krusinga, 231, 263
buildings, 18, *36, 44, 59, 99*
  cost of *(see* construction budgets)
  fireproof, 52, 77, 125, 151, 208
  found, xiv, 166–173*(8),* **167**–255, **172–173**
  foundations of, *21,* 84–*85,* 95, *99, 113, 163, 191*
  human relationships with, xiii–xv, 2–6, 59–60, 75, 204, 210, 211, 223, 245
  integrity and, xiv, 9, 87, 201
  lost, xiii–xiv, *xvi,* **1,** 1–*3(2),* 9–164

buildings *(continued)*
  moving, to save them, 173, 200, 243
  multipurpose, 19, *46,* 62, 176*(2), 216(2),* 219, 245*(2)*
  multistory, xvi, 1–24*(9),* 9, 29–41*(22),* 45–56*(12),* 59–71*(13),* 73–85*(10),* 90–104*(14),* 109–119*(12),* 166–173*(4),* 174–210*(24),* 211–254*(21)*
  one-story, xv, 11–20*(8),* 31–38*(2), 54, 65, 92,* 125, 174–210*(9),* 211–254*(8)*
  reuse of, 32, 49, 68, 71, 75–76, 83, 88, 94, 96, 104, 116, 118 *(see also* adaptive use)
  shapes of *(see* footprints, building)
  two-story, 11–25*(4),* 29–56*(10),* 62–71*(4),* 79–83*(4),* 87–101*(13),* 107–120*(14),* 166–173*(5),* 174–210*(20),* 211–254*(33)*
  See also types, e.g., commercial buildings
bull's-eye corner block, *246*
bungalows, *194,* 213*(2), 252,* 258, 259, 261
  features of, *178,* 179, *217,* 233
  hybrids of, 238
Burdick, Cyren, 9
Burdick, Justus, 9, 123, 130
  mansion, 50, 87, 130, 131
Burdick Hotel, 128–129*(2)*
Burdick House (hotel*),* 128
Burdick Street, 5, 159, 160
Burdick Street, North, 9, 108, 178–179
  100 block, 125*(2)*
  200 block, 137
  300 block, 43, *52,* 254
  400 block, 227
  1200 block, 18*(2)*
  Kalamazoo Mall, 125*(2),* 142
  transport stations on, 20, *22–23*
Burdick Street, South, 56, 114, 119
  200 block, 203
  300 block, 145
  400 block, 187, 206
  500 block, *1*
  600 block, *226*
  900 block, 63
  1100 block, 177
  1600 block, 134*(2)*
  1700 block, 134*(2)*
  1800 block, 134*(2)*
  activities on, 137, 145, 190

Burdick Street, South *(continued)*
   businesses on, 9, 13, 21*(3)*, 103, 134, 134*(2)*, 187
   Kalamazoo Mall, 21, *46, 49,* 89, 145*(4), 203, 228*
   South St. and, *46,* 89, *124*
Burham, Giles, and Mary, 92
Burham House, site, 92*(2)*
burial receiving vault, 164*(3)*
Burns, Dr. John B., 226
Burns Hospital, KSH, 36, 36, 37m
Burr Oak Street, 123, 160
Burrell & Son Carriage and Wagon Shop, *73,* 74
Burtt Manufacturing, merger, 95
buses, 20*(2), 22, 160,* 161, 227
Bush, Frederick, 5–6, *6,* 78, 148
   See also under builders/contractors, firms of, Bush & Paterson
Bushouse, Nicholas, 13
Bushouse Hardware, 134
business districts, xv, 3, 9, 12–13, 25, 76, 123–134*(23)*
   neighborhood, 99, 123, 127, 133, 249, 252
   See also downtown
business schools, 5, 104, 108, 114, 263
businesses
   lost, 10, 13, 17, 19, 24, 74, 79*(4),* 83
   success and, 12, 21, 73, 80–81
   See also specifics, e.g., J.R. Jones Sons and Co.
butcher shops. See meat markets
Butterfield, Walter S., 146, 149
buttresses, 164*(2)*
Byers, Walter, and Doris, 195*(2)*

C

Cahill, Leroy, *132*
Cameron Street, 144
canopies, *180, 230,* 242
Capitol Hotel, 67
Capitol Theatre, iv, 67, 138, 146*(2),* 260
Carder, Edwin, 229
carpenters, 5–6, 60, 71, 239, 263
Carr-Ciadella Photography (firm), 250
carriage houses, rehabilitation of, 197
carriage steps, curbside, 206*(2)*
carriages
   businesses associated with, *73,* 74, 176, 216
   porte-cocheres for, 87–88, 90, *97, 104,* 227

carriages *(continued)*
   successors of (see automobiles)
Casteel, Bill, and Andrea, 104, 199
"Castle, The," Monroe St., 239*(2),* 259, 262, 263
cathedrals, 70, 71, 96–97*(2)*
Catholic churches, 60, 70–71*(4),* 116, 117
Catholic Family Services, house, 169
Catholic schools, 108
   elementary, *70,* 71, 109*(2), 114,* 116, 117*(3),* 252, 260
   secondary, *70,* 97
Cavender, Jim, 237
Cedar Street
   East, 33
   West, 65, *88, 95,* 173
Cedar West Apartments, 95
ceilings, *65,* 201, 234, 244
   paintings on, *148,* 149, 188, 198, 199, 219, 242
   skylights in, *192,* 215
   stenciled, 198, 199
   tall, *50,* 51, *192,* 193
   tin, 187, 254
Celery City Cycle Co., *9,* 10
celery farms, 134, 177, 252
cement blocks, 12
cemeteries, *157,* 161*(2),* 164*(3)*
Central Christian Church, 68
Central Church of the Nazarene, *63*
Central Corners, Kalamazoo, *249,* 257, 258, 260
Central Fire Station, *43,* 49*(2)*
Century Plaza, *46*
chandeliers, 92, 148*(2)*
chapels, church, 59–60, 64, *68,* 69, 218
chapels, college, 112, 113, 172, 245*(2)*
Chapman, Don, designer, 216, 258
Chappell House, site, *199,* 257
Charlotte Avenue, 119, 213, 259
Chase, Nehamiah, 11
Chase Block, site, 9, 11*(2),* 114
chase egress, as stairway, 203
Chateauesque Style, 96, 97
Chicago, Kalamazoo and Saginaw Railroad (CK&S), depot, 23*(2)*
Chicago brick, 237
Chicago Musical Instruments (firm), 208
Chihuly, Dale, glass artist, 235, 258
Child Welfare League, 28, *31*
Children's Home, 38*(2),* 96

chimneys, *32,* 219*(2), 246*
   multiple, on one house, *97, 110,* 181
   Tudor Revival and, 204*(2),* 244
Chormann, Richard F., legacies, 180
Christian Church—Disciples of Christ, site, 68
Christian Reformed churches, 59–60, *61,* 63
Christian Reformed schools, 108, 115*(2)*
Church of Christ (denomination), 68
Church of God in Christ Pentecostal, 69
Church Square, 59, 218
Church Street
   North, 20, 51, 84, 87, *179*
   South, 54, 59, 64
churches, 43, 59–65*(12),* 68–71*(7),* 252
   additions to, 60, 61, 62*(2),* 64, *65,* 68
   downtown, 59, 60, 62, *62,* 64, 68*(2),* 70–71*(4), 151,* 218, 240
   education funding from, 107, 112, 116
   (see also parochial schools)
   "mother-daughter" congregations and, **60**
   neighborhood, 31, 61, 63, 65, 69, 116, 117, 220, 234
circuses, 144, 252
cisterns, 56
"Citadel, The," Salvation Army, *247,* 257, 258, 260
Citizen-Soldiers. See National Guard
Citizens Street Railway, 139
City Beautiful Movement, 18
city halls. See under Kalamazoo, City of, administrative quarters for
City Union Brewery, 79
civic buildings. See public places
Civic Theater, 168
Civilian Conservation Corps (CCC), 140
CK&S. See Chicago, Kalamazoo and Saginaw Railroad (CK&S)
clapboard, *63,* 197*(2), 217, 233*
Clarage Foundry, 5
Clark, Dr. O.H., 28
Classical Revival Style, 9
Clinton Street, Tudor Revival on, *252,* 253
clocks, *210,* 228*(3),* 262
clothing stores, 92, 131, 214, 228
Clover Street, Lustron house on, 222
Cobb, James, *1*
Cobb, Thomas, 23
Cobb Avenue, 60, 140–141
Cobb Street, 115
code violations, 125, 187

Coldstream Brewery, 79
College of Business Library, WMU, 121
colleges and universities, 50, 101, 107, 108, 114
   See also specifics, e.g., Kalamazoo College; Western Michigan University (WMU)
Colonial influence, *103*, 119*(2)*
Colonial Revival Style
   adapted use and, *180, 198–199, 225*
   characteristics of, *54, 63, 224*
   Georgian, *210,* 245*(2), 257*
   homes, 87, *178,* 225
   hybrids of, *186,* 250*(2)*
colonnades, *67, 120*
   See also columns
Colony Farm, KSH, 40–41*(5),* 101
colony system, mental illness treatment with, 35–36, 40–41
Columbia Sled Co., 77
columns, 129, *191*
   decorative, 182*(2), 190*
   entrances and, *82,* 151
   interior, 110, 245*(2),* 250
   Ionic, *49,* 94*(2), 99, 224, 234,* 245*(2)*
   paired, *90,* 229
   porches with, *90,* 94*(2), 99, 217, 233*
   porticoes with, *178,* 225*, 229*
   style, Colonial Revival, *178, 210, 225*
   style, Neoclassical, 94*(2), 99, 229*
   style, Queen Anne, *90, 217*
Comerica Building, *149*
comfort stations, 54*(2),* 141*(2)*
Commerce Building, 11*(2)*
commercial blocks, **9–10**, 11*(2), 25,* 128–129*(2),* 133, 176*(2)*
   one-part, *249*
   two-part, 13, *25,* 176*(2), 187,* 249*, 254,* 263
   three-part, *21*
commercial buildings, 9–25*(36),* 12, 16, 103, 125–134*(20),* 146–152*(6),* 166–173*(5),* 174–210*(11),* 211–254*(16),* 252
   block design and, **9–10**, 21, 25, 129*(2)*
   condemned, 125
Commonwealth Power Co., 78
Community Education Center, *110*
Comstock, Village of, *43*
concrete
   artistic use of, *190, 196, 198,* 199, 240
   bridges and, 158*(2)*
   cast, *190, 196, 198,* 199, 227

concrete *(continued)*
   reinforced, 74, 78, 80, 158, 198, 208–209
   stabilization with, 163, 182, 230
concrete blocks, 16, 192–193*(2)*
condominiums, 103, *203, 223*
Congregation of Moses, 66, *67,* 259, 263
Congregational churches, *151*
Connable, Alfred, Jr., 99
Connable, Alfred B., 99, 224
Connable, Frances Peck, and family, 99
Connable House, Alfred and Frances, site, 99*(2),* 259
Conservation and Museum Services (firm), 188, 258
conservatories, botanical, *177*
construction budgets
   commercial buildings, 15, 20, 224, 242
   education, 112–113, 115, 116, 205
   healthcare, 28, 29, 33
   industrial facilities, 73, 208
   public places, 45–47, 49–55
   residences, 211, 219, 223, 251
   sacred places, 66, 69, 71, 245
   sources of, 112, 116, 219
Consumers Power Co., Power Plant, 78*(2)*
contaminants, cleanup of, 184, 243
Conti, Annette, 198–199, 200, 219, 238, 258
Conti, Louis, 198–199
contractors. See builders/contractors
Cooley Street, 70
copper use, 196*(2),* 215, 227, *230*
corbels, *75,* 76*(2),* 79*(2),* 109*, 246*
corduroy roads, **158**
Corinthian columns, 210
cork flooring, 81
Cork Street, East, 74
Cornell residence, YWCA, 180
corner treatments, *65, 186, 189, 246*
   crenelations, 68–69*(3)*
   entrances, *12,* 65
   finials, *11,* 148
   pilasters, *50,* 197*(2)*
   pinnacles, *148,* 164*(2)*
   towers, *11, 59, 61, 64,* 68–69*(3), 75, 90,* 93*(2), 95,* 114
cornices, *249*
   brackets at, *24, 47,* 50–51*(2), 96, 254*
   brackets (paired) at, *39(3), 150,* 184–185*(3),* 232*(2)*
   commercial/industrial buildings, 73, 80*(2),* 84–85, 130*(3),* 146, 224, 254

cornices *(continued)*
   corbel course at, *75,* 76*(2), 109*
   decorated/ornamented, *37, 40, 73, 119,* 130*(3),* 148–149*(2), 180,* 184–185*(3),* 188, *214, 216,* 262
   deep/wide, *29, 37,* 89*(2),* 102–103, 206
   dentiles and, 84–85, 94*(2), 99, 146, 210, 224*
   as horizontal design element, 176, *189*
   returns and, *63,* 94*(2)*
   style, Colonial Revival, *180, 210*
   style, Italian Villa, *39(3)*
   style, Italianate, *29,* 89*(2),* 102–103, 130*(3), 150,* 206, *216,* 232*(2)*
Corporation Hall, 43, 53, 54–55*(2),* 148, 257
corset companies, 84–85*(3)*
Cosmopolitan Hotel, 128
Cosmos Restaurant, *172*
cottages
   homes as, 204*(2),* 215*(2)*
   hospitals and, *27,* 30, 35, 36, *39,* 40–41*(4)*
Courthouse Square, 47*(2),* 50–51*(3),* 54, 240
courthouses, *19,* 43, *100*
   courtrooms in, 50–51*(2),* 188
   good business locations near, 11, 21, 131
   Kalamazoo County, 43, 50–51*(5),* 54, 130, 257, 259, 263
courts and judges
   Michigan, *19,* 21, *100,* 205
   municipal, 53
   U.S., 46, 91, 110
Craftsman Style, *54,* 87, *98, 175*
   homes, 87, *98*
   hybrids of, *186,* 204*(2)*
craftspeople, 82
Cramer, W.B., manufacturer, 95
Crane, Dr. Augustus W., 32, 98, 100
Crane, Caroline Bartlett, 28, 62, *98,* 100
   collected photographs of, homes, 88, 98*(2),* 100*(2)*
   before marriage, 62, *102,* 102–103*(2)*
Crane, Jacob, 167
Crane, Julia, *98*
Crane, Dr. Warren Bartlett, 98
Crane House, Augustus and Caroline Bartlett, sites, 98*(3),* 262
crenelations
   churches with, *65,* 68–69*(3)*

crenelations *(continued)*
　roofline with, *247*
　towers with, *52, 163, 212*
cresting, *11, 56,* 92*(2), 97,* 174*(2),* 181*(2), 185*
Creston Avenue, 233
Crosstown Parkway, East, 56, 77
Cummings, Kim, 200
cupolas, *56,* 89
　dual, *80–81(3)*
　finials atop, *29, 110,* 232*(2)*
　Italianate homes with, *29, 89, 150,* 211*(2),* 232*(2)*
　multiple windows per side, *29,* 89, 150
　rounded, *150*
Curry, Sam, 83

D

Dahl, Dennis, cabinetmaker, 233, 258
dams, 78
dance halls, 11, 52, 80
D'Arcy, Frank, 82, *128,* 129, 198
D'Arcy Spring Co., 82*(2)*
"daughter" churches, **60,** 68
Davenport College, 114
Davis Street, *120*
day-light construction, 74, 76*(2),* 78*(2),* 82*(2),* 208–209*(3)*
D.C. Byers Co., 230
DDA. *See* Downtown Development Authority (DDA)
Dean, A.L., 68
Dean, Vernon, 250, 258
Decker, Fred and Leslie, family homes, *197*
decorative elements
　cast concrete, *190, 196, 198,* 199
　cast iron, *89*
　medallions, 219, 242, 248
　paint schemes, 181, 190–191, 197, 199, 211, 221–222, 233, 237–239, 247
　tile work, *249*
　trim, *82,* 148–149*(2), 190,* 208–209*(2),* 220–221*(3),* 242, *246*
　wrought-iron, *251*
　See also associated architectural features, *e.g.,* moldings
decorative motifs
　floral, *188,* 242
　historical, *188*

decorative motifs *(continued)*
　serpentine, *206*
　shell, *180*
　sunburst, 181*(2), 246*
Den Adel, Homer, 189
Den Adel Court, 169
den Bleyker, Dimmen, 246
Denner Street, 30
dentils
　beltcourses with, *214*
　cornices with, *84–85, 99, 146, 151, 210, 224*
　moldings with, 94*(2)*
　pediments with, 245*(2)*
　triglyphs with, *82*
dentists, 9, 21, 214
department stores. *See* dry goods stores
Desenberg families, 62, 66
Designer's Showcase, fundraiser, 211
Detroit Automobile Inter-Insurance Exchange, 71
Dewing, Carrie, 96
Dewing, Chapin, 242
Dewing, William G., and Jane Tuttle, 38, 96
Dewing, William S., 38, 96, 125
Dewing Building, *125,* 262
Dewing Hall, Children's Home, 38
Dewing House, William G. and Jane Tuttle, site, *96–97(3)*
Diekema Hamann Architecture & Construction, adaptive use and, 173, *234,* 258
Dietz Movers (firm), 243
District Court Building, *19, 100*
doctors. *See* physicians
Doctor's Row, 206
Dodge Hall, Michigan Female Seminary, *116,* 257
domes, 66*(2),* 67, *132*
Donovan Funeral Home, 198
door handles, custom-made, *254*
doors, 3, *49, 163, 247*
　arches and, 59, 130*(2), 164(2)*
　front, *32,* 211*(2)*
　multiple, 202, 211*(2)*
　pediments above, *102–103*
　pocket, *103*
　style, Italianate, *102–103,* 211*(2)*
　style, Queen Anne, *118,* 202
　windows above, *32, 94, 210 (see also* fanlights)

doors *(continued)*
　wooden, *145,* 221
　See also entrances
dormers, *32, 33(2)*
　eyebrow, *186*
　front, 94*(2)*
　gabled, *233*
　multiple, 38*(2), 40, 41, 97,* 184, *185, 191,* 239*(2)*
　portholed, *148*
　Queen Anne style, *118, 132, 238,* 239*(2)*
　rebuilt, 244
　shed, *118,* 174*(2), 178, 197, 233*
　windowed, *212*
Dormitory Road, 39
Dosker, Rev. H.N., 65
Doubleday, Fred, home, 191
Douglas, Stephen, memorials, 217
Douglas Avenue, 40, 101, 178, 182, 191, 196, 217
Douglass, Frederick, memorials, 62, *137,* 137–138, 178
Douglass Community Association, 178
Douglass Community Center, *137,* 137–138
downtown
　business district, xv, 9, 21, *46, 49,* 53, 88, 89, 123, 125*(2),* 128–131*(11),* 228
　fires in, 11, 17, 22, 24, 89, 125, 128–129, 131, 138, 149, 151, 212
　gas stations, 17, *18–19(4),* 215
　hotels and inns, 9, 17*(2),* 67, 68, 128–129*(3), 198–199(2)*
　industries, 75*(2),* 84–85*(3),* 91, *94,* 184, *185*
　office space, 9, 11, 21, 32, 89, 103, 181, 184–185*(2), 206*
　parking, iv, 11, 19, *24,* 33, *52,* 53, 60, *66,* 67, *75, 85, 96,* 131, *146,* 150–152*(3),* 184–185, xv
　sacred places, iv, 59, 60, *62, 64,* 66–67*(3),* 66–68*(5),* 70–71, 218, *240*
　theaters, iv, 21, 66, 67, *128,* 129, 142*(3),* 145–146*(7),* 148–149*(5)*
　tornado damage, 15, 68, 128
Downtown Development Authority (DDA), 142, 171, 184–185, 203, 236
Doyle, James, mason, 237, 258
Doyle House, James and family, site, *237,* 258
Drake, Benjamin, 21
Drake, Soledad Dela Vega, 152

Drake Road, 40–41
dressmakers, 9, 21, 89, 194
drug stores, 9, 10, *25*, *127*, *128*, 129, *133*
dry goods stores, 24*(2)*, 46, *49*, *55*, 89, 131, *133*
Dunbar, Willis, Ph.D., 143, 167
Dunkley Street, 178
Dunwell's Drug Store, *127*
duplexes, *189*, *253*
Dutch Colonial Revival Style, *186*
Dutch culture
    celery farming and, 134, 177
    churches, 61, 65, 234
    distinctive roofs, 117*(2)*, 186
    residential areas and, 190, 198
Dutton Street
    East, 187, 200
    West, 59

E

Eames, Mrs. Lucia, 107
East Avenue Elementary School, 108, 118–119*(2)*, 258, 259
East Campus, WMU, 168, *201*
    East Hall, *108*, *120*, 121, 152
    North Hall, 121*(2)*, 263
East Hall, Normal School, *108*, *120*, 121, 152
Eastern Michigan Motorbuses (firm), 20
Eastside neighborhood, 119, 213*(2)*, 259
eaves, 244
    boxed, 94*(2)*
    bracketed, *54*, 211*(2)*, *217*, 219*(2)*
    cantilevered, 192–193*(3)*
    deep/wide, 16*(2)*, 29, *100*, *102–103*, *113*, *175*, 189, *191*, 192–193*(3)*, *217*, 227*(2)*
    knee braces under, *186*, 204*(2)*
    rolled, 204*(2)*
    set, *98*
    style, Craftsman, *54*, *98*, *175*, *186*, 204*(2)*
    style, Italianate, *100*, *102–103*, *113*, 211
eavestroughs. *See* gutters, rain
Economic Development Corporation, 234
Edgemoor Avenue, 163
Edison Environmental Science Academy, 252
Edison neighborhood, 118, 144, 161, 252–253*(4)*
    Washington Square in, 6, 123, 133*(3)*, 252, 253
Edwards, Dr. William, 36

Edward's Gulf Station, *18*
Edwards Hospital, KSH, 36, 37, *37*, 37m
Edwards Street, 9, *159*
    North, 59, 108, 176*(2)*, 261
Egleston Avenue, *252*
Eleanor Street, 56
    West, 84, 142, 184–185, 247
electricity
    providers of, 78, 108
    uses of, 17, 73, 75, 79, 120, 160–161, 175
elevators, 17, 21, 46, 116, 188, 209, 231, 242
Elgin Street, *253*
Elite Theatre, 21, 138, 145*(4)*, 261
Elizabeth Street, *178*, 179
Elks Temple and Lodge Hall, site, 152*(4)*, 258, 260, 261
Ellis, Miron, *228*
Ellison, Roy, and Josephine, *226*
E.M. Sergeant Co., 23
Emerson Street, 119
Emporium Antiques, The, *83*
energy conservation technology, 193, 205, 237
English Gothic Style, *218*
English Tudor Style, *54*, 61, *63*
entablatures, *234*
entertainment, 137–138*(2)*, 139–154*(48)*
    adult, businesses, 133
    amusement parks, 138, 139*(3)*, 144*(2)*, 144m
    chautauquas, 137, 153*(3)*
    dance halls, 11, 52, 80
    home venues for, 99, 137, 138, 141, 146
    recreation facilities, 138–141*(9)*, 143*(3)*, 147*(3)*, 151–152*(6)*, 154*(2)*
    social clubs, 137–138*(2)*, 150–151*(6)*, 152*(4)*
    streetcars and, 137, 138–139, 144
    theaters, 137, 138, 142–149*(5)*
    See also parks
entrances
    arched, *25*, 44–45*(3)*, *49*, 73, 75, *85*, *189*, *242*, *244*, 250*(2)*, 252–253
    arched (triple), 70*(2)*, 71
    canopies over, *180*, *230*, *242*
    central, 65, *99*, *224*, *225*
    columns beside, *82*, *151*, *210*
    dual, *69*, *102–103*, *189*
    front, 64, *102–103*, *186*, *189*
    hospital, *190*, *230*

entrances *(continued)*
    multiple, *102–103*, *190*
    pediments above, *50*, *51*, *67*, *77*, *80*, *81*, *224*
    pergolas over, *54*, *186*, 204*(2)*
    piers beside, 204*(2)*
    porte-cocheres (mansions), 87–88, 90, *97*, *104*, 219*(2)*
    porte-cocheres (nonresidence), *190*, *218*, 227*(2)*
    porticoes at, 33*(2)*, *61*, *63*, *251*
    redesigned, *151*, 175
    school, 119*(2)*, *210*
    unique, *12*, *77*, *94*, *157*, *185*, *235*
    vehicles and, 20, *49*, 182*(2)*
    windows adjacent to (*see* fanlights; sidelights)
    See also doors
Eriksen, Roger, supervisor, 213, 258
Esterman, Edward, 139
Evangelical Lutheran Latvian Church, 220
Everard, Herbert H., and Althea Vande Walker, 140
Everard, H.H., family, *181*
Everyman's House, site, 98
Exchange Place, 24, 130
exterior design
    appearance in, 73, 78, 80
    asymmetry in, *104*, 197*(2)*, *237*, *248*
    balance and, *225*
    changes in, commercial buildings, 10, *11*, *12*, 14–17*(9)*, 20–21*(4)*
    changes in, healthcare and human services buildings, 29*(2)*, 31, 32*(4)*, 34–35*(2)*
    human relationships and, 2–4, 75
    materials in, clapboard, *63*, 197*(2)*, *217*, *233*
    materials in, metal, 222, 242
    materials in, stucco, 31, *175*, *182*, *226*, 252–253*(2)*
    symmetry in, *54*, 59, *63*, 68*(2)*, *95*, *180*, *210*
    temple front, *67*
    texture in, *202*
    See also facades

F

facades, 14–15*(3)*, *53*, *145*, *164*, *250*
    brickwork, 36, 55, 110–111*(2)*, *198*, 199
    broken, *113*, 114, *189*, *246*
    decorated, 36, 79, 110–111*(2)*, *190*

facades *(continued)*
　　front, *49, 54,* 55, *63, 67, 82,* 142, *180*
　　limestone and, *36,* 224, 245*(2)*
　　multiple, 55*(2), 238*
　　siding and, *31,* 74
　　stucco and, *31, 198,* 199
　　style, Art Deco, *152,* 242*(2)*
　　style, Colonial Revival, *54, 63, 180*
　　style, Greco-Roman, *67*
　　style, International, *16*
　　style, Queen Anne, *113,* 114
　　symmetrical, *54, 63, 180*
factories. *See* industrial buildings
Factory Street, *2*
Fair Oaks. *See* Colony Farm
Fairmount Hospital, 30, *30,* 257, 263
fairs, 133, 144m, 252
fanlights, *32, 63,* 82, *94,* 145
　　Colonial Revival, *54,* 250*(2)*
　　Dutch gable and, 117*(2)*
　　Georgian Colonial Revival, *210,* 245*(2)*
Farm Bureau, agricultural businesses and, 83
Farmer's Alley, iv, *66*
Farmer's Market, 162, 252
farms, 40, 83, 109, 134, 162*(2),* 204
Farrell, Charles, mayor, 162
Featherbone Corset Co., 84
Federal Building, Michigan Ave., *68, 73,* 74
Federal Emergency Relief Administration Act, 140
Federal Housing Administration, 251
Fedesna, Nicholas, 226
females, education of, 38, 96, 100, 108, 109, 116, 232
fences, *157,* 232*(2)*
fenestration, **3,** *103,* 190
　　Chicago-style, *214*
　　English Tudor and, *54,* 61, *63*
　　Romanesque Revival and, *64*
　　symmetry and, *54, 63,* 68*(2)*
　　See also doors; windows
Ferdon Road, Lustron house on, 222
Ferris, Gov. Woodbridge, 52
Fidelity Federal banks, 21, *145*
Fifth Third Bank, 242
finials, *148, 158, 164*
　　corners with, *11, 148*
　　gables and, *91, 197*
　　multiple, 239*(2)*
　　towers with, *48, 90,* 96*(2), 219, 237*

fire escapes, *84,* 152
fire protection
　　fire departments, 43, 49
　　fireproofing, 52, 77, 125, 151, 201, 208
　　steel construction for, 222
　　water for, 56, 163
　　water supplies for, 163, 212
fire stations. *See* firehouses
firehouses, 4
　　Central, *43,* 44, *49*
　　Corporation Hall and, 55, 137
　　No.2, Portage St., 172, 250*(2),* 259
　　No.5, Douglas Ave., 182*(2),* 263
　　No.7, Parkview Ave., *207,* 258, 262
fireplaces, *94,* 100, *103, 121,* 189, *192,* 193, 244
fires, 12, 34, 77, 139
　　churches and, 64, 69, 234
　　downtown and, 11, 17, 22, *24,* 89, 125, 128–129, 131, 138, 149, 151, 212
　　homes and, 89, 191, 243
　　schools and, 111, 118, 200
First Christian Reformed Church, 234
First Congregational Church, *60, 151*
First Federal Savings and Loan Association, 20
First National Bank, 9, 14–16*(5),* 130, 231, 257, 263
First of America Bank (FOA), 15, 180, 184–185*(2),* 259
First Unitarian Church, 110
First United Methodist Church, 64, *240*
Fischer's Orchestra, 52
Fleming, Andrew, 102
Fletcher Hospital, KSH, 36, *36,* 37m
Flexnit Co., 85
flooring, 110
　　cement, 12, 182
　　hardwoods, 175, 189, 198, 202, 232, 250, 251
　　marble, 232, 242
　　mosaic, *45,* 242
　　pine, 186, 237
　　tile, *45,* 254
　　unique materials as, 81, 121, 232
Florence Street, 118
Flynn, Cale L. "Bud," and Margrete, 12
Flynn's Soup'er Burger Restaurant, 12*(3)*
FOA (First of America Bank), 15, 180, 184–185*(2),* 259
Folz, Sam, 214, 228

Foote, James B., 78
Foote, W.A., 78
footprints, building, 100, 101, *238*
　　box, 124, 191
　　changes in, 67, 215*(2)*
　　cubic, 206, 211*(2), 229,* 232*(2)*
　　Italianate style, *150,* 197*(2),* 206, 211*(2), 229,* 232*(2)*
　　L-shaped, 177, 197*(2)*
　　rectangular, 124, *189, 192,* 193, 222
　　solar-hemicycle, *193*
　　T-shaped, *113*
　　triangular, *192,* 193, 236
formula architecture, 10
foundations, community. *See* Kalamazoo Foundation
foundations, structural. *See under* buildings, foundations of
"Fountain of the Pioneers," Bronson Park, 240–241*(3),* 259
Four Corners, Kalamazoo, 5, 114, 131
Fox, Scott, and Terri, 198
foyers, 202, 232, *235,* 242
frame buildings, 87, 194
　　sacred places, iv, *63,* 69
　　school facilities, 107, 116, *120*
Frank Street, East, 59, 108, 160
Frank Street School, *107,* 108
Fraternal Order of Police, 65
fraternal organizations, 138
　　college-based, 39*(3),* 49, 101, 181, 200, *232*
　　lodges for, 11, 65, 131, 139, 152*(3),* 170
　　regalia for, 75, 239
Frederick Douglass Community Association, *137,* 137–138
Frederick Douglass Literary Club, 62
Free Holland Christian Reformed Church, *63*
frescoes, *148,* 149
friezes, 78*(2), 82, 99, 103*
Fuller Brush Co., 242
functional architecture, 9, 40, 52, *53*
　　transportation and, 18, 23, 49, *182, 189, 207,* 250
Functionalism, **52**
fundraising, 33, 112, 116, 158, 211, 212
funeral homes, *94,* 96, 150, 191, 198, 231
furniture, *94,* 263
　　manufacture, 75, 77
　　stores, 75, *92,* 214
　　uses, 108, *142*

G

gables, *22, 23, 33(2), 207*
   bungalows with, *178,* 179, *217*
   cross-, 197*(2)*
   decorated, *91, 246, 248*
   duplexes with, *253*
   Dutch, 117*(2)*
   finials on, *91,* 96*(2)*
   multiple, *113,* 116
   parapeted, *36,* 164*(2)*
   position, 83*(2), 246*
   position, front, *175, 178–179, 220–221(3), 244, 246, 252–253*
   position, porch, 181*(2)*
   position, side, *244*
   shingled, *104, 220–221(3)*
   style, Craftsman, *98, 175*
   style, English Gothic, *218*
   style, Italianate, 197*(2)*
   style, Minimal Traditional, *178–179*
   style, Queen Anne, *90,* 92–93*(4),* 95–96*(3), 104,* 113, 116, *118, 132, 179,* 181*(2),* 217, *220–221(3), 237–239(4), 243, 246, 248*
   style, Richardsonian Romanesque, *45*
   style, Second Empire, *91*
   style, Tudor Revival, *244, 252–253*
   style, Victorian Gothic, 164*(2)*
   width of, 68*(2), 98*
   windows in, *177*
Galesburg Country Homes (development), 192, *193*
gambrel roofs, **186,** *252,* 253
garages, *189, 243, 250*
gardens
   businesses associated with, 176, *177*
   private, *82, 90, 94, 104,* 199
   public, *47,* 210
gargoyles, *174*
Garrett, Charles H., family home, *220*
Garrett-Shell House, *220–221(3)*
Garside, John, 236
Gary Center, WMU, 121
gas lighting, 61, 108, 148*(2)*
gas stations
   buildings replaced by, 56*(2),* 96, 100*(2),* 127
   downtown, 17, *18–19(4),* 64, 215
   former, and adaptive use, 173, 215*(2)*

Gate Cottage, KSH, 35
Gateway Golf Course, 147, 211
gazebos, *207*
Geilfuss, Bertha, 102
George F. Barber and Co., 238
Georgian Colonial Revival Style, *210,* 245*(2),* 257
Gernant, Harry, businesses, 13*(2)*
Gernant and Laning Meat Market, 13*(3)*
Gibson, Orville, 208
Gibson Building
   Mandolin-Guitar Company in, 208–209*(3),* 263
   rescue of, 172, 209, 257
gift shops, *127, 200,* 235
Gilbert House, Henry, site, *246*
Gilmore, Donald, and Genevieve, 132, 235
Gilmore, Irving S., 219
Gilmore, Jim, mayor, 21
girls schools, 38, 96, 108, 109, 116*(3)*
Gladding Corporation, 77
Gladysz, Victor, 12
glass use, 149, *177,* 185
   architectural styles and, 142, 205
   art and, 45, 235, 258, 262
   facades and, 15, *45,* 145
   See also windows
Globe Casket Co., 97
golf courses, 121, 126, 152, 211
Goodwill Industries, *195*
Gothic Revival Style, *22–23, 64,* 65*(2), 201*
   hybrids of, *196*
Gothic Style, *69,* 164*(3)*
   hybrids of, 59, 64
Gougler, Marceline, artist, 240
Gown Shop, 92
Grace Christian Church, 59
Grace Christian Reformed Church, adaptive use of, 173, *234,* 258, 261
Grace Corset Co., 84–85
grain businesses, 83, 90, 92, 132
Grand Avenue, 99, *194*
Grand Prairie Avenue, 67
Grand Rapids and Indiana Railroad, 17, 23
granite, *46,* 188, 242
Gray, Dr. John, 34
Graybiel, Lester, and Doris, 16
Greco-Roman Style, *67*
Greek Revival Style, *50,* 59, 87
Greenleaf Capital Inc., merit award, 231

Greenleaf Trust, Retirement Division, 231
greenspaces, *47,* 50*(2),* 152*(3), 190*
   See also gardens; parks
greenstone, hand-carved, *92*
Gregory Commercial College, 108
Greyhound Bus Station, 20*(2),* 257, 261
Grinwis, Brett, craftsman, 194, 259
grocery stores, 9, 13, 25, 75, 96, *134,* 249
Grofvert, Cornelius, cigarmaker, 134
growleries, **104**
Gull Road, 29, 109, 116, 230
Gull Street, 28, *31,* 178
gutters, rain, 227, 230, *233*
gymnasiums, 116, 119, *147, 151*

H

Haas, Orley, 204
Hahn, Nicolette, 200
Hall House Bed & Breakfast, *198–199,* 261, 263
Halley, Rev. H.H., 68
Halls of Finance. *See* banks
Hanselman Building, 128–129*(2)*
Harding, Pres. W.G., 108
Harding School, 118
hardware stores, 133, 134*(2)*
Harper Funeral Home, 191
Harrell, Michael, designer, 216, 259
Harris Hotel, 17
Harris Motor Inn, *17*
Harry L. Harris & Associates (firm), 17
Harvey, Leroy, and family, 186
Harvey-Macleod House, site, *186,* 259, 260, 263
Hastings, T. William, 236
hay markets, site, *52,* 53
Hayden, Michael, artist, 244, 259
Hayes, Orrin B. "Pug," and family, 224
Haymarket Building, 137, *170*
Haymarket Historic District, *166,* 168, 169, 176, 216, 227
Hays, Charles, developer, 17, 21, 144, 147, 252, 253
Hays, Charles B., realtor, 39
Hays Drive, 39
Hays Park Avenue, 144
healthcare services, 71
   mental illness treatment, 27, 34, 35–36, 37, 40–41

healthcare services *(continued)*
   physical illness treatment, 27–28
   specific institutions, 29–30*(5)*,
     32–37*(14)*, 40–41*(5)*, 190*(2)*, 230*(2)*
hearths, *192*, 193
Henderson, Frank, and family home, 239
Henderson-Ames Co., 75*(3)*
Henderson Castle, 239*(2), 259, 262, 263*
Henderson Park, West Main Hill, 186, 194, 198
Henehan, Brendan, 170
Henrietta Street, 94, 107
Heritage Co., architectural salvage, 176
Heritage Guitar Inc., 209
Hicks, Weimer K., Ph.D., 225
Hilbert Street, 163
Hildreth, Dr., Kalamazoo Radiology, 32
Hill, Rev. Moses, 29
Hill, Thomas, artist, 121
Hillcrest Avenue, 98
Hillcrest neighborhood, 204*(2)*
Hind's farm, 40
Hinman Corporation, 46
historic architecture, xiii–xvi, **xv,** 1–255
   community essence in, xiv, 2–4
   found, in Kalamazoo, xiv, 166–173*(8)*,
     167–255, 172–173
   lost, in Kalamazoo, xiv, *xvi,* **1,** 1–3*(2)*,
     9–164
   photographs of, xiv–xv, 1, 87–88, 169
   preservation of, 37, 167–173
   relationships and, xiii–xv, 2–6, 211
historic districts, Kalamazoo sites
   Local Register, 111, 169, 171, 176, 189,
     195, 199, 211, 216, 217, 234, 237, 248
   National Register, 111, 166–170*(2), 180,*
     186, 188, 194, 195, 198, 216, 248
   state legislation for, 169
historic places, Kalamazoo sites
   National Register, 5, 81, 168, 170, 174*(2)*,
     184, 187, 199, 201, 209, 211–212*(4),*
     217, 223, 227*(2),* 242*(2),* 245*(2), 246,*
     250(2)
   State Register, 168, 170
historic preservation movement, xiv, 6,
   167–173
Hoben, Allan, Ph.D., 225, 245
Hoben Hall, Kalamazoo College, 112
Hoben House, Kalamazoo College, *225,* 258,
   262, 263
Holden, Perry, *160*

Holland Reformed Church, school, 117
Holly, Birdsill "Burt," inventor, 56
Holly Waterworks, site, *56*
homes, 87
   abandoned, 220, *221*
   architectural style of (*See specifics, e.g.,*
     Italianate Style; Queen Anne Style)
   businesses in, 82, 231
   as entertainment venues, 99, 137, 138,
     141, 146
   institutions in, 29, 30, 33, 37, 38–39*(7)*
   mansions, 50, 87–88, 90, 96–97*(5),* 104,
     130
   middle-class, 98, *167,* 213*(2),* 233, 243,
     252–253
   offices in, 32, 55, *98,* 175, 189, 226, 239
   photographs of, 1, 87–88
   prefabricated, 213, 222, 238, *252*
horses
   buildings associated with, 49, 51, 175,
     182, 197
   racing, 144, 211, 252
   vehicles and, *49, 182* (*see also* carriages)
Horton, Harrison, 92
Hospital Hospitality House, site, *229*
hospitals
   local (*see corporate names that begin*
     with Burns; Borgess; Bronson Methodist;
     Edwards; Fairmount; Fletcher; Kalamazoo
     State; Potter; Queen City; Van Deusen)
   U.S., linear plans, 34–36*(9)*
Hotelling, Ethol, 246
hotels
   city, 17, 67, 68, 198–199*(2)*
   downtown, 128–129*(3)*
   village, 9, 17, *198*
House, William, 150
House Block, acquisition of, 14
housing types, 124
   boardinghouses, 89, 133
   fraternity, 39*(3),* 49, 101, 181, 200, *232*
   inns, *17,* 68, 198–199*(3), 229, 239*
   senior citizen, 90–91*(3)*
   student, *112,* 116, *121,* 151, 200, *232*
   See also apartment buildings; homes; hotels
Hubbard, Mary Loomis, 100
Hubbard, Silas, 62, 100, 204
Hubbard Homestead site, 100*(3)*
Hudson Motor Car, 82
Huff, Tom, and Gitti, 214

Hull, Latham, and family home, *231*
"Human Fly," as entertainment, 137
human services institutions, 28, 30–31,
   38–39*(7)*
   alcoholism recovery and, 63
   Children's Home, 38*(3)*
   Infant Welfare Station No.1, *31*
   "Social Christianity" and, 62
   Wilbur Home and School for the Feeble-
     Minded, 39*(4)*
Humphrey, Gen. Bissel, legacies, 214
Humphrey Block, 114, 214*(2), 262, 263*
Humphrey family, 109
Humphrey Products, 68
Huston, Hosea, 128
Huyser, Dr. William C., 206
Hybels, Adrienne, 189

I

Iannelli, Alfonso, artist, 240–241*(3), 259*
ice rinks, 138, 143*(3)*
Ihling, Otto, 62
Ihling Brothers and Everard Co., 76
Illinois Envelope building, 5, 81
imposts. *See* moldings
industrial buildings, *xvi,* 75–85*(30),* 252
   arched entryways on, *75, 85*
   businesses success in, 73, 80–81
   design and construction specialists for,
     73–74
   downtown, 75–76*(6),* 83–85*(7),* 91, 184,
     185
   rehabilitation of, 195*(2),* 208–209*(2)*
Industrial Relations Center, University of
   Chicago, 225
Industrial State Bank, 149
Infant Welfare Station No.1, 28, *31*
infill, as "found" category, *169,* **173,** 178,
   184–185*(2),* 191, 200, 207, 213*(2),* 243
Inkster Avenue, 163
inns
   bed and breakfast, 104, 198–199*(3)*
   hospital hospitality, *229*
   motor, *17,* 68
integrity, buildings and, xiv, 9, 87, 201
interior design
   commercial, 9, 13, *14,* 20, *200,* 247, 254
   growleries in, **104**
   human relationships and, 2, 245

interior design *(continued)*
    industrial, *73*, 81
    institutional, *35*, *45*, 108
    renovations to, *12*, *216*
    residential, *48*, 88, *100*, *102–103(2)*, 104, 216, 258, 259
    sacred places and, *61*, 62, 64–65*(2)*, *66*, *70–71*, 245
    theaters and, *142*, 146, 148*(2)*
Intermodal Transportation Center, 20, 227*(2)*, 257, 258, 260, 262
    original depot and, *22–23*, *227*, 257
International Harvester Co., 195
International Style, 16, *19*, *100*, 205
Ionic columns, *49*, *94(2)*, *99*, *224*, *234*, *245(2)*
iron use, *89*, *158*, 244, *251*
    See also under concrete, reinforced
Israel, Mannes, 24, 66, 131
Italian Renaissance Style, *14*
Italian Villa Style, *39(3)*, *219(2)*
Italianate Style, *34–35(4)*, *152(2)*, 243
    apartment buildings, *102–103*
    characteristics of, *150*, 206, 211
    commercial buildings in, *17*, *24*, *128(2)*, 129, *130(3)*, *142*, *214*, 216, *231*
    education facilities in, 108, *110*, *113*, *116*
    homes in, *29*, *87*, *89(2)*, *93*, *100(2)*, *132*, *197(2)*, *211(2)*, *229*, *232(2)*
    hybrids of, *248*
    public places in, *47*, *55*
    rehabilitation awards and, *231*, 262, 263

J

Jackson, Dr., Kalamazoo Radiology, 32
Jacobson's Department Store, *49*
jails
    city police station and, *53(2)*
    Kalamazoo County, 43, *47*, *51*, 240
    mental illness and, 27, 34
James River Corporation, 82
Jasper Street, 190
J.C. Penney Co., 46, *55*
Jefferies, Rev. Robinson, 69
Jefferson Avenue, 191
Jim's Barbershop, Central Corners, 249
John Street, 33, 190
Johnson, Tobias, mason, 34, 259

Johnson House, Dr. William and family, site, 232*(2)*, 263
Johnson-Howard Co., 15
Joldersma and Gilman Funeral Home, *94*
Joldersma and Klein Funeral Home, *94*
Jones Dry Goods (firm). *See* J.R. Jones Sons and Co.
Jones Gift Shop, *127*
Jon's Barbershop, Central Corners, 249
Josephine's European Dining, *226*
J.R. Jones Sons and Co., *24(2)*, 130
Judaism, branches of, 66–67
judges, 53, 91
Junior League of Kalamazoo, 229
Justice (statue), *50*, 51
Justus Burdick House. *See under* mansions
J.W. Bosman Building, *187*, 263

K

Kalamazoo, City of, 17, 143
    administrative quarters for, *54–55(2)*, *93*, *172*, *188*, 258, 260, 262, 263
    building committees, 54, 59, 69
    central business district (*see* downtown)
    courthouses in, 43, *51*, *100*
    departments of, 31, 43, 81, 140, 141, 183, *187*, *188*, 207, 219, 243
    development and growth in, 44, 60, 74, 129, 142, 171, 184–185, 203, 234
    employment in, 75, 77, 80–81, 83, 84–85, 92
    historical preservation in, 167–173
    marketing of, 2, 44, 48, 87, 107
    planning, 167, 171–172
    property owned by, *30*, *31*, 53, 83, 93, 95, *100*, 139, 161, 162, 228
Kalamazoo, Lowell and Northern Co., 23
Kalamazoo, Village of, 104
    administrative hall for, *55*
    central business district, 128–131*(6)*, *214*, 228
    growth in, 9, 88, 118, 124
    healthcare services in, 27, 34
    homes in, 87, 89–102*(7)*, 197–198*(2)*, 206, *211*, 219*(2)*, *229*, *231*, 232*(2)*, *243*, *248*
    nonresidences of interest, 174*(2)*, 184–185*(2)*
    public places in, 43, *47*, 50–51*(4)*, 56, 240

Kalamazoo, Village of *(continued)*
    sacred places in, 59–60, *66*, 69, 70–71*(2)*, 218
    schools and colleges in, 55, 107–108
Kalamazoo Academy of Medicine, 28
Kalamazoo Antiques (firm), 176
Kalamazoo Avenue, 104
    East, 83, *173*, 215
Kalamazoo Avenue, West, 101
    200 block, *18*, 19, 173
    400 block, 70–71, 76
    500 block, 195
    700 block, 237
    industries on, xvi, 76, 195
    rehabilitation area, 237, 254
Kalamazoo Brewery Co., *79*
Kalamazoo Buick Sales, 224
Kalamazoo Building, 131*(3)*, 263
Kalamazoo Business and Professional Women's Club, 240
Kalamazoo Business College and Telegraph Institute, 114
Kalamazoo Central High School, 110–111*(3)*
Kalamazoo City Savings, banks, 129, 133
Kalamazoo College, *91*
    athletic facilities, *113*, 147
    brick street through campus, 183, 262
    building professionals and, 258, 260, 262, 263
    chapel, 172, 245*(2)*
    classroom facilities, 112–113*(8)*
    community development and, 200, *225*
    property owned by, 99, 219, 239
Kalamazoo Community Mental Health Services, 71
Kalamazoo Corset Co., 74, 84–85*(3)*
Kalamazoo County, 144, 171, 192–193*(4)*
    Chamber of Commerce, *75*, 80
    energy sources in, 73, 78
    governmental agencies of, 43, *47*, 50–51*(5)*, 71, *85*, 240, 259
    ownership by, 30, 54
    townships, 54, 60, 62, 67, 219
    villages in, 9, 27, 34, 43
Kalamazoo Creamery Building, *79(2)*
Kalamazoo Custom Metal Works, 228, 259
Kalamazoo Electric Co., 78
Kalamazoo Enterprise Center, 209
Kalamazoo Foundation, grants, 132, 143, 235

Kalamazoo Hall, Kalamazoo College, 112–113*(2)*
Kalamazoo Heating and Plumbing (firm), 203
Kalamazoo Historic District Commission, 169, 170
Kalamazoo Historic Preservation Commission
  activities of, 170, 228
  Merit Awards from, 176, 191, 200, 201, 211, 213, 215, 231, 247, 248, 250, 254
  origin of, 168–169
Kalamazoo Historical Commission, 168–169
  See also its successor, Kalamazoo Historic Preservation Commission
Kalamazoo Hospital. *See* Bronson Methodist Hospital
Kalamazoo House (hotel, 19th century), 9
Kalamazoo House (inn, 20th century), *198,* 199, 258
Kalamazoo Institute of Arts (KIA), *132,* 211, *235,* 239, 257, 258, 260, 262
  previous locations, 32, 48, 132, 180, 235
Kalamazoo Interior Finish Co., 98
Kalamazoo Jockey Club, 144
Kalamazoo Land Co., 253
Kalamazoo Laundry Building, 184–185*(2),* 259
Kalamazoo Light Guard. *See* National Guard
Kalamazoo Literary Institute, 112
Kalamazoo Loose Leaf Ledger Co., 74, 76*(3),* 261
Kalamazoo Mall, 129
  North, 125*(2),* 142
  South, 21, *46, 49,* 89, 145*(4), 203,* 228
Kalamazoo Motor Coach Co., 224
Kalamazoo Musical Instruments (firm), 231
Kalamazoo Neighborhood Housing Services, 171, 178, 213, 249, 259
Kalamazoo Northside Non-Profit Housing Corporation, 178
Kalamazoo Opera House Co., 148
Kalamazoo Paper Co., *74,* 80, 100
Kalamazoo Probation Enhancement Program, 65
Kalamazoo Public Library (KPL), 43, 44–45*(5), 48,* 85, 131, 235, 248, 260, 261, 263
  Northside branch, 178
  Washington Square branch, 133, *244,* 252, 257, 259, 260
Kalamazoo Public Museum, *45,* 48*(2),* 85, 260
Kalamazoo Public Schools, 107–108

Kalamazoo Public Schools *(continued)*
  elementary, 110–111*(2),* 118–119*(8),* 207, *210,* 252
  library-museum ownership by, 45, 48
  naming of, 108, 205
  secondary, 110–111*(4),* 205, 259, 260, 261, 263
Kalamazoo Radiology, 32*(2), 61*
Kalamazoo Regional Psychiatric Hospital, 212
Kalamazoo Riding Club, 17
Kalamazoo River, 73
Kalamazoo Rotary Club, 241
Kalamazoo Savings Bank, 21
Kalamazoo Sled Co., 77*(3),* 259
Kalamazoo State Hospital (KSH), 37m
  Brook Farm part of, *27,* 40–41, 101
  Burns Hospital for men, *36,* 37m, 261
  Colony Farm part of, 40–41*(5),* 101
  colony system for, 35–36, 40–41
  cottages, *27,* 35, 36, 40–41*(4)*
  Edwards Hospital for men, 36, *37,* 37m, 260
  Female Department, 34–35*(5),* 37, 37m, 259, 262
  Fletcher Hospital for men, *36,* 37m, 259
  linear plans for, 34–36*(9)*
  Male Department, 35–37, *36,* 37m
  Michigan Asylum for the Insane, 27, 34–37*(8),* 101
  Potter Hospital for women, 36–37, *37,* 37m, 261
  Van Deusen Hospital, 36, *37,* 37m
  water tower, 7, 36, 163, 169, 212*(2),* 248, 259, 260, 261, 262
Kalamazoo Stove Co., 214
Kalamazoo Street Railway Co., 160
Kalamazoo Symphony Orchestra, 211
Kalamazoo Tank and Silo Co., 90
Kalamazoo Town Agricultural Society, 144
Kalamazoo Township, Kalamazoo County, 67
Kalamazoo Trust and Savings Bank, 242
Kalamazoo Valley Electric Co., 78
Kalamazoo Valley Museum, 48, *50,* 51, 142
Kauffer family, 235
Kauffer House, site, 45
Kehoe & Nicols (firm), plasterers, 36, 260
Kellogg, W.K., 114
Kendall, Lyman, 148
Kennedy, John F., 240
Kennedy, Robert, 240
Kent Avenue, 139

Kent grain elevator, 83
Keystone Community Bank, 130–131
keystones, 80, *81,* 84, *85, 145,* 182*(2), 187,* 250*(2)*
KIA. *See* Kalamazoo Institute of Arts (KIA)
Kidder, George, 23
Kilgore Road, and Lovers Lane, 154, 205
kindergartens, 62, 117
King, John, superintendent, 80
King Paper Co., 80
Kirby, Lewis, 242
Kirkebride, Dr. Thomas, 27, 34, 35
Klein's Bagels, 249
Kleinstuck, C. Hubbard, family home, 204*(2),* 257
KM Industrial Machinery, *195,* 261
Knight, John J., 67
Knights Hotel, 67
Knights of Columbus, *11*
Knights of Pythias, 139
Korab, Balthazar, photographer, 169
KPL. *See* Kalamazoo Public Library (KPL)
Krone, Amy, 224
KSH. *See* Kalamazoo State Hospital (KSH)

L

L. Lee Stryker Center, Kalamazoo College, *225*
Label, Fr. Anthony, 60, 70
label stops, *97*
LaCrone, William L., 138, 141
LaCrone Park, 138, 140–141*(2)*
Ladies' Library Association, 55, 168, 169, 172, 174*(2)*
  building professionals and, 257, 258, 259, 260, 261, 262
Ladies Soldiers' Aid Society, 144
LaFourche Realty, 152
Laird Avenue, 207
Lake Farm for Boys, 38, 96
Lake Street, 79*(4),* 117, 143, 162
Lake Street School, 154
Lake View Park/Casino, 139
Lakeshore and Michigan Southern Railroad (LS&MS), 22*(2)*–23
Lakeside Boys and Girls Residence, 38, 96
Lakeway Avenue, Lustron house on, 222
Land Ordinance (1785), 107
land use, automobile effects on, 18, 138
landscaping, 34, 141, 163, 238, 240

Lane Boulevard, *252–253*
Langereis, Rev. Henry H.D., *63*
Laning, Claus, 13, *13*
Larsen, Martin, decorator, 186, 260
laundromats, 25, *121,* 250*(2)*
Lawrence and Chapin Iron Works, 73, 91, 170, 184–185*(2),* 257, 259
Lawrence Education Center, Borgess Hospital, 230
Lawrence House, site, *93*
Lawrence Street, 118
lawyer's offices, 9, 11, 21, 32, 68, 75, 206
League of Women Voters, project input, 54
Lee, Jeff, and Honore, 175
LeFevre, Bish. Paul, 70–71
LeFevre Institute, *70,* 71, 109
Levin, Robert and Rae, Usonian home, 192
Levine & Levine (firm), 206
Lew Hubbard Store, fire, 131
libraries
    church, 218
    college and university, 112, 113, 121*(2)*
    homes with, 91, 198, 199, 232
    public, 43, 44–45*(5), 48,* 55
    school, 38, 45, 48
Light, Rudolf, mayor, 242
lighting, artificial, 108, 201
    artistic, 188, 204, 215
    electric, 17, 75, 78, 175
    floodlights, 142
    fluorescent, 74
    gas, 61
    streetlamps, *158,* 204
lighting, natural
    day-light (factory), 74, 76*(2),* 82*(2),* 208–209*(3)*
    fanlights, 32, 54, 63, 82, *94,* 117*(2), 210,* 245*(2),* 250*(2)*
    sidelights, 32, 54, *94,* 225
    skylights, 129, *192*
    See also windows
Lilienfeld, David, and family, 198
Lilienfeld & Brother (firm), 128–129
Lilienfeld families, 66
Lilienfeld House, site, *198,* 199
Lilley-Ames Co., 75
limestone
    decorative use of, 164, 188
    facades of, *36,* 224, 245*(2)*
    Indiana, 242, 245*(2)*

limestone *(continued)*
    rusticated, *36*
    Victorian Gothic use of, 164, 174*(2)*
Lincoln, Abraham, visit, 240
Lincoln School, 108
Linden Park (development), 253
lintels, *85,* 115–116*(2),* 184–185*(2),* 248, *254*
Little, William, mason, 186, 260
Little, William T. "Ted," 223
Little family, **83,** 83*(3)*
Little Michigan Restaurant, The, 16*(2)*
lobbies, 202, 232, *235,* 242
Local Register Historic District
    sites on, 111, 169, 171, 176, 189, 195, 199, 211, 216, 234, 237, 248
Lockwood Street, 59, 69
loggia, *145*
Loomis, Mary O. *See* Hubbard, Mary Loomis
Loren's Lake. *See* Asylum Lake
Lovell Street, East, 28, 33, 94, 118
Lovell Street, West, 49, 55, 90, 120
    200 block, 218
    400 block, 243, 246
    700 block, 243
    Park St. and, 59, 62, 132
    Rose St. and, 19*(2),* 32, 53, 64, 87, *98,* 102–103
Lovell Street School, 110, 118*(2),* 260, 261
Lovers Lane, 126*(2),* 154, 205
Lower Hall, Kalamazoo College, 112–113*(2),* 258
Loy Norrix High School, 172, *205,* 259, 261
LS&MS. *See* Lakeshore and Michigan Southern Railroad (LS&MS)
Lustron Corporation, steel prefabs, 222
Lutheran Student Center, WMU, *39*
Lutten, Nicholas, 254
Luyendyk, Peter and Sam, butchers, 134
lyceums, 107, 137
Lyons Drug Store, *133*

M

Mabel Street, *178,* 179
Macleod, Dr. A. Garrard, family, 186
Macleod, George, and Linda, 186
Magic Maid (firm), 250
Maher's Business University, 108
Main Street, 45, 50, 123, 167
    See also later-named portion Michigan Avenue

Main Street, East, 119, 163
    100 block, 9, 14–15*(5)*
    300 block, 17*(4)*
    500 block, 22, 23*(2)*
    600 block, 158*(2)*
    700 block, 158*(2)*
    as commercial center, 9, 22*(2)*–23, 24
    See also later-named portion Michigan Avenue, East
Main Street, West, 60, 151*(3)*
    100 block, 128–131*(11)*
    200 block, 11*(3)*
    300 block, 20*(2)*
    400 block, 150*(2)*
    700 block, 127*(2)*
    800 block, 127*(2)*
    1400 block, 164
    churches on, 59, 218
    commercial buildings on, 9, 20*(2),* 24, 24*(2),* 127*(2)*
    improvements along, *123,* 159, 163, 170
    notable homes along, 101, 104
    See also later-named portion Michigan Avenue, West
Majestic Gardens (theater), 146
Majestic Theatre, 138, *145*
Mansion Row sites, 96–97*(5)*
mansions
    Justus Burdick House, 50, 87, 130, 131
    gardens and, 90
    Henderson Castle as, Queen Anne Style, 239*(2)*
    Mansion Row sites for, 96–97*(5)*
    porte-cocheres with, 87–88, 90, *97, 104,* 219*(2)*
Manvel, Homer, manufacturer, 90, 95
Manvel, Ida, 90
Maple Street, West, 151
marble
    exterior walls, 14, *15,* 20
    interiors with, 14, 46, 129, 188, 232, 242
    Italian, 188, 198
    terrazzo, 242
    Travennielle Clair, 14
    travetine, **188**
    Vermont, 46
    white, 14, *15*
markets
    farmers' produce, 162*(2),* 252
    hay, *52,* 53

markets *(continued)*
　meat, 9, 10, 13*(3)*, *127,* 134*(2)*
　Rose Street Market, *168*
Marlborough, The, 32, *223,* 243, 257, 262
marquees, rehabilitation of, *203*
Masonic Temple, *11,* 162, *168,* 170
masonry, 195*(2),* 250*(2)*
　cleaning and repairing, 227, 236
　Depression-era, in city parks, 140–141*(2),* 154
　See also bricks
masons
　J. Doyle, 237, 258
　T. Johnson, 34, 259
　W. Little, 186, 260
　Rickman & Atkins, 62
　B. Roe, 36, 46, 212, 261
　J. Sherman, 183, 262
　J. Shirlaw, 224, 262
　volunteers as, 60, 69, 71
　A.J. White, 5
massiveness, architectural styles and, 49–50*(2),* 51, 101, *188*
Mastercraft (firm), 76
May, Charles, 148
Mayfair/Uptown Theater, 142
McCalmont, Dr. Harriette. *See* Stone, Mrs. Dr. Harriette
McCartney, Ward and Helen, Usonian home, 192–193*(2)*
McCarty, Ted, 208
McDonald's Restaurant, Kalamazoo Ave., *18*
McDuffee, Alice, 104
McDuffee House, Louis and Harriet, site, 104*(2)*
McKessy, Gerald, 251
McKinley, Pres. W., 108, 119
McKinley Elementary School, 119*(2),* 257, 258, 263
McNair, Noel, 94
McNair, Dr. Rush, 102
McNair Building, 177
McNair House, site, 94*(3),* 263
meat markets, 9, 10, 13*(3),* *127,* 134*(2)*
medallions, 219, 242, 248
Mediterranean influence, *145,* 189, *223*
Meinert family home, *238,* 258
melodeons, 137
memorials
　organizations, 62, 132, 137–138

memorials *(continued)*
　street names, 123, 217
　structures, 49, *70,* 94, 108, 225, 245
mental disabilities, treatment of, 27, 39
mental illnesses, treatment of, 27, 34, 35–36, 37, 40–41
Merrihew, Lucille, 102
Merrill, David, and Ida, 90
Merrill residences, 90*(3)*
metal structures
　artistic creations as, 215, 240–241, 242, 244, *254*
　nonresidential, 20, 121, *158,* 163, 196*(2),* 208–209, *210,* 212, 230*(2),* 244, 247
　residential, 77, *89, 195,* 198, 222, *251*
　See also under concrete, reinforced
metals, structural
　aluminum, 74, 77, 244
　brass, *254*
　bronze, 240–241
　copper, 196*(2),* 215, 227, *230*
　iron, *89, 158,* 244, *251*
　lead, 242
　steel, 20, 121, *158,* 163, *195,* 198, 208–209, *212,* 222, 242
Methodist churches, Kalamazoo, *59,* 60, 64*(2),* 69*(2),* 240
Methodist Episcopal Church, 33, 59, 60, 64, 64*(2)*
　building professionals and, 258, 259, 260
Meulenberg, Tim, and Janine, 248, 260
Meyer, Curtis and Lillian, Usonian home, 193
Michigan, 34, 50, 52, 107, 108
　courts and judges, *19,* 21, *100,* 205
　historical sites and, 168, 169, 170, 212
　legislation, 27, 28, 33, 34, 112, 126
　state agencies, 118, 141, 158, 167
　tax credits or exemptions, 209, 234
Michigan and Huron Institute, 107, 112
Michigan Asylum for the Insane. *See under* Kalamazoo State Hospital (KSH)
Michigan Avenue, 5, 83
　See also previously-named portion Main Street
Michigan Avenue, East, 23*(2),* 162
　100 block, 242
　200 block, 216*(2),* 228
　600 block, *158*
　700 block, 78*(3), 158*
　Burdick St. and, 114, 125

Michigan Avenue, East *(continued)*
　Portage St. and, 114, 124, 137, 214
　See also previously-named portion Main Street, East
Michigan Avenue, West, 39, 68, 71, 121
　100 block, 129
　200 block, *10,* 228
　500 block, 224
　homes of note on, 96–97
　Lovell St. and, 16*(2),* 112, 120
　Park St. and, 46, *73,* 74, 75, 96–97
　Rose St. and, 47, 50
　south of, 120, 147
　See also previously-named portion Main Street, West
Michigan Bakeries, site, *162*
Michigan Bell Telephone Co., *64*
Michigan Central Railroad, depot, *22–23,* 159, 162, 181, 227*(2),* 257, 261
Michigan Electric Railway Co., 160, 161
Michigan Female Seminary, site, 116*(3),* 257, 261
Michigan National Bank, *11,* 14
Michigan State Agricultural Society, 144
Michigan State Armory, 258, 259
Miles Avenue, Lustron house on, *222*
Milham, Frank, 80, 93, 114, 140
Milham, Frank and Elizabeth, home, 55, 93
Milham Park, 126, 138, 140*(2),* 141, 154*(2)*
military personnel, 43, 52, 114, 120, 137, 144
Mills Street, 162
Milwood neighborhood, 12, 60, 222
Minimal Traditional Style, *178–179*
mint oil refining, buildings for, *xvi,* 196*(2),* 257, 260, 262, 263
Mirror Lake, Kalamazoo College, *113*
mirrors, plate glass, 149
Mission influence, *189, 195*
Mitchell Cottage, KSH, *41*
modernization
　construction materials and, 94, 207, 213
　fashionable upgrades as, *142,* 185, 203
　Modernist theory and architecture, 205, 235, 242
Moeller organs, 61
moldings, *50,* 184–185*(3)*
　arched, 38*(2),* 39*(3)*
　carved, 96*(2)*
　decorative, *47, 61, 179,* 206, 232*(2)*
　hood, *97*

moldings *(continued)*
  masonry, 250*(2)*
  picture-frame interior, *103,* 189
  stone, 89*(2),* 117*(2), 146, 163*
  style, Italian Villa, 39*(3), 219(2)*
  style, Italianate, 206, 232*(2)*
  style, Queen Anne, *118, 179*
  style, Richardsonian Romanesque, 250*(2)*
Monroe, Stephen, 242
Monroe Cottage, KSH, 36
Monroe Street, 112, 183, 186, 239
Montague Estate, 37
Morrow Dam, Kalamazoo County, 78
"mother" churches, **60,** 68
motorbuses. *See* buses
Mt. Carmel, West Main Hill, 91
Mountain Home Cemetery, *157,* 161*(2),* 164*(3),* 217
Murphy, John and Pegg Osowski, home, 238, 258
museums, *45,* 48*(2)*
music study, 9, 89, 99, 116
musical entertainment, 52, 137, 139, 152, 211
musical instruments, *61,* 64–65*(2), 100,* 137, 208–209, 231, 246

N

National City Bank (NCB)
  Arcadia Commons, 184–185*(2),* 259
  Chormann Building, *180,* 258, 260
  Michigan Ave., *15,* 263
National Driving Park, 6, 160, 161, 257
  Washington Square and, *133,* 144*(2),* 144m, 252
National Guard, 43, 52
National Historic Preservation Act, 37, 168–171
National Industrial Recovery Act, 140
National Register Historic District, 248
  Kalamazoo sites on, 111, 166–170*(2),* 180, 186, 194, 195, 198, 199, 216
National Register of Historic Places, 5, 168, 222
  Kalamazoo sites on, 81, 170, 174*(2),* 184, *198,* 199, 209, 211–212*(4),* 217, *223,* 227*(2),* 242*(2),* 245*(2), 246,* 250*(2)*

National Storage Building, *236,* 263
National Trust for Historic Preservation, 167, 253
natural gas, 61, 73, 108
Nazareth Academy, 108, 109
Nazareth Road, 109
NCB. *See* National City Bank
neighborhoods, 18, 124
  business districts in, 9, 12, 123, *249,* 252, 257, 258, 260
  improvement associations and, 171, 178, 217, 249, 253
  See also specifics, e.g., Edison neighborhood; West Main Hill neighborhood
Neoclassical Style, 94*(2), 99, 229*
Netherlands Reformed Church, 63
Neumaier, Fred, 79
Neumaier, George, 79
New Bronson Methodist Hospital, The, 190*(2),* 257, 262
New Theatre, *128,* 129
Newman, Kirk, artist, 241, 261
Newton Carriage Co., 176
Nicholas Kik Pool, 141
Nicholson, Mrs. N.H., 102
Nicholson pavement, 129, 159*(2)*
Nielsen, Ian, cabinetmaker, 194, 261
Noble, Dr. Alfred, 36
Noble House, James and Hattie, site, *202*
Noel's Place, 94*(3)*
Norlin Corporation, 208
Normal Hill, trolley, *120*
Normal School, Kalamazoo. *See* Western State Normal School
Norrix, Loy, Ph.D., 205
North Christian School, 115
North Hall, WMU, 121*(2),* 263
North Street
  East, 31
  West, *25,* 60, 210, *217*
North West Street Christian Reformed School, 117
North Westnedge Elementary School, site, 118*(2),* 257, 258, 261
Northside neighborhood, 118, 178–179*(4),* 182
nurses, 27, 30, 37, 230
Nurse's Home, Fairmont Hospital, 30

O

Oakland Drive, 127*(2),* 139, 204
  KSH on, 34–37*(10),* 37m, 41, 169, 212
  Michigan Ave. and, 96–97, 112, 113
  schools near, 38, 120
  streetcar route on, *160,* 161, 204
"Oaklands, The," WMU, 147, 211*(2)*
Oakwood Elementary School, 207
Oakwood neighborhood, 60, 207
Oakwood Park, 138, 139*(3),* 152, 161
O'Brien, Fr. Frank, 28, 29, 109
O'Connor, Terry, and Pamela, 198
Octagon Style homes, 87
oculus windows, *24, 47, 49,* 70–71*(3), 91,* 117*(2),* 219*(2)*
O'Duffy's Pub, *172*
office space
  downtown, 9–11, 21, 89, 103, 131, 146, 148–149*(3),* 181, 184–185*(2)*
  in homes, 32, 55, 175, 189, 226, 239
  industrial, 75, 80, *81,* 260
  neighborhood upper-story, 25, 127
  professionals in, 9–10, 21, 25, 32*(2),* 68, 75, 103, 181, 189, 190, 206, 225, 242
  public buildings with, 43, 46*(2),* 49, 50, 53, 55, 55*(2),* 201
  rehabilitation and, 10, 234, 250
Old Central (high school), 110–111*(3)*
Old Kent Bank-Southwest, 242
Olde Peninsula Brewpub & Restaurant, *214*
Oliver, Adam, 240, 261
Oliver Street, 37, 121
Olmsted Brothers, 108
One-Part Commercial Blocks, *249*
Orcutt home, 55
organs (musical instruments), *61,* 64–65*(2)*
Orrin B. Hayes, Inc., 224*(2),* 262, 263
Oshtemo Township, Kalamazoo County, 60, 62, 219
Osowski, Pegg, and John Murphy, home, 238, 258
Owen Group, Ltd. (firm), 247

P

Page Manufacturing Co., 77
Pagenstecher, Felix, 80
pagoda roofs, *22–23, 150*
Palmer, Charles, 145

Palmer, Dr. George, 35, 36
Palmer Cottage, KSH, *40*
paneling, *45*, 81, 201, 222, 226
paper companies, *74*, 80–81*(4)*, 82, 252
parapets, 33*(2)*, 113
    crenelated, *65*
    factories with, *82*, 208–209*(2)*
    gables with, *36*, 117*(2)*, 164*(2)*
    stepped, 195*(2)*
    towers and, 68*(2)*, 208–209*(2)*
Parish Associates (firm), 247
Park-American (hotel), 17, 263
Park Club, *93*
Park Street, North, 20, 76
    churches and, 68, 70
    Michigan Ave. and, 46, *73*, 74, 75
    Water St. and, 68, 75
Park Street, South, 32, 132
    300 block, 235
    500 block, 65
    600 block, iv, 66–67*(2)*, 234
    Academy St. and, *60*, 64
    Cedar St. and, 65, 173
    Lovell St. and, 59, 60, 62, 132
    Main St./Michigan Ave. and, 96–97, 151*(2)*
    sacred places and, iv, 59, 60, 62, 64, 65, 66–67*(2)*, 218, 234
    Walnut St. and, 61, 65
Park Street Church of Christ, 60, 68, 68*(3)*, 257, 263
Park Trades Center, 76
Parker homestead, 117
Parker House, Harry B. and Pearl, site, *175*
Parker's Mammoth Store, *130*, 131
parking lots
    buildings replaced by, 11–24*(5)*, 52–53*(2)*, 60–71*(3)*, 75–82*(3)*, 91–98*(4)*, 109–120*(6)*, 131, 150–151*(2)*, 167, 249
    downtown, xv, 11, 19, *52*, 53, 60, *75*, *96*, *131*, 150–151*(2)*
    off-street, 16, 249
parking structures, iv, 33, *66*, 67, *85*, *146*, *152*, 185, 230
parks
    automobile effects on, 139
    business/industrial, 41, 74
    city-owned, *30*, *31*, 138, 140–141*(6)*, 143*(3)*, 154*(2)*
    golf courses in, 126, 138

parks *(continued)*
    replaced by gas stations, 17
    water-type, 138, 140–141*(6)*, 143*(3)*
    zoos in, 138, 154*(2)*
    See also specifics, e.g., Bronson Park; National Driving Park
Parkstone Properties, 180
Parkview Avenue, 139, *160*, 161, 207
Parkview Drive, 40–41
Parkwyn Village (development), 192*(3)*, 193
parochial schools, 107–108
    Catholic, *70*, 71, 97, 108, 109*(2)*, 117*(3)*, 252
    Christian Reformed, 108, 115*(2)*
Parsons, William Frederick, 114
Parsons Business College/School, *5*, 104, 108, 114*(3)*, 214, 263
Parsons Street, 172, 208
Partners Building Community, 253
Parzyck, Rodger, 176, 200, 261
Paterson, Thomas, carpenter, 5–6
    See also under builders/contractors, firms of, Bush & Paterson
Paterson Street, 75
    East, *82*
    West, 18*(2)*, 117, 138, 140–141, *178–179*
patios, 194
Patricia White Interiors (firm), 200
Paw Paw Road. *See* Michigan Avenue, West
Pearson Construction Co., 20
Peck, Charles and Mary, home, *132*, 235
Peck, Horace M., 48, 99
Peck Building, *21*, 145, 263
Peck House, Horace and Helen, site, 45, *48*, *87*, 88, 235
pedestrians, 60
    display windows and, 195, *224*, 254
    orientation of, and streets, 3, 24, 124, 129
pediments
    central roof and, 54–55*(2)*
    columns support, *210*, *234*, 245*(2)*
    Dutch-church design, *234*
    entryways below, *50*, 51, 77, 80, *81*, *102–103*, *224*
    Greco-Roman style, *67*
    Italianate style, 54–55*(2)*, *102–103*
    Revival styles, *50*, 51, *178*, *210*
Peeler Street, 123
Peninsula Building. *See* Humphrey Block
Pension Board, 46

People's Church, 59, 60, 62*(3)*, 67, 234, 259, 261, 263
pergolas, *54*, *82*, *186*, 204*(2)*
Perrin, Joel J., 93
Perrin-Milham House, site, 93*(2)*
pest houses, 27
Peters, Jahai "Gahy," paver, 159, 261
Pettiford, Rev. Joseph, 59–60, 69
Pewabic Pottery (firm), 198, 261
Pharmacia, Inc., *29*
Phelps, Edwin, 60
Philadelphia brick, *148*
photographs
    building interiors, 88, *100*, 102–103*(2)*
    local buildings, 1, 87, 88, 169, xiv–xv
physical illnesses, treatment, 27–28, 30, 164
    See also hospitals
physicians, 28
    offices, 9, 10, 21, 25, 32*(2)*, *98*, 128, 206, 226
    roles of, 27, 28, 33, 34–36, 39
Piebalgs, Rev. Arturs, 220
Pierce, Dr. Della, 27
piers, *191*, 204*(2)*, *233*, 252
pilasters
    brick, 51, *82*, 247
    capped, 78*(2)*
    corners with, *50*, 197*(2)*
    decorated, *50*, *190*
    stucco, 94*(2)*
    windows between, 78*(2)*, 110–111*(2)*, *210*
Pine Street, 118
pinnacles, corner, *148*, 164*(2)*
Pitcher Street, North, 59, 69, 82
plaster uses
    ceilings, 244
    frescoes, *148*, 149
    medallions, 248
    walls, 198–199, 251
    See also stucco
plasterers, Kehoe & Nicols, 36, 260
Pleasant View Primitive Baptist Church, 31
Plow, St. John, home, 82
Plymouth Church, 110
police stations, 43, 52–53*(2)*, 259, 260
    in public safety buildings, 19, *100*, *178*, *179*, 227
poorhouses, 27, 34
porcelain-enamel paneling, 222
porches, *104*, *132*, 200, *246*

porches *(continued)*
  columned, 94*(2)*, *99*, *217*
  covered *(see* porticoes*)*
  front, 38–39*(5)*, *41*, *90*, 92–93*(4)*, *95*, *100*, *116*, *152*, *178*, *179*, *191*, *202*, 211*(2)*, *217*, 233*(2)*, *252*, 253
  gabled, 181*(2)*
  screened-in, 194
  second-story, 94–95*(2)*, 98–99*(2)*, 197
  shaped, *36*, 94*(2)*
  side, *179*, 211*(2)*, 253
  sized, *150*, *202*, *238*
  style, bungalow, *178*, 179, 194, 217, 233*(2)*, 252
  style, duplex, 253
  style, foursquare style, *191*
  style, Italianate, *100*, *116*, *150*, *152*, 211*(2)*
  style, Neoclassical, 94*(2)*, *99*
  style, Queen Anne, *90*, 92–93*(4)*, *95*, *132*, *179*, 181*(2)*, *202*, *217*, *238*, *243*
  style, Tudor Revival, *252*, 253
  wraparound, 40–41*(3)*, 181*(2)*, *243*, *252*
Portage Avenue, village road, 252
Portage Creek, 80, 81, 123, 140
Portage Road, 94
Portage School, name change, 108
Portage Street, 144
  200 block, *19*
  300 block, 28–29
  1200 block, 244, 250
  2000 block, 12*(2)*
  commercial district spreads south along, 9, 79, 133
  Michigan Ave. and, 114, 124, 137, 214, 228
  paper companies near, 74, 80, 81
porte-cocheres, 231
  churches and, *218*
  depots and, 227*(2)*
  hospitals and, *190*, 230
  mansions with, 87–88, 90, *97*, *104*, 219*(2)*, *229*
Porter, D.D., 48
Porter Street, 22, 23, 59, 69
porticoes, 33*(2)*, *61*, *63*, *210*
  supports for, *178*, *229*, *251*
post offices, 4, 21, 44, 46*(2)*, 128, 248, 257, 258, 261
Potter Hospital, KSH, 36, *37*, 37m
Potter Street, 13*(3)*, 243

poultry businesses, 83
power plants, 78*(2)*, 80–81*(3)*, 262
Prairie School Style, 101, 193
  hybrids of, *196*
Prairie Street, North, 30
Prange, Henry T., 103
Prange Building, 102, *103*, 257
Pratt Cottage, KSH, *41*
Prentice, Arthur, 234
Presbyterian church schools, 116*(3)*
preservation
  awards for, *211*, *254*
  as "found" category, *93*, **172,** *177*, *188*, *205*
  government and, 37, 167–173, 253 *(see also* Kalamazoo Historic Preservation Commission*)*
  integrity of buildings and, xiv, 87, 201
private schools, 107–108
  elementary, 62, 117, 252
  gender-based, 38, 96, 116
  mental disabled and, 39
  secondary, 116*(3)*
produce markets, city-owned, 162*(2)*
prohibition movement, 79
Prospect Street, South, 99
public places, 4, 9, 11, 43–56(34)
  See also types, e.g., courthouses; parks
public safety buildings
  International Style, *19*, 100
  mini-stations, *178*, 179, 227
  renovation of, 182*(2)*, 263
  Station No.7, 173, *207*, 258, 262
  See also firehouses; jails; police stations
public schools, 107–108
  elementary, 110–111*(2)*, 118–119*(8)*, 154, 178, 207, *210*, 252
  indoor swimming pools in, 140
  secondary, 110–111*(4)*, 172, *205*
Public Works Administration, 47, 51

Q

Queen Anne Style, *161*, 191
  adaptive use of, homes, 198–199*(2)*, 239*(2)*, *246*, 258
  characteristics of, 114, 181, *237*
  homes in, *1*, 48*(2)*, 87, *90*, 92–93*(4)*, 95–96*(3)*, *104*, *132*, 198–199*(2)*, 202, *217*, 220–221*(3)*, 239*(2)*, 258
  hybrids of, 238, 243, *248*

Queen Anne Style *(continued)*
  institutional facilities in, *36*, 40–41*(4)*, 62, *113*, *138*
  rehabilitated, homes, 198–199*(2)*, 202, *217*, 220–221*(3)*, 239*(2)*, 258
  schools in, 108, 110, 111*(2)*, *116*, 118
Queen City Hospital, 28
Quick to the Rescue Hall. *See* Corporation Hall
quoins, *210*, 219*(2)*

R

radiant heating systems, 192–193, 251
railings, *89*, *217*, 232, 233*(2)*
railroads, 23, 70–71, 126
  depots, 17, 22–23*(7)*, 227*(2)*, 248
  industrial success and, 73, 77, 82, 92, 192
railways. *See* streetcars; trolleys
Ranney Street, 38
Ransom, Gov. Epaphroditus, 34
Ransom Street, West, 138
Raseman, Edgar, Sr., 236
Read Fieldhouse, WMU, *121*
real estate developers, 9, 11, 17, 89, 142, 145, 261
real estate offices, 2, 9, 12, 175
recreation facilities
  active, *47*, *113*, *121*, 138, 139–141*(5)*, 143*(2)*, 147*(3)*, *151*, 152
  passive, *41*, *47*, 50*(2)*, 138, *140*, 154*(2)*
rectories, 70–71, 97, *117*
Redpath Chautauqua, 152*(3)*
Reed Street, *2*, 134*(2)*
Reedy, Ryan, 103
Reformed Christian churches, 60
Regent Theater, 149
rehabilitation, adolescent, 38
rehabilitation, building, 164, 166–168*(2)*, 191
  awards for, 176*(2)*, *191*, 200–201, 215, *231*, 248
  bed and breakfast inns, 198–199*(2)*, 239*(2)*, 258
  commercial sites, *173*, 176, 203, 215*(2)*, 224, 227*(2)*, *254*
  education sites, *201*
  federal standards, 171, 234
  homes, *197*, *202*, *217*, 220–221*(3)*, *231*, *243*, 248

rehabilitation, building *(continued)*
    neighborhood improvement associations and, 171
    shop-houses, *203*, 216*(2)*, *226*
    tools for, xiv, *167*, 171–173, 200
    See also adaptive use
Reisch Bakery, 254
Remington-Rand Co., *76*
Renaissance Revival Style, 49–50*(2)*, 51
Republican Party, Kalamazoo, 100
residences. *See* housing types
residential areas, 18–19, 49, 124, 163
    changes in, 88, 132*(2)*, 190
    in commercial districts, 9, 25
    See also neighborhoods; suburbs
restaurants
    Kalamazoo Ave., *18*, 215*(2)*
    loss of, 10, 226, 227
    Michigan Ave., 11, 16*(2)*, *17*, *214*
    neighborhood, 9, 12*(3)*, 172
    in shop-houses, 25, 214, 226
retail businesses. *See specifics, e.g.,* dry goods stores; meat markets
retail space, 9, 11, 21, *24*, 249
    See also business districts
Rice, Lester, 215
Richards, Linda, 27
Richardson, Henry Hobson, 190
Richardson, Ralph and Charlotte, home, 194
Richardson, Stephen, 240
Richardson Garment Co., owner, 194
Richardsonian Romanesque Style
    commercial buildings, 11, 227*(2)*
    hybrids of, 250*(2)*
    public places, 43, 44–46*(4)*
Rickman House, George and Jane, site, 197*(2)*, 261
Ringling Brothers, circus, 144
Ripe (specialty store), *203*
Riverview Drive, 116
Roamer and Velie (firm), 82
Roamer automobiles, plant, *2*
Roberts & Hillhouse (firm), *128*
Rochford Building, St. Joseph Parish, *117*
Rockwell, Ethel, 141
Rockwell Park, 141*(2)*
Roe, Benjamin, mason, 36, 46, 212, 248, *248*, 261
Roman Style, arches, 25

Romanesque Revival Style
    characteristics of, *64*, 70–71*(4)*
Romanesque Style, *49*
    hybrids of, 59, 64, 250*(2)*
    Richardsonian, 11, 43, 44–46*(4)*, 227*(2)*
Rood, H.R., and Rood Row, 125
roofs
    candlesnuffer, *97*
    central, *47*, *50*, 54–55*(2)*
    conical, *45*, *95*
    crenelated, *247*
    cresting on, *56*, 92*(2)*, *97*, 174*(2)*, *185*
    cross-gabled, *61*, 197*(2)*
    cross-gambrel, *252*, 253
    duplex, 189
    flat, *102–103*
    gabled, 22, 23, 33*(2)*, *90*, 92–93*(4)*, 95–96*(3)*, *113*, *116*, *118*, *132*, *161*, *175*, *178*, *179*, *202*, *207*, *217*, *218*, 230*(2)*, 237–239*(4)*, *243*
    gambrel, *186*
    glass, *177*
    high-pitched, *212*, 253
    hipped, 32, *32*, *54*, 54–55*(2)*, *100*, *175*, *178*, 206, 227*(2)*
    irregular, *90*, *104*
    jerkin head, *36*
    low-pitched, 54–55*(2)*, *100*, *101*, *110*, 189, 196*(2)*, 232*(2)*, *252*
    mansard, *32*, 38*(2)*, *50*, *91*, *130*, *148*, *184*, *185*
    metal, 196*(2)*, *222*, 230*(2)*
    pagoda, *22–23*, 150
    parapets on, *113*, 195*(2)*
    pitched, *77*
    shed, 125, *143*, 262
    slate, 184–185*(2)*, 219*(2)*, 227
    sloped, *98*, 195*(2)*
    steeply-pitched, *63*, *65*, 96*(2)*, *97*, 164*(2)*, 204*(2)*, *218*, *244*, *248*, 252–253*(2)*
    stone coping at, *119*
    style, bungalow, *178*, *179*, *252*
    style, Colonial Revival, *178*
    style, Craftsman, *54*, *98*, *175*
    style, duplex, *253*
    style, Dutch Colonial Revival, *186*
    style, English Gothic, *218*
    style, Gothic Revival, *65*
    style, Italian Villa, 219*(2)*

roofs *(continued)*
    style, Italianate, 54–55*(2)*, *100*, *102–103*, *110*, *130*, *150*, 197*(2)*, 206, 232*(2)*
    style, Queen Anne, *90*, 92–93*(4)*, 95–96*(3)*, 104, *113*, *116*, *118*, *132*, *179*, 217, 237–239*(4)*, *243*, *248*
    style, Renaissance Revival, *50*, 51
    style, Richardsonian Romanesque, *45*, 227*(2)*
    style, Second Empire, 38*(2)*, *91*, *184*, *185*
    style, Tudor Revival, 204*(2)*, *244*, *252*, 253
    style, Usonian, *192*
    style, Victorian Gothic, 164*(2)*, 174*(2)*, 230*(2)*
    style, Victorian period, *56*
    tile, *189*, 227
    tower, *45*, *50*, 51, 68*(2)*, *95*, *185*, *212*
    triangular, 68*(2)*, *192*
    trim along, *190*
Roosevelt, Pres. F.D., 140
Roosevelt, Pres. T.R., 119
Roosevelt Elementary School, 108, 119
Roosevelt Hill Apartments, *118*, 119
Rose Parkway, 221
Rose Place neighborhood, *167*, 168, 169
Rose Street, North, 9, 48, 124
    100 block, 11*(3)*
    200 block, 184–185, 247
    300 block, 11
    400 block, *18*
    industrial sites, xvi, 82
    public places along, 20, 22, 162
    Water St. and, 51, 73, 184
Rose Street, South, 45, 130
    100 block, *9*, 10, 148
    200 block, 150, 180
    300 block, 48, 88
    400 block, *19*, 98
    600 block, 200
    Lovell St. and, 32, 53, 64, *98*, *102–103*
    Michigan Ave. and, *24*, *47*, *50*
Rose Street Market, *168*, 170
Rosenbaum, Simon, 24
Rosenbaum families, 66
Rounds, Charles, 68
Royce, Fred, 232, 239
rusticated foundations, *36*, *99*
Ryan Hall, Barbour Hall, *109*

S

St. Ambrose (statue), *70*
St. Augustine Cathedral, sites, 96–97*(2)*
St. Augustine Roman Catholic Church, site, 60, 70–71*(4)*, 97, 259
 school and, *114*
St. Augustine (statue), *70*
St. Camillus Nurses' Home, 230
St. James Parish, 117
St. John's Episcopal Church, 218
St. John's Place, 93
St. Joseph Elementary School, site, 117*(3)*, 252, 260
St. Joseph (locomotive), 22
St. Joseph Roman Catholic Church, 117
St. Luke's Episcopal Church, site, *218*, 258, 260, 261, 262
St. Mary's Roman Catholic Church, 116
St. Mary's School, 116
St. Monica (statue), *70*
salons, 131, 187, 246
Salvation Army, 119
 The Citadel, *247*, 257, 258, 260
Sam Folz One Price Clothier, *214*, 228
sandstone, 20, 227
sanitariums, 28, 30, 41
Saniwax Co., 76
Sarkozy, Ken, and Judy, 254
Sarkozy Bakery, *254*, 263
Sattem, Steve, 237
Schaberg family, 186
Scheid, Fred, and Anna, 91
Scheid, Winifred, 91
Scheid's Meat Market, *10*
Schlee, William, 189
Schmidt House, Peter and Julie, site, 233*(2)*, 258, 261
Schmitt, John, and family, 223
Schmitt, Peter, Ph.D., 168
schools
 boarding, *109*
 lyceums as, 107, 137, 153*(3)*
 parochial, 70, 71, 97, 107–108, 109*(2)*, 115*(2)*, 117*(3)*, 252
 private, 38, 39, 62, 96, 107–108, 112–114*(11)*, 116*(3)*
 professional, 5, 104, 108, 114*(3)*, 263
 public, 107–108, 110–111*(4)*, 118–121*(15)*, 252

Schram, Peter, 142
Scott, Doerschler, Messner & Gauntlett (firm), 247
Scott Tribby Violins, *246*
screening, window, 175
scrollwork, *91*
Scudella, Bill, glass artist, 223, 262
Sears Roebuck and Co., *195*, 213, *252*
Sebring, James, *132*
Sebring, Jay, 92
Second Empire Style, 38*(2)*, *91*, 184, *185*
Second Holland Christian Reformed Church, *63*
Second Reformed Church, 59, 60, 61, 65*(3)*, 117, 261, 263
Seminary Hill, *116*
Senior Citizens Fund, 90
Sergeant's (firm). *See* E.M. Sergeant Co.
Severns House, Henry and Sarah, site, *91*, 259
Shakespeare, William, Jr., 246
Shannon, Bob, 223
Sharpe's Colonial Furniture, *92*
Shauman, Bill, and Sandy, 219
Sheldon, Theodore P., 242
Shell, Bobby Joe, and Barbara, 220–221
Sheridan Drive, 126
Sherman, Jeff, mason, 183, 262
shingles, *31*, *104*
 asphalt, 244, 250
 circular, *161*
 decorative, 181, 243
 fish-scale, *90*, 93*(2)*, *132*, *179*, *207*, 220–221*(3)*, 237–238*(2)*
Shirlaw, James, mason, 224, 262
shop-houses, *176*, *181*, *187*, *263*
 Burdick St., *134*, *226*, 254
 in commercial districts, 25, 103, 127, 131, 214
 rehabilitated, 216*(2)*, *226*, 258, 259, 263
Shoup, Harold, 16
shutters, *50*
sidelights, *32*, *54*, *94*, 225
siding materials, *246*
 metal, 74, *195*
 vinyl, *194*, 207
 wood, *31*, *63*, 197*(2)*, *233*
Sigma Alpha Delta, WMU, 39
signs. *See under* advertisements
Sill, Dr. Joseph, 102
Sill Terrace site, 102–103*(4)*
sills, stone, 115–116*(2)*, 254

Simons, V.D., engineer, 80, 262
Simpson House, site, *88*
Simpson Methodist churches, *59*, 60, 69
Sinclair gas stations, *19*, 100
Sisters of St. Joseph, 27, 108, 109, 117
skylights, 129, *192*, 215
skyscrapers, 128–129*(2)*, 131*(3)*, 212, 263
Sloan, Samuel, 27, 34, 262
Smith, Trish, 200
Smutek, Mark, 215, 262
"Social Christianity," 62
softball, fast-pitch, sponsors, 12
soundproofing, *65*, 81, 142, 237
South Burdick School, 119
South Burdick Street Historic District, 169
"South Side News" (weekly), 133
South Street, 79, 99
South Street, East, 107
 100 block, iv, 66, 66*(3)*, 138, 146*(2)*, 152
 300 block, 66
 commercial buildings on, *19*, 21*(3)*
South Street, West, 112, 132
 200 block, 188
 400 block, 32, 198–199, 223, 231
 500 block, 219, *229*
 800 block, 181
 Burdick St. and, *46*, 89
 notable homes on, 89, 92, 93, 181, 198–199, 219, 223, 229, 231
 public places, 45, 46, 55
South Street Historic District, 168, 169, 171, 219
South Westnedge neighborhood, 222
Southside Park, 141
Southwestern Michigan Tuberculosis Sanitarium, 41
Spalding, Brian, 191
Spear, Marion R., 27
Speyer, Joseph, 24
spindlework, porches with, 93*(2)*, 96*(2)*
spires, *64*, *66*, 70–71*(3)*, *97*
Sprau Hall, WMU, 120
Spring Street, 28
Spruce Drive, notable homes, 175, 204
Spruce Park (development), 204
stability, as design element, 9, 43
stables, 49, 51, 175
Stadium Drive, 65
stained-glass windows, *69*, 92, 202, *218*, 223, 239, 262

stainless steel, Art Deco and, 20, 142, 242
stairways, indoor, 92, 202
    circular, 203, 211
    hardwood, 110, 189, 211, 219
    towers for, 208–209*(2)*
stairways, outdoor, 232
    fire escapes, *84, 152*
    matched, unusual on Queen Anne style, *95*
    stone materials for, *46, 95, 120,* 211*(2),* 219*(2),* 239
    WMU and, 120, 211*(2)*
Stancati, Ross, 251
Standard Federal Bank, 20, *21, 145*
Standard Oil stations, *18, 19*
standpipes, water towers as, 162*(2)*
Star Bargain (firm), 129
Star Brass Works, 91
Starkey & Gilbert Furniture Co., 214
State Charities Act, 33
State Historic Preservation Office, 168, 170
State Hospital. *See* Kalamazoo State Hospital (KSH)
State Register of Historic Places, 168, 170
State Renaissance Zones, 209
State Theatre, ceiling lighting, 215
Statler Ready Mixed Concrete (firm), 196, 262
statues, *50,* 51, *70, 71,* 241
Stauffenberg, Otto, painter, 188, 242, 262
steel use
    nonresidential, 20, 121, *158,* 163, 208–209, *212,* 242
    residential, *195,* 198, 222
stenciling, 181, 198, 199, 219, 232, 239, 263
Stetson, Herbert Lee, Ph.D., memorials, 245
Stetson Chapel, Kalamazoo College, 172, 245*(2),* 258, 260, 263
Stevens Block, *149*
Stewart, Edgar C., 114
Stockbridge, George, and family, 181
Stockbridge Avenue, 134, 162
Stockbridge-Everard House, site, 181*(2),* 261, 263
Stockwell, Madeleon, before marriage, 232
Stone, Mrs. Dr. Harriette, 101
Stone, Lucinda Hinsdale, 100, 112
Stone, Dr. William Addison, 101
Stone House, William and Harriette, site, *101,* 260

stone materials
    aggregate, 240
    Amherst stone, *218*
    Berea stone, 148–149*(2)*
    cement, 12, *120,* 182
    cobblestone, *159*
    granite, 46, 188, 242
    graystone, 68*(2)*
    greenstone, *92*
    sandstone, 20, 227
    terra cotta, 14, *15,* 129, *180*
    See also brick; concrete; limestone; marble; stucco
stone (unspecified), *119*
    beltcourses, 95, 110–111*(2),* 148–149*(2)*
    brick and, 29, 51, 56, 234
    building foundations, 36, 95, *99, 113, 191*
    exterior trim, *82,* 151*(2), 190*
    facings, *178–179*
    fireplaces, 154, 244
    lintels, *85,* 115–116*(2),* 254
    moldings, 84, *85,* 89*(2), 146, 163,* 244
    park facilities, 140–141*(3),* 154
    piers, *191*
    sills, 115–116*(2),* 254
    transoms, 45
    voussoirs, **177**
stoves, *50,* 194, 214
Strandlund, Carl, 222
Streamline Moderne Style, *18,* 19
    hybrids of, *196*
street impact, 67, 123–134*(26)*
    aesthetics and, *66, 177,* 194
    building foundations and, *84–85*
    fenestration and, 3, *12*
    massiveness and, 49–50*(2),* 51, 101
    pedestrians and, 3, 24, 124, *195, 224,* 254
street life, 3, 9, *24*
street-surfacing materials
    asphalt, *159*
    brick, 159, 183, 262
    logs, 158
    Nicholson pavement, 129, 159*(2)*
    planks, 126
streetcars, 160–161*(5)*
    entertainment and, 137, 138–139, 144
    routes of, *133, 134, 160, 161,* 204
Streeter, Daniel, 211
streetlights, *158,* 204
Stryker, Dr. Homer, and Mrs. Mary Jane, 225

Stryker, L. Lee, memorials, 225
Stuart, Charles, 34
Stuart Avenue, 104, 199, 210
Stuart Avenue Inn, 104, *199,* 257
Stuart neighborhood, 138, 143, 182
    business districts in, 123, 127
    classic Italianate in, 197, 232*(2)*
    Historic District registers and, 168, 169, 195, 199, 211, 217, 237
    property improvement in, 202, 237
    schools in, 118, 210
stucco, 94*(2),* 194, *198,* 199, *253*
    brick and, 112, *198,* 199
    covered by siding, 31, 194, 233
    exterior, Craftsman style, *175, 186,* 204*(2)*
    exterior, Tudor Revival style, 182*(2),* 204*(2), 226,* 252
    half-timbered, 61, *175,* 182*(2),* 226, 252
    trim as, *251*
Student Recreation Building, WMU, *121, 147*
Studio of Architectural Sculpture, 188, 262
Style Shop, building rehabilitation, *203,* 261, 262
substantiality, idea of, 101
suburbs, 146, 233
    development of, 60, 62, 67, 74, 81, 83
    streetcars and, 138–139, 199
Summer Street, *217*
sun porches, 197
sun rooms, *186,* 189
Sutherland Paper Co., 82
swimming pools, 138, 140–141*(6),* 180
symbolism, 4, 44, 52, 129
    building design and, 9, 14, *15,* 101
    historical values and, xiv, 6
symbols, logos as, *151,* 254
symmetry, *95*
    asymmetrical, *104,* 197*(2), 237,* 248
    fenestration and, *54, 63,* 68*(2)*
    Gothic styles and, 68*(2), 218*
    Revival styles and, *54, 63, 180, 210*
    Romanesque style and, 59
synagogues, Orthodox Judaism, 59, 66
Syrian arches, 227*(2)*

T

Taft, Pres. William Howard, 99, 151
tailors, 214
tax credits, 234, 249

Temple B'nai Israel, iv, 59, 60, 66–67*(5)*, 259, 263
temple front, **67**
temples
    fraternal organizations and, *11*, 152*(3)*, 162, 168, 170
    Reform Judaism, iv, 59, 60, 66–67*(3)*
terra cotta, 14, *15*, 113, 129
terrazzo, 242
Texaco gas stations, *19*
theaters, 80, 138
    downtown, iv, 21, 66, 67, *128*, 129, 142*(3)*, 145–146*(7)*, 148–149*(5)*, 168
    other performance stages, 99, 133, 139, *241*
Theta Xi fraternity, WMU, 101
Third Christian Reformed Church, 59, 60, 61*(3)*
Third Street, Kalamazoo. *See* Crosstown Parkway, East
Third Street Studio, Cincinnati, 239, 262
Thomas, Seth, clockmaker, 228, 262
Thompson Street, 198
Thorne, James M., engineer, 181
Thorne, Thomas, 189
Three-Part Vertical Blocks, 21
Three Rivers Plank Road, *126*
Thurman's Restaurant, *18*
tile use, *45*, *189*, 198, 227, *249*, 254
Todd, Albert M., legacies, xvi, 48, 121, 196
tombstones, 49
tornadoes, 15, 68, 128
towers, *45*, *46*, *95*, *97*, 169, 174*(2)*
    bell, *69*, 110, *111*, 117*(2)*, *118*, 218, 245*(2)*
    central, 39*(3)*, *50*, 51, 59, *63*, *91*, 96*(2)*, *118*, *185*, *210*, *218*, 219*(2)*
    corner, *11*, 59, *61*, *64*, 68–69*(3)*, 75, *90*, 93*(2)*, *95*, 114
    crenelated, *52*, *163*
    finial on, *48*, *90*, *132*, *219*
    hose-drying, *49*, *55*, *207*
    industrial buildings with, 73, 79*(2)*, 208–209*(2)*
    more than four-sided, *113*, 227*(2)*
    rear, *50(2)*
    side, 40–41*(3)*, *65*, *116*, *237*
    three-story, 208–209*(2)*, 239*(2)*
    water, 17, 157, *163*
Towsley, Dr. Maltilda, 27
toy manufacturers, 77
Trailer Village, WMU, 121*(2)*, 147
transoms, stone, 45

transportation, modes of. *See specifics, e.g.,* automobiles; buses; railroads
Trask Cottage, KSH, *27*, 40
Travis, Anna Boyland, 92
Travis, Armond, 246
Triangle Service Station, 215*(2)*, 262
Tribby, Scott, 246
triglyphs, friezes with, *82*
Trimble Avenue, 141*(2)*
Troff, Garrett, 251
Troff, Nancy, 216
trolleys, 18, *120*, 157, *161*
Trombley, Albert, and Susan, 187, 263
Trowbridge, Silas, 132
Trowbridge Dam, Allegan County, 78
Truesdale Funeral Home, 150
Tudor Revival Style, 33*(2)*, *226*, 244
    characteristics of, 182, 252–253*(2)*
    hybrids of, 204*(2)*
Turn Verein Hall, 137
Turner, Charles, and Madeleon Stockwell, 232
Turner, James, 60
Tuscan columns, *191*
Tuttle, Jane, after marriage, 38, 96
Two-Part Commercial Blocks, *25*, 176*(2)*, *187*, *249*, *254*, 263

U

Union Hall, 137, 148
Union School, 107, 108, *110*, 118
Unitarian churches, 62*(3)*, 100, 110
U.S. Bicentennial, 169, 241
U.S. government, effect of
    agencies, 46, 47, 51, 114, 138, 140, 154, 234, 241, 242, 251
    courts, 46, 91, 110
    legislation, 37, 46, 107, 140–141, 168–171
    presidents, 108, 140, 151
University of Chicago, Stryker Center program, 225
University of Michigan, 107, 112, 232
Upjohn, Burton H., memorials, *225*
Upjohn, Dr. James, 199
Upjohn, Dr. William E., 219
    legacies, *92*, 132, 151, 171
Upjohn Co., *29*, *94*
Upjohn Estate, 132, 235
Upjohn Park, 141, 252
Upjohn Pill and Granule Co., 219

Upper College, Kalamazoo College, *112*
Uptown Theater, 142*(3)*, 262, 263
urban renewal, rehabilitation and reuse, 172
Usonian Style, 192–193*(4)*

V

Valley Inn Motel, 68
Van Avery, Charles and Elsie, 25
Van Avery, Gerald, 25
Van Avery Drug Store Building, Ray and Ella, site, *25*
Van Deusen, Dr. Edwin, KSH, 34–35
Van Deusen, Dr. Edwin and Cynthia, benefactors, 45, 218, 229
Van Deusen Cottage, KSH, *40*
Van Deusen Hospital, KSH, 36, *37*, 37m
Van Hamersveld, Mrs. Angie, artist, 232
Van Hamersveld, Herm and Angie, family home, *232*
Van Werden, Harold, and Patricia, 206
vandalism, 99, 154
Vande Walker, Althea, after marriage, 140
Vander Horst, Henry L.
    builder, 14, 17, 119, 125, 131, 224, 230, 263
    contractor, 5, 21, 125, 142, 226, 242
    home and roles, 198, 223, *226*, 236
Vander Salm, Jacob, designer, 177, 263
Vander Salm family, greenhouse businesses, 177
Vander Salm's Flower Shop, 172, *177*, 257, 263
Verburg Park, 141
vergeboards, *91*, 197
Vermeulen's, furniture businesses, 75, 170, 184
Veterans Administration, 114
Viavi (firm), 176
Victorian Gothic Style, 68, 164, 174*(2)*, 230*(2)*
Victorian period, characteristics of, 56
Victor's Restaurant, 12
Village Street, 238
villages, Kalamazoo County. *See specifics, i.e.,* Bronson, Village of; Comstock, Village of; Kalamazoo, Village of
Vine neighborhood, 60
    business districts for, 13, 123, 249
    Historic District registers and, 168, 169, 189, 234, 248

Vine neighborhood *(continued)*
    property improvement in, 220–221, 238, 249
    schools in, 107, 110, 118
    winter ice rinks in, 138, 143
Vine Street
    East, 190
    West, 87, 107, 110, 131, 249
Volderauer, Dr., Kalamazoo Radiology, 32
voussoirs, *177*

W

Waber Development (firm), 142
wainscoting, 81, 198, 201
Waite family, farmland, 204
Waldo, Dwight B., legacies, 121, 201
Waldo Library, WMU, 121
Walgreen Drugs, *21*
Walker, Jess, and Jane, 239
Wall, John, *160*
wall coverings
    paneling, *45*, 81, 201, 222, 226
    wainscoting, 81, 198, 201
    wallpaper, 148, 199, 219, 237, 244
Wall Street, 177
walls, 3, 16, 110, *212, 233,* 247
    brick, 74, 78
    finishes, *113,* 198–199, 251
    half-timbered, 61, *175,* 182*(2),* 226, *252, 253*
    interior, 81, *103,* 189
    stenciled, 219, 239
    window-, *224, 235*
Walnut Street, 117
    East, 190
    West, 61, 65
Walter, James, and Eliza, 29
Walwood Hall/Union, WMU, *201,* 215, 259, 260
Washington Avenue, 133, 144
Washington School, 108
Washington Square
    Edison neighborhood and, 6, 123, 133*(3),* 252, 253
    KPL branch library in, *244,* 252, 257, 259, 260
    National Driving Park as part of, 6, 144*(2),* 144m, 252
Washington Writer's Academy, 252

Water Street, East, 59, 69, *159,* 224
    100 block, 43, *52, 53*
    300 block, 215, 236
    400 block, 83
Water Street, West, 20, 129
    Church St. and, 51, 87
    Park St. and, 68, 75
    Rose St. and, 51, 73, 184, 185
Water Street Cafe/Coffee Joint, The, 173, 215*(2),* 262
water supplies, *56,* 163, 212
water tanks, 163, *212*
water towers, 17
    as architectural accessories, 157, *163*
    KSH, 7, 36, 163, 169, 212*(2),* 259, 260, 261, 262
Water Works, 56*(2), 157*
Waterman, Harry, 145
W.E. Upjohn Institute for Employment Research, *92, 171*
Weisblat, David and Christine, Usonian home, 192, *193,* 259
Wendy's Restaurant, Michigan Ave., *17*
West Douglas neighborhood, 182, 191, 202, 217
West Douglas Neighborhood Association, 217
West End business district, 123, 127*(2)*
West Main Hill neighborhood, 60
    business districts in, 99, 123, 127*(2)*
    National Register Historic District, 168, 170, 186, 194, 198
    notable hilltop houses, 91, 99, 239
West Street, after 1918. *See* Westnedge Avenue
West Street, North, *25,* 114, 117, 118
West Street, South, 161, 163
    notable residences on, 38, 87, 90, 92
    Vine St. and, 87, 107, 110
Western Michigan University (WMU), 16
    East Campus and National Historic registers, 168, 201
    facilities, *39,* 120–121*(8),* 147*(2),* 152, 200, 211*(2),* 259, 260, 263
    faculty as community consultants, 168, 169
    fraternities, *39,* 101
    Normal School origins, 108, 120, 152
    property ownership by, 37, 39–40*(2),* 41, 121
Western State Normal School, 108, 120, 152*(3)*
Westfall Avenue, Lustron house on, *222*

Westnedge, Col. Joseph, 52, 132
Westnedge Avenue, before 1918. *See* West Street
Westnedge Avenue, North, 96–97
Westnedge Avenue, South
    200 block, 200
    400 block, *189*
    2000 block, 251
    infill houses on, 169, 173, 200
    Vine St. and, 131, 249
Westnedge Hill Apartments, *251,* 258, 261, 262
Westnedge Hill neighborhood, 98, 233*(2)*
Wheaton Avenue, 248
Wheeler-Blaney Co., 142
White, Albert J., *5,* 29, 67, 111, 114, 263
White, L.V., 18
White, Patricia, 200
Whitechapel Bell Foundry, London, 245, 260
White's Lake, Lakeside, 38
wicker furniture, *94*
widows, 89, 90*(2),* 91, 93*(2)*
Wiegand, Peter
    contractor, 214, 216, 263
Wilbur, Dr. Charles, 39
Wilbur, Dr. Edward, 39
Wilbur, Joseph, and Helen, 39
Wilbur Home and School for the Feeble-Minded, 39*(4)*
Willard Street, *22–23,* 178
William Street, 115*(2),* 140–141
William Street School, site, 115*(2)*
Williams, Bradley, 95
Williams, Dean Clarke Benedict, 112
Williams, Dave and Kim, 202
Williams, Mae, 95
Williams, Malcolm, 95
Williams Hall, Kalamazoo College, *112*
Williams Manufacturing, 95
Winchell Avenue, churches on, 61, 68
Winchell neighborhood, 222
window walls, "enframed," *224*
windows, 14, *79,* 94*(2),* 200
    arched, *36, 46, 56,* 61, *63, 64, 65,* 68*(2),* 70–71*(3),* 80, *81,* 93*(2),* 174*(2),* 177, *218*
    bay, 33*(2),* 39*(3),* 89*(2),* 95, 100*(2), 102–103, 104,* 110–111*(2), 113,* 150, *191, 197,* 206, 219*(2),* 244
    box, *197*

windows *(continued)*
  brick details above, *49,* 110–111*(2), 187*
  casement, *36, 101,* 244
  clerestory, *235*
  crowned, *113*
  decorative, *89,* 239*(2)*
  display, 3, *24,* 195*(2),* 224, *254*
  dormer, *94(2), 212*
  double-hung, 74, *77, 84–85,* 117*(2), 178, 217, 252,* 253
  double-storm, 237
  front, *39(3),* 70*(2),* 206, 243, *244*
  full-height, *78(2), 102–103,* 247
  gabled, *177*
  grouped, *98,* 248
  hooded, *97, 100, 102–103, 109, 110–111(2), 187, 211(2), 248*
  keyhole-shaped, *132*
  long narrow, *39(3), 47,* 152*(2),* 184–185*(3),* 206, 219*(2),* 232*(2), 248*
  louvered, *50, 218*
  metal, *247*
  moldings above, *11, 24,* 38*(2), 39(3), 47, 50,* 89*(2),* 96*(2), 97, 116,* 117*(2), 118, 163, 179,* 184–185*(3),* 206, 219*(2)*
  mosaic, *45*
  multiple, *29, 89,* 181, *202,* 239*(2)*
  narrow, 38*(2), 50,* 51, 89*(2), 113,* 116, *214, 218*
  oculus, *24, 47, 49,* 70–71*(3), 91,* 117*(2),* 219*(2)*
  paired, *56,* 96*(2), 118, 150*
  Palladian, *94(2)*
  paned, *32, 55, 77, 244, 252,* 253
  picture, 243
  pilasters between, *78(2),* 110–111*(2)*
  rectangular, *94(3)*
  rose, *70(2)*
  round *(see* oculus *above)*
  rounded, *39(3), 64,* 70–71*(3),* 76*(2), 77, 131, 150,* 184–185*(3)*
  screened, 175
  side, *50, 191*
  stained-glass, *69,* 92, *202, 218, 223,* 239, *262*
  stone details above, *84–85,* 89*(2),* 110–111*(2), 115,* 117*(2), 163,* 184–185*(3), 248*
  stone sills below, 115–116*(2), 254*
  trefoil, *174*

windows *(continued)*
  two-story, 100*(2), 150*
  See also fanlights; sidelights
Winn, Robert and Winifred, Usonian home, 192
Wise's Hardware Store, *133*
WMU. *See* Western Michigan University (WMU)
Wolthuis, Ralph, shoemaker, 134
Women's Auxillary, Bronson Hospital, 27, 33
Women's Civic Improvement League, 28
Women's Medical College, Philadelphia, 101
Wood, Henry, 60
Wood, Leslie, Ph.D., 201
Wood, William, family home, 219
wood blocks, paving with, 129, 159*(2)*
Wood-Upjohn House, site, 181, 219*(2),* 257, 258, 261, 263
Woodbury, Potter & Wood (firm), 14
Woodruff, James, 236
woods, 189
  birch, 239
  cherry, 110, 148, 198
  fake, 226
  fir, 237
  mahogany, 151, 198, 239
  maple, 239, 250
  oak, 175, 181, 197, 198, 210, 237, 239, 244
  pine, 186, 237
  refinished, 175, 194, 197–199, 202, 219, 221, 237
  replacement of, 16, 120, 182
  sycamore, 239
  walnut, 81, 211, 219, 242
woods, use of
  beams and joists, 74, 77
  commercial districts and, 22, 23, 130
  flooring, 110, 148, 175, 186, 189, 198, 202, 232, 237, 250, 251
  furniture, 75, 77, 77
  Nicholson pavement, 129, 159*(2)*
  paneling, 45, 81, 201
  shingles, *31,* 207
  siding, *31, 63,* 197*(2), 217,* 233
  stairways, 110, 120, 189, 211, 219
  See also frame buildings; woodwork
Woodward Avenue, notable homes on, 191, 197, 202, 232
Woodward Elementary School, *210,* 257

Woodward School for Technology and Research, *210,* 258
woodwork, 3, 92, 96, 229
  hardwood, cherry, 110, 148, 239
  hardwood, mahogany, *151,* 219, 239
  hardwood, oak, 181, 197, 210, 237, 239, 244
  hardwood, sycamore, 239
  refinished, 197–199, 219, 221, 237, 239, 250
  salvaged, 215, 218
  softwood, birch, 239
  softwood, fir, 238
  softwood, pine, 237
woodworking plants, 75
Woolsey, Dr. Paul, 25
Works Progress Administration (WPA), 138, 140, 154, 241
Wyckoff, Joseph, and family home, *231*

Y

Ye Olde Central Laundry, *38*
Yenner, Lloyd, 143
Yonkman, Leonard, carpenter, 239, 263
Yorkville, Michigan, 83
"Yosemite Valley" (painting), *121*
YMCA (Young Men's Christian Association), 111, *138,* 151*(4), 178*
YWCA (Young Women's Christian Association), *17,* 150*(2), 180,* 235, *261*

Z

ziggurats, effect of, 242
Zinn, A.K., 83
Ziobron, Judith, artist, 181, 199, 219, 232, 239, 263
Zomor's Market, *127*

Designed and composed in Kalamazoo, Michigan, using the fonts Garamond Book Condensed for text and Onyx for titles and headings. Printed and bound by Edwards Brothers, Inc., in Ann Arbor, Michigan.